Music in American Life

A list of volumes in the series Music in American Life appears at the end of this book.

CHOSEN VOICES

CHOSEN VOICES

The Story of the American Cantorate

Mark Slobin

University of Illinois Press
Urbana and Chicago

© 1989 by the Board of Trustees of the University of Illinois
Manufactured in the United States of America
C   5   4   3   2   1

This book is printed on acid-free paper.

All music examples used by permission of
Transcontinental Music Publishers.
A tape of all music examples is available in cassette form.

Library of Congress Cataloging-in-Publication Data

Slobin, Mark.
    Chosen voices : the story of the American cantorate / Mark Slobin.
        p. cm. -- (Music in American life)
    Bibliography: p.
    Includes index.
    ISBN 0-252-01565-7 (alk. paper)
    1. Cantors, Jewish—United States.   I. Title.   II. Series.
ML3195.S55 1989   88-17310
783.2'096'0973—dc19   CIP
                                                                         MN

This one's for Mom and Dad
—and Maya too

Contents

Preface

There has been an American cantorate for three hundred years, ever since Saul Brown became the first known leader of Congregation Shearith Israel, New York, in 1685. In the course of those three centuries, no one has ever attempted a comprehensive history of this significant Jewish-American institution.[1] To do so in the late 1980s is asking too much of any one book, so the present effort must be understood as a preliminary study of a complex, fascinating, and neglected topic.

This volume is subtitled the "story" rather than the "history" of the American cantorate for two reasons. First, it is too early to produce *the* history. Second, there is more to the cantorate than a history—using the term in the strictly chronological sense. Unlike other religious institutions, such as the Catholic church, or religio-musical units like the Canterbury Cathedral Choir, the American cantorate has little recognizable structural continuity; indeed, the word *cantorate* itself is of quite recent coinage. It is an institution buffeted by external forces: waves of immigration, government policies, Jewish sectarianism, and major historical events, such as the Holocaust. These factors tell us more about what happened to the cantorate than would any account of its internal evolution. But that is not all—we also have to reckon with the aesthetic and psychological factors that shape the world of the sacred singer, and this book uses the insider's perspective as much as possible.[2] We are dealing with people whose mission it is to express the longings of their community, as represented by synagogue worshippers, and to serve as *sheliach tzibbur*, the "messenger of the congregation," to God. They are also interpreters of sacred text, performers and sometimes improvisers in a long line of musicians with a rich heritage of repertoire, terminology, and aesthetics. In this sense, the cantorate is particularly amenable to current from-the-bottom-up historical and anthropological approaches, which build an analysis from a counterpoint of overlapping, sometimes dissonant voices, rather than laying out a formal series of documents and events. *Chosen Voices* tries to balance history and ethnography, sociology and musicology, the past and the present, to tell the "story" of the cantorate as it emerged from a three-year research project undertaken by a team of investigators with the enthusiastic backing of a large number of the professionals who make up today's American cantorate.

Studying the cantorate means looking at intersecting and overlapping worlds: the Jewish, composed of pre- and non-American traditions, languages, texts, institutions, and music; the American, featuring geographic isolation, attitudes towards foreigners, local religious and secular traditions and laws, and a volatile history; and the Jewish-American, influenced by a Jewish past and an American present, all the while in touch with world Jewry. As an institution deeply concerned with expressing a people's consciousness and intimately associated with ritual, the cantorate is not just a reflection of the state of American Jewry, but forms an important building block of group identity. Yet nearly all the basic sociological works on American Jewish life, down to recent reevaluations of the 1980s, not only shortchange but actually ignore the cantorate's contribution. Perhaps this is because the best work on the Jewish community began to be done in the 1950s, when the rabbi was assumed to be not just the leading, but the *only* Jewish clergyman, a spokesman to his people and to the larger world. Another reason might be the traditional view of the sacred singer as a figure who is both necessary and unimportant, perhaps even comic, an attitude partly born of the fact that only scholars could stand at the pinnacle of respect: an issue of "mind over voice."[3] I will detail such attitudes below; what should be said now is that nearly everyone has overlooked a rich vein of data and a path of insight into the expressive culture of American Jewish life. Partly as a result of this neglect, I decided to make *Chosen Voices* as much a sourcebook as a story, relying heavily on quotations to let the reader into the professionals' own world, citing leading thinkers like Isaac Leeser for the nineteenth century and today's hazzanim in the chapters based on interviews. I hope that readers will weigh the various accounts to make their own judgements in addition to accepting my interpretation.

To lay out the story of the cantorate in this introductory study, a background chapter on the institution as a part of Jewish culture must come first. Chapter 1 provides the framework for understanding why the Jews have a cantorate at all, to the extent that fragmentary evidence allows us to frame the question that way. In describing the nineteenth-century background, I have tended to stress the Ashkenazic (western, central and eastern European) Jews who form some 95% of today's American Jewish population. Nevertheless, the following chapters will show that the Sephardim (descendants of Jews exiled from Spain beginning in 1492) dominated the original community in what is now the United States and their ways of institutionalizing prayer set the tone well into the nineteenth century.[4]

Part 1 presents a historical review of the American cantorate. Beginning with the colonial period and moving through the age of mass immigration (1880s–1920s), I draw on early documents and memoirs, then, approaching the period reached by living memory, turn increasingly to oral histories as source material. The history is in outline form, with key figures and moments highlighting major trends.[5] Chapter 2 covers the first era of the cantorate, from colonial times through the turbulent period of the mid-nineteenth century, when the *hazzan*, the basic, often multipurpose community leader, began to be supplanted by the ordained rabbi with the arrival of the German wave of immigration and the rise of Reform Judaism. Chapter 3 takes the story from the onset of the eastern European wave in the 1880s through World War II, focusing on the phenomenon of the "star cantor," the fate of the everyday hazzan, and the lively interchange between Europe and the United States. Chapter 4 is set in the post-Holocaust age of recent decades, when the American cantorate re-created itself as a native-born institution, centering on the newly founded training programs and professional organizations. Chapter 5 takes up American-based change, such as the appearance in 1976 of the first accredited female professional, and presents a "group portrait" of the various strata of today's cantorate.

Between chapters 3 and 4, an "interlude" presents the life histories of three fascinating European-born hazzanim who illustrate generations of immigrant sacred singers.

Part 2 turns towards ethnography and sociology as I examine the cantorate in the workplace—the synagogue—looking at aspects of being the *sheliach tzibbur*, which is the core of the cantorate's mission. Here I stress elements of continuity with earlier generations and centuries. Chapter 6 lays out the various ways that hazzanim function within the American community, both within and beyond the congregation, with a particular focus on the recent relationship of rabbi and hazzan within the synagogue. Chapter 7 details the nature of the job, considered contractually and actually. Chapter 8 moves into the sanctuary to examine the heart of cantorial activity: the building and musical leading of services.

Finally, part 3 looks inward to the music itself, which is the voice of the cantorate, an institution built on song, once again primarily from the insider's point of view. Chapters 9, 10, and 11 draw on the rich musical data gathered for the present project and look at specific pieces to understand the issues of participation, presentation, and improvisation, ranging from the congregational hymn through the crafted work of the composer to the traditional notion of the soloist's own inspired improvisation.

Throughout, I focus on the individual, whom I call the *hazzan* rather than the *cantor*. There are two reasons for this decision: First, hazzan is an in-group term rather than a borrowed one, and a term preferred by American Jewish communities until the late nineteenth century. Second, *hazzan* is the title of choice among the largest group of today's full-time practitioners, the members of the Cantors Assembly (despite the organization's name, which is left from the 1950s). However, *cantor* will appear whenever it is used in quotations from written or interview sources.

Finally, a note about format. Since a central point I make is that the cantorate is part of a large cultural pattern related to interpretation of text, it seems suitable to mirror that process in the book's organization. Like some Jewish texts, parts of this volume present a range of opinions on a topic, then provide an apparatus of commentary in the form of my remarks in the body of the text plus the footnotes as counterpoint. I realize that this means the reader cannot always sit back and have the author narrate, but I have three reasons for this approach: (1) I enjoy the cultural resonance just described; (2) the sourcebook nature of the volume; and (3) I think the primary source materials are inherently interesting in themselves, whether they be cast in highflung nineteenth-century style or in the self-revelatory flow of oral history. Consequently, I have tried to keep secondary sources not written by hazzanim to a minimum.

A Note to Ethnomusicologists

This part of the introduction will lay out what I think are the main lines of ethnomusicological inquiry. Because I want the body of the book to be accessible to nonspecialists, I will henceforth address "theory" largely in footnotes.

The fact that this study is an example of in-group ethnomusicology needs some comment. Marshall Sklare, a major sociologist of American Jewry, has said that "there is no way around the fact that the sociology of Jews will be written by Jews" (1982:269).[6] The fact that it is almost always Jews that write about Jewish culture—including the Jewish-American subculture—means two things: (1) the author somehow expresses insider sensibilities and addresses the group's concerns as well as those of scholarship; (2) non-Jews take less interest in the work, as they tend to think of Jewish matters as being special-interest or esoteric. The two factors are interdependent, since despite one's best intentions, the insider author at times tends either to take things for granted or to overexplain.

First, a word about myself. I feel comfortable writing this book in the period of "reflexive" ethnography, long being an advocate of the position that the scholar must throw off his mask—at least in the introduction. I grew up in Detroit in a mildly observant, largely secular Jewish-American household that was so ensconced in an ethnic neighborhood that degree of individual affiliation seemed less relevant than the larger ethnic boundary. It was a classic second-generation community well described by Deborah Dash Moore (1981) as feeling "at home in America." My father was American-born, but my mother was an immigrant, and her extensive kin set the tone for family life.[7] Yiddish songs and Russian poetry were performed, along with Broadway tunes and classical music. The fact that numerous synagogues with widely varying denominational and sectarian differences dotted the neighborhood was simply a fact of life, as Moore points out. My parents taught part-time in the Hebrew school of the largest bourgeois centrist synagogue, where we sometimes went to services, so I absorbed the atmosphere of cantorial grandeur Shaarey Zedek provided, whereas my grandfather might be leading services over a storefront for a group with different tastes. Once or twice an extremely orthodox relative from Brooklyn who resembled Santa Claus was imported by another congregation that appreciated his way of *davening* (praying). Only since embarking on this project have I discovered that I also have ancestors who were hazzanim in the Ukraine. I was tutored for my bar mitzvah by my father, so participated in the old-style oral tradition. The melodies of the family Passover seder were rich in variants from different relatives, a truly folk amalgam that was typical of domestic celebrations in that generation, before institutionalized melodies from Jewish schools and summer camps infiltrated the home.

I left this intensely ethnic atmosphere when I went to college and only returned to it after years of work on the music of Afghanistan and central Asia (1965–73). The elation and frustration of studying the Other left me looking for a brief respite, and I fell into the renaissance of eastern European Jewish studies that began to blossom in the mid–1970s, emanating largely from the YIVO Institute for Jewish Research in New York, conveniently located near my university. It seemed that there were a great many sophisticated academics and helpful friends who were now confronting the Self, and I found it congenial to join them, particularly since almost no one of my generation was working on the music. This phase culminated in my book *Tenement Songs: The Popular Music of the Jewish Immigrants* (1982c), along with brief studies of the secular instrumental (*klezmer*) tradition and other writings.[8]

In 1983, approached by the Cantors Assembly to help them formulate a research project and write grant proposals for a history of the American cantorate, I found that while it was not a subject I knew much about, it was highly suitable from the ethnographic standpoint: I was far enough from the mindset of the musicians to ask the right questions and close enough to sympathize with the answers. It also felt much more complete to view the sacred Jewish world as well as the secular, since anyone will tell you that the two are inseparable, as I know from personal experience in Detroit. At the same time, the project vastly extended the range of my research, since it entailed setting up and running a research team, as well as making raids into history, into the sociology of the professions, and even into gender studies. Without going into further personal detail, I should stress how important I think it is for any ethnomusicologist to confront both the Other and the Self in fieldwork situations, and I recommend it to all my students.

Turning to professional issues, one of the satisfactions of working on the cantorate is that it fills a very large lacuna in Jewish studies, a fact easily illustrated by a single quote from a 1982 anthology dedicated to what should be studied about American Jewry:

> We know a great deal about the ritual observance of American Jews—
> how much is observed by how many . . . we know relatively little about
> the specifics of observance and their demographic correlates and even
> less about the dynamics of abandoning or undertaking ritual observ-
> ance. . . . We know a little but not much about the dynamics of synagogue
> life, roles and changing roles of rabbi and layman, the correlates of in-
> creased professionalization among laity, the changing role of women and
> its implication for male participation, ritual aspects of the synagogue that
> do or do not engage the laity, what can and cannot be changed, and the
> dynamics of change (Liebman 1982:113–14).

To me, the most striking fact of this quotation is the complete lack of the word *cantor*. It seems to have occurred to almost no one, from the pioneering Jewish-American sociology of the 1950s to today, that studying the hazzan would be a wonderful forum for addressing the many issues listed above; the equation "rabbi-laity" is missing a key third component.[9] This seems to me to be an elegant illustration of the way the ethnomusicologist, by thinking about the musician first, can easily make a significant contribution to any given area of ethnography, history, or sociology that has ignored the performer, in this case the sacred singer. The same article makes a point that leads directly to the suitability of an ethnomusicological approach: "There is no recognized field of study called American Jewish life. Students of contemporary American Judaism come from a variety of fields, bringing with them the tools and theories of their particular disciplines" (Liebman 1982:96).

Another sentence from the same article points out a second ethno-musicological theme: "A growing body of data supports the notion that religious observance is the most powerful measure of Jewish commitment" (Liebman 1982:114).[10]

Here we begin to move from the particular Jewish case to the general "ethnic" situation in America. While we have some studies of preaching and music in the black and rural white church, much of it only recent and unpublished, ethnomusicology has ignored the mainstream, middle-class American church, ethnic or otherwise. The present study would seem to be the first full-length volume in this area. At the same time, studies of "ethnic" (usually Euro-American) musics tend to concentrate either on "survival" of Old World repertoires (Erdely 1978) or on the transformation of those materials into American popular, secular styles (Klymasz 1973; Keil 1977, 1981; Leary 1984; Slobin 1984). The fact that the ethnic church was a main rallying point for classic immigrant groups and continues to be so for many current-wave newcomers has been overlooked, certainly in terms of its musical implications, with occasional exceptions for a look at the more "exotic" urban forms like Hispanic *santeria*, just as within American Judaism, the colorful Hasidim have garnered a great deal of attention from scholarship (Koskoff 1978) and even the mass media. Outside the American frame, I am unaware of serious study of mainstream religious music in Europe or elsewhere today, the emphasis there also tending to be on folk-based or popular styles. In short, the study of contemporary societies has tended to assume that, in our times, the dominance of secularism has rendered music in the context of middle-class worship so irrelevant as to be hardly worthy of scholarly inquiry, a notion undiscussed and unchallenged in the literature.

To a certain extent, this is part of our continued fascination with the marginal. Practically no attention has been paid to standard mainstream musicians, like the countless workaday performers who turn out music for middle-class rituals such as weddings (McLeod 1978, the exception, is an unpublished dissertation). It was a sociologist, not an ethnomusicologist, who tackled the Hollywood studio musician and filmscore composer (Faulkner 1967, 1981), and those are elite, not garden-variety musicians. Everyday musicmakers, such as the thousands of barbershop quartet enthusiasts, tend to be described only in the *New York Times,* not in scholarly periodicals. Given the fact that folklorists have long since recognized the potential of studying office folklore and college folktales, even devoting chapters in textbooks to the subject, it seems ethnomusicologists remain all too wedded to their older view of music cultures.

Chosen Voices is somewhat unusual ethnomusicologically in combining so many spheres of research. While the study of "non-Western" musics often mixes history and oral history, it rarely also includes quantifiable data (questionnaire results) and internally generated archival sources dating back to the eighteenth century, such as are available for the American Jews. Combining all this with a formidable synchronic musical data base (a core repertoire sample from some 30% of practicing professionals) and performers' own publications (from "cantor's columns" in synagogue newsletters through scholarly articles) has made the data on tap extremely rich and varied, on the order of the materials for Indian or Middle Eastern "classical" musics. I say this not so much to vaunt the authority of what follows, but to point out the wealth of materials Western middle-class musical professionals can supply as well as to excuse the fact that in this introductory survey of the topic, no one area is covered in depth. Those looking for definitive musicological analysis of contemporary Jewish sacred song or a comprehensive survey of the career paths of professional clergy-musicians will find that while I have blazed trails and made clearings, I have not built settlements.

This relates to one more issue regarding approach: contextualization vs. generalization. I tend to support the general ethnomusicological approval for maximal contextualization and have, with students, faulted the discipline for being less precise in this respect than sister fields, say sociolinguistics. Nevertheless I found myself disguising the specifics behind interview remarks in favor of presenting them as examples of trends. I did this intuitively, in response to a simple lack of clear-enough parameters to establish their interdependence; as a historian has said, we should try to avoid reductionism by assuming "that all variables are independent and interdependent and, consequently, that their actual relationships cannot be formulated in advance" (Phillip 1983:351). I simply do not feel that I/we know enough about the independent variables of synagogue and community size and location, denominational affiliation, in-house politics (rabbi, lay leadership), and the factors of age, gender, temperament, and abilities of individual hazzanim to tell which cluster of variables is the "right" one to explain a given remark about professional life I have quoted. In this situation, to say "said a middle-aged male Conservative hazzan of a medium-sized eastern seaboard city" would probably be more harmful than helpful in understanding the cantorate.

Finally, because this is the most collaborative scholarly venture I have ever undertaken, I have tried throughout to distinguish between my own first-hand investigation and the findings of consultants and correspondents. I discovered that while it is glorious to have other people slog through archives, it partly limits the yield to their interpretation of your interests, putting limits on the personalized serendipity that is so basic to scholarship. Though the research assistants turned out to be excellent interviewers, the need to standardize their questioning perhaps left untapped promising areas of inquiry I would have followed up on a hunch. Some areas of the research never got plumbed simply because some collaborators never delivered, for which one cannot blame a consultant who is going to get only an honorarium and reflected glory. My general feeling is that we should do more of this joint inquiry in ethnomusicology, but be wary of the dangers. Finally, it is hard for me to gauge what was lost and what gained by smoothing the disparate data into a single authorial—perhaps too authoritative—voice.

Acknowledgments

The idea for a study of the American cantorate came from Samuel Rosenbaum, for many years the executive vice-president and guiding spirit of the Cantors Assembly, the professional organization of the Conservative movement. Funding came from the National Endowment for the Humanities in the form of a three-year Basic Research grant (1 January 1984–30 June 1987). I am also grateful for sabbatical leaves from Wesleyan University during the spring of 1984 and again in 1987.

As project director and principal investigator, it fell to me to define the questions, to design the methodologies, and to pick the team to do the research. For history, I relied most heavily on the American Jewish Archives at Hebrew Union College, one of the most hospitable havens a scholar could ask for, as ably mined by Douglas Kohn with advice from Jonathan Sarna and Jacob Rader Marcus. Abraham J. Karp was an overall historical consultant. For earlier periods, we had congregational histories, nineteenth-century periodicals, Yiddish newspapers, personal letters, and standard secondary sources like the works of Marcus, whereas for recent decades we tapped materials from professional organizations and trade journals. Joseph Lipner scanned Yid-

dish-language newspapers, and Charles Bloch made available the archive of the Jewish Cantors Ministers Association.

For ethnography, we took several tacks. Some 125 oral histories form
the backbone of the data, most heavily gathered at the annual conventions of the Cantors Assembly (Conservative) and the American
Conference of Cantors (Reform) in 1984 and 1985. Able assistance
came from Louis Weingarden, Jeffrey Summit, Lionel Wolberger, and
Marcie Frishman. The total also includes two special series of interviews, by Sheyna Mueller on the Women Cantors Network and by
Jeffrey Summit on part-time hazzanim in greater Boston. Another approach was the questionnaire, several of which went both to practitioners and to synagogue presidents, as representatives of the lay leadership. Return in each case (detailed below) was above expectations,
indicating wide sympathy for the project from those most closely involved in synagogue life. Abraham Karp undertook a valuable survey
of rabbinic opinion about hazzanim to further balance the perspective.

Another direction was musicological: the creation of a core repertoire
survey via cassette. The sample requested from members of the Cantors
Assembly was selected in consultation with senior hazzanim to cover
items that would indicate both homogeneity and heterogeneity in Jewish-American sacred song, and the yield of ninety-three cassettes far
exceeds anything available in the study of Jewish liturgical music. Fol-
low-up letters and interviews enabled more precise assessment of the
musicological findings.

A number of special studies were commissioned from individual
senior scholars or graduate student researchers. These are cited in the
relevant sections below as sources for discussion of specific topics, but
are summarized here (in random order) to give an overview of areas
surveyed and personnel recruited: Kay Kaufmann Shelemay (New York
Sephardim), Carol Merrill-Mirsky (Los Angeles Sephardim), Jeffrey
Summit (M.A. thesis, Tufts University on part-time hazzanim), Lionel
Wolberger (M.A. thesis, Wesleyan University on the Conservative Saturday morning service in the Northeast), Louis Weingarden (composers
and the cantorate, cantorial improvisation), and the late Lois Ibsen al
Faruqi on the Islamic quran-chanter.

Some scholars helped immensely by looking at the data and giving
their reactions, in longer or shorter form, particularly in the area of
musicology, including Judit Frigyesi, Max Wohlberg, Pinchas Spiro,
Hanoch Avenary, and Harold S. Powers. Akiva Zimmerman kindly
provided copies of materials from his extensive archive and Amnon
Shiloah helped with orientation, as did Henry Abelove. I am partic-

ularly indebted to Barbara Kirshenblatt-Gimblett for her overall response to the manuscript.

Among those who work in the cantorate itself, Samuel Rosenbaum must be mentioned first. His dedication to the project's highest standards and his organizational ability were a constant comfort. Morton Shames was the geographically closest major hazzan and gave unstintingly of his time and wisdom. The doyen of cantorial authorities and teachers, Max Wohlberg, was particularly patient and unfailingly helpful. Samuel Adler, Miriam Gideon, and Hugo Weissgal were kind enough to illuminate the composer's point of view. Lenny Wasser and Freide Gorewitz of the Cantors Assembly and American Conference of Cantors offices, respectively, were most responsive to inquiries, and successive directors of the School of Sacred Music (Hebrew Union College-Jewish Institute of Religion) Jon Haddon and Lawrence Hoffman, as well as Bernard Beer, director of the cantorial training program at Yeshiva University, were helpful to the project. Many hazzanim sent in special materials from personal files, for which I am extremely grateful. The following listing represents the full-time and part-time hazzanim who were most active contributors to the project (an asterisk marks those who have passed away since being interviewed): David Aptowitzer, Penny Aronson, Lawrence Avery, Vicki Axe, David Bagley, Shlomo Bar-Nissim, Jacob Barkin, Maria Barugel, Tyrone Bauer, Ben Belfer, Kerry Ben-David, Emil Berkovits, Gabriel Berkovits, Bruce Benson, Janet Bieber, Frank Birnbaum, Sheri Blum, Joyce Bonen, Jacob Bornstein, Burton Borovetz, Richard Botton, David Brandhandler, Alan Brava, Margaret Brenner, Samuel Brown, Joel Caplan, A. Lopez Cardozo, David Chack, Jack Chomsky, Sheila Cline, Bette Cohen, Doris Cohen, Sanford Cohn, Baruch Cohon, Phyllis Cole, Renee Coleson, Barbara Collier, Don Croll, Louis Danto, Walter Davidson, Gerald De Bruin, Irving Dean, Elliot Dicker, Joshua Elkins, Steve Epstein, Abraham Ezring, Irving Feller, Kalman Fliegelman, Edward Fogel, Mimi Frishman, Edwin Gerber, Maynard Gerber, Sherwood Goffin, Isaac Goodfriend, Edward Graham, Daniel Green, Harieta Gross, Erno Grosz, Saul Hammerman, Mordecai Heiser, Errol Helfman, Rochelle Helzner, Anita Hochman, Mark Horowitz, Barbara Ostfeld Horowitz, Joshua Jacobson, *Oscar Julius, Simon Kandler, John Kaplan, Patrice Kaplan, Sidney Karpo, Aaron Katchen, David Katchen, Deborah Katchko-Zimmerman, Alane Katzew, Paul Kavon, Samuel Kelemer, Robert Kieval, Sherman Kirshner, Harold Klein, Louis Klein, Jeffrey Klepper, Jerome Kopmar, Kenneth Koransky, Arthur Koret, Paul Kowarsky, *David Koussevitsky, Morton Kula, Edmond Kulp, Mark Kushner, Nathan Lam, Morris Lang, Moshe Lanxner, Alan Lefkowitz, David Lefkowitz, Harold

Lerner, Sheldon Levin, Morris Levinson, Harold Lew, Ivor Lichterman, William Lipson, Leon Lissek, Abraham Lubin, Ben Maissner, Yehuda Mandell, Moshe Meirovich, Saul Meisels, Solomon Mendelson, Sheldon Merel, Abraham Mizrahi, Philip Moddel, Sheyna Mueller, Edward Mulgay, Richard Nadel, Rochelle Nelson, Maurice Neu, Macy Nulman, Harold Orbach, Emanuel Perlman, Gordon Piltch, Irving Pinsky, Marshal Portnoy, Sidney Rabinowitz, Samuel Radwine, Neil Ram, Donald Roberts, Neil Robinson, Elias Roochvarg, Jules Rosenberg, Henry Rosenblum, Roy Rosenzweig, Ruth Ross, *Louis Rothman, Judith Rowland, Max Rubin, Zindel Sapoznik, Noah Schall, Robert Scherr, Morris Schorr, Neil Schwartz, Seymour Schwartzman, Charles Segelbaum, Elli Shaffer, Morton Shenok, Abraham Shapiro, Jody Schechterman, Robert Shapiro, Philip Sherman, Linda Shivers, Irving Shulkes, Shlomo Shuster, Benjamin Siegel, Kurt Silberman, *Moses Silverman, David Silverstein, Abraham Salkov, Max Shimansky, Jeffrey Shiovitz, Hyman Sky, Judah Smolack, Raymond Smolover, Robert Solomon, Pinchas Spiro, Stephen Stein, Jodi Sufrin, Reuven Taff, Peter Taormina, Moshe Taube, Louis Teichman, Howard Tushman, Larry Vieder, Samuel Vigoda, Moshe Waldoks, Isaac Wall, Harry Weinberg, George Weinflash, Roger Weisberg, Bruce Wetzler, David Wisnia, Richard Wolberg, Gregory Yaroslow, Robert Zalkin, Paul Zim, Sol Zim, and Nathan Zimri.

A Note on Transliteration and Translation

Translations from the Yiddish are mine or those of my parents, Judith and Norval Slobin, who have kindly spent time over the years making primary sources available. Yiddish orthography follows the standard YIVO system. Hebrew transliteration is a problem; there are multiple systems, even in the area of liturgy. For example, two standard sources on Jewish religious practice I refer to often (Klein 1979; Millgram 1971) have radically different systems. I have simply picked one easy to read for nonspecialists and easy to type. To simplify things, I have standardized the transliteration of basic terms in quotations from secondary sources (e.g. *chazan, hazan, khazn,* and other variations are all rendered *hazzan*). Non-English terms are italicized at their first appearance.

A Note on Identities

For various reasons, living hazzanim are only exceptionally cited by name throughout the book. The initials that appear after quotations from interviews (e.g., D.T., C.E.) were selected randomly.

A Note on Statistics

Questionnaire responses generated enough numbers to allow for modest statistical input. The data were processed with DataEase 2.5r2 by Lionel Wolberger, in consultation with staff of the Wesleyan University psychology department. The statistical base includes the following: Cantors Assembly (Conservative): 68 of 382 listed members; American Conference of Cantors (Reform): 41 of 188; Cantorial Council of America (Orthodox): 32 of 99. It should be noted that the totals, based on membership directories, include emeritus, retired, and unemployed or otherwise inactive hazzanim, so represent a larger number than the total of full-time active American professionals. Thus our sample, submitted by those who are interested in professional life and its history, represents a somewhat greater percentage than it would appear.

A second database came from a questionnaire to presidents of synagogues listed in the above directories as having professional hazzanim. Two hundred ten responded, certainly a significant figure, though the fact that presidents received the questionnaire but may have had others fill it out must be borne in mind; we know of at least one case where a president handed the form to the hazzan to complete.

Concerning another database, the musical core sample that forms the basis for part 3 was gathered from ninety-three members of the Cantors Assembly. The breakdown of participants is as follows (for those who contributed information on their background): (1) generation: 22 born before 1925, 28 born 1925–39, 20 born 1940–49, and 13 born 1950–55; (2) place of birth: all but 14 American, Czechoslovakia 4, Poland 4, Germany 3, and Hungary, England, France, Israel, and Latvia/Lithuania, 2 each; (3) schooling: 19 at Jewish Theological Seminary, 15 at Hebrew Union College, 2 at both, 4 at Yeshiva University, and 5 with father/family. Many also list private schooling, three of whom cite Joshua Weisser, two Gregor Shelkan, and two Alan Michelson; another two studied with one of their fellow contributors.

NOTES

1. Indeed, there is only one book on the hazzan (cantor), as opposed to various (though hardly numerous) works on sacred music: Landman (1972). This brief monograph sketches out the topic in a helpful way, but it is neither comprehensive nor definitive.

2. Although it is easy to do this in part 2, which is based largely on oral histories, for the historical survey of part 1, firsthand accounts by hazzanim are hard to come by. However, the fact that Isaac Leeser, himself a hazzan,

published the mid-nineteenth century journal *Occident* was very helpful and forms part of the reason I drew so heavily on that source.

3. I am grateful to Barbara Kirshenblatt-Gimblett for this formulation.

4. To be precise, different layers and waves of Sephardim are involved. In colonial times the Sephardim drew on London and Amsterdam for inspiration. In the late nineteenth and early twentieth centuries, a small wave of Mediterranean Sephardim arrived, originating anywhere from Morocco to the Balkans and Turkey. Today the scene is further complicated by the arrival of "Afro-Asian" Jews from places like Yemen and Bukhara, so a thorough study would have to take a great deal of communal variation into account, only some of which can be suggested here.

5. The small size of early Jewish-American communities—fifty prominent families in New York in colonial times—means that well-known individuals played an outsized role, further justifying a methodology based also on paucity of data and the limited scope of the enterprise.

6. The same may, largely, be said of the anthropology of the Jews, as witnessed by the contributors' list to a new volume of such studies (Goldberg 1987).

7. Moore's definition of "second generation" as a state of mind, not a demographic fact, is borne out by my parents. Born in 1943, I was just old enough to witness the second-generation pattern break down, which it did in 1954 in Detroit with the building of freeways and suburbs, while nationally, the period saw the opening of all fields of American achievement to Jews for the first time, all this helping create a "third-generation" sensibility.

8. One of my projects was aimed at establishing my own scholarly genealogy via presenting the work of Moshe Beregovski, the scholar of Jewish music I found most comfortable to acknowledge as ancestor (Slobin 1982a, 1982b, 1986). For a telling account of why Jewish-American anthropologists failed to take stock of their ethnicity in their work—so could not serve as founding fathers for me—see Kirshenblatt-Gimblett (1987); it would be nice to have a similar account for the many Jewish pioneers of ethnomusicology. At any rate, experience shows that the issue goes well beyond Bruno Nettl's generalization that although ethnomusicologists "believe we must study all of the world's music, the fact that we have not done so results [merely] from convenience of certain sources, locations of peoples availability of time, and other incidental factors" (1983:9, addition mine).

9. This bypassing of the hazzan is part of the larger historiographic issue of the role of religious life among American Jews in earlier decades, brought to a head by Jenna Weissman Joselit's critique of Moses Rischin's classic work on the immigrant age, *The Promised City*. Joselit notes "Rischin's relative neglect of American synagogue life" as "a conspicuous omission" (1983:165), and in his response to her critique, Rischin concedes that "*The Promised City* gives little attention to religious continuities" (1983:199). That Joselit has moved on to full-scale study of the Orthodox before World War II indicates that a reexamination of the role of religion is well under way.

10. Since I wrote this passage, Goldberg's *Judaism Viewed from Within and from Without* (1987) appeared, which quite explicitly points out the usefulness of Jewish materials in the anthropology of religion, as well as the problems: "Both anthropology, and the modern study of Judaism, have shown complex, ambivalent, and sometimes contradictory attitudes toward the topic of religion" (Goldberg 1987:14).

CHOSEN VOICES

1

The Cantorate in Jewish Culture

From its inception to the present, the cantorate has been
the center of debate, sometimes of communal strife, but
also the source of exultation and of spiritual revival.
—Eric Werner,
A Voice Still Heard . . .

*Ale yidn kenen zayn khazonim, ober di maysten zaynen hey-
zerik*—Any Jew could be a hazzan, but most of them are
hoarse.
—Yiddish proverb

Twenty-three Jews came to America in 1654 and some five million live
in the United States today. Though this seems like a long story, it is
but a short chapter in the history of Judaism. Anything Jewish-American must first be understood as something Jewish, that is, having roots
millennia before there was an America. This chapter places the cantorate in the Jewish historical and cultural landscape, from the nebulous
beginnings of the *hazzan* as a recognizable figure through the heyday
of the superstar sacred singer in the early twentieth century.

There is a second reason, beyond antedating America, to look at the
cultural setting of the cantorate. After all, for the past three hundred
years, the American and European histories have overlapped and intertwined. Although we use the terms *Old World* and *New World* for
the transatlantic spheres of Jewish development, they mislead us into
thinking that anything European is ancient and everything American
is modern. Yet when emigrants leave Europe, they do not slam the
door. To understand Jewish culture in the United States until 1939,
when the Holocaust really made Europe the Old World, one has to
remember that the Atlantic was a two-way ocean, crossed and recrossed
by Jews and their culture. In short, European sounds and values are
inextricably wound up with the fate of American Jewry. And remember
that for Jews (unlike, say Hungarians), "Europe" is not a unitary con-

cept. There are many European pasts for American Jews, ranging from the patricians of Amsterdam through the barefoot villagers of the Ukraine, a contrast I have picked to show that class, as well as geographic, sectarian, and ideological, contrasts marked the Jewish millions of a continent.

This chapter is divided into three parts, each addressing a different aspect of the points just raised: (1) the rise of the cantorate as an institution; (2) the cantorate as part of Ashkenazic expressive culture; and (3) the European cantorate at the time of the great period of emigration (1840s–1930s).

The rise of the cantorate

In earliest times, Judaism as a religion focused on a cult, centered on sacrifices offered in a main sanctuary—the Temple—with a priesthood that performed impressive multimedia services at least as early as the times of King Solomon.[1] The Temple singers' status grew in the times of the Second Temple, after the Exile (De Vaux 1961:457). Although we are relatively informed on Temple music, we know less about what went on in the synagogue, the local house of prayer and instruction, and are not even clear on the synagogue's origins. Authorities tend to agree that the two religious centers were very different in character: "the attitude of the Temple was theocratic and ritualistic, that of the Synagogue anthropocentric and democratic" (Werner 1959:22). Of particular importance for the development of the cantorate was the question of control: the synagogue relied on the local congregation for leadership, as opposed to the official hierarchy of the cult center. With the destruction of the Second Temple in 70 C.E., the entire apparatus of sacrifice disappeared, and the surviving leadership—the rabbis—had to refashion the day-to-day practice of the religion. They turned to individual prayer as the answer, based on a portable sense of religion. Each Jew's personal prayers were declared equal to the old system of sacrifices, which meant that everyone, everywhere, could substitute for the devotion formerly offered by the priesthood.

The evolving attitude towards prayer paved the way for the gradual emergence of the hazzan.[2] Prayer was defined as being most effective if it was communal, rather than private, and sung rather than spoken:

> Although in the absence of an alternative, one is permitted to pray privately, synagogue attendance and participation in communal worship is mandatory. Indeed, we are warned not even to dwell in a place that is without a synagogue. . . . But our liturgy was not merely recited in a monotone, it was chanted *binei'imah*—pleasingly. It is remarkable how replete our ancient literature is with references extolling the importance

of song. . . . God, we are assured, loves to hear a pleasant voice (Wohlberg 1984:35, 38).

Another aspect of synagogue life that bears on the cantorate was the combination of fixity and freedom in the liturgy. Certain prayers were obligatory from the very beginning, but there was also a principle that "a rigidly fixed liturgy was frowned upon by the sages as engendering routine-praying" (Werner 1959:5). This issue can be conceived of as a polarity between *keva*, here understood as deadening routine, and *kavanah*, a state of intense spirituality.

Thus four historical conditions set the stage for the invention of the hazzan, based on the absence of a cult center and the geographic dispersion of the Jewish population in the Diaspora: (1) emphasis on prayer, particularly if communal; (2) emergence of the synagogue as the dominant "house of prayer"; (3) stress on the melodic, aesthetic quality of prayer; and (4) the notion that the liturgy combined the fixed and the free, allowing for creative insertion and improvisation.

The term *hazzan* itself was ready for specialization, since in earliest times it was ambiguous. Though the word was in use by the rabbis as early as two thousand years ago, the man who held the title was not a musically gifted prayer leader, but "just a general synagogue official whose duties included matters as diverse as sweeping the sanctuary, on the one hand, and engaging in religious debate with non-Jews on the other" (Hoffman 1984:14). Slowly, the notion of hazzan comes into sharper focus as part of a classification of prayer leaders and crystallizes by around the year 600. What happens is that congregations begin to rely on someone to help them through the long sequence of Hebrew prayers that forms the backbone of the service. Remember that Hebrew was already not the Jewish vernacular when the Diaspora began. So worshippers let someone step forward—or elected a congregant—to serve as an "ideal" projector of prayer. This person was known as *sheliach tzibbur*, "messenger (envoy, emissary) of the congregation," and was required to be a particularly pious and upstanding Jew. The position of sheliach tzibbur was "formally created by Rabban Gamaliel II (fl. c.e. 90)" (Werner 1976:10). To what extent this person was felt to be not just a model worshipper, but a mediator, is unclear;[3] what is known is that each congregant could feel "covered" by the prayer leader's acknowledged ability to recite everything appropriately: "The individual worshiper needed only listen carefully and attentively to the precentor, and by saying the prescribed responses, especially the 'Amen' at the end of each benediction, he fulfilled all his obligations. This is easily understood when one realizes that the writing down of prayers was not permitted until the eighth century" (Werner 1976:10).

In contrast to the voluntary, relaxed role of the sheliach tzibbur, the hazzan had quite a different status. This prayer leader was paid and appointed by the community, a kind of sacred civil servant, a situation that jelled by around the year 600 (Werner 1976:10). Why communities wanted the hazzan, whose contribution equaled and exceeded that of the sheliach tzibbur, is not totally clear, but many scholars feel the rise of this new sacred singer is tightly connected to the emergence of the *piyut* as a vital expression of Jewish aesthetic and religious feelings. It is a rhymed, metric hymn that grew as a genre around the fourth or fifth century, with one of its most outstanding exponents, Eliezer Kallir, flourishing ca. 600. This novelty in the prayerbook was somewhat complex, introducing legal and tale material from the great rabbinic commentaries, but also expressing strong devotional feelings, all set to beautiful melodies. To create or sing a piyut required extra skill, so it is not surprising that the rise of the piyut and of the hazzan are co-incidental, since they are probably interdependent. This means that aesthetic satisfaction began to take on ever greater importance in worshippers' notion of why they went to services, an issue that has remained germane down to our days. It also became an ever-present question in terms of the job expectations of the sacred singer: "It was inevitable that as the liturgy developed and the role of the Hazzan as leader in worship grew ever greater, emphasis was placed on the requirement that he have a pleasant voice. Only comprehension of the text took precedence over a pleasant voice" (Wohlberg 1974:17).

Yet the piyut was not just a solo for the hazzan; a twelfth-century observer named Samuel ibn Yahya notes that when the hazzan sang the piyutim, he was "accompanied by the congregation with shouts and songs" (Freelander 1979:62). The issue of congregational participation is one we will find still alive in the American context (see chapter 9). This popular appeal of the piyut matches trends in other religions: "Hymn writing and singing must be regarded . . . as an elementary religious force, effective in Jewry as in every other faith" (Avenary 1971:570).

Another similarity with surrounding cultures was the dislike for soloists and grassroots enthusiasm in sacred music. Much like their Christian ecclesiastical counterparts, the rabbinic authorities[4] distrusted enthusiasm and excess on the part of worshippers.[5] They also worried about expanding the role of a prayer leader who might be more interested in personal prestige or sensual delight than in the power of prayer; having a beautiful voice may have been a job requirement, but "the possessor of this unique gift, maintains Rabbi Judah, the Pious, should devote his talents only to lofty purposes and while singing His praises must refrain from a display of vanity" (Wohlberg 1974:17). As a result, "There is hardly a medieval rabbinic book about synagogal liturgy that does not sharply inveigh against the liturgical and secular misconduct of the hazzanim" (Werner 1959:122).[6]

The parallel to the Christian situation is continuous, and is nicely summarized by Werner:

> In many respects the status and the function of the Jewish cantor parallels that of the Christian lector. He was the paid (not honorary) reader and singer of the Synagogue since the time of the seventh century; like the lector, he preferred to sing; very frequently, we find two hazzanim, one for reading, one for singing, as was the case with the lectors; the hazzan too, was often at odds with his superiors. Even the complaints about the immodest life of the hazzanim parallel those about the lectors; the *Constitutiones Apostolorum* warn the cantors and psalmists to lead a modest life, and admonish them not to indulge in throwing dice and other immoral pastimes (Werner 1959:121–22).

Perhaps these anticantorial outbursts contributed to a streak of folk humor directed at hazzanim; there are numerous proverbs and jokes at the expense of sacred singers, none more famous than the Yiddish saying *ale khazonim zaynen naronim* ("all hazzanim are fools"). However, as the case of the piyut shows, when congregations want charismatic aesthetic leadership, they choose it, despite rabbinic objections or low evaluation of the hazzan as an individual, for very good emotional reasons: "During the Crusades and the never-ending persecutions the cantors and their moving songs could give more comfort than the best *halakhic* [legal] decisions" (Werner 1959:13). Looking back, later generations imbued the hazzan with special powers based on this ability to voice the mood of the masses: "The creative hazzan did not only enthrall his congregants by his free imaginative flow of Jewish musical expression, he voiced also our people's suffering and tribulation. . . . We are told how Hazzan Hirsch so moved the Tartars (in 1648–9) by his emotional chanting of the 'El mole rachamim' [prayer for the dead] that they saved 3,000 Jews from the hands of the raging Cossacks" (Ephros 1976:23).[7]

It was perhaps this legendary prowess that made the position of hazzan "the most permanent and continuous synagogue office, one which underwent relatively few changes after the early Middle Ages" (Baron, in Avenary 1971). Of course, all this tells us little about the work conditions or daily life of European hazzan in premodern times, and Baron's generalized time frame is perhaps a bit too pat to allow for regional and temporal shifts in the status and work of the sacred singer. We do know that the requirements and rewards for hazzanim were quite diverse, varying from place to place and over time.[8] Though the rabbinic sources stipulate modesty and poverty as essential characteristics, even these might not have been essential, since each community could choose its own prayer leader for its own reasons.[9] If there is a basic fact to be learned from our scanty knowledge of the early cantorate, it is that the institution is a grassroots phenomenon. Judaism mandates no ecclesiastical hierarchy, so it is only by agreement of a congregation and a community that a fellow-worshipper is raised to a position of authority. The importance of the hazzan rises and falls with the enthusiasm of the laity for its sacred singers. The hazzan and the congregation are engaged in a dialogue, both figuratively and literally, as in the communal response to a hymn.

This capsule history of the cantorate yields a few points that remain valid for the American situation:

1. The hazzan is chosen and paid by the laity.

2. The hazzan is one of a group of possible prayer leaders filling the niche of sheliach tzibbur ("messenger," or "delegate," or "emissary" of the congregation). The particular specialty of the hazzan is not just to know the prayers, but to perform them with exceptional skill and beauty.

3. The community's or congregation's interest in having a hazzan, or how he should be regarded and rewarded, may fluctuate drastically across space and time.

4. There is always a "strict-constructionist" segment of the Jewish population that distrusts the cantorate, most often on the grounds that the sensuality of the voice may take precedence over the understanding of sacred text.

5. Developments in the cantorate may well parallel social situations for Christian sacred musicians.

6. The hazzan is an innovator: "In most cases it was the cantor who championed new fashions, and in fact often engendered them himself" (Werner 1976:9).

The hazzan in Ashkenazic expressive culture

Like many traditions within a society, the cantorate fits into a broad cultural pattern, a way of conceptualizing the world that cuts across several fields of action. One of the most general of Jewish patterns is the primacy of sacred text. The only thing that holds together all the Jews of the Diaspora, living worldwide for millennia, speaking different languages and carrying on diverse customs, is shared texts.[10] Within each traditional Jewish community, the texts were the wellsprings of group existence and infused many aspects of daily life, a remarkably resilient approach to living in exile: "In retrospect we realize what a remarkable tool the halacha books [sacred texts] of various types were for the maintenance of the continuity of the Jewish community without a centralized hierarchy and final authority at the top. Simultaneously we have here an imposing monument of unceasing adjustment to constantly changing times" (Weinreich 1980:210).

Since to be a hazzan is to be a master of texts, the cantorate lies close to the core of the culture, particularly *expressive* culture, which, roughly defined, means the aesthetics of everyday life. The aesthetic component enters the picture because mere routine performance of known texts is not enough; what this culture particularly values is commentary, interpretation, exegesis—the reworking of sacred texts as a daily and lifelong activity.[11] This is worked out as a cultural pattern that involves two components. One is relatively fixed, timeless, spaceless: the sacred text. The other is improvisatory, current, locatable: a form of commentary that may be linguistic, musical, or even, in the case of handicrafts, material, snowballing its way through history, enlarging through gradual accretion, as well as varying from place to place at any given time. Weinreich calls this "variety within stability" (1980:216) and identifies it as the underpinning of "the Way of the SHaS," where "SHaS" stands for *shisha sedarim*, the Book of Books, (technically, the Babylonian Talmud or the six orders of the Mishnah), or what we are calling sacred texts here.

To understand how the cantorate and its music fit into this pattern of Ashkenazic life, we need to look at parallel examples from other expressive media. First, let's look at Weinreich's analysis of the Yiddish language in its cultural context. Weinreich was a champion of secular studies of Ashkenazic culture and was the great historian of the Yiddish language. Inevitably, he recognized that sacred text lay behind the patterns of life and thought of the Ashkenazic Jews to such an extent that he could not understand their vernacular, secular language without reference to the influence from what Yiddish speakers call *loshn-koydesh*, the "sacred tongue," meaning elements from the sacred texts (in Hebrew or Aramaic). This is not just a matter of borrowing words, but of adapting whole concepts from the sacred world into everyday life, and doing it creatively. Particularly interesting from our point of view is the influence from the language of prayers. For example, "In reciting the prayer *vayoymer dovid* the eyes are covered with the forearm; schoolboys therefore called skating downhill with closed eyes *vayoymer-dovid-glitsh* (*vayoymer-dovid* skating)" (Weinreich 1980:222).

From the homely example of kids sliding on a shtetl hill, we can turn to how the pattern works in the most valued grownup activity, learning to improvise commentary on sacred texts. Adin Steinsaltz, an authority on the Talmud, is quite clear about the cultural pattern involved in *lernen,* a concept of studying that "is so specific that it is untranslatable into a 'Christian' language" (Weinreich 1980:211). Heilman's definition, "a spiritual meditation on and lifelong review of Jewish books," comes close (Heilman 1983:1). The Talmud is an immense compendium of commentary on the Bible, handed down from the past, but that is only the beginning, since talmudic scholars have a special view of time:

> It is understood organically as a living and developing essence, present and future being founded on the living past. Within this wide-ranging process, certain elements take on more stable form, while others, pertaining to the present, are flexible and much more changeable; the process as such, however, is based on faith in the vitality of each element, ancient as it may be, and the importance of its role in the never-ending, self-renewing work of creation (Steinsaltz 1976:8).

What flows naturally from this open-ended conception of the sacred text is the obligation of every male to continue the task: "True knowledge can only be attained through spiritual communion, and the student must participate intellectually and emotionally in the talmudic debate, himself becoming, to a certain degree, a creator. . . . The Talmud is perhaps the only sacred book in all of world culture that permits and even encourages the student to question it" (Steinsaltz 1976:9).[12]

Yet there is a strong brake on this innovation: "Every scholar tries to prove that his own revelations are not totally new but are implied in the remarks of his predecessors" (Steinsaltz 1976:266). In this process of self-expressive interpretation of text, then, there is a constant tension between the concept that "everything that the distinguished scholar creates anew has already been said to Moses on Sinai" and the principle that "the Talmud is unfinished" (Steinsaltz 1976:273).

Steinsaltz's Talmud provides a provocative analogy to the work of the hazzan, who, based on the past, moves ever forward into a musical present as part of an unfinished commentary on the sacred text. This parallel to talmudic study is strongly suggested by another description of Steinsaltz: "The talent for studying Talmud resembles artistic ability in some ways: any man who has a predilection for the subject may become a passive savant, and if he is more proficient, may become creative, but greatness depends on a special skill, what in other spheres is called artistic genius" (Steinsaltz 1976:265). Translated to the world of prayer, Steinsaltz's insight cuts two ways. First, it helps distinguish the ordinary worshipper from the hazzan, but second, it is very useful in dividing the role of the everyday sheliach tzibbur—the competent but uninspired prayer leader—from the charismatic hazzan, the grass-roots favorite.

Let me move from the exalted, exclusively male domain of the Talmud to the female world exemplified by a ritual handicraft, the making of the Torah binder, analyzed by Barbara Kirshenblatt-Gimblett (1982). Here sacred text becomes what she calls "a performed object" as developed among Western Ashkenazim. A strip of cloth, inscribed with relevant passages from sacred text, is prepared for an infant boy who, some years later, presents the binder to the synagogue to wrap a Torah scroll. In some cases, the boy may even use that particular scroll as the one from which to read at his bar mitzvah, continuing an intimate association with the binder. The mothers who embroider these ritual objects are as imbued with a sense of tradition and commentary as are their husbands and fathers, who help select and draw the texts. The passages they illustrate are not in the least arbitrary, but depend on individual and local aesthetic choices and folkways; as Kirshenblatt-Gimblett says, "there are many ways that a text may be approached in the quest for its meanings." This form of cultural expression, then, also uses the fixity of sacred text as a springboard for improvisation. The Torah binders "exemplify in the extreme the interplay of text, commentary, symbolism, and style of representation in the wordbound image" (1982).

It is not just in the Torah binder, but in the entire world of Jewish art that similar concepts flourish. Surveying the early centuries of European Jewish art, Sed-Rajna finds she can generalize about cultural concepts: "In the majority of communities artistic production was tolerated and even encouraged when a didactic purpose was involved or when a beautiful setting was imparted to the precepts (*hiddur mitzvah* [enhancement of a mitzvah, or meritorious act]), the two goals often going together. . . . In fact, in displaying adorned objects, it is as if one is embellishing the precepts themselves" (Sed-Rajna 1975:11, 147).[13]

Didacticism involves a connection to sacred text; the very hymns we saw as integral to the rise of the cantorate turn out to be involved in the visual arts as well: "Very decorative in itself, the Hebrew script was adapted in various ways to serve as an ornament. . . . The illustration of ritual manuscripts (*mahzorim*) gave rise to an entirely new repertoire . . . the liturgical hymns (*piyutim*) . . . were headed by narrative scenes created for this purpose" (Sed-Rajna 1975:176, 181).

The impulse to use graphic interpretation is quite old, being present in the most important ancient synagogue art we have, the frescoes at Dura-Europos (ca. sixth century). "These details [of wall panels] are based on Midrashic texts, an influence that can be perceived in other panels as well. Their presence may indicate that the text of the model was a Biblical paraphrase" (Sed-Rajna 1975:75).

I have purposely jumbled the historical continuity of this discussion of visual interpretation of sacred text to make the point that a profound cultural concept has little to do with the history of style and everything to do with deeply felt internal values. The pattern we have been discussing for Ashkenazic Jewry (equally true for Sephardim) had a real survival value, according to Weinreich: "The secret of Ashkenazic flexibility, of the capacity to bear shocks and to constantly absorb new variants, is inherent in the initial pattern" (1980:241). This, then, is the context of the hazzan's work; sacred music is yet another form of commentary, of interpretation and reinterpretation of the ever-present matrix sacred text provides. The hazzan's approach is more demanding than that of the average member of the Jewish community, for his is a chosen voice, evaluated on the basis of aesthetic, rather than intellectual or everyday norms. He is expected to improvise on the spot, so as to give ever-fresh meaning to old words. As one hazzan who taught improvisation for years puts it: "Improvisation, to my estimation is: pick up a page in the *siddur* [prayerbook] and he starts singing something that he never done before. He is just reading the words; according to the meaning of the words, you are trying to interpret the word . . . try to put it over to the listener. He should know what you are talking about" (F.C.). Or, as another veteran expresses it: "The word has to be interpreted. Otherwise, I'd rather hear a violin play, because they can do it better and they don't have to breathe" (A.C.).

We have seen historical and cultural reasons for the rise of the cantorate and the expressive role of the hazzan. No one has summarized the way these forces have shaped the sacred singer's role better than Max Wohlberg, doyen of hazzan-teachers today. Wohlberg sees four interlocking factors that drive the musical interpretation of text, all producing constant vitality and change over the centuries:

> 1. *Hiddur mitzvah* ["beautification of a meritorious act"]—the desire to add an esthetic dimension to a mitzvah; 2. The attempt to eschew monotony, as evidenced in the dictum of Rabbi Simeon: *Al taas tefiltacha keva*—"Do not make your prayers routine [i.e., not *meaningful*]"; 3. The absence of a universally accepted *minhag* ["customary way"] prompting— during a millennium (between the sixth and sixteenth centuries)—the proliferation of new piyutim; 4. The irrepressible urge of the individual precentor for artistic self expression (Wohlberg 1977).

Only Wohlberg's fourth concept addresses *individual* aesthetic satisfaction; the others form part of a communal consensus, a core understanding of aesthetics that is part of what I am calling expressive culture. Thus, though everyone may be expressively engaged in "the way of the SHaS" through language, study, crafts, or other media, Ashkenazic culture also allows for specialists who are respected for particular skills. To take one regional example, in eastern Europe, there were three such specialists: the hazzan, the rabbi—a master of the legal interpretation of texts—and the *maggid,* the preacher. The maggid was an itinerant sermonizer who came to a town and drew a crowd and a fee through extraordinary skill in live performance based on sacred text, somewhat in the Protestant tradition of far-famed preachers who wandered the American countryside or who still populate the airwaves.

Individual excellence, even to the point of allowing for professionals, coexists uneasily with strongly felt values of communal consensus. Those who make a living by performing—whether hazzanim, maggidim, or *klezmorim* (secular instrumentalists)—are suspect in two ways: first, because they tend to travel about, so lack the steadiness of the solid citizen, and second, because they may flaunt their separatism or vaunt their skills. These considerations lead us to our third area of interest, the development of the modern cantorate.[14]

The modern cantorate: 1820s–1930s

We have no comprehensive history of the European cantorate. This is not an institution historians have felt drawn to, perhaps because they tend to shy away from expressive culture. The only purpose of trying to provide even a sketch here is to have a backdrop for discussing the cantorate in America. The emphasis will tend to be on the eastern European context, the source of the vast majority of American Jews, but we need also to take account of western Europe, whose approach to the modern cantorate was strongly influential as well.[15]

We begin with the East, where in the smallest Jewish community there was not likely to be a hazzan at all. Zavel Kwartin (1874–1953), who grew up to be a giant among hazzanim, describes the way he absorbed liturgical music in his *dorf* (village) of Khonorod near Tolna and Uman' in the southern Ukraine. This community had eighty Jewish families surrounded by 10,000 peasants. The local services were run by four men with the title of *ba'al tefillah* ("master of prayer"), the usual term for the volunteer sheliach tzibbur described earlier as a basic type of prayer leader. Kwartin explains that these men "influenced my entire musical career deeply" through their knowledge of tunes. Each had a distinct style, some being influenced by hearing hazzanim when they went to big cities (Kiev, Odessa) on business trips, whereas others simply were inspired spinners of improvised sacred song. Every Friday night, there was wrangling in the single synagogue over who would lead the prayers (Kwartin 1952:38–39). Khonorod was such a backwoods shtetl that Kwartin was eight before he ever heard a hazzan, one of the many itinerant professionals who plied the Ukrainian countryside. These men were based in a town but assembled a group of *meshoyrerim* ("choirboys") and toured the provinces to make a living, because their home synagogue provided minimal support. Kwartin sang for the visitor and showed he could improvise, but the boy's father refused to let him go off with the hazzan: "The departure of the hazzan and his meshoyrerim left an open wound in my childish heart" (Kwartin 1952:46). It took the future superstar another twenty years to become a hazzan.

Some boys were pluckier than Zavel; when the great David Roitman's (1884–1943) father refused to let him become a meshoyrer, he knew what to do: "[Roitman] stole a few rubles from his father, put on three or four shirts to have something to change to and was on his way. He came to Uman' and became a meshoyrer with Yankel Soroker. . . . Cantors fought over him and resorted to various tricks to steal him away from each other" (Linder 1925).

Life in the towns made it possible for a child like Roitman to survive— barely—as another former meshoyrer describes:

> At the end of the nineteenth and the beginning of the twentieth century, every hazzan in every city and town in East Europe had a permanent choir of meshoyrerim. The hazzan did not pay them any wages. They drew their support by going every Friday with a sealed collection box from door to door; by singing at weddings and circumcisions—and after the hazzan had sung a special blessing for the father of the bride and the father of the groom, the choirboys circulated among the guests asking for *misheberach* money; by spending the entire month of Elul [High Holiday time] with trips to the cemetery waiting for people who came to visit the graves, to sing for them, with a wailing melody, the "El mole rachamim," made a special effort to elicit tears from the mourners and then extended their hands for *"mole* money"; by going on Chanukah evenings from house to house with a lantern asking for money; by putting a collection plate in the vestibule of the synagogue just before Yom Kippur, and the like. The hazzan didn't have to feed the choirboys either. They had "eating days" [rotating meals at local homes, like religious-school students]. If a day wasn't covered, the choirboy went hungry (Gelbart 1942).

Many societies grant a special role reversal to nominally weak people who have ritual power (see Turner 1969). This allowed the meshoyrerim to turn the tables on the community:

The choirboys were always cheerful. They mocked everything and everyone in town. . . . No one was sure of not becoming the next target. . . . [On Chanukah, after collecting money they] cunningly extracted quite a bit of the silver, hid it away . . . and came to the hazzan with glum and angry looks because the "stingy housewives this year had put only coppers in the boxes." They survived the fiery cross examination of the hazzan, who still remembered very well what he himself had done as a choirboy. (Gelbart 1942).

In his early novel *Yosele Solovey* (1888), which has a hazzan as hero, the great Yiddish writer Sholom Aleichem supports this view:

The meshoyrer gang, you should know, are a good bunch. . . . Going out in to the wide world, these guys are like wild horses; they don't know what to do first. . . . Whoever they were before, now they're all together, and they're one-for-all. . . . Usually they get rid of Jewishness, and do whatever they please . . . in their free time, they go around town, smoke cigars, have fun, and who cares for work—in general, it's: this is the life! (Sholom Aleichem 1942:112).

Making the transition from meshoyrer to hazzan was not something every boy did,[16] nor did it necessarily make their lives easier. In small communities such as the fictional hometown of Sholom Aleichem's novel, life was rough on men like Yosele's father, Shmulik the hazzan, compared to the star singers, for whom the author uses real names:[17] "Shmulik the hazzan might have a rare throat and produce something like Nisi, or Pitzi, or even like Yerukhom Hakoton, but when Chanukah comes, he can take a walking stick and a lantern and amble around the city, wishing everyone individually 'seasons' greetings' and take—alms" (Sholom Aleichem 1942:20). Like his choirboys, the town hazzan had to scrape together a living from a variety of jobs, including the cemetery singing already mentioned. Despite the great praise showered on a local hazzan, he was very low on the social scale. The fact that he was dependent on handouts seems to have played a part in this evaluation.[18]

When Kwartin married into a wealthy merchant's family, his father-in-law refused to allow him to become a hazzan, exploding:

What, a hazzan, a beggar, in our family? And my coddled and delicate daughter should become a *khaznte*, a beggar, so every *yidene* [gossip] can look into her pot, and my son-in-law should go around to *brisses* [circumcisions], weddings, and *pidyon-habens* [a ceremony for a first-born son], funerals and *yortsayts* [anniversaries of a death], delivering misheberachs [blessings] and el mole rachmims, and then stretching out his hand, so maybe someone will feel sorry and throw him a dollar? (Kwartin 1952:175).

In this domestic drama, Kwartin quotes his father as defending him by using the grassroots argument: "We cannot stand against the will of my child, which . . . is also the will of the people, who have displayed such enthusiasm for him although he is still young" (Kwartin 1952:175). Indeed, it is that enthusiasm which Kwartin cites almost rapturously as the real reward of being a sacred singer, particularly in smaller cities unspoiled by cosmopolitan airs. He found greatest happiness in the Galician town of Yaroslaw:

> I fell into a trance from wanting to display all my wonders. . . . I felt that I gave everything I was capable of. . . . I davened [prayed] with a true ecstasy. . . . Only in this small, dirty and not too wealthy shtetl did I feel what a hazzan can be among Jews. There I saw for the first time, what a powerful figure the hazzan is and what place he occupies in Jewish life. Burdened Jews, who fight tooth and nail all week for a little living, collect in the shuls Sabbaths and holidays, and the hazzan is the one who helps them unburden themselves of all the weekly cares and transport themselves to a purer, higher world of spirituality. . . . They see the hazzan as a true spokesman for their buried feelings, who evokes with his prayers their longing for a better future (Kwartin 1952:248).[19]

This sweet memory of Yaroslaw is particularly impressive coming from Kwartin, who became a major recording star and cashed in on his celebrity in America as well as in Europe over a long career. He takes pains to point out the two-way nature of the hazzan-average Jew relationship and stresses the interpretive side of his work: "This also had a reciprocal effect on the hazzan himself, who felt a terrible responsibility to his listeners. . . . In all my more than fifty years of practice as hazzan, I never stopped, day and night, to think, to improvise, to study, and to immerse myself in the inexhaustible source of melody. I tried to pour myself into every word of the prayers, to interpret them the better to listeners" (Kwartin 1952:249). This is a perhaps idealized, even romanticized portrait of the classic eastern European situation of the hazzan. However, it is reinforced by popular fiction, like the Sholom Aleichem novel cited, and forms part of the myth of the golden age of the cantorate continued by immigrants and their descendants in America, as we shall see.

Meanwhile, in central and western Europe, developments had produced a somewhat different situation that began to affect the East. When the German/Austrian Jews were "emancipated," that is, were granted citizenship by the state in post-Napoleonic times, they began to shift their sense of how to practice Judaism. They felt a need to accommodate to the new situation in religious as well as in civic life. The role of the rabbi as legal authority gave way to the state-approved concept of a "religious representative" who was expected to have a secular as well as sacred education and to become a community leader (see Schorsch 1981). At the same time, the fervor of the Orthodox service slowly changed into a "modern" synagogue ritual in an attempt to achieve the decorum that ought to go with recognition by the state. This meant that as early as 1810 in Cassel "unsuitable traditional singing which interrupts the prayer" was curtailed, and congregants were "reminded and ordered to follow the cantor's prayers quietly and silently" (Petuchowski 1968:109). Not only were congregants quieted, but also the high- and low-voiced singers who used to accompany the hazzan were replaced by a decorous chorus as change spread across the German lands community by community throughout the first half of the nineteenth century. Hymns in German replaced the old piyutim, which began to be curtailed or proscribed altogether (Lowenstein 1981). Even synagogue architecture was affected by the decorum movement, as fixed seating supplanted the old movable chairs; reformers "wanted to tidy up visual irregularities, just as they wanted to replace individual cantillation with uniform prayers" (Krinsky 1985:23).

This German modernism took two directions. On the one hand, the emerging German Reform movement, which became prominent in America, felt that the hazzan was a relic of the past. Closely observing the "cultured" behavior of their Christian fellow-citizens, Reformers decided that an organist, choir director, and congregational hymns were all they needed for an up-to-date "Mosaic" religion.[20] On the other hand, a more traditionally oriented wing felt uncomfortable moving out of the old house of worship and remained content with redecorating it. Musically, these "liberal," still rather orthodox Jews supported the work of pioneering hazzan-composers in Vienna (Salomon Sulzer, 1804–90), Berlin (Louis Lewandowski, 1821–94), and Paris (Samuel Naumbourg, 1815–80), whose influential works are cited in later chapters. Sulzer was the pacesetter. Becoming Oberkantor (chief cantor) of Vienna in 1826, he devised a new role to go with the respectable title; Bach, after all, was a cantor by trade.[21] In large cities, the modern central/western synagogue evolved a contemporary, classical music-based performance style solidly grounded on chorus and organ. The resulting bourgeois *chorschul* (Yiddish *khorshul*) was far from the old-time synagogue, with its overlapping, individualized congregant/hazzan/high- and low-voiced soloist interplay of voices. But it was also deliberately distanced from the newfangled, clean-cut, nonparticipatory Reform "temple." The khorshul slowly made its way east to Hungary and the Russian Empire in the nineteenth century along with the general influence of emancipated Western Jewry. By 1869, the narrator of a classic Yiddish novel (Mendele's *Fishke the Lame*) could be over-whelmed and also suspicious of the high-tone choral style as compared to his hometown hazzan's style: "[Back home] Reb Jerechmiel put his heart and soul into his singing and was soaking wet . . . but the cantor here . . . hardly did a thing. As soon as he sang a note, the chorus caught up the cue and dished it out on a little platter . . . that's what they called 'services' here" (quoted in Slobin 1982c:20).

We see the transition in an Easterner like Kwartin during the first decade of the twentieth century. Having worked in Vienna where he was at first hard-pressed to shift styles from his Russian upbringing, he then became a champion of modernism when he was invited to Budapest: "I had already become used to the modern service, which demanded praying facing the people, using a mixed choir and an organ," so he fought the local conservatives and won a compromise, whereby he could use Eastern style in a Western context. What is important here is not just the style wars, but the fact that every community supported a variety of local synagogues, ranging from the purposely plain *shtiblakh* of Hasidic sects, who scorned ornament, through a badly heated *shnaydershul* (tailors' synagogue) to the grand edifices of the middle class. By the late nineteenth century, this jumble of houses of prayer was lightly regulated by the *kehillah*, the Jewish communal structure, who appointed "civil servants."[22] Local governments expected Jews to run their own affairs, and the kehillah was a fractious, possibly corrupt agency given to factional disputes. Hazzanim were often caught up in the resulting shenanigans and the clever ones, like Kwartin, used the kehillah to their advantage wherever possible.

The reason Kwartin had room to maneuver was due to his status as recording star. Having heard the very first cantorial discs (by Cerini and Sirota, ca. 1903), he jumped into the market, recording first the "modern" repertoire of the West, then the down-home Eastern style. Suddenly, he was receiving fantastic offers and having wildly successful tours. He reports that one distributor in Russia had sold one-half million cantorial records in just a few months, topping the sale of all other records in the previous five years.

Part of the success of recordings in the East had nothing to do with the civic emancipation of Jews or with the new synagogue style of the West. The former never came to the Russian Empire, while the latter was very slow to develop, except among a small, secularized circle. It lay in the interests of a rising urban Jewish bourgeoisie who could afford gramophones and who were greatly impressed by the sound of opera. Odessa was the most cosmopolitan of Russian provincial cities and the first Eastern city to have Jews flocking to the opera house, as early as the mid-nineteenth century. As should be clear from the description of the Odessa khorshul above, this lively port favored the emergence of the star hazzan, a figure basic to the European backdrop of the American cantorate. Samuel Vigoda (1981:54), himself a star hazzan who has gathered the legends of the old-time greats, provides a colorful and probably accurate portrait of Ephraim Zalman Razumni (1853–1918),[23] an early Odessa favorite:

> He was perhaps the most representative, most characteristic, almost classic example of the personal cult. He was considered the glamorous matinee idol of the cantorial profession, who bewitched audiences and remains a legendary figure to this day. . . . Notwithstanding the fact that he had a pock-marked face, he had a way . . . to impress people; he was at all times elegantly decked out in a flowing cape . . . and a silk hat. . . . In winter, he would wear a furlined coat, the collar of which was mink. . . . Strutting in the street, he would unconsciously rock his body back and forth in the manner of a dance master. . . . His whole comportment was more like that of an opera singer than a cantor. . . . In the synagogue he donned an extra high cantorial hat, which together with the elevated footstool tended to accentuate his towering presence, adding a regal touch to his appearance. It was all calculated to heighten the suspense and evoke the reverence and awe of the assembly. . . . Razumni knew every trick in the book and played on the heartstrings of his audience at will (Vigoda 1981:98–99).

While bourgeois patrons and proletarian camp followers thronged to hear Razumni, the rabbis had not lost their ancient distrust of the sacred singer:

> As much as he was adored by the general public, he was shunned by the members of the Rabbinical fraternity, who were looking askance at his rather unconventional, irreverent personal conduct that did not jibe with his status of sheliach tzibbur. [But] the overwhelming majority of music lovers were little concerned with Razumni's personal life . . . all that interested them was that he was a great artist of liturgy (Vigoda 1981:103).

This large pool of enthusiasts engaged in fierce rivalry over who should be appointed to their synagogue, reminiscent of the nearly simultaneous fights in New York over who was the leading star of the Yiddish stage. The similarity is not surprising; for the late nineteenth-century synagogue-goer who was too pious to go to the theater or lived in a community too small for a stage, the synagogue was the main show in town.[24] With so much at stake, the hiring process could turn into a public brawl. When Zeidel Rovner (Jacob Samuel Margovsky,

1856–1946) was up for his first job, in the town of Zaslov, all hell broke loose:

> Violent quarrels broke out which gradually degenerated to such an extent that the rabbinical authorities felt obliged to intervene, and a *bet din*, a religious court of law, placed the whole community of Zaslow in *cherem* (state of excommunication) . . . finally they . . . agreed to appoint a neutral arbitrator . . . a Makarover Hasid. First of all he made a pilgrimage to the court of the grand rabbi of Makarov (Vigoda 1981:199).

The neutral party here belongs to the extensive network of Hasidic sects, groups who were uninterested in mainstream religion or its cantorate, and who believed in the authority of their charismatic leaders. Zeidel Rovner had grown up in Makarover circles, so was known to the rabbi, who, according to legend, prophesied that the boy would one day become a world-famous sacred singer. His word carried weight, and the community appointed Zeidel, starting him on his road to renown.

But in the cosmopolitan centers to which Zeidel eventually moved, the natural point of reference was not some Hasidic rabbi, but opera, as the preceding description of the great Razumni suggests. Tales connecting famous hazzanim to the opera world are legion, stretching back well into the nineteenth century. The first, semilegendary figure that comes to mind is Joel David Loewenstein-Straschunsky (1816–50), known by his nickname *"der vilner balabesl,"* supposedly seduced into secular music by an attachment to a Polish noblewoman, only to die alone, heartbroken, after repenting of his folly. Such was the appeal of this romantic hazzan that he became the hero of a Yiddish play and film. Somewhat more historical is the story of Selmar Steifmann, known as Cerini. According to a biography published in 1900 (Mirsky 1900), Cerini was born in 1861 in Warsaw and vacillated continuously between the cantorate and the opera stage. He sang first from behind a curtain to hide his identity and was assigned the stage name Cerini accidentally. He copied opera libretti into the Hebrew alphabet while simultaneously serving as a soloist under Lewandowski in Berlin. The lack of a secure, well-paid cantorial position kept drawing him back to opera to show his independence from the synagogal lay leadership. He is said to have gained German citizenship at the hands of Kaiser Wilhelm himself, and to have been the very first hazzan to make a record.

Time and again, both European and American legends of the hazzanim have sacred singers performing for greats of the opera world and of the government, who are immensely impressed. Kwartin considered the stage seriously as a young man, but was dissuaded by an interview with Vinogradov, a convert-opera star who told Kwartin of the inner emptiness he felt at having abandoned his tradition for the hollow world of opera stardom. Opera even took some hazzanim to America. Herman Davidson (1846–1911), born in Russia, joined a traveling opera company, touring to the Middle East and Europe. He studied under Sulzer in Vienna and came to New York with his opera company in the early 1870s. Frightened by the Wild West, Davidson refused to go along to Mexico, stayed in California, and became a hazzan in Stockton, where he ended life as a gentleman farmer. In this case, opera and the new Sulzer style, indebted to Jewish operatic composers like Halévy and Meyerbeer, paved the way for success in the New World. Later in America, the most famous cantorial superstar, Yosele Rosenblatt (1880–1933), was said to have been offered a highly lucrative contract by the Chicago Opera and to have turned it down due to religious scruples. Still later, younger cantorially trained men like Jan Peerce and Richard Tucker took the opera offers and quite comfortably continued to serve occasionally as hazzanim as well, and today, cantorial children like Neil Shicoff can still be found at the Metropolitan Opera.

The high degree of contact with non-Jewish musics implied by the opera syndrome was not limited to westernized hazzanim. Even the lowliest hazzan might well be in a category of eastern European Jews most in touch with the gentile world, as Weinreich points out:

> The lower, sometimes half or more than half declassed strata that drifted from place to place, maintained a broad contact level; these were unsuccessful yeshiva students, inferior cantors and singers-actors, *pekhotne magidim* (itinerant preachers . . .) and ordinary poor people. On the roads and in the inns these wanderers met with non-Jewish wanderers of similar social caliber, and they exchanged experiences superstitions, ideas and language (1980:180).

Music might well be added to this list of exchanged items; well before the advent of opera and widespread secularization, hazzanim were bringing the outside world into the Jewish community at the same time they were maintaining the old ways; as Weinreich notes: "one could indulge in free variations, because one was sure of the fundamental principle" (1980:228), a sentence which can stand as summary of the present chapter's viewpoint on the hazzan in history.

This brief overview of the modern European cantorate provides several keys for understanding America:

1. "Europe" is a multiple area, and each region, sect, and class of Jews contributed its approach to the American cantorate. The Am-

sterdam burghers, German Reformers, Polish Hasidim, and Ukrainian hazzan-fans all played out their parts on American soil.

2. European change occurred simultaneously with emigration to America. The revolutionary shifts in German thinking about the Jewish clergy peaked in the 1840s, precisely at the moment the "German wave" began to stream towards America. Similarly, the rise of the star hazzan in the East synchronized with the massive movement of Easterners to the United States, beginning in the 1880s. This means that "Old" and "New" Worlds are particularly inapt terms for the cultural trends in which we are interested.[25]

3. The favorite musics of each European region and group became the roots of a new American sacred song, which still shows the effects of multiple influences. One of the characteristically "American" aspects of sacred music in the United States is the combination or the prominence of particular European styles and melodies.

4. A pattern of varied, possibly competing synagogues in a community, each serving a different class/denomination membership, was duplicated in America by mid-nineteenth century and remains the norm today.

5. The fact that the rise of the star hazzan coincided with the eastern European emigration meant that the stereotyped American image of the hazzan was an historical accident. For example, Hollywood's notion of the "cantor" as the soul of the Jewish community, as in that perennial property *The Jazz Singer*, has outlived the phenomenon it describes.[26] The prominence of the star hazzan has meant we know infinitely more, both in Europe and America, about a handful of celebrities than we do about the everyday sacred singer who faithfully served a thousand Jewish communities. It also means we know exclusively about eastern European stars and songs, since no Mediterranean or Middle Eastern performers came to public consciousness despite their early prominence and continued presence in America. This has ramifications for those communities even today, as we shall see below.

6. The further coincidence of both the star and the emigration with the birth of the recording industry meant that stars could become superstars, and that certain brand-name sounds have survived to our times as the most vivid remnants of a great period of cantorial art. Those who did not record, like Razumni, have come down to us as little more than a vague memory.

These and many other echoes of Europe still resonate in the American cantorate; but to make transcontinental connections, both sides must be clear, so it is time to turn to the western shores of the Atlantic.

NOTES

1. Two aspects of Temple music recur in the later cantorate. First, it seems that non-Jewish influence on music-making was strong: "The court and temple orchestras of Mesopotamia in this period [the Exile] are the prototype for the Temple music established in Jerusalem after the return" (Bayer 1971:557). Second, there may have been competition between priests and levite/musicians, (Bayer 1971), foreshadowing the conflict between rabbi and hazzan that continues down to our day.

2. It is perhaps typical of the long-term refashioning of post-Temple Judaism that there is no one date for the emergence of the hazzan, rather a process by which a recognized prayer leader slowly comes into focus. Of course, a precise, comprehensive historical study could help pin down the time frame.

3. DeVaux feels there might be philological evidence for thinking that the prayer leader has a mediating function: "the terms most commonly used for prayer are the verb *hithpallel* and the noun *t'pillah*. . . . In Hebrew, the root seems to mean "to decide, to arbitrate, to intercede. . . . The person who pronounces a prayer on behalf of the people or of an individual is a mediator" (1961:459).

4. I realize that I am being somewhat vague about precisely which rabbinic authorities said what when about the hazzan. This is largely due to the lack of a comprehensive study of subject, which would be greatly enhanced by close study of the approximately 1,500 responsa (Avigdor Herzog, personal communication) that can be culled from the now-computerized compilation of rabbinic decisions of past centuries.

5. For a fine account of the Christian situation, see Hayburn, who summarizes the establishment viewpoint this way: "More than all the other arts, music unfortunately affords the opportunity to interject a personal element into the house of God" (1979:389)

6. Nevertheless, the relationship between the medieval rabbinate and cantorate is unclear, since Avenary notes that "in northern Europe eminent rabbis served as hazzanim, among them Jacob Moellin ha-Levi (Maharil) of Mainz (c. 1360–1427)" (1971). Sources agree that the Maharil, who is credited with creating the Ashkenazic *minhag* ("customary way"), was remarkably well disposed towards the cantorate.

7. Citing the hazzan's role as a response to catastrophe is reminiscent of David Roskies's eloquent study of the important role of expressive behavior in providing continuity in the face of destruction. For our generation, he mentions searching for "meaning, language, and song as a much more promising endeavor" than other paths in seeking to grasp the Holocaust (1984:9).

8. Landman (1972) provides the most comprehensive account to date of these issues, but is only a point of departure. I have not gone into detail concerning the traditional sources on the qualifications of the hazzan, but I am grateful to Avigdor Herzog and Jeffrey Summit for pointing out the intrinsic interest and extensive data surrounding the topic.

9. Within Christianity, there are interesting overlaps between the hazzan and various sacred music officials that deserve separate study. The experimental quality of Protestantism has lent itself well to a wealth of prototypes, for example the parish clerk in rural England, whom Temperley describes as "the natural leader of the singing . . . psalms could be related to folklore and superstition, important local events and everyday human problems. A clerk by his choice could make a psalm an expression of current popular feeling" (1979:77). His description of the rise of congregational singing seems analogous to the appeal of the piyut: "people welcomed with delight a verse form and a musical form which they could understand and enjoy and which let them express hearty feelings" (46). Finally, his stress on the localism of parish music is an important antidote to the conventional sense that Christian music was more centralized than Jewish: "local customs have crept in to provide forms of expression more spontaneous than those devised by a remote authority" (1).

10. For a new and helpful survey of the importance of text in the anthropological study of Judaism, see the epilogue in Goldberg (1987).

11. Of course, this part of the pattern—at least as it relates to worship—is not uniquely Jewish, being shared by various cultures that center on sacred text; for example, Islam, where "it is not possible to perform the worship without recitation of several verses from the scripture, verses which tradition has dictated should be rendered in the most beautiful manner possible—therefore, with at least a modicum of chanted elaboration" (al Faruqi 1986:23).

The general description of the text-centered lifestyle in the following section also resonates with an account Terry Ellingson gave me in conversation about Tibetan Buddhism and everyday life (1986), raising the possibility of a cultural parallel worth following up.

12. This is where the Jewish system differs from, say, the Islamic world. While "every practicing Muslim is a potential or actual reciter of the Qur'an" (al Faruqi 1986:23), he or she is not expected to go beyond recitation to commentary, and even gifted amateurs (*qari*) or professional Qur'an chanters restrict their creativity to criteria such as "correct pronunciation . . . singular dignity . . . a beautiful voice . . . musicality . . . and breath control" (al Faruqi 1986:30–33).

13. Sed-Rajna's evocation of didacticism as a motive for expressive culture is echoed by Schwarzbaum (1969), who opens his magisterial study of Jewish folklore by citing didacticism as one of its distinctive features. Because a large proportion of the folktales are based on plots or characters from sacred text, it is possible to view folklore as a whole as yet another system of commentary.

14. The marginality of performers is a standard issue in ethnomusicology, so needs little comment here. The particular nature of the hazzan as one involved with ritual would seem to separate him from the klezmer, but the latter's principal function was to perform at weddings, a rite of passage, blurring the distinction. The *badkhn*, a wedding bard, should be mentioned here, as he customarily filled a niche somewhere between sacred and secular by performing mock commentary on sacred text along with insulting verses directed at

guests. The extent to which hazzanim also functioned as badkhonim lies beyond our historical reach, though it is clear there was some overlap from one performance sphere to another; since both jobs hardly paid a living in smaller communities, they could easily be filled by the same expressively gifted person. For a general survey of the eastern European scene in modern times, see Slobin (1982c, chapter 1).

15. Admittedly, having the West stand for modernism and the East for traditionalism is clichéd and downplays opposite trends in both regions. From the American point of view, however, it is the nineteenth-century modernizing thrust of Reform that largely marks the Western contribution, which makes the subsequent turn-of-the-century Eastern influx of old-time improvisational solo hazzanim seem all the more traditional.

16. Nevertheless, the American cantorate depended for decades on the many meshoyrerim produced in eastern Europe. In places as far off as the wilds of Saskatchewan, the local hazzan for the tiny Jewish community "around 1917 or 1918 (had been) a choir boy for Cantor Sirota . . . he had a beautiful cantorial voice and style and I still remember his *Ashrei* and his *Unetane tokef*" (Feldman 1983:17).

17. Sholom Aleichem uses the term of his day, *veltkhazn* (world-class hazzan), for these people, strongly implying the universal recognition accorded outstanding sacred singers. While his description—and other fictional accounts of the life of hazzanim—should not be taken literally, it is highly evocative of a cultural atmosphere.

18. This view is corroborated by the Yiddish proverb *dray mentshn zingn far tsores: a betler, a badkhn, un a khazn* ("three people sing out of/because of troubles: a beggar, a badkhn, and a hazzan").

19. This and similar descriptions of the Jewish "masses' " enthusiasm for the sound of the hazzan are echoed in Islamic accounts of the impression made by talented readers of the Qur'an: "When someone finds a reader with an especially good voice and brings him for some occasion, the village in its entirety rushes to hear him, the men surrounding him and the women sitting on the roofs of the houses or in any other place where they can hear the beautiful voice that reads the Qur'an" (al-Naqqash, in Danielson 1987:30).

20. Here the Jews were following a generalized western European Protestant trend towards gentility. For example, in England, the centralized church's attempt to control parish musical behavior was summarized by the introduction of the organ and decorum. In 1820 a Dr. Busley called the organ "an instrument powerful enough to drown the voices of parish clerk, charity children, and congregation . . . an inestimable blessing," and decorum was felt to be "the enemy of extremes, of enthusiasms, of spontaneity, and often of sincerity" (Temperly 1979: 5, 100). Thus the Jewish quest for an acceptable "church" style coincided with the embourgeoisement of the Protestant tradition.

21. The literature is unclear as to exactly when and how the new term *cantor* was applied to the hazzan. At any rate, it is ironic that the title apparently meant upward social mobility for the Jews, because in German society the

kantor had sunk in estimation after the Enlightenment, being offered only to petty organists and teachers in small communities.

22. Meyer Gimblett (personal communication), who grew up in Opatow/ Apt, Poland, a town of some 10,000, summarizes the situation of diversity in even a small community, which included: (1) a *shtot-khazn*, official "town hazzan" paid by the kehillah, who came to the *kheydr* (Jewish school) to pick out choirboys, who were lightly paid for the High Holidays; (2) three *bes-medresh* houses of study and prayer, which each had two to four ba'al tefillah nonprofessional prayer leaders; (3) several Hasidic *shtiblakh* (Ger, Lubavitch, etc.) who all tended to travel to the "court" of their *rebbe* (charismatic leader) for holidays. Tryouts for shtot-khazn attracted "the whole town," which went home humming the tunes.

23. It is typical of the legendary quality of the hazzanim of the time that while the dates given here are Vigoda's, the *Encyclopaedia Judaica* gives the years as 1866–1904 and prefers the spelling Razumny; the name comes from the Russian adjective meaning "intelligent" and is itself the source of legend.

24. This situation is reminiscent of the usual notion that Bach's passionate cantata and oratorio style was an outlet for his pietistic congregants, who eschewed the immensely popular Italian opera of the day; perhaps here the overlap between German and Jewish *cantor* is socially grounded.

25. The same is true of the growth of Yiddish popular culture, particularly theater and its music (see Slobin 1982c).

26. This is particularly clear in the 1981 Neil Diamond remake, in which, of all actors, Laurence Olivier plays the hazzan-father, who seems as out of place on the Lower East Side of New York in the film as he would be off-camera.

PART 1

The Cantorate in American History

2

~~~~~~

1680s to 1880s: Colonials Through German Reformers

Though officially Jewish-American history begins with the twenty-three people who landed in New Amsterdam in 1654, the story of the cantorate starts in New York, under English rule. In 1674 the duke of York told the governor to "permit all persons of what religion so ever, quietly to inhabit within the precincts of yo'r jurisdiccion w'thout giving them any disturbance or disquiet whatsoever for or by reason of their differing opinion in matter of religion" (Marcus 1961:48). So it was that the first community felt free to organize the first synagogue, Shearith Israel, and to select as its leader one Saul Brown, who had translated his name from Pardo. This name change can stand as a convenient symbol of one of our main themes: Americanization, or how European Jews reshape their core religious institutions on American soil. Pardo was Dutch-born and named for a prominent ancestor who was one of the judges at Spinoza's excommunication trial, so he certainly had credentials for becoming what an English observer of 1697 called "minister" of the fledgling New York community, then just twenty families strong. It is important to keep numbers in mind when thinking about colonial Jewry. For those of us used to counting American Jews in the millions, it is not easy to consider that up to the Revolution, Shearith Israel "probably never had more than fifty active members," and that in 1776 there were only 2,500 Jews in a national population of 2.5 million (Marcus 1970a:389).

As an institution serving such small numbers, the early American synagogue developed quite differently from its Old World counterpart. As noted in chapter 1, in Europe, within one community and often under the umbrella of the *kehillah* (communal body), any number of tiny places of worship and sacred study could flourish, each with or without named or salaried functionaries and with a class/sect orientation. Belonging to a synagogue was not necessarily the key component of one's Jewish identity in the European condition of densely settled Jewish populations. By contrast, "no colonial American Jewish community ever sheltered more than one permanent synagogue, and the local synagogue naturally exercised a monopolistic control overy every Jew within its ambit" (Marcus 1970a:857). A natural situation in seventeenth-century New York with its twenty families, this pattern of "synagogue equals community" remained fully in force until the early nineteenth century, when new waves of immigration caused competing synagogues to spring up, each serving a different—an almost "ethnic"—group of worshippers who often grouped together according to area of origin as well as socioeconomic level. Even when New York became a checkerboard of congregations, the idea of an overarching community structure never got off the drawing board, the only serious—and failed—attempt being made in the early twentieth century (see Goren 1970).

Although the synagogue's immense gravitational pull was a result of Jewish demographics, it also suited the American religious landscape. Protestants came to the New World to escape being stifled by community control in the form of established churches and, like Jews, were content to let local variety flourish: "Localism, then, was the essential characteristic of the clerical office in eighteenth-century New England. . . . Ministers were all ambassadors of God, but they were ambassadors to a specific place" (Scott 1978:16–17).

Though this urge differed from the Jewish reasons for congregational dominance of community life, it shaped a religious and political landscape that was well tailored to Jewish needs. The notion of free-standing institutions like the American synagogue fit naturally into Judaism's lack of an ecclesiatical structure, and the intense ferment of Protestant religious activity in the United States provided an example of vigorous denominationalism that did nothing to check the internal turbulence of nineteenth-century Jewry's approach to the problems of faith in a modern world. This eventually created a religious landscape that paralleled the Protestant patchwork of denominations and individualized churches.[1]

But we anticipate. Let us return to the colonial scene to lay the groundwork for understanding the figure called *hazzan*, who was the sole leader of small and scattered congregational communities. These men were pioneers in the creation of Jewish-American culture and represent a major phase in the development of the cantorate—or do they? The question is: were they cantors in today's sense at all? Today we are used to thinking of someone called *rabbi* as the basic congregational leader, hence for us *cantor* is the other member of the clergy team. Yet until the 1840s, no ordained rabbi lived and worked in the

United States. As we shall see, each generation of Jewish-Americans has its own understanding of what we are calling the hazzan. If we translate hazzan as "cantor," we cannot make sense of the position. For the early era of American Judaism, hazzan is the sole congregational and hence community leader, so he functioned rather more like a rabbi, in today's terms, than like a cantor.[2] In fact, he held both jobs, plus others, so he does not look like today's rabbi either. Marcus provides a convenient summary of the work of the early hazzanim:

> They circumcised the male children, taught them in a makeshift school and prepared them for bar mitzvah. Often they acted as *shochatim*, men who slaughtered cattle in approved ritual fashion. They married and buried, but above all they were the men who chanted the Hebrew services. . . . When they had a moment's leisure they scurried around augmenting their salaries by petty trading or language instruction (Marcus 1970a:4). . . . [The hazzan] even attempted to fatten his income by playing the lottery . . . [and] fees for marriages, burials and bar mitzvahs were an important source of income for him (27). . . . The only time a hazzan would be called upon to make a formal address was on a public commemorative occasion (4).

All of this activity barely enabled the hazzan to make ends meet, nor did he command particular respect from the congregation. Part of the reason the hazzan was underpaid was because he was not seen as an authoritative and distinguished person, except in individual cases where a strong man could make his presence felt. Here Old World sentiments held firm. Although there was no ecclesiastical hierarchy, neither were all clergy equally valued. As we have seen, among Ashkenazim the hazzan was valued, but not necessarily highly respected, nor was he among the Mediterranean Jews, the Sephardim who shaped early America's religious institutions, who also tended to have greater regard for the scholarly expertise of the rabbi than for the expressive power of the hazzan.

But there was an equally strong institutional reason for the lack of hazzanic power: the dominance of lay leadership in the London/Amsterdam Sephardic tradition that shaped early American Judaism: "synagogal tradition and the authoritarian character of the Board made it very difficult for any hazzan to develop leadership qualities" (Marcus 1970a:7). In short, the board, often called the *adjunta*, and its director, the *Parnas*, ruled the roost. These men were the heads of the leading families of the city, who assigned the best seats in the synagogue and positions on the board to their "clan" while keeping the hazzan on a very short leash.[3]

A letter written in 1849, in the latter part of the period we are covering here, nicely summarizes the difference between Europe and America. The writer, one Jacob Rosenfeld, starts by explaining the power of the Jewish ministry in a generalized and somewhat imaginary Old World:

> [T]he Jewish ministers there are, for the most part, invested with some powers from the government of said [European] countries, to enact such laws and make such regulations respecting synagogue discipline and other religious matters, as they may deem wholesome or necessary. In this country it is different, the Jewish minister is but a *dead letter*, because all matters of the congregation, even such points of religion which require deep learning, are decided by a majority of the members, whether they understand anything about it, or whether they take the least interest in it or not. The minister in this country is, therefore, properly speaking, governed by his flock instead of his leading them (Rosenfeld 1849:563).

In the final analysis, we must turn to portraits of individuals to understand how the cantorate worked. In a limited population, a handful of impressive individuals can be as influential as the standard rules of governance in shaping the fate of an institution like the cantorate. No man better summarizes his day than Gershom Mendes Seixas (1746–1816), hazzan of Shearith Israel: "Seixas was American's first native American Jewish clergyman. That he was born here is of itself of no import; significant is the fact that he lived and thought and aspired in an overwhelmingly American milieu. . . . Seixas was a prime example of what the colonial American Jewish melting pot had produced. He was a descendant of both Ashkenazim and Sephardim . . . this breed of Jewish ethnic amalgam was uniquely American" (Marcus 1970b:64).

Marcus perhaps exaggerates, since Jewish regional populations mixed and influenced each other in Europe as well, but in American terms, Seixas is indeed a Janus-faced figure, looking back to the Sephardic-dominated, pioneering congregation Shearith Israel, and ahead to a new, post-Revolutionary age of greater Jewish diversity and a more individualized ministry. We get to know Seixas best through his letters. He had retired to Philadelphia during the British occupation of New York in the Revolutionary War, and in 1783 we find him writing to his New York congregation about reclaiming his job: "As I have now a Family to provide for, I can not think of giving up this Place till I meet with some Encouragement from you that my Salary will be made equivalent to what I receive here [in Philadelphia]—for unless I can obtain a Sufficiency to support my Family in a decent manner, by being Hazan—I must inevitably give up the Calling, and endeavor with the

Blessing of God, to procure it by Industry & an Application to Business" (Seixas, letter of 21 Dec. 1783).

Two years later, having returned to New York after presumably being promised that he would be properly paid, he complains bitterly about lack of support:

> You can not but be sensible of the many Disadvantages I laboured under to return here from Philadelphia, the Expences that attended my moving from there, & the continued sickness in my family ever since I have been here—from these Circumstances you must necessarily Judge I require some certain assurances of my Salary being punctually paid. . . . I expect to be punctually paid whenever my Quarter becomes due, at the Rate of fifty pounds every three Lunar Months, & the sum of Money equal to the Purchase of six Cords of Hickory Wood and Perquisites as usually allowed to the Hazan. You will be pleased to remember there is yet a Balance due to me since the year 1776 (Seixas, letter of 22 Sept. 1785).

Seixas's assertiveness, even including a reminder of pre-Revolutionary debts, is unusual and tells us just how strong a figure he was in an age of hazzanic meekness. To be sure, he was *the* New York Jewish community leader, yet he was unable to assert real authority under the rules of the game despite his status and his forceful character.

What sort of man was Seixas intellectually and theologically? He knew enough Hebrew to get by and was a commanding enough figure to become a trustee of Columbia University, yet Marcus notes that by modern standards, Seixas's level of learning (like that of his congregants) was small and his sermons wooden. What is important to remember is the extent to which he was Americanized: "he was completely receptive to the influences which blanketed him" (Marcus 1970b: 64). Looking at materials Seixas presented to children, Marcus observes: "There was nothing specifically Jewish in this talk. It could have been written by any churchman and delivered in any Christian school. It was . . . utterly neutral and nondenominational, indeed almost secularly Americanistic" (Marcus 1970b:6).

Marcus summarizes Seixas's theology as "a mishmash of rabbinism and the Enlightenment. He seasoned this melange with dashes of Calvinism and liberal Protestant thought" (Marcus 1970b:31). We should not be surprised at this evaluation; like their fellow-citizens, Jewish-Americans experimented with their social organization and their theology alike, responding to the social and intellectual climate. At the same time, this improvisatory pattern is not that far removed from the flexible way of life discussed in chapter 1, which seems well suited to the American opportunity.

The early hazzan (pre-1840) is a complex figure. Bound by convention and encumbered with rules, he nevertheless led his flock into uncharted territory, both literally in the case of the frontier hazzan and figuratively back in the settled seaboard centers. It was not easy to find suitable leaders, as shown by the frequent, eloquent pleas to London and Amsterdam for job candidates. An 1805 letter to London from an American congregation seeking a hazzan provides a trenchant summary of the need for a community leader of real substance:

> In a free and independent country like America, where civil and religious freedom go hand in hand, where no distinctions exist between the clergy of different denominations, where we are incorporated and known in law; freely tolerated; where, in short, we enjoy all the blessings of freedom in common with our fellow-citizens, you may readily conceive we pride ourselves under the happy situation which makes us feel that we are men, susceptible of that dignity which belongs to human nature, by participating in all the rights and blessings of this happy country; to which nothing could add more than having a Hazan of merit and classical education, who would reflect honour on himself and stamp an additional degree of dignity and respectability upon our congregation" (*Occident* 1, no. 7, Oct. 1843:389–90).

The demands made on anyone shouldering such a responsibility were considerable and reflect the contemporary European interest in a modern ministry combining Jewish and secular education. Throughout this early period the hazzan's integrity and courage were tested in ways we can hardly imagine, as in the issue of whether he stayed with his flock during a raging epidemic of yellow fever. Heroism in the face of disease was expected of all American clergy in the nineteenth century; Catholic priests were expected to help their parishioners "in every pesthouse and focus of contagion" (Dolan 1975:64). Two letters separated by sixty years vividly illustrate this situation. In the first, from 1793, Samuel Hays writes to his fiancee, Richea Gratz, about the cowardly behavior of the local hazzan, Mr. Cohen:

> Like other persons of his cloath [he] gives precepts they dont mean to follow, one afternoon he was at Jonas Phillips's and preached for half an hour to put the trust in the Almighty, that there was not such thing as flying from his hand, that he would protect those who put his trust in him, and that he meant to stay, he made Mr. Phillips conclude to do the same, when the first thing Mr. Phillips heard next morning was that Mr. Cohen with all his morality, had flown, and left his congregation to put their trust in that being, himself put no Faith in (Hays, letter of 27 Nov. 1793).

The second letter, from 1853, shows the hazzan in a better light: "We have also learned that our friend the Rev. James K. Gutheim [of New Orleans] had been seized with the yellow fever, but was recovering at last accounts, a fact which will gratify many who have been alarmed at the account of his illness. It is truly grateful for us to record that our ministers and physicians did not fly from their post at the approach of the fell destroyer. May they be blessed for it" (*Occident* 11, no. 6, Sept. 1853: 329).

Nor was congregational life tranquil even in trouble-free times. Conflict between the hazzan and the lay leadership was often exacerbated by partisans of both sides. On one occasion in 1812 in Charleston, Hazzan Carvalho, recently arrived from London, took drastic measures when he was suspended for insubordination: "[He] collected a rabble composed of all the vagrant jews & had a petition signed by them to give him redress, this petition was handed the Parnass who could not act upon it being in express violation to the constitution. Mr. Carvalho in person aided and abetted the confusion and riot which took place in a short time, the whole meeting parnass & all were battling with clubs & bruising boxing etc. during which his reverence . . . came off with a few thumps" (Wolf and Whiteman 1957:249).

However, on the whole the interest in synagogue decorum and in improving the hazzan's lot increased in the early nineteenth century. An acute shortage of hazzanim produced a seller's market that raised salaries: "The difficulty was not that congregations wanted a man of great learning, but that they could not find even qualified readers willing to serve for the modest pay given to hazanim. The shortage was national" (Wolf and Whiteman 1957:251).

At the same time, Americanization—as well as modernization—meant that Jews began to follow the Christian model of giving more respect to their clergymen. For example, in 1784 New York State "permitted and encouraged the incorporation of every religious group and accorded a certain official character to the chief religious functionary," so that by 1786 Seixas's congregation began to refer to him as "the Rev. Mr." (Marcus 1970b:21). Another early instance of respect for the hazzan came in the instruction given to attendees at the dedication of Congregation Mikveh Israel, Philadelphia, in 1782. This was a major festive occasion. Haym Salomon, a national figure due to his active support of the Revolutionary cause, led the procession and ceremonially opened the door of the new sanctuary. When the congregation settled down in their new pews to sing, they kept their voices down: "They all chanted the *Baruch haba* [blessing of the house], following it with the customary Psalms, the members having been warned on this occasion 'to be particularly careful not to raise their voices higher than the Hazan's who will endeavor to modulate his Voice to a proper Pitch so as only to fill the building' " (Wolf and Whiteman 1957:121).

Even here, where the hazzan's authority is assured, we have a double-edged injunction: the congregation is charged to sing less loudly than the hazzan, but he himself is also told to modulate his voice, no doubt a carryover of the age-old worry that the hazzan would take over the services and impose his musical sensibility on the worshippers.[4] This ancient concern now coincided with a heightened interest in decorum; the procession in Philadelphia moved towards its goal, the new building, "without any band of musick" (Cohen 1976:19).

The earliest American cantorate, then, was western Sephardic in origin and shows a uniformity of approach and conservatism of outlook, being a creature of the lay leadership. The *adjunta*, the ruling body of the synagogue-by-synagogue organization, was temperamental and capricious, consisting largely of eminent families who insisted that hazzanim minister to their members first, or who even gave synagogue posts to close kin. It would take an increase of size and diversity of the Jewish population to change this situation.

As the nineteenth century unfolds, the cantorate slowly emerges into the light of history due to the arrival of the large wave of German immigration (1840s–1880s) and the resulting efflorescence of Jewish publication, especially periodicals. The pages of these journals are filled with accounts of the doings of hazzanim and the continuing, often strident debate over the nature of the Jewish clergy, which was undergoing major change. Most useful here is the *Occident*, begun by Isaac Leeser (1806–68), a hazzan and a major intellectual leader of American Jewry. So dominant was Leeser that one scholar says "it is no exaggeration to call the antebellum period in American Jewish history, the 'Age of Leeser' " (Sussman 1986:3), while another states unequivocally that "Practically every form of Jewish activity which supports American Jewish life today was established or envisaged by this one man ... almost every kind of publication which is essential to Jewish survival was written, translated, or fostered by him" (Betram Korn, quoted in Sussman 1986:4).

Among Leeser's creations, the *Occident* is immensely helpful, since this magazine is something of a trade journal for the cantorate, so will be frequently quoted here. We begin our survey with a number of quotations that speak eloquently to the great divisions within Jewish America over what a hazzan does and what he might do, beginning with letters from contributors before turning to Leeser himself:

In its present state, the Reader's desk presents no higher claim upon the respect and affection of the congregation than a musical voice and graceful inflections may create. Its moral power owns no existence. Regarded as a salaried official, whose duties are plainly indicated by the terms of his contract, the Reader is held to a rigid observance of mere technical trifles, whilst the greater objects of his service are totally disregarded. There is a necessity for a thorough reform commencing at the very foundation of the structure ("A Moralizing Layman" 1847:25–27).

In this country, where we have about sixty Hazanim, perhaps there are not more than ten among them, that could answer the most plain or simple question about their religion [while] in the United States we are multiplying congregations faster than perhaps in the whole of the rest of the world; it becomes absolutely necessary that the greatest care should be taken in selecting and appointing proper persons for that most important office (Abrahams 1847:89).

Is it really so, that the highest religious office yet among us in America is so insignificant, as to possess no power, beyond vocal abilities, to chant a set number of tunes, to be the registrar of births, marriages, and deaths, to pay a number of visits to their respective members, to have a friendly chat with the female members, and to perform other trifling matters? Is it true that we have so far departed from the custom of our pious ancestry, as to have no shepherd to guide us, none to warn us, no one to strike the sinful with heart-saddening conviction, to cheer others in their soul-desponding moments, to be equally regardless of the opinions and favours of their brethren, and to exhort them to give their children a religious education? (Isaacs 1844:592).

Leeser, interested in detaching the functions of teacher, preacher, and pastor from the hazzan's duties, points out the problem of over-burdening the clergy:

[The hazzan] will have enough of ministerial duties, including *visiting* the people, as this seems lately to be viewed, though with doubtful propriety, as a part of the Hazan's functions, to perform, without the superadded labor of preaching and giving instruction. If any one had been present in a large synagogue in a certain city on the last Day of Atonement, he could easily have satisfied himself that the minister has [been] taxed enough to read the Kol Nidre, Shacharith, Moosaph, half Mincha, Ne'ila, and the concluding evening service, beside an almost endless number of offerings . . . without expecting a sermon of him in addition. Human nature cannot bear so awful a strain very long, and it is cruel to tax any man beyond his strength (*Occident* 12, no. 10, Jan. 1855:42)

Note Leeser's impatience with leading the services, which we might have considered the primary function of the hazzan. While this may partly be based on the fact that he himself was an undistinguished singer, it is a political position, tied to his enthusiasm for a more complete Jewish culture in America, grounded in religious teaching (he helped start the first Sunday school in 1838), Bible study (he translated the Bible into English in 1853–54), and preaching, of which more below. All of this was to be guided by a sensitivity to the New World context, since Leeser was sure "there should be a conscious and selective acceptance of American cultural elements into Jewish life, lest the unconscious, unthinking and unselective espousal of Americanism go too far" (Joseph Blau, quoted in Sussman 1986:6). In other words, Leeser thought that since the Jews had to Americanize, they should do so deliberately and wisely.

Leeser's dream took decades to be realized. Congregations simply were not ready for radical change, though the fact that they were dissatisfied is obvious when we look at hiring practices: it was very hard to decide on a leader. One congregation adopted a novel solution after receiving fifty reponses to their advertisement:

> The Trustees were puzzled which one of the multitude to hire, as they were all strangers to them, when one of the Trustees . . . proposed that an inquiry in the former occupations of each applicant should be instituted. . . . One was found among them whose profession had been that of "soul" mending, in fact, a cobbler . . . and a very happy selection it was, for the man had a fine voice, and was just wise enough to know his duties and his predecessor being a learned man with a cracked voice, and knowing what was right and what not, perhaps too often caused his unpleasant voice to be heard in places where it was not over-welcome. The only qualification for a hazzan is an agreeable voice. Whether he understands what he reads or not, is but a matter of small moment (Abrahams 1857:400).

If this congregation seems cynical, perhaps it is partly due to certain abuses of the profession which alarmed Leeser: "We are sick and disgusted with the adventurers who have occasionally got into office, and sincerely hope that hereafter we shall not see placed into prominent positions men who come hither because they found nothing to do in their native land, or who deemed it convenient to go away for reasons of their own, be these moral or political" (*Occident* 15, no. 10, 1858:495).

Indeed, sometimes hazzanim politicked for their jobs too strongly; one H. A. Henry of Cincinnati made his overtures to a Louisville congregation so vehemently that he was rejected: "He made his appearance again in this city, and canvassed most vigorously among the majority of the members of this congregation, soliciting their support at the coming election for hazzan, promising them, at the same time, that *if elected* he would commence a good school" (Strauss 1851).

Politics within congregations was robust, at times litigious or even violent. The Jewish press was very interested in the spicy details of communal wrangling,[5] so we are well informed on some specific cases, of which the Rosenfeld controversy in Cincinnati in 1852 can stand as an example. Hazzan A. L. Rosenfeld was accused by a congregant, Mr. N. Bing of Congregation B'nai Jeshurun, of having eaten guinea fowls (a nonkosher food), having arrived in Cincinnati by railroad on the eve of the first day of Rosh Hashanah, and of having a Christian cook. Rosenfeld defended himself, drawing on a book of religious law called the *Magen Avraham*, declaring that guinea fowl were indeed allowable, the employment of a Christian cook could not be regarded as an infringement, and the railway is nowhere mentioned as being unlawful. Now the *Magen Avraham* was a seventeenth-century rabbinic work by a Polish authority, a commentary on part of the standard Ashkenazic reference source, the *Shulcan Aruch*, so looked authoritative. Nevertheless, a closer examination reveals that the book does not involve itself with dietary laws and was written prior to the development of the train, so was quite useful for Rosenfeld's purposes; historian Douglas Kohn feels that "the whole incident smacks of the less-blind leading the more-blind" (personal communication, 1985), since Rosenfeld's accusers, more ignorant than he, could not return his challenge. He was acquitted.

The chaos in the cantorate is aptly reflected in any given congregation's hiring history. The Baltimore Hebrew Congregation had thirteen cantors in nine years (1835–44), while in the same city, Oheb Shalom arranged to have three trial hazzanim on one Sabbath (Fein 1971:112). A detailed case history of one congregation—Savannah, 1862–71—can serve as model here. In 1862 they failed to attract or agree upon a much-needed hazzan. In the meantime "we will keep the synagogue open and have the service regularly performed." Mr. Amram, the *shochet* (slaughterer), was asked to cover Sabbath and High Holy Day services for $87.50 a quarter; meanwhile, they advertised a salary of $400 a year for a hazzan. A year later they asked Mr. Millhauser to serve as reader for $200 per quarter on top of his salary as *shammash* (sexton), if he would get someone else to do the job. Finally, a Mr. Lewin accepted the hazzan's position, but resigned after two years due to his leading the congregation towards Reform Judaism (see below) too quickly. The Hebrew teacher, E. Fisher, led services for six months at $150 per month. Applications continued to arrive, but no choice was made, one of the lay leaders saying the congregation was "badly in want of a lecturer and I fear if we are much longer without one that our congregation will be broken up and our place of worship closed." In 1871 Reverend Rosenfeld was chosen for one year, dependent upon his continuing a musical program. Fortunately "the Rosen-

feld family was very musical; the children and extended kin constituted
the choir." However, Reverend Rosenfeld did not last, as the congregation decided to move towards Reform after all, so they brought back
Mr. Lewin (Rubin 1983:151–53).

The Savannah situation makes it clear that the nature of the cantorate
was under constant question in many congregations by the mid-nineteenth century. Growing, more-sophisticated communities exposed to
a variety of musical and theological orientations focused their uneasiness on their spiritual leader, leading to considerable confusion, as
one 1847 observer notes:

> Turn to our various congregations . . . and what a spectacle do their
> ministers present to us! Here we find one chosen for his fine voice, there
> one who can lecture well; here one because he can read the Sepher Torah—
> there one because he was the best that could be procured. . . . However
> widely separated the office of a chazan from a spiritual guide in Europe
> may be, the case is very different in America. Here the offices in most
> cases must be combined together in the same person; for our spiritual
> guidance must partake in a measure of the republican simplicity of our
> social laws, as citizens of this free republic (Ritterband 1847:548).

Yet it seems that laymen as well as leaders like Leeser began to chafe
at having all the clergy functions concentrated in a single individual.
After all, in the 1840s, ordained rabbis (albeit some self-proclaimed)
began appearing regularly as part of the German influx. It became clear
that one person might take over the leadership role, as exemplified by
preaching in the Protestant, soul-rousing manner coming into favor in
Germany, while another could take care of the music, as happened
little by little in many congregations, for example Shaaray Tefillah of
New York in 1865:

> In order to relieve their minister of the many duties devolving upon
> him, the members resolved to engage with the least possible delay an
> assistant hazzan, who is to conduct the service according to the ancient
> liturgy with the accepted tunes, leaving the duties of Preacher more es-
> pecially for the veteran of the New York pulpit. . . . The Reverend Mr.
> Isaacs, at whose suggestion the office of Assistant was established, will
> thus obtain more leisure to prepare the discourses which have afforded
> his audience so much edification and instruction ("B" 1865:43).

Not surprisingly, the board turned to an Americanized young man
to take over the musical responsibilities:

> The choice has fallen on Mr. Phillips, son of the Rabbi Eleazer Phillips,
> who may be called an American, since he immigrated hither at a very

early age with his parents, and obtained consequently his education and musical training in this country. . . . The piety of his parents resident in New York prohibited his entering on the stage as a public singer; he therefore perfected himself under the universally known chief Hazzan of the principal Berlin Synagogue, Mr. Lichtenstein, for the office of minister ("B" 1865:43).

In his day, Phillips had to go to Berlin for training, just as the new "ministers" with higher education came from Germany. There, the pioneers of modern synagogue composition, Louis Lewandowski of Berlin (1821–94) and Salomon Sulzer of Vienna (1804–90), were creating melodious, solo-plus-choral works that encompassed the entire liturgical year. These grand, modern works were patterned on the work of Jewish-origin composers like Mendelssohn, Halévy, and Meyerbeer who had become famous in the mainstream world. Up-to-date congregations in the United States immediately recognized the impression that classical musical training can make on a synagogue audience:

> [Mr. Phillips] officiated with much applause in several cities of Germany, but at length resolved to return to America. His fine base [sic] voice of a rare compass and guided by good taste, whether with or without choir, in both ancient and modern melodies, accompanied as it is by a good pronunciation and intoning of the Hebrew, makes an agreeable impression on ear and spirit. His rendering of the hymns is not only an entertainment for the ears, not a mere pleasant delivery of words in a senseless musical strain which does not penetrate to the heart, but one feels at the same time that the reader purposes to move the recesses of the soul. . . . He ought to endeavor to devote himself entirely to his calling, which opens for him a fair and wide field as a spiritual master of song, and to avoid all pursuits unconnected with his profession ("B" 1865:43).

Notice that "B," in his letter to the *Occident*, is already worried about an outstanding young singer deserting the synagogue for the concert stage. Opera was newly established in New York, and there was even a flourishing German-language theater with some actors of Jewish background. As we have seen for Europe, in America Jews were beginning to measure their liturgical "performers" by the yardstick of mainstream music—but were also expecting their preachers to live up to the standard of star Protestant ministers. In short, congregations were demanding more and more of their clergy, expecting one man to rouse them with stirring rhetoric and another, musically trained, to stir them with sacred song.[6]

The power of the preacher particularly fired the imagination of mid-century American Jews. Leeser led the way in this area with particular zeal, since "of all his accomplishments, his role as the pioneer Jewish preacher in the United States was closest to his heart" (Sussman 1986:8). Like Seixas before him, Leeser's preaching was not exciting, nor was it much encouraged by his congregation. But he "viewed preaching as the central activity of the Jewish religious leader in America and advocated the transformation of the office of hazzan into a Jewish ministry based on the Protestant model" (Sussman 1986:10), the two ideas going hand in hand. Even if he did not have the charismatic power needed to stir his listeners deeply, he was a good judge of others' work and recommended it highly to the readers of his magazine, as this description of Solomon Jacobs of Charleston (1818–60) vividly illustrates: "His style is bold, fluent, eloquent, argumentative, and heart-touching. His forte is pathos . . . vivid and glowing in his imagination, he possesses all the feeling that lends its magic touch to the chords of sympathy. Clear and distinct in his enunciation, chaste and natural, yet fervid in his gesticulation, possessing a commanding and dignified person, he is in fine an orator in the full sense of the term" (*Occident* 10, no. 7, Oct. 1852:401).[7]

Conflict between the old-time hazzan and the new, lionized preacher was bound to develop, particularly where congregations invited outside oratorical stars to liven up weekly services. Through midcentury, "readers" were confined to chanting prayers, and the resident hazzan had to listen to itinerant preachers hold forth. In Easton, Pennsylvania, the hazzan could "deliver a discourse" only with the express consent of the Parnas, who might "direct" him "at any time he should think fit" to preach, which normally only occurred on holidays. At least once (in 1862) the local hazzan "asserted himself and forcibly prevented the guest, a Rev. L. Delbanco, from delivering his sermon" (Trachtenberg 1944:46). Despite the hazzan's strenuous efforts, the congregation's attention turned increasingly to the preacher. Even worse, given this strong appeal of the gifted sermonizer, the hazzan was bound to be evaluated ever more sharply. We begin to find critiques of "readers" who either go overboard in vocal display or seem entirely uninterested in moving the audience; Leeser rejects both extremes:

> Is it not evident that many read the prayers in a manner which seems to say, "Come and admire my chaunting?" Is it not palpable that humility and devotion have little or no part in the performance? . . . [T]here are some who seem to regard their style of reading, their beautiful intonation, their wire-drawn chaunting as all in all, through which they stand before the people as unrivalled incomparable "sweet singers of Israel." We should have devotion, but they give us song; we should have elevation of feeling, but they display their vocal powers. . . . [S]ong, and nothing but song is continually presented as the sole spiritual food to a famishing people.

Another class of readers are those who hurry through the service as though the greatest merit consisted in the utmost rapidity of utterance. But our catalogue is not yet complete. We must revert to the very indifferent manner in which the blessed words of the law are read to the people. . . . [T]he errors are often approaching to blasphemy (*Occident* 10, no. 4, July 1852:179–81).

Certainly this drive for upgrading the cantorate stemmed from internal sources, particularly the new tastes of the incoming German Jews, influenced by Emancipation and Protestantism. But we should not underrate the importance of wanting to look like the local Christians as well, a symptom of a desire to appear worthy of the equal citizenship offered the Jews:

When . . . nobody but Israelites came to our places of public worship, it was comparatively a matter of small consequence who acted as the reader; because his co-religionists alone saw him during the time of divine service, and however ignorant, immoral, or improper he might be for such a calling, it was then a matter of but little importance, because the world at large knew little or nothing about it. . . . But now that we are free, and have the privilege to raise our Holy Temples where we please, and that many respectable persons, of various religious opinions, with whom we have daily communication in commercial transactions, friendly visits, etc., come often among us at our places of worship for the purpose of witnessing its rites, etc., how great is the necessity that they in their visit should not be allowed to see anything that would in any manner tend to our national degradation. And how, sir, can this be prevented? Surely but by the adoption of one measure, which is to have none but moral, respectable, and well educated men fill the office of Hazzan (Abrahams 1847:88).

Leeser, always the spokesman for the profession, explained what Jews should learn from their neighbors about the clergy. Writing in 1850, he first quotes an article in *The Jewish Messenger* to the effect that "the Christian clergyman is better fed, better clothed, and better lodged, and made independent in the management of his flock—without waiting for orders—in every particular he is superior." This is exactly what Leeser thinks should be the case among the Jews: "Now we hold it as self-evident that if the Jewish ministers be placed on a certain and firm basis, they would become every way equal to those of other denominations—self-respected, and esteemed by others" (*Occident* 7, no. 1, Jan. 1850:568). Leeser's opening phrase, so resonant of the Declaration of Independence, eloquently illustrates the impact of American thinking on Jewish minds.

Attacks on the old-style hazzan increase both in numbers and stridency as the century wears on. A certain Simon Hecht of Evansville, Indiana, nicely summarizes the contempt felt by reformers of the cantorate towards the old hazzan, now replaced by figures called, for the first time, *cantor*. Writing in German, Hecht says the old hazzan was sloppy, dirty, and disorganized, singing "tavern music and real Gypsy song," using tunes from the "military drum and the night watchman's horn," very Teutonic but hardly surprising references, since Hecht was writing in German. For the High Holidays, the earlier hazzan matched tunes to text by adding a strong "pum, pum, pum or la, la, la, da, da, di" after every other syllable if the melody was too short. He spent nights drinking and days gossiping. The synagogues were settings for "crudity and boredom," so grew ever emptier (Hecht 1879a:2). In a final peroration, Hecht sums up the differences between the old and new clergymen: "The hazzan and the cantor are naturally worlds apart. Whereas in the hazzan we knew the village fool, sponger, and tippler at circumcisions, weddings, etc., we find in the cantor the worthy man of honor, who is conscious of his holy task in all respects" (Hecht 1879b:2).

The most famous rebuke to the older cantorate was penned by Isaac Mayer Wise (1819–1900), a giant of early American Reform Judaism who edited the journal to which Simon Hecht wrote (*Die Deborah*). Wise found the old-time hazzan a stumbling-block in his path to a new American Judaism:

> The hazzan was the Reverend. He was all that was wanted.... [H]e was teacher, butcher, circumciser, [shofar]blower, gravedigger, secretary. He wrote the amulets with the names of all the angels and demons on them for women in confinement, read *shiur* for the departed sinners, and played cards or dominoes with the living; in short, he was a *kol-bo* [jack of all trades], an encyclopaedia, accepted bread, turnips, cabbage, potatoes as a gift and peddled in case his salary was not sufficient. He was *sui generis*, half priest, half beggar, half oracle, half fool, as the occasion demanded. Among all the hazzanim who I learned to know at that time, there was not one who had a common-school education or possessed any Hebrew learning (Wise 1901:45–46).[8]

Leaving aside the fact that Wise's own educational credentials were not altogether clear, this denunciation epitomizes the attitude of the major Reformers towards the old-time American hazzan. Put simply, they wanted to run the show themselves and had no use for competition. Fleshed out, their approach summarizes the whole Reform agenda, which saw the kind of "folk" practices Wise lists as anathema for forward-looking Jews.[9] Wise sees the old ways as discrediting the

Jewish clergy as a whole: "There was an antipathy at that time in America [1847] to rabbis and preachers in general, just as there was a prejudice against cultured people of any kind" (Wise 1901:45–46). However, it was not easy to replace the older cantorate, which is what Wise and his colleagues wanted, because the lay leadership was still hard to move: "At the beginning of the 1850s virtually every religious leader of standing was repudiated by his congregation. Lilienthal, Isaac Mayer Wise, and Leeser lost their positions, Leo Merzbacher's post at Emanu-El was in serious jeopardy, and Abraham Rice resigned and went into the dry goods business" (Sussman 1986:15).

Although these early years of Reform Judaism, which arrived in America simultaneously with its explosive growth in Germany, may have been difficult, by the 1860s, the movement was well on the way to consolidation, and by the 1880s, when the great wave of eastern European Jews arrived, it had achieved a position of dominance. The milestone dates are perhaps the Philadelphia Conference, at which a core group of German immigrant Reformers set the stage for action, followed by the establishment of Hebrew Union College (Cincinnati) in 1882, the crucial Pittsburgh Platform of 1885, which outlined basic principles, and finally the formation of the Central Conference of American Rabbis (CCAR), originally more general in membership, but eventually (and still today) the voice of the Reform rabbinate.

In this formative period, issues relating to the modernization of Judaism in every sphere were touched upon, but the role of the hazzan received little direct attention. Instead, the key musical trend seemed to be the establishment of the choir direction and organist[10] (both often non-Jews) as the main authorities, clearly subordinate to the new type of eloquent, educated Reform rabbi/minister. The congregation's role, already restricted to docile, decorous hymn-singing in early German modernism, was cut back so far that by 1892 the CCAR began to worry that the spirit was going out of congregational worship by comparison to Christian practice. Isaac Mayer Wise, who, we have seen, had little interest in hazzanim, nevertheless wanted some expressive music in his services: "Music is the language . . . of humanity and we have as yet been . . . too intellectual and too little emotional. . . . We need not become Methodists . . . but we should touch the soul, make people do what they seldom do in our synagogues, cry. Dr. Kohler [another major Reformer] has referred to the great strength of Christianity, their hymns" (quoted in Hoffman 1977a:32–33).[11]

Under the new ground rules, what space was left for the cantorate in terms of musical leadership if his pastoral function was to be taken over by the rabbi and the music was the province of the choir and organ? The answer was that some Reform congregations could indeed get along for generations without a hazzan, but if a musical leader came along who knew how to reshape and revitalize the service, the laity might be swayed by his personality. Such activists created a basis for the emergence of new Jewish music and musicians in the twentieth century and allowed for a time when, beginning in the late 1920s, the Reform movement—under eastern European influence—would again find the hazzan a useful adjunct to the rabbi and an adornment to the service. The case of one congregation, Oheb Shalom of Baltimore, is instructive in illustrating the ways that strong musical leaders could put their stamp on a synagogue despite early waffling about the cantorate. Our chronicle starts in 1850:

> Isaac Hamburger, a young man of 28 who had opened a clothing store on Harrison Street, acted as reader and officiated regularly until the election of Mr. Altmeyer as Cantor. The functions of Mr. Altmeyer in the Congregation were somewhat complex. First, he was appointed to read the Torah and perform marriages for a salary of $50 per year. Then the duties of collecting dues and keeping the synagogue clean were added [the normal duties of the shammash]. Later [1854], when Reverend Salomon was elected as Cantor and Preacher, Altmeyer was continued in office as shammes or sexton. . . . Rev. Salomon remained for only ten months and his connection with the Congregation was severed in a very abrupt manner [he said he was divorced, got engaged to a local girl, and then his wife turned up in town] (Cahn 1953:21–22).

Here we have the familiar picture of the mixture of duties, nicely combined with an incident tailor-made to support Wise's notion of the old-time hazzan as scoundrel. However, in 1866 Oheb Shalom hired Alois Kaiser (1842–1908), the exact opposite of Hamburger and Co. A major figure in the composition of new synagogue music, he served the congregation for forty-two years, working closely with the rabbi on service building. They stripped down the liturgy and stressed decorum, using Szold's prayerbook and Kaiser's music, which became a legacy for their successors. Jacob Schuman, who began in 1908, arranged "much of the music used in the synagogue service today. . . . Following the example of Cantor Kaiser, he transposed operatic arias and classical composition to be used as melodies for the synagogue" (Cahn 1953:55). Repertoire, then, had to be consistent with the respectability of the clergy and congregational decorum, and was based on contemporary European classical favorites, above all the music of the bourgeoisie, tastefully performed by the cantorial soloist while the worshippers sang hymns directly inspired by four-square, four-part Protestant standards.

Kaiser's work was paralleled by that of Edward Stark (1856–1913) in San Francisco's prestigious Temple Emanu-El. Stark insisted on conducting most of the service in English and stressing music. He hired leading non-Jewish singers for his choir and demanded perfection, as did the audience. One choir member, Homer Henley, describes the choir's state of mind at the onset of the High Holy Days around 1900: "The gentile singers . . . were in fine form, thoroughly trained for the tremendously exacting work of the day. They sang with nervous eagerness, anxious to measure up to the critical standards of the musical Jews in the congregation. . . . The numerous orchestra laid a rich background of meshed gold for the singing music of Israel" (Zucker 1985:235–36). Jeffrey Zucker, himself a hazzan, summarizes Stark's music: "Many of the works performed were his own, and he frequently included the compositions of Salomon Sulzer. . . . [T]here were adaptations of works of Haydn, Gounod, Auber, Flotow and Reinecke as well as a few compositions by Schubert and Mendelssohn. A significant portion of the music heard at Emanu-El was from the Protestant tradition of anthems and hymns" (Zucker 1985:248).

Stark also produced religious school operettas that "combined selections from grand opera, light opera, and popular song with 'quaint Jewish traditional melodies' " (Zucker 1983:19). Apparently Stark felt free to draw on the same sources for both sacred and secular music within the synagogue walls, displaying a considerable sophistication— or degradation—of synagogue music depending on one's point of view. The fluidity with which hazzanim crossed this boundary was already clear in the choice of the classically trained Mr. Phillips described earlier, who took over musical duties at a major New York synagogue in 1866, and the colorful character Herman Davidson (1846–1911) who was described in chapter 1 as moving from being a Russian opera trouper on tour to becoming a respected hazzan in California:

> Reverend Davidson, the hazzan, has an excellent baritone voice, and it is a treat in itself to listen to it. His grand baritone voice and his Hebrew reading are faultless. . . . It is a very creditable fact that a place of worship in such a small place should possess such a well trained choir as does this synagogue. . . . A more honest and charitable man I have never met, and above all he maintains his reputation and dignity as a man in his calling should. Such men are rare among the Jewish clergy in California (Clar 1983:74–75).

Davidson eventually brought over his family from Germany and went into farming as well as cantoring to assure a decent income: "he looks forward to the day when he will be able to sing for pleasure for his old congregation. . . . [B]uy land! Be a goy—and buy land!" wrote the local columnist (Clar 1983:85).

With men like Stark and Davidson at the helm of congregations by the late nineteenth century, we find synagogue life and the cantorate radically changed from the colonial situation. The expansion of the American Jewish population had broken down the "one town, one synagogue" model. The opening up of new areas, such as California, was one reason for substantial adaptation to new conditions. Another was the shift in the balance of the Jewish population from the dominant Sephardic to the emerging Ashkenazic majority. Seats in the old-line Sephardic synagogues became increasingly filled by newer Ashkenazic members who enjoyed the prestige of the patrician past. Already by the 1840s, congregational variety was vigorous and noticeable; by 1857, the diversity of the community could be vividly portrayed as a sub-ethnic bedlam at a concert of hazzanim for the consecration of a new synagogue: "The whole hazzan-army appeared. . . . Mr. Pape sang Polish, Noot screamed Dutch, and Morais trilled Portuguese, and Leeser and Dropsie spoke English and the community is German. Fortunately the ruins of the Tower of Babel were recently discovered, or Philadelphia would certainly have been dug up by archaeologists looking for the Tower" (*Die Deborah*, 20 Feb. 1857, 213).

Thus on the eve of mass immigration from eastern Europe (1880), American Judaism was rife with competing communities, sects, and orientations.[12] This is not surprising in the American atmosphere, as Karp has noted: "The divisions in American Judaism were pronounced, the polemics sharp, and the controversies continuous . . . and small wonder. Religious controversy, the sharpest polemics and the vilest accusations were part of the nineteenth century American religious scene. Religious controversy was [also] rife in European Judaism. American Judaism being part of both responded and participated" (1984:I–14). The late nineteenth century saw the consolidation of Reform power, but also dynamic activity among Jews of other persuasions. Just a year after the Pittsburgh Platform of 1885, a more traditionally oriented group of scholars and laymen founded the Jewish Theological Seminary, a counterweight to Reform's Hebrew Union College and, a generation later, the flagship of the middle-of-the-road Conservative movement. Meanwhile, in 1890 the right wing of American Judaism brought an Orthodox rabbi to be "chief rabbi" on the European *kehillah* (community) model. American Jews were to continue a strong penchant for dividing themselves along lines reflecting place of origin, socioeconomic status, and ideological/denominational identity.

All of this affected the cantorate deeply. Until the new eastern European immigrants could find their own ideals for the role of the hazzan, a process to which the next chapter is devoted, the cantorate was in a parlous state. The old hazzan was discredited, whereas the new, pacesetting Reform congregations dispensed with all but the most creative and dignified "cantors." Of course, in many farflung provincial settlements, the tried and true traditions lingered; we are aware of only the tip of the iceberg in trying to assess the evolution of the nineteenth-century cantorate. Even for New York we are informed only about prominent clergymen, as Grinstein notes in his list of hazzanim: "We list here only those ministers who were regularly paid officials; volunteer ministers are not mentioned. . . . On the whole we know more about the ministers engaged by the larger synagogues; the ministers of the smaller congregations are rarely mentioned in the periodical press or elsewhere" (1947:488).

It is true that many features of the older nineteenth-century cantorate "go underground" in the as yet under-researched history of more recent generations. Even for the period of the twentieth century that lies beyond living memory, we know less than we would like about the situation of the hazzan. Probably the cantorate was livelier than it looks in the 1880s; the wave of eastern European immigration simply floods our historical consciousness at this point and radically revises the role of the hazzan, and it is to this drastic development that we now turn.

NOTES

1. It is tempting to offer the reader a concise set of dates to sort out the eventual denominational spread among Jewish-Americans, but I would rather the reader followed the figure of the hazzan through the labyrinth than try to pigeonhole, because even within denominations the role of the sacred singer has hardly been consistent.

2. I am grateful to Jacob Rader Marcus for making me think through this issue.

3. Here again, the Jewish situation paralleled Protestant practice: "Protestantism in America . . . has been almost from the first strongly lay-centered and lay-controlled" (Michaelsen 1956:275).

4. As we shall see below, the question of whether the hazzan performs a preset service or helps create it is a steady issue in the cantorate. The feeling one gets from this earliest period is that cantorial creativity was quite circumscribed, partly due to the authority of the *adjunta* but perhaps also because hazzanim do not seem to have been chosen for musical skills.

5. Critiques of communal behavior parallel the contemporary European situation; this is exactly the period of the emergence of modern Yiddish literature,

in which caustic descriptions of the arrogance of Jewry's officialdom played an important part.

6. The issue of whether the hazzan is also a preacher is an old one; Landman notes that it was often "considered the duty of the cantor to preach and reprove his congregants, should their failings make this necessary" (1972:38) in medieval times. However, in the nineteenth century, the Jews' interest in the preacher probably came more from the Protestant influence than from ethnic memory. Meanwhile, in America as in western Europe the old-time rabbi who lived by making legal decisions was but a minor factor in the new sense of a ministry.

7. Barbara Kirshenblatt-Gimblett has pointed out to me the distinction between this American Protestant/German Reform Jewish notion of the preacher and that embodied in the eastern European *maggid*, the former stemming from a new interest in a highly educated, secularized ministry and the latter based on the old values of textual interpretation described in chapter 1. The "orator" type worked on an uneducated modern laity, whereas the "interpreter" simply did, albeit in a virtuoso way, what any traditionally educated male could and did do. The Jews were not the only ones to feel the pressure of the preacher in America; "as a minority religion in a hostile Protestant environment, Catholicism had to measure up to the level of preaching in the United States or suffer the disgrace of public ridicule" (Dolan 1975:413).

8. Wise's diatribes could be even more fantastic. In one sally of 1858 in *Die Deborah* (1, no. 12, p. 158) he describes God creating the hazzan late, so he is doomed to work on the Sabbath and rest the other six days; the hazzan will also lack free will, so will be dependent on others all his life.

9. For a tabular summary of the Reformers' abolition of older practices within synagogue life, see Lowenstein (1981). The fact that Lowenstein's data show the *cantor* was given authority over the laity ("no chanting between words of the Cantor") in early German Reform rules of order strikes me as indicating that Wise's frustration with the hazzan was partly a matter of wanting to rule out a role for the *cantor* in favor of the new American Reform rabbi, but I am not an expert on the rabbinate.

10. The introduction of the organ, beginning in the 1840s, is a separate branch of study in American Jewish music and has been discussed as such elsewhere. It is worth noting that that already by 1844 in Charleston, the breakup of the local synagogue into two congregations—representing moderate and radical Reform currents and leaders—was precipitated by the introduction of the organ, a situation oft-repeated nationwide thereafter.

11. The shift to an interest in hymns is perhaps directly related to the stress on preaching; for Protestantism, one observer has noted: "in denominations that concentrate more on preaching, on the spoken word, hymn-singing is the predominant congregational contribution to the music" (Gray 1986:1).

12. "National" denominational differences were not unique to Judaism. Even the highly organized Catholic church felt the same pressure: "In the United States the principal solution to the issue of religious nationalism was the formation of national parishes" (Dolan 1975:71), and as among the Jews, German immigrants were at the forefront of pushing for a separate identity as part of a continuation of trends back home (Dolan 1975:69).

3

~~~~~~

1880s–1940s: First- and Second-Generation Eastern Europeans

An unprecedented, almost impossibly large number of Jews—2.3 million—came to the United States in the great immigration of 1882–1924 (Goren 1980:1). It began when growing persecution in the Russian Empire made more and more Jews desperate enough to abandon Europe, and it ended only when the United States Congress yielded to a long anti-immigrant campaign. To indicate the size of this wave, it is enough to note that while New York City housed some 80,000 Jews in 1880, it found room for perhaps 1.75 million by 1925, creating the largest metropolitan Jewish population in history. New York became the heart of American Jewry, and certainly the center of the cantorate: seventy percent of the Jews who landed in New York between 1881 and 1911 stayed there (Goren 1980:43), principally in the meganeighborhood called the Lower East Side, or usually just "the East Side," or "the Ghetto." As in the case of the similarly centralized Yiddish theater and press, the rest of the country was simply called "the provinces," even though this defined the backwoods as starting at Philadelphia. That cities were the major focus of settlement was a major shift in consciousness. Whereas the German Jews had located themselves around the United States, the eastern Europeans tended to stay in the big cities, forming large neighborhoods that acted like miniature East Sides.

This impressive demographic shift radically reshaped the structure and inclination of American Jewry, since the urban eastern Europeans swamped both the original Sephardic layer and the dominant German group that had formerly set the tone. The cantorate changed drastically and quickly. In New York, the newcomers founded dozens of small synagogues, many named for the town of origin of their congregants, producing the well-known "Rumanian Shul" or more localized entities like the "Bialostok Shul." This meant that synagogue life became part of a cluster of fraternal activities centered on where you came from,

not where you were, designed to support immigrants—both econom-
ically and spiritually—in their transition from Europe to America. The
statistical back-up for this picture is impressive: "A 1917 study of the
365 Lower East Side congregations estimated that 90 percent owned
cemetery plots, nearly half had free-loan societies, a third had sick-
benefit societies, and nearly half sponsored traditional study groups"
(Goren 1980:46). Of course, even these very European houses of prayer
were susceptible to American lifestyles: "Many [society] constitutions
also reflected the impact of American middle-class decorum in matters
of public prayer. The Kletzker society, which maintained its own synagogue building, insisted that: 'Every member is required to conduct
himself quietly, and not to wander about the synagogue during services
. . . he must also refrain from conversation with others' " (Moore
1981:125). In 1885, one of these countless brand-new congregations
hired a hazzan at the impressive figure of $1,000. This innovation had
an electrifying effect on the cantorate:

> Reports of the New York cantor and his thousand dollar salary spread
> through Russia and Poland, and set off a cantorial migration to America.
> Each cantor left his home, filled with the hope that he would gather up
> "fistfuls of gold" in the New World. Many arrived in 1885–6, and most
> quickly learned the ways of New York: to inflate and to publicize them-
> selves, in manner proper, and even not so proper. In advertisements they
> hailed themselves as "king of the cantors. . . ." Synagogues began to com-
> pete with one another, and to "snatch" the cantor of its competitor (Ma-
> lachi 1937).

Around this time, one émigré Polish congregation decided not just
to wait and see who stepped off the boat, but to take the initiative,
and thus began the tradition of directly importing European hazzanim.
"The first congregation to bring a cantor was the Anshe Suvalk Synagogue. It had just built an elegant edifice and was deep in debt. To
meet expenses, its leaders decided to [engage] a 'star' cantor whose
name would attract new worshippers and increase membership" (Malachi 1937). The man they chose was Chaim Weinshel (grandfather of
the famous radio commentator Walter Winchell), and his arrival fulfilled the congregation's hopes: "the first Sabbath he officiated, the
streets surrounding the synagogue were crowded with worshippers
struggling to enter" (Malachi 1937). Weinshel was a sophisticated, well-
educated man who was amused and repelled by the small-town atmosphere of American Judaism. In 1891 he published a scathing account of his experiences as a hazzan. He had been in New York and
in the "provinces" (Rochester) and had seen it all. Writing in Hebrew,

the language of eastern European literati, he described the good-for-nothings from Poland who become community leaders in the New World. Not surprisingly, he picked the town of Suvalk, hometown of his first American congregation, as his target. The centerpiece of his epic poem is a miller's assistant who becomes hazzan:

There [in Suvalk] they bang with hammers like their fathers. Here they become instant hazzanim praying for the well-being of their brethren.

In a language he has not mastered, he lifts his voice in prayer. An ignorant person, how can he pray well?

And there is one who never thought to lead in prayer till a friend, calculatedly, declared him one—and he became ordained and led! . . .

When his uncle found no work for him, he said: "I'll make you a hazzan. You'll pray for your people. You'll live in comfort, eat your bread with dignity."

He objected: "How can I be a hazzan? I shouted at the millstones, but I don't know any Hebrew—how can I be a hazzan, a master of prayer? "

The uncle answered: "My son, calm yourself. I am the master here, head of the congregation. I'll call a meeting of my herd, my sheep and donkeys. Then you'll see my power, how my flock fears me. . . . I have spoken—who will question my words? You are the chief cantor of my synagogue, so cease your foolish idle words. You are the hazzan, and your salary is five hundred a year."

The mill worker opened his mouth, roared and shouted in a gravely voice that grated on the ears like an owl's shrieking.

"Is there a better hazzan?" the uncle stated. "He is the best of all: musical, sweet-voiced, hazzan, the one we'll choose."

The miller became a hazzan and informed his wife in the Old Country; the poor woman went into shock and ran to the rabbi: "Save me from my demented husband. He claims to be a hazzan—he must have lost his mind! "

At the rabbi's behest, the wife sent a letter imploring her husband to return home, where there are doctors who could cure him . . . but *there*, the miller, now a noted hazzan, was singing at weddings, circumcisions and at gravesides, and money was pouring in from all directions.

The women carried him on their fingertips. He received a new tallit with a large silver embroidery as a present. . . .

The hazzan sent an answer to his wife: ". . . Weep not, my sweet one, fear not that your husband has lost his mind. My mind is clear—it's the congregation that's gone crazy!" (Weinshel 1891, translated by A. J. Karp).

Meanwhile, Weinshel's appearance in New York caused quite a furor: "The success of the Anshe Suvalk congregation roused the envy of the other congregations, and they began to import cantors . . . even when a cantor fell into disfavor, the congregational leaders were often reluctant to let him go, not knowing whether they would be able to find a replacement" (Malachi 1937).[1]

What could have caused this cantorial craze in America, which raged throughout the 1880s and 1890s? It is too early to understand completely why many of the incoming eastern European Jews put so much store in the hazzan, just when this congregational leader was being dethroned or transformed by the resident American Jews. True, it was the age of the star hazzan in Europe, as described in chapter 1, and no doubt the immigrants used the hazzan as a comforting transitional figure as they oriented themselves in America. A close look at the internal workings of immigrant synagogues might help here. Fortunately we know a great deal about Beth Israel of Rochester, where Weinshel himself worked briefly before moving on to bigger things, because Abraham Karp has done an exemplary study of this one congregation for the years 1872–1912, the formative period of Americanization. It is very instructive to know how at least one group of lay leaders handled the question of the cantorate. Karp sees the hazzan's importance in terms of a fledgling congregation's basic needs: respectability in the Jewish community, financial stability, and "consumer satisfaction" for the membership:

> The cantor was a congregation's most cherished possession, chief contributor to its standing and popularity. His utility was constantly visible to all members of the congregation. For some he provided aesthetic pleasure, to others spiritual uplift, to most a combination of both. Beyond that, he provided the community with a subject for critique and conversation. . . . Income from sale of tickets for the High Holy Day Services was an important factor in congregational financing, and it depended in part on the quality and fame of the officiating cantor. . . . In difficult times as in times of well-being the cantor remained till the end of the century the central functionary in the east European Orthodox congregation (Karp 1984:III–58, 61).

For Beth Israel, having a terrific hazzan came before all other business of the board: "It is no wonder that the minutes disclose that more discussion time was devoted at meetings to the office, search, election, compensation, tenure and critique of the cantor than to all other functionaries combined" (Karp 1984:III–55). What we see in microcosm in Beth Israel is the turbulence of a community of Europeans who are becoming Americans, focusing their collective energy on an institution they believe in passionately. Among nonobservant Jews and in large cities, it was possible to find other channels for this energy, ranging from the Yiddish theater (Sandrow 1977; Slobin 1982c) to the trade union movement and other political causes (Howe 1976). For the believers, the synagogue was where they wanted to enact a communal ritual of identity, and they were not alone: all ethnic groups thought of the church as a central place for making choices about their new life in America. The older neighborhoods of the Frost Belt are dotted with the towering spires and humble halls of a hundred Jewish and Christian denominations, all built on the hopes of immigrants:

> The ethnic church has been singled out [by historians] for the role it played in giving the immigrant parishioner the feeling of security which comes from a sense of community . . . for providing for him instruments and experiences of continuity in the New World where discontinuities marked his personal and communal life; and presenting him with a safe arena in which he could act out the dramas of interpersonal relationships— or contention for power, status and influence . . . —in an atmosphere of fraternal concern (Karp 1984:I–9).

In tracing Beth Israel's perpetual search for the ideal hazzan, then, we are watching a daily drama that took place in dozens of congregations across America. Here are the details for the early immigrant years:

> When Beth Israel sought a "good cantor," it did so by advertising in the Yiddish press, the candidate to appear and be chosen after a "two Sabbaths trial. . . ." The popular Cantor Jospe announced his resignation because . . . "he was elected in New York for much more money," and it took a full year to find an acceptable replacement. . . . Hayim Weinshel is elected hazzan for two years at a salary of $800 per annum [1891, the year Weinshel wrote his indictment of the American cantorate]. An extra $100 is voted for a choir; he is given $25 for expenses and . . . when he signs the contract he is granted $50 to bring his family. By the spring, however, he has financial problems. He asks [for] a grant above his salary because he needs a new suit for Pesach, but cannot afford it. Instead of money the Trustees grant him permission to sell tickets for Passover services [and] he is granted a leave of three weeks to lead prayer as a visiting cantor [elsewhere]. But problems mount. A special meeting is called on July 31, 1892, to decide whether to give the cantor his salary in advance, since there are rumors that he is planning to leave the city. . . . [T]ry as it may the congregation can not retain their "star" cantor. . . . [I]t is informed that the cantor was away from his pulpit without permission to try out for a position in another city, and it is voted to declare his contract null and void. Hazzan Weinshel leaves and once again candidates and negotiations arouse interest during the entire year (Karp 1984:III–58–59).

This is a description of the seller's market of the early immigrant era. The congregation certainly got its share of diversion from trading in the "Cantors' Exchange." Yet not all hazzanim were so much in demand as Weinshel, and in New York the stiff competition eventually made life rough for sacred singers in the center of American Jewry:

> The Anshe Kalvaria synagogue engaged Rev. Yisroel Cooper [famous cantor of Vilna]. The high salary offered by American synagogues caused him to try his luck there. After initial success, his good fortune faded, and he was dismissed. Thereafter he lived alone and forsaken, until in one impetuous moment he brought an end to his life. . . . When the novelty of "star" cantors wore off, synagogue attendance began to decline. . . . [B]y the end of the eighties, . . . those who could not find a position even in cities outside New York went to work in the shops or became peddlers (Malachi 1937).

However jaded New York may have become within a few years, for the rest of the country, the record shows that towns like Rochester remained fascinated by its hazzanim:

> Finally, on May 28, 1893, Hazzan Samuel Joseph Cantor[!] is elected for a period of two years at an annual salary of $900, but he is to provide a choir. . . . The Spring 1896 quarterly meeting heard the president report that their hazzan was planning to open a liquor business in Syracuse. It was voted that he be called to the meeting and asked about it. He appeared and verified the report. It was thereupon voted to void the contract [but] it was agreed that he remain through the High Holy Days and be paid $600 (Karp 1984:III–60).

What we are seeing is constant cultural improvisation. A constituency—a congregation—wants to have the hazzan, for organizational, financial, and aesthetic/spiritual reasons. Yet there are no ground rules. Salary, job description, personality—all are open to discussion, or even violent argument, and the situation holds coast to coast, as a California example will show. At Congregation Sherith Israel, San Francisco, the hazzan's wife was so incensed when a board member insulted her husband that she punched him in the nose. Shortly thereafter, the husband, Hazzan Max Rubin, resigned after being accused of smoking a cigarette in the men's room on Yom Kippur while "dressed in his white robe and tallith" (Zwerin 1985:144). By contrast, in the same congregation, Benjamin Liederman rose from $75 to $175 a month by 1915 and received an alpaca robe, being called only "choir leader" and not "cantor." Despite the fact that this Reform congregation insisted it did not have a "cantor," Liederman was given the title in 1916 at

$2,100 a year and served forty-eight years, leaving over one million dollars.

Clearly there is no simple way to categorize the cantorate in the immigrant age. Yet despite all the confusion, even a glance at views from the end of this era, in the 1930s, confirms the unchanging image of the cantorate as a marketplace. We shall see that for selected stars, life was easy, but even they had to struggle with the competitive, bruising world of job hunting and board pleasing that lay at the core of the cantorate and to some extent still does. One leading hazzan, Joshua Weisser, explained it to his colleagues back in Poland in a 1938 article for a Warsaw trade journal:

> Here business takes a front seat, and the hazzan becomes a sort of employee. He, naturally, is in a worse position, since the need for a hazzan is not so strongly felt in the shul, as the need for an employee in a business. In addition, there's the sad situation in which a coach-driver can take the hazzan's place, as long as he can shout. [Auditions] look like a slave market. You can't blame the lay leadership either, since the majority of those who come are not really hazzanim. They are tailors, or other artisans, whose colleagues have talked them into becoming clergymen (Weisser 1938:16).

Over and over, hazzanim rail against the system of *proben*, auditions, try-outs for an available position, as in this precise, damning account by a prominent hazzan:

> Many synagogues which are in need of a cantor . . . start competitive hearings right after Passover. Considering the fact that there are only approximately 22 Saturdays from Passover to New Year, the congregation cannot afford to grant hearings to every applicant (which might be over 100). They . . . stage preliminary hearings during the week . . . to determine who shall be the lucky winner for the coming Saturday. As the time towards New Year approaches, the Congregation resolves to divide one Saturday service even among as many as four or five applicants. [They may decide] after having exploited about 100 Cantors under false pretenses, not to engage a Cantor at all for the coming year (Adolf 1935:8).

A certain A. D. Egoz, writing in the Yiddish press, carries the notion of hazzan as employee much farther, using the natural comparison of the immigrant age, the sweatshop:

> To make an analogy with the tailors' trade: there are bosses who will not allow their workers to feel so safe about their jobs that they will ask for raises, so they hang out help-wanted signs and get great numbers of applicants who are really not needed or wanted but are used as a threat to discourage requests for raises. This is the way many shul administrators

deal with their hazzanim. A congregation, though satisfied with their hazzan, will often bring in others from the outside for a trial performance to intimidate the one they have (Egoz 1910:5).

The effect of this sort of treatment can be severe on the incumbent hazzan, even leading to disaster:

> It may . . . break their hazzan's heart, making the grief in his voice more real when it comes to the prayers asking for forgiveness for the congregation. Here is an example: the hazzan of a large synagogue had a couple of opponents. One Saturday of the new moon in the prayer "God is my helper and I will be avenged on my enemies," he chose to repeat, several times, the words "I will be avenged on my enemies," and coincidentally in conducting the choir he happened to move his hand in the direction of his adversaries; although he did not do this intentionally . . . he lost his job (Egoz 1910:5).

Advertisement became the main weapon in the battle to get, keep, and sell hazzanim, and the language of commerce is plain in the Yiddish press; we hear about Leib Shlossberg "who astounded all of New York with his lion-roaring voice; [he] will *daven* [pray] in the big, airy Beethoven Hall. When a lion roars, who will not hear?" (*Morgen zhurnal,* 7 Sept. 1906). Another ad of 1906 shows how the cantorate had become part of Jewish-American entertainment. Edelstein, Thomashefsky, and Friedsell, manager, actor-writer, and composer respectively of the People's Theater, a bastion of the Yiddish stage, announce the transformation of their hall into sacred space for the upcoming holidays:

> After strenuous effort and great expense, we finally succeeded in engaging the world renowned hazzan Reb Israel Fine, former hazzan of the Hungarian Norfolk St. Synagogue, the Bes Hamdresh Hagodol, the Sephardic Synagogue on Willette St. and the present hazzan of the Bes Medresh Hagodol of Brooklyn for the Rosh Hashanah and Yom Kippur to daven at the People's Theater with a magnificent, trained choir under the direction of the famous composer Mr. Louis Friedsell. Do you want to get pleasure for your money this year? Then come to the beautiful, airy People's Theater Synagogue. You will hear good singing, beautiful davening, Jewish and sweet. The management guarantees good service (*Yidishes tageblat,* 16 Sept. 1906).

The provinces were not exempt from hype either: "Good tidings for Detroit, Michigan! At the demand of the general public, the well-known manager Morris Wolf has consented to comply with the wishes of the public and bring to Detroit the favorite of cantors, Berele Chagy" (*Der Tog,* 24 Sept. 1920).

Managers were the main means of placement if you were an ambitious hazzan, and managerial maneuvering continued unabated until the advent of professional cantorial organizations in the 1950s. The sacred singers who wrangled with agents and boards and who rose to the top of the hazzanic heap raked in rich rewards, at least in the early decades when immigrants identified the cantorate with the deepest feelings of their European past. Not only impoverished immigrants, but also the Jewish upper crust and assorted dignitaries made their way to the debuts of the latest cantorial sensation, as we read in a Yiddish newspaper account of the great Gershon Sirota's first New York appearance (in 1912):

> Carnegie Hall was packed from top to bottom. The crowds which remained outside were even greater; men and women, young and old who tried without success to get in to hear the concert by the great tenor and the choir under the direction of Herr [Leo] Loew. New York has never witnessed such a scene. The police had their hands full in keeping order on the street. Among the gentile members of the audience were such personalities as Baron Shlimenbach, the Russian Consul-General, State Senator Tom Sullivan. . . . Also present were Rabbi Stephen S. Wise . . . and the famous star of the Metropolitan Opera, Alma Gluck (reprinted in Fater 1969:20).

The spectacular splash made by such superstars led to the creation of many legends, with the favorite point of comparison, opera, reappearing constantly. The most celebrated gentile singer of the age, Enrico Caruso, had his name linked with the appearance of major hazzanim; for example, at Sirota's debut, which included the operatic aria "Celeste Aida," Caruso was quoted as saying: "Thank God he has chosen to employ his heavenly gift in a different field and I do not have to compete with such a formidable challenger in opera" (Vigoda 1981:585). The most popular of hazzanim, Yosele Rosenblatt, was often called "the Jewish Caruso," and it was said that Caruso secretly came to hear Rosenblatt.[2] There are various versions of a story about Rosenblatt being offered a lucrative opera contract and turning it down because of religious scruples, a testimony both to his gifts and his integrity, from the traditionalist point of view.[3] Yet observant Jews were not happy with the apotheosis of the star hazzan.[4] True to the tradition of suspecting any singer who raises his voice for purely musical rather than religious effect, they denounced the commercialism and vanity surrounding the superstars, asking how Sirota could sing only in concert halls at events open to gentiles on his first sensational tour. Responding to this criticism, Sirota started his next tour with a Sabbath service, though still on a stage decked out with an Ark (Vigoda

1981:585). The purists remained unsatisfied: "He was taken to task for his frequent use of banal and cheap effects and for his sudden outbreaks of unrelated, stunt-like roulades and coloratura acrobatics . . . and falsetto. . . . [T]hey also looked askance at his too frequent repeating of the text and . . . throwing around the words in arbitrary disorder" (Vigoda 1981:600).

If star hazzanim left the straight and narrow path of their calling, they were certainly well rewarded for it. In 1914 Zavel Kwartin, whose early European career we followed in chapter 1, laid down stringent conditions for a projected American tour: (1) only three months for the entire tour, which is to start only after the High Holy Days (so he could travel while on vacation from his job in Vienna); (2) first-class ship tickets for himself and his daughter, who is to get featured billing as singer at all concerts; (3) thirty concerts across America, outside extra Sabbaths to be arranged; (4) each performance at $1,000; (5) deposit of $2,000 in advance; (6) bank guarantees for the balance; and (7) not more than two concerts a week, including Sabbath services. All the conditions were met—but the outbreak of World War I cancelled the whole project, which was rescheduled only in 1920. This six-year delay did not hurt Kwartin's marketability: the first five Saturdays of his tour went for $1,700 each, the first day of Pesach netted $2,500, while the two days of Shavuot added another $4,500 (Kwartin 1952:372, 413).

However, just as the first rush of enthusiasm for hazzanim in the 1880s and 1890s cooled quickly, this new passion for the recording-star virtuosos began to fade.[5] By 1925, a newspaper critic could already lament the fact that "*hazzanut* [the cantorial art] has become so uniform, it has acquired such a 'phonographic' character, that there is very little to write about" (Goldblum 1925). Goldblum picked his adjective well: new technologies could produce what we would now call media overexposure. As mentioned in chapter 1, cantorial recordings date back to the earliest days of widespread commercial disc-making, with Sirota and Kwartin taking the lead. Initially there was some doubt as to the suitability of electronic dissemination of the liturgy. One respectable hazzan, Pinye Minkowsky of Odessa, wrote tirades against commercial recording of hazzanim, citing reports that one could hear sacred hymns coming out of the rooms of prostitutes in the city's pleasure quarters. Kwartin and Sirota countered with fan mail from Jewish soldiers out in the Far East during the Russo-Japanese war who said hearing the beloved sounds of sacred song kept up their morale. Like it or not, sales figures in Europe and then America showed that the ordinary Jew was eager to buy up all the discs the companies could produce (Kwartin 1952).[6]

With the advent of radio in the 1920s and Yiddish-language "talking pictures" in the 1930s, a well-placed hazzan could get even more media coverage, as this 1937 announcement about Leibele Waldman indicates: "To date he is the only cantor who is under contract to make Jewish talking pictures. . . . Samuel P. Mogelewsky, President of the World Clothing Exchange, gave Cantor Waldman his greatest opportunity by bringing his remarkable talent, by means of the radio, to a new and enlarged public" (Chazanut 1937:48).

Here, the garment industry tie-in only underlines the commercialization of the cantorate. The question was how long a "new and enlarged public" would maintain an interest in listening to cantorial music, and what impact this media blitz would have on live performance at concerts or services. By 1938, a noted hazzan writing for his European colleagues says, "if you get hit in the head with hazzanut from all sides, and free, just by turning a knob, then why should you go hear a hazzan, and even pay for it?" (Vigoda 1938:9). With the onset of hard times in the 1930s, the lot of the hazzan deteriorated considerably. Even concerts became passé: "If you arrange a concert, you have to bring a half-dozen 'world-famous cantors' to get ahold of someone's 'quarter' [the basic ticket price] because otherwise you can't draw a crowd" (Vigoda 1938:9). In the same magazine, another American hazzan bemoans the change of fortunes of the cantorate: "We remember the recent past, when every shul in New York, whether real Orthodox or 'modern,' supported a rabbi, a cantor, a shamash, and a choir director and choir the whole year long. . . . Now, when the finest hazzanim are in New York [due to the influx of refugees from Nazism] and there are about 400 hazzanim in the *Hazanim-farband* [cantors' association], young and old, many shuls remain without hazzanim" (Kirshenbaum 1938:14).

According to Vigoda, in 1938 there were 300 hazzanim in New York, of whom only fifty had full-time positions. The others hung around, starving, because they hated to go to the "provinces," where, however, there were a lot of good jobs and where hazzanim were more appreciated. His reason for this disparity was simple: in New York there was no communal pressure to join a congregation, because it was easy to lead a fully encompassing ethnic life in the metropolis as an unaffiliated Jew, whereas in the rest of the country, belonging to a synagogue was essential to one's ethnic/religious identity:[7]

> The times when a [New York] hazzan could get four to eight, even ten thousand a year are gone with the wind. Today, $3000 is about the highest price for a well-known hazzan. . . . It's become "the style" for the big hazzanim to daven the High Holy Days not in New York, but in other

cities, which pay more. In the provinces there are a number of hazzanim who get $4000 a year and even more. The same hazzanim couldn't get half as much in New York, and would have to look for a new position every year, whereas in the provincial cities they stay for years, and some for a lifetime. . . . In a word, the relationship of the provincial communities to their hazzanim, as to their clergy in general, is more mentshlikh, more respectful (Vigoda 1938:9).

A good example of "provincial" generosity supporting Vigoda's point can be found in Kansas City's Congregation B'nai Jehudah. In 1939, they hired a refugee hazzan, Alfred Rosbach, though they were a Reform synagogue, hence not given to the notion of a permanent cantorate, as we have seen. The results were extraordinary: "With skillful musicianship he brought a glow of beauty and warmth to the whole ritual. It seemed to us that all the pathos and all the hope of a tormented world were integrated in the lovely tones of his baritone voice and the traditional melodies he sang" (Adler 1972:184).

Most hazzanim of the late 1930s did not fare as well as Rosbach. Another dispatch to Warsaw colleagues points out that in the struggle for jobs between the refugees and those already in place in America, "the young ones have the advantage, first because you have to be able to read certain prayers in English, which is a bit stiff for the older hazzanim, and second, because you have to please the 'ladies' " (Cohen 1938). In 1940 Joshua Weisser detailed the predicament of the hazzan in telling terms for the Yiddish press:

> This year, the cantor's status is worse than ever. The bitter competition between long-time resident hazzanim and newly arrived refugee hazzanim [means that] only 20% of all hazzanim have established annual positions. . . . [M]any of those who are finally chosen were selected on the basis of a few shticks they picked up from listening to phonograph records, since to them being a hazzan was only a means of picking up a little extra income on the side. The genuine hazzan, who had spent most of his life studying, and who really knew music, was overlooked. . . . He and his family had had to borrow all summer long and live on the credit extended by grocers and friends who counted on repayment of a couple of hundred dollars from cantor's fees expected to come in after the High Holy Days. Imagine how the family felt when the hazzan, the provider, remained without a job. . . . But what hurt even more was the spiritual insult when he found himself passed by for the first time. For shame, he felt obliged to hide out in a tiny synagogue in a remote neighborhood for fear of being recognized. . . . I would like to have the shul leaders visit the office of the Cantor's Union and see the beautiful honored hazzanim who have not been hired, and the dark and hopeless expressions on their faces. When these shul leaders . . . beat their chests [on Yom Kippur] to

ask forgiveness for their sins, they would do well to ask forgiveness for one more sin: the sin they have committed against these hazzanim! (Weisser 1940).

The memoirs of immigrant hazzanim bear out Weisser's description. Zeidel Rovner (born Jacob Samuel Margovsky, 1865–1946), whose early career was cited in chapter 1, was one of the true cantorial giants, known for his compositions as well as for his singing. His arrival in America was immensely gratifying, as he was greeted not just by the general public, officials, and music critics, but by his former choirboys, now successfully Americanized, who invited him to a reception: "He found there . . . a large crowd among whom were . . . not only cantors, choir leaders, professional singers and members of the musical world, but also physicians, attorneys, dentists, manufacturers, bankers, merchants, mechanics and shopworkers. . . . Once more they had become the choristers of Rovno, Kishinev, Berditchev and Lemberg. Zeidel, baton in hand, began directing and the gigantic chorus, following his lead, sang song after song" (Vigoda 1981:229). However, after the initial sensation wore off, Zeidel's fortunes declined. He was invited to return to Europe, being offered a lifetime contract in Vienna. Enthusiasts created a fund to keep him in America: "A mammoth chorus and larger orchestra [were assembled in 1923]. Six thousand people jammed the huge auditorium. . . . Zeidel was also the recipient of the honor of a visit to the White House [where] he was given a warm reception by President Calvin Coolidge. [However] there was mismanagement galore. The well-intentioned plan turned into a complete fiasco" (Vigoda 1981:232–34). Old and embittered, Zeidel wrote memoirs for a Yiddish newspaper in which he described sitting in a lonely tenement, visited by his only colleagues, the shades of hazzanim past. Vigoda cites an anecdote about Zeidel Rovner that sums up the old man's feelings about the American cantorate: "Once . . . Reb Zeidel posed the question: 'How is it that all societies usually own a cemetery, but the Cantors' Association does not?' He answered the question himself: 'They do not need a cemetery for the reason that they all are trying to bury one another' " (Vigoda 1981:234). Vigoda adds: "Most of the renowned and celebrated figures of the cantorial fraternity, having in one way or another squandered their considerable earnings . . . became indigent paupers, living in straitened circumstances, dependent on charitable contribution and dying, as the saying goes, *in fremde takhrikhem* [in strangers' shrouds]" (Vigoda 1981:153).

Some attempts to help floundering hazzanim were made by those who managed to remain successful in America:

> In those years [early 1920s] a club was organized to which belonged about a dozen of the most prominent cantors like Kwartin, Hershman, Roitman, and others, which had as its purpose the support of Karniol, Bromberg, and other cantors who were in need. These colleagues saw to it that he received a regular weekly stipend and he was even provided with a vacation during the summer. Shortly before his death, the cantors of New York arranged for [Karniol's] benefit an appearance. . . . The synagogue was packed to the rafters. . . . When Karniol began in a trembling voice *Tefilo leoni* (the prayer of a poor man) . . . the choir of over 100 cantors responded (Vigoda 1981:111–12).

As we have seen, such possible sources of comfort were hit or miss affairs. Much more useful for all hazzanim, young and old, might have been a tough professional organization, dedicated to placement and enforcement of decent treatment by synagogue boards. One such society did exist: the Jewish Cantors Ministers Association of America, familiarly known by its Yiddish appellation, the *khazonim-farband*. Nominally founded in 1897 and incorporated in 1919, this organization continues to exist in our own times and has served the cantorate to the best of its capabilities over the years. Overshadowed since the 1950s by the larger, denominationally sponsored professional organizations, in the immigrant decades it stood alone in trying to help hazzanim of all ages and origins find their footing in America. The degree of the Farband's success is disputed. Some former members feel it was never more than a patronage club, and that it compromised itself greatly by taking in not just full-time professionals, but any part-timer of whatever qualifications and interest in the cantorate. Max Wohlberg, today a major teacher of hazzanim and leading authority on cantorial music, but then a young aspiring professional, has a jaundiced view of the Farband:

> During the thirties the preponderant number of cantors in New York and its environs were members of the Farband. Unfortunately, the Farband saw fit to open its ranks to even such as were but remotely related to hazzanut, so long as they were willing to pay dues. As a result our colleagues included *shamoshim* (sextons), *shochtim* (slaughterers), *melamdim* (Hebrew teachers), *mashgichim* (supervisors of kosher food), *mohelim* (circumcisers), kosher delicatessen clerks and whoever functioned or aspired to function as a hazzan for as few as three days a year (Wohlberg 1976:3).

The hard core of the membership, was about thirty percent who "at least grew up in the profession, served as singers." These true professionals had to put up with some hard-fisted tactics on the part of the president, Jacob Rapaport, a gifted hazzan and composer but an autocratic administrator: "He brooked no opposition . . . he managed the organization under the rule of his thumb. And they did as he pleased. Then anyone whom he didn't like was ignored, disregarded or declared null and void, doesn't exist . . . your name didn't appear, you were not sent for a position where you wanted to apply" (D.A.).

Dissenters from this mode of organization were not hard to find:

> Progressively the cantors ceased to look to the Farband for the solutions to their problems . . . and thus was laid the foundation for the cantors cultural organization [among whose aims were] monthly musicales where new compositions of our members be performed discussed and analyzed; improvement of the ethical standards in our profession and the formation of an Arbitration Committee; refining the forums of publicity employed by our members; social and fraternal help for our colleagues; erection or purchase of a cantors' old-age home in *Eretz Yisrael* [Palestine] (Wohlberg 1976:6–7).

Thus was born the short-lived Cantors Ministers' Cultural Organization, which served as a bridge from the old Farband to the aspirations of the post–World War II period, when the Cantors Assembly (Conservative), American Conference of Cantors (Reform), and Cantorial Council of America (Orthodox) were established.[8] Looking back from the comfortable vantage point of 1974, a later cantorial leader can be particularly scornful of the old Farband: "Even in its heyday it was not concerned about hazzanut, but about the private success of individual hazzanim. . . . [T]he building on Second Avenue was called the *kibbetzarnyeh*, the hangout, a place to come to shmooze, to play a game of cards, to hold impromptu vocal contests" (Rosenbaum 1974:73).

Of course, the Farband's own publications portray a different notion of what had been achieved by the late 1930s than do the writings quoted above;[9] here is President Lipitz, writing in the fortieth anniversary jubilee volume of 1937:

> When the Jewish immigrants arrived at the shores of America forty years ago . . . the Synagogue became their rallying center. . . . How heartened the immigrants felt upon entering the synagogue after a hard week's work in the shop or factory to hear the Cantor intone the *Kedusha*. . . . The immigrants of forty years ago have become captains of industry and commerce. The humble synagogues have been transformed into great community centers and magnificent Temples. The power of the voice of Israel still holds its magic sway . . . wherever Jews gather in celebration of social, cultural, communal, or philanthropic events, there the Cantor is featured as the principal attraction (Lipitz 1937).

The gulf between Lipitz's view and that of the organization's critics is to a certain extent understandable; it is indeed the case that "captains of industry" built huge bourgeois synagogues, and that at many social and ceremonial occasions, hazzanim were asked, as a matter of course, to set the tone for the occasion. Yet Lipitz himself, in writing back to Warsaw about developments, had to admit that the association failed to find jobs for most of its members, and that they have had to resort to an unthinkable tactic—restructuring as a union:

> Our protests were, until now, a voice in the wilderness. It can't go on this way. Now we have 65% of the hazzanim who are completely un-employed. The others are always in danger of losing their positions. So after long discussion we decided to join the American Federation of Labor [AFL] and the Yidishe Geverkshaftn [Jewish Trade Unions]. Hazzanim, who until now were dreamers, fantasizers, will from now on have to be practical people and devoted union members. They'll have to carry out the decisions of our union one hundred percent. We have also decided to help the shuls this way, since the union will fit the appropriate hazzan to each shul according to its needs (Lipitz 1938:4–5).

Thus was created Cantors Ministers Union No. 20804, chartered by the AFL on 21 August 1942.[10] The decision to affiliate was made with only one dissenting vote, that of Max Wohlberg, who today still recalls his reasons for opposing the move:

> First of all, the union as such cannot . . . do anything actively against the congregation. They can do something against a manufacturer who makes a living from my work. But the congregation . . . none of my *bal-ebatim* [lay leaders] make a living from my singing, so what are they going to threaten them with? . . . Number two, we're still supposed to be cler-gymen. . . . If you're clergymen, what do we do with this labor. . . . And after about three years or four years, I believe, it was found that they really can do nothing for us, and we dropped the association.

Meanwhile, hazzanim helped themselves as well as they could. If commercialism guaranteed professional longevity, they were willing to indulge, as the following item about David Roitman, a celebrated, much-recorded hazzan, shows:

> What Famous New York Cantors Say about Maxwell House Coffee: After vacation I am happy that I can again enjoy the richer, better Maxwell House Coffee regularly. In thousands of Jewish homes, where the families are now reunited, the "summer bachelors" feel again the same thrill as Cantor Roitman and other well-known New York cantors—the enjoyment of coffee that they had been missing . . . with milk or cream for breakfast, and black after a *fleyshige* [meat] meal. *Gut bizn letstn tropn* [good to the last drop]. The favorite coffee in the Jewish home (*Morgen zhurnal*, 5 Sept. 1940).

Maxwell House, then, sees Roitman as part of mainstream, well-to-do Jewish America, which has its men stay in the city and work while the women and children go on summer holidays to the mountains or the seashore. The assumption that most families keep kosher (no milk in the meat-dinner meal) keeps the proper spirit of decorum that the company extended to the Passover holiday, when it distributed thousands of complimentary copies of the *haggadah* prayer-book for the *seder*, the family service, a service the company still offers today.

Less well known hazzanim went into other sorts of moneymaking ventures. The High Holidays, the bread and butter of the cantorate, drew in so many Jews that there was often not enough space in the local synagogues. Describing one of the more observant New York neighborhoods, Moore points out that whereas attendance at synagogues was light in general, it flourished in the fall:

> Brownsville reflected a pattern of Jewish religious behavior characteristic of New York Jews. Its synagogues regularly attracted a mere 8 percent of the neighborhood's adult Jewish males. . . . Only on Rosh Hashanah and Yom Kippur did Brownsville Jews flock to the synagogue. On those holidays, Brownsville's synagogues could not accommodate all worshippers, so individual rabbis and cantors transformed movie theater and private halls into makeshift synagogues. In these improvised quarters they conducted services for a modest fee to the overflow crowds (Moore 1981:127).

A typical advertisement for a catering halls run by a hazzan shows the sales pitch: "Cantor Gershen Spund, New York. Big reception rooms for weddings, Bar Mitzvahs. Singing, music, and organ. Air conditioning system installed. Recognized as the best mohel [circumciser]" (*Morgen zhurnal*, 11 Aug. 1950).[11]

In the midst of the scramble for steady jobs and of large-scale shifts of population from old central neighborhoods to new, more middle-class sites, the very make-up of the American cantorate began to change. Native-born Jewish boys were finding their way into the profession, learning from the old-timers and beginning the reshaping of the tradition on American terms. For despite all the volatility of the Jewish community and its increasing secularization, it still clung to the synagogue as its symbol: "Although the synagogue enrolled only a minority of New York City Jews as members, lack of formal affiliation with one did not destroy its symbolic importance. It served as the Jewish home which Jews conveniently could take for granted and ignore. A neighborhood synagogue announced not merely the presence of Jews, but their commitment to group survival. Activities carried out under its auspices bore the stamp of Jewish authenticity" (Moore 1981:123).

The synagogue itself was changing from the immigrant society, based on kinship and European town of origin, to an Americanized, symbolic institution. No longer the spiritual home just for immigrant men, it was now meant to serve families as a rallying point for identity: "second generation Jews reconstructed the synagogue into an institutional bulwark of middle-class ethnicity, but no longer an ethnicity based on town of origin." This led to the development of a new type of institution, the synagogue center, sketched out as early as 1918 by Mordecai Kaplan, a major spokesman for the second generation and a towering figure in twentieth-century Jewish-American thought. Kaplan articulated the need for a new type of synagogue as part of his notion of Judaism as a "civilization," rather than as either purely a religion on the one hand or a "race" on the other. He founded a new branch of American Judaism—Reconstructionism—which has remained small, but his thinking also heavily influenced the older Reform and emergent Conservative movements. Kaplan's insistence on the aesthetic side of Judaism is telling, and the fact that the following assessment of Kaplan is from an important Reform thinker underlines his influence: according to Kaplan, "the Jewish religion needed to be seen as but one aspect of an entire range of ethnic activities. Much of the revival of Jewish music, art, dance, and other cultural activities among us in recent decades has been due to Kaplan's insistence that we are an ethnic group and need to take up the full gamut of cultural responsibilities which derived from that identity" (Borowitz 1977:87). As Kaplan saw it, "In an age such as ours, religious rites are likely to be accepted only when they are regarded as customs and folkways" (Kaplan 1981:437). "The Jew will demand of his civilization many more meaningful and esthetic folkways and a greater variety and range from which to choose means of Jewish self-expression than it offers at present" (Kaplan 1981:439)

This meant that synagogues would have to turn into "centers," as he called them, proferring a wide variety of activities that would both lure Jews in and keep them through appealing both to their American need for recreation and their Jewish need for grouping as a people: "The Jew must learn to utilize his leisure in such a way that it shall enhance his life physically, mentally, and morally" (Kaplan 1981:429). The hazzan thus becomes just a small part of the larger aesthetic expression of his people, so would necessarily have to change with the times to keep up. Kaplan's ambitious musical agenda is a harbinger of the increased demands to be made in the postwar era on the hazzan's musical leadership skills: "Simultaneously with the preparation of the musical material there should be formed various choral societies, glee clubs, quartets, etc., to provide entertainment and develop a taste for Jewish music in the various synagogues, men's and women's clubs and centers" (Kaplan 1981:456).

Even without Kaplan's urging, Jewish-Americans had already begun, since the 1910s, to form a vast variety of socio-musical groupings either espousing specific causes, such as the Workmen's Circle Chorus with its leftist bent, or as the kind of recreational outlet just described. All of this made the hazzan's job increasingly ambiguous and challenging, as the fashions and trends of the various denominations swirled around the sanctuary. It is not easy to sort out the complex sectarian and institutional religious activity of second-generation Jewish-Americans, part of a whole complex of social patterns summarized succinctly by Moore: "The second generation shares in common the experience of growing up American in Jewish immigrant homes. While not a compact group in time—since mass immigration from eastern Europe extended uninterruptedly for 33 years beginning in 1881—the second generation occupies a similar point in space in their relationship to each other and to their immigrant parents" (Moore 1981:9).

To summarize the basic outlines of the period 1920–50, the rapid expansion of a new middle class among American Jews led to the opening up of new neighborhoods and the experimenting with new forms of association and identification. The synagogue changed, as we have seen, along with this general trend. Most particularly, the Conservative branch of American Judaism was born and began to make its presence felt, becoming the dominant denomination by the end of the period. Having grown up in observant homes, the men and women of the second generation gravitated towards Conservative Judaism, which promised tradition and modernization simultaneously.[12] Though constantly expanding in this era, the Conservative movement was far from clear about its aims and goals, neither internally nor in the view of the older Reform and Orthodox wings. The latter have consistently faulted Conservatives for inconsistency, since often the movement has known more about what it wanted to avoid than what it wanted to affirm. Its success—as well as its weakness—came from consensus and compromise and a talent for defining the center.

Conservative Judaism made the role of the hazzan ambiguous. The movement was no more precise about what the "cantor" should do than it was about other areas of doctrine. It appears from all accounts that the generation that swelled the Conservative ranks wanted shorter services and fewer solos, but at the same time, some leading thinkers stressed the importance of the aesthetic component of American Judaism, which by implication might have included the hazzan's contribution.

Meanwhile, Reform Judaism began to move away from what is called its "classic" phase: "about 1928, we note the beginnings of a new direction in the Reform rabbinate in which there is a conscious effort to uncover traditional elements for the enrichment of Jewish life" (Polish 1983:322), which brought new challenges in that wing of American Jewry. Here the urge for an aesthetically oriented American Judaism expressed itself not in relationship to the cantorate, which—with notable exceptions—Reformers had formerly tended to downgrade and even eliminate, but in the appreciation of modern composition as practiced by a whole school of gifted composers, including Heinrich Schalit, Isidor Freed, Herbert Fromm, Max Helfman, Hugo Adler, and many others.[13] These men, many of whom came from Europe as Nazi refugees in the wave of artists and intellectuals that included Einstein and Kurt Weill, brought about a great efflorescence of formal, written synagogue music (see chapter 10) putting pressure on the Reform hazzanim to raise their musical sights. Meanwhile, even the Orthodox began to ask for some streamlining of the service. A somewhat experimental branch of that wing, appealing to second-generation sensibilities by calling itself Young Israel, insisted that congregations do most or all of the singing themselves. Some hazzanim feel that this started a decline of the Orthodox cantorate which has accelerated down to our day.

Along with its other innovations, the second generation produced the first corps of American-born hazzanim. Whereas there were very, very few indigenous members in the earlier decades of the Farband, the group that came of age in the late 1940s and early 1950s represented the spirit of Americanization so apparent in all aspects of Jewish life in the post-immigrant age. This helped the push towards a dominance of the cantorate by the Conservative hazzanim:

> It was not only that the Conservative element became stronger, it was also that the Orthodox element grew weaker, both financially and numerically. . . . The synagogues of the East Side which used to play the big, big honor gradually couldn't afford, because people moved away, so they played a lesser and lesser role, and most of the members of the Hazonim farband were without positions. . . . [By] the end of the forties and fifties . . . there were probably in New York City no more than about five or six Orthodox cantors who held annual positions . . . and it was the Conservative congregations that grew in stature and number and financial security (D.A.).

We get a lively sense of how the cantorate was part of a large so-ciological shift by listening to the life histories of hazzanim born in the twenties and early thirties. They describe how sacred and secular musical influences mixed freely in their early years and the way they were trained in an unofficial, oral tradition that combined family in-fluences, learning by osmosis from attending a wide variety of services, and a paid apprenticeship—mostly just a set of lessons and choral back-up work—with a European-born master hazzan-teacher. By and large, the terms of entry into the profession were dictated by the old-timers and their ways; there were no Americanized professional training pro-grams for the cantorate as there had been for the rabbinate for decades. The old system prevailed, based on family background and appren-ticeship, or at least private lessons, with Old World masters.

We have reached an era where we can finally turn to living voices to describe the making of hazzanim. We begin with Lawrence Avery, today a distinguished senior hazzan and instructor at the School of Sacred Music (Reform); his childhood was in many ways typical of the age:[14]

> There was always a record spinning on the Victrola when I was very young. . . . My mother had an extraordinary kind of voice. . . . She would play for my father and my father would sing and eventually as soon as I got to be past four or five, I knew that I was a singer. So I sang and I was belting out songs from the roof of our car. . . . I had the proper musical background from age eight or seven. I had the religious background, that is, I went to a yeshiva (religious day school). For my bar mitzvah I davened the whole service. My father hoped I would be a cantor after all. He was a [part-time] cantor, my mother's father was a cantor. What greater con-tribution could I make?

But Avery was all too conscious of other possibilities as well, partic-ularly the prestigious realm of opera: "My dreams were really greater than that. I wanted to be something important in the real musical world." The adjective "real" illuminates Avery's musical map, on which classical music holds a privileged place despite a strong emotional pull to sacred song, strongly rooted in childhood family experiences:

> I always sang with my father on the High Holidays. As I grew older, I still sang the little duets with him that I sang as a child. . . . I spent a year and a half in the Navy and very wisely found the chaplain, and like I said when I was six years old, "Hey, I can sing, I can help you." It was a very cushy job from there on in. . . . When I finally got out of the Navy, I began to study even more seriously . . . mostly my passion was opera. At that point when I was home my father said to me again, wisely: "now you will study hazzanut [cantorial art] seriously." . . . There were teachers,

Hazzan Lipitz there, Berman there, Raisin there, and Beimel here, and he
said "I'll find you one." He found me Shimon Raisin, who was a wonderful
and a fascinating old man. He was positively ancient by that time. Katchko
was another one . . . he wrote me the entire repertoire, handwritten. . . .
I think we paid him . . . $750, spread out over two years. We'd give him
five bucks at a time.

The names Avery cites were among the most important teachers of
the day, all born in Europe and steeped in the nineteenth-century
traditions of cantorial composition and pedagogy. Americanization is
evident in the method of acquisition: a quick purchase of an entire
repertoire rather than the years of living with the hazzan, away from
home, experiencing the joys and hardships of the meshoyrer's life
described in chapter 1. Avery's combination of parental tutelage and
formal lessons makes his story a nice microcosm of this period of
emergence of a new American cantorate. Again and again, his father
pops up in the narrative: "My father was like the deus ex machina.
He would say he had a job someplace, he'd say, 'you know, I'm tired
of that job. You're about ready to take it over.' . . . I got the little job
. . . stayed there about three years. . . . They didn't expect much from
me, I didn't expect much from them. They paid me like $2000 for the
whole year. I used to go out there weekends and sleep over." Another
way in which Avery is a transitional figure is the fact that he only
completed his training when the new School of Sacred Music opened
in 1949, and that eventually he became a faculty member there in
addition to holding down his first full-time position, a job which became permanent. He summarizes his career in a simple statement: "I've
been in New Rochelle thirty-two years and realized that my father was
right. . . . I was not destined for an operatic career."

Of course, some kids who started in the synagogue did become opera
stars, most notably Richard Tucker and Jan Peerce, of the generation
before Avery. Those who did manage to leap the footlights into prominence were immensely successful; it is said that Tucker was paid upwards of $30,000 in the 1950s for doing holiday services in the Cats-
kills, not a bad side income for an opera singer at that time. But we
are more interested in those who stayed within the community. Like
Avery, they were often drenched in hazzanut and star-struck by the
heroic halo surrounding the great hazzanim of the day: "I remember
as a kid we used to come home from school and play khazn—stand
in front of a mirror with a tallis. My adulation was the great hazzanim. . . . [Family background is] like cream cheese on a bagel. . . .
Our home was filled with hazzanim all the time, and they were always

singing. [One day he told his father] 'Pop, I can improvise' " and he did a "Tsur Yisroel" to his father's satisfaction.

School and neighborhood were also prime places for soaking up cantorial atmosphere, even outside the intensely Jewish atmosphere of New York's ethnic concentrations. One hazzan who grew up in small-town Passaic, New Jersey, recalls the atmosphere in which one could absorb a cantorial background:

> In Passaic, there were eight shuls within a five-block area. So on Rosh Hashanah, Yom Kippur, I remember as a youngster of eight or nine [mid–1930s], they'd actually block off the five square-block area, the police. . . . On *slikhes* night [beginning of the High Holiday period] we went from one shul to another. We'll hear this hazzan halfway, and then we'd pick ourselves up and we went to another shul. We always made the rounds because one shul started at 12, another one would start at 12:30 (F.A.).

For New Yorkers, Williamsburg, an intensely Jewish neighborhood of Brooklyn, often appears in the biographical accounts of older hazzanim. As a historian notes, "by the 1930s Williamsburg was known as an Orthodox neighborhood. . . . Orthodox Jewish activities overshadowed those of socialist and Zionist Jews. . . . By the end of the decade, observers noted that 'every second man wears a beard and the children on Lee Avenue are Jewish and most of them have a *yarmulke* and go to a Yeshiva' " (Moore 1981:72–73). It had a major role as a "school" of hazzanut, where there were sixty synagogues in a twenty square-block area, twelve of them enormous. The inquisitive child could hear the full gamut of sacred song, from Hasidic chant in tiny *shtiblakh* (storefront synagogues) through the coloratura of the superstars in monumental bourgeois edifices. Local boys who went to *yeshiva* could be spotted by choir leaders on the lookout for new faces:

> At that time choir leaders were like talent scouts, you see. They used to go to the various yeshivot looking for talented yeshiva *bocherim* (boys). If they found one, they would train them . . . to become alto soloists. We needed the money. It had an economic effect. The fifty cents that I received for singing *Vimale* or "I love you truly" at a wedding was important. . . . At the same time, we were hearing the greats. I sang with Pinchik, Kapov-Kagan, Ganchoff (J.B.).

The hazzan just quoted also relates the anecdote of singing "I love you truly" with a thick Yiddish accent even though he was American-born, since he learned it from an immigrant choir leader. This worked to his benefit: he got more tips because wedding guests thought he was a poor boy just off the boat. At the same time, he also worked in the Yiddish theater, which another hazzan who doubled in weddings and melodramas as a child has called "a unique admixture of the Yiddish soul and the synagogue" (M.E.).[15] Second Avenue, as the Yiddish Broadway was called, was closely allied to the cantorial world in several ways. First, as we have seen, theaters were rented out as sacred concert and service spaces. Second, theater performers, of whom Moishe Oysher (1907–58) is the most famous example, could cross over and become sacred song stars. Of course, like the line in the Afro-American community between sacred music and the blues, those who tried to cross back and forth were subject to close scrutiny. Oysher, for example, took witnesses to walk to the synagogue with him when he sang for Friday night services to prove to the congregation that he had not taken a shortcut by driving and desecrating the Sabbath (F.E.). Third, cantorial numbers popped up repeatedly in the plots of Yiddish melodramas and musicals, and were recorded.[16] Either genuine liturgical items being sung on stage by actors, sometimes with remarkably good sense of style, or pseudosacred songs were composed by secular tunesmiths. Even in this latter case, the dividing line is hard to draw, as many of those who made a living writing for the Yiddish stage also produced large amounts of sacred music on the side.[17] Finally, there was considerable overlap in "audience" between the Yiddish theater and the synagogue. Except for the ultra-Orthodox and those too Americanized to straddle two languages and cultures, many listeners enjoyed and criticized performances on the stage and in the sanctuary every week.

For those who remained within the yeshiva walls, one could still gain a reputation as an up-and-coming hazzan in the interwar period, as the son of a star, Leibele Waldman, recounts:

> My father started out as a boy hazzan on the East Side . . . when he was nine. . . . He was in the yeshiva and the yeshiva had its own choir. The choir was composed of kids below the age of thirteen and they would appoint one of their own to be hazzan . . . and he was appointed. . . . Every once in a while they would go to various places, not so much for davening but for concerts or for presentations to raise money for the yeshiva. In that way he soon gained a reputation on the East Side as Leibele (Waldman 1980:17–18).

Thus training in the United States before World War II was not that different from becoming a hazzan in Europe. Though the long-term apprenticeship served by living with a hazzan and touring with him was not a factor, career development still centered on home, neighborhood, religious school, and oral transmission, with a strong dose of admiration for the giants of the pulpit. For the men trained this way, today's formal training programs are "like saying 'potatoes' instead of *kartofl*—there's a ring to *kartofl*" (J.B.).

In summary, the immigrant age and its extensions through World War II were yet another period of great upheaval and regrouping of the cantorate at all levels, from the cultural through the organizational. The initial effervescence of the Lower East Siders jolted the profession out of the torpor induced by the social and cultural developments sketched in the preceding chapter, leading to an unprecedented flourishing of the sacred singer's art and large-scale importation of hazzanim. When the ebbing of immigration coincided with upward social mobility and the move to new neighborhoods, the old-style cantor became part of a surplus labor pool in New York, though he apparently continued to maintain his hold on the "provincial" Jews of large and small cities nationwide. A weakly organized profession, the cantorate was unable to press its case to its constituency or even to close its own ranks behind a unified position. Teaching continued to be done in the time-honored apprenticeship system, modernized to the extent of speeding up the learning process by the purchasing of repertoire. At the same time, denominational currents suggested the hazzan might be swept into new channels of activity.

All of these trends would have continued to push the cantorate in new, Americanizing directions even without the disastrous impact of a major historical event: the Holocaust. What the period of 1939–45 did was to drastically accelerate the change in orientation and activity initiated in the previous two decades, because the destruction of European Jewry severed the precious transatlantic link that had kept American Jews in touch with Old World sensibilities and that had brought a steady flow of new talent to the cantorate. How the institution was refashioned in the face of this emergency is the subject of the following chapter. But before that, it seems altogether appropriate to celebrate the pathway to America followed by thousands of hazzanim by highlighting a small sample of extraordinary individuals whose life stories can stand for many. In the following interlude, three sacred singers tell their own tales.

NOTES

1. For another biting commentary on the cantorial craze, see the remarks of Moses Weinberger, translated by Sarna (1982).

2. Rosenblatt was the chief "icon" of the cantorate in this period, largely due to the great success of his recordings, but I have not concentrated on his contribution here because it is so well documented elsewhere, especially in the only full-length biography of a hazzan, prepared by Rosenblatt's son (Rosenblatt 1954).

3. An anecdote told by Jan Peerce supplies a fine counterpoint to the Caruso story: In 1930 the young Peerce suggested to Yosele Rosenblatt that the great hazzan might teach him the cantorial art. Rosenblatt declined, saying that he foresaw Peerce as a great [operatic] tenor and that if he learned the tricks of Rosenblatt's art as well, he might eclipse him (Levy 1976). The tale shows that already by the early post-immigrant period, an old-time sacred singer like Rosenblatt acknowledged the fact that talented Jewish tenors could be comfortable as bicultural singers. There might even be a suggestion that Peerce's future success in opera would lend him greater stature if he chose also to continue as an in-group artist, as opposed to Rosenblatt's own refusal to "go secular."

4. The same is true for orthodox Muslims and the reciters of the Qur'an: "There is a consistent effort to guard against any association of Qur'anic recitation with show business. . . . [However] a few reciters have also been famous as singers. . . . [S]ome reciters of particular skill gain such reputations that they command superstar fees for a performance, and achieve international fame. . . . The unacceptable 'overlap of melodic recitation with the business of entertainment' is seen as an important issue in contemporary Egypt" (al Faruqi 1986:28–30).

5. This, along with the fact of quick secularization of certain immigrant boys, may help to explain the fact that so many cantorial sons fled the field. The children of Israel Cooper, the early star who sank into despair and suicide, ended up in the pop group Empire City Quartet, and there are more celebrated examples, like Al Jolson and the deceptively named Eddie Cantor, who rose to the pinnacle of American show business. Their careers are beyond the scope of this book, though one should not minimize the possibility that the famous "tear in the voice" recognized by non-Jews in Jolson's singing came from early immersion in the cantorial art. In Jolson's case, of course, this connection became part of personal legend and cultural metaphor through the vehicle known as *The Jazz Singer* (see Slobin 1983).

6. It should be remembered that New York Jews became a sophisticated audience for their sacred music tradition some two decades before any local ethnic music was available to the vast majority of rural black and white Americans.

7. The argument may not be so simple. Moore (1981), as corroborated in my own experience growing up in Detroit, indicates that any medium-sized second-generation enclave had an encapsulated atmosphere in which the existence of synagogues was taken for granted, but pressure to join may not have been severe, the latter situation holding only in the smallest Jewish communities.

8. There was another, little-known organization best remembered today by its long-time president (1928–53), Walter Davidson. As Davidson recalls, it was a small group "with a peculiar name" that he suggested renaming Modern Cantors Association, later changed again to Board of American Hazan-Ministers. This group had some distinguished members, such as Adolph Katchko, and in 1934 put out a pamphlet entitled *The Ministerial Status of the Cantor:*

A Collection of Facts Upholding the Cantorial Right in Religious Functions, which served as forerunner to the legal stance of the Cantors Assembly in its postwar fight for recognition of the profession.

9. Today the Jewish Cantors Ministers Association is a small society of limited resources that maintains an office in New York with some out-of-town branches and helps place largely part-time hazzanim. Membership is estimated at 100.

10. I am grateful to Hazzan Charles Bloch for making the archives of the Cantors Ministers Union available to me. Time and shortage of assistants to read through the organization's notes, handwritten in flowing Yiddish, made it impossible to fully mine this source.

11. Even full-time hazzanim might be forced into self-promotion. One veteran remembers having to quit his job in 1928 because "I always had to wait two months before I would get a check for one month," so "I hired a Jewish theater in the Bronx, I got a choir and a choir leader and I got someone to preach, and I did the High Holiday services" (M.C.).

12. This position, established by Marshall Sklare (1955), has recently undergone revision by younger historians, but holds up well enough for understanding the hazzan in the sense that his role was redefined along second-generation lines among Conservatives earlier than among the Orthodox, and well before significant reappreciation of the cantorate by the Reform.

13. According to a veteran Reform hazzan, in 1928 there were only four Reform congregations with hazzanim (Emanuel, Shalom, Israel, and Central Synagogue) and very few others nationwide (e.g., Emanu-El of San Francisco) (M.C.).

14. The following quotations were recorded during a 1984 interview with Lawrence Avery.

15. For an account of how the composer of the Yiddish theater emerged from the meshoyrer world, see Slobin (1982c).

16. There were also whole Yiddish shows with hazzanim as protagonists. A 1919 Boris Thomashefsky production called *Two Cantors*, for which I unfortunately do not have the script, has a list of characters that includes "Yiruchem, an orthodox cantor" and "Mordecai Silbert, a reformed cantor," the latter played by Thomashefsky himself. The synagogue trustees have the ridiculous names of Hyam Spodack, Moses Bock, and Isaac Kugel. Very likely there was a scene about furious disputes among the board members over choosing a hazzan, such a stock item on the Yiddish stage that it infiltrated Yiddish films and even Hollywood, in the landmark *Jazz Singer* of 1927. There is a chance that this scene grew out of the well-known folksong *A khazndl oyf shabbes*, which describes how various small-town tradesmen describe a visiting hazzan's performance; the song was recorded frequently in the period under discussion and is still viable today on concert programs.

17. The situation is reminiscent of a Duke Ellington, who felt his career, no matter how successful, was not complete without making a contribution to the religious music of his people.

INTERLUDE

~~~~~~

Paths to America

So that the intensely personal, individualized path that brought each European hazzan to America is not lost in our overview, this chapter takes full account of biographical detail, presented by three hazzanim who represent generations of immigrants. The three accounts are all from Project oral histories, so have the richness of autobiography rather than the sketchiness of archival reconstruction. The aim is not to analyze, but to present these lives, so my commentary is restricted to the notes.

The first witness is Samuel Vigoda (b. 1893), who stands for those whose lives were shaped before World War I. Vigoda was among the last members of the star hazzan generation, and he has also been a commentator on the cantorate from whom I have quoted in earlier chapters. The second, David Koussevitsky (1912–85), was an outstanding performer, but became well known as an arranger and teacher of cantorial music as well. He was one of four famous brothers (Moshe— the most celebrated, Jacob, and Simcha), so has an entire family saga attached to his account and represents those who came on the eve of World War II. The third hazzan, Isaac Goodfriend (b. 1927), is a survivor of the Holocaust and is part of a special group of sacred singers who share that experience, as well as who arrived in America in the early postwar period. For Vigoda and Koussevitsky, the colorful days of each man's youth in Europe are the part of his life story each has stressed, whereas for Goodfriend the postwar adjustment in Europe and America has come to overshadow his Polish childhood. Elements stressed in chapters 1 to 3 should resonate in these biographies, but will be deepened and amplified by the living detail of these hazzanic histories.

Samuel Vigoda

I was born in Russian Poland . . . near Warsaw. My father was there cantor and shochet—he wore two hats, and with the two hats he didn't make a living,[1] so when I was four years old, my father left for Hungary, and he became a cantor in what's now Slovakia; it used to belong to Hungary . . . near Pressburg. . . . I was exceptionally good in Talmud and so forth, and in the Pressburg yeshiva there was a rule they wouldn't accept yeshiva bocherim below eighteen years old. . . . [Although] I wasn't yet fifteen years old, they made an exception for me. . . . At that time already I [had] published *chidushim* ["answers to Talmudic problems"]; I really did not intend to become a cantor, never, because I saw the *glikn* ["joys"] which my father had. . . .[2] One day Yosele [Rosenblatt] came to town [for a wedding.] Yosele sang at the *sude* ["banquet"] and my father sang something and we assisted. . . . So Yosele says to my father, *git mir di tsvey yinglakh* ["give me the two boys"] to sing in my choir, I'll take them to Pressburg.[3] I was about seven years old. . . . My father says, "you should promise me you'll keep them in your home, they'll eat at your table, they'll sleep at your bed, and you'll enroll them in the *talmud torah* ["school"], they wouldn't be just loafing around and you'll take good care of them, I'll give them to you." So we lived in the home of Yosele Rosenblatt. Yosele stayed in Pressburg another two and a half years, then he went to Hamburg, so then we went home.

Every day after dinner my father took down the big folios of music and he took me and my older brother and we had to read. . . . [M]y brother always said "I'm going to become a hazzan" and I said I'm going to be a rabbi . . . they thought of me as a genius. . . . I saw that the yeshiva bocherim in Pressburg, besides Talmud, they also studied worldly sciences. They wanted to become *doktor-rabbiner* ["doctor-rabbi"], it was that time in vogue, like . . . in Germany. . . .[4] I intended to go to Germany, but at that time the war broke out, 1914, the First World War. . . .

I was in Transylvania [then part of Hungary, now Rumania] in Klausenberg, Cluj, so I finished this *matura*[5] ["secondary school final exam"] together with a very dear friend who decided to enroll in the university and study for medicine. . . . After I studied three semesters in the University of Cluj, medicine, I was called in, and I became a soldier, and since I had the matura. . . . I was entitled to become an officer. I became the assistant to the doctor since I was a medical student. . . . One day the general came to visit our division. We used to eat together with the officers and they knew that I can sing; I sang the Hungarian songs very well. So when the general came with his wife, my colonel said to me I should prepare to sing something. . . . [T]he general's wife sent down, asked if I know her favorite song. . . . She was so enthused with my singing that the general said to the colonel that I should be pro-

moted out of order. Because of my song, I was promoted to become a
sergeant. . . .[6]

At the end of the war I became a first lieutenant. All right. Now
what am I going to do? Of course, Cluj became Rumania; I couldn't
go back to the university. . . . I wanted to finish my studies in the
University of Budapest, but then because of that great anti-Semitism
[under the Horthy regime], they promulgated the law of *numerus clau-
sus* ["quota"] . . . so I couldn't get in. . . .[7] Always I was singing . . . so
there was one friend who said . . . "I know Cantor Tkach, maybe he
can get you a job for the High Holidays. . . ." I got a job for the High
Holidays. Very fine . . . but this was only temporary. But a few weeks
later, Tkach called me . . . and he says, "If you want to really make
the cantorate your profession, there's an opportunity for you to get a
job. Cantor Tarnowski . . . has some relatives in America who have
big stores and they're taking him out, and he's quitting his job. . . ." I
got the job; that was the beginning.[8]

I became the sensation of Budapest: that a medical student that could
not get into the university had to become a cantor . . . one of the biggest
newspapers, the main dissident paper against the government, they
took this up. . . . People flocked to my synagogue, and all the cantors
became jealous of me. . . . [In 1921] I was called to give an audition in
the Rambach shul. . . . everything went fine. . . . You had to be approved by the Chief Rabbi, he had to first examine you, whether you
are worthy. It's not like in America [where] I wanted to show my *ksuvim*
["documents," "credentials"] to the President [of the congregation], an
amhorets ["ignoramus"]. . . . [S]o he said, *"ksuvim, shmuvim—a gutn
hashkivenu kent ir avekleygn?"* ["—but can you knock off a good 'Hashkivenu,' "] (a standard prayer for cantorial solos)]. . . . Anyway, I was
elected as a cantor of the Rambach synagogue.[9]

But at that time I had an uncle in America . . . and another uncle I
had near Budapest, a little cantor, a shochet, he couldn't make a living
there, so . . . the [American] brother-in-law sent him *shifskartn* ["ship
tickets"]; he says come over to America, you'll make a living as a cantor,
as a shochet. So he came into Budapest and he says "If you want to
go with me, I'll give you the shifskarte. . . ." I said, OK, I'll go with
you; I was a single fellow. . . . I had to go back to Czechoslovakia [now
an independent country] because I was a resident, and I talked to my
parents. . . . [T]hey were against it . . . so my father instigated my brother
he should prevent me going to America. So when I wanted a passport
. . . they made [it] only valid for Europe, so I couldn't get the visa to
America. Meanwhile, I left the job anyway . . . before [the High Hol-

idays]. . . . When I came back with the passport, the uncle decided he's not going because his wife won't let him go by himself.

So one night I packed my baggage. I knew I couldn't go to America straight, so meanwhile, I decided I'll go to Zürich, Switzerland. . . . I heard of Zürich. There was another man in the train . . . "What are you, a khazn? All right, I'll take care of you. . . ." [10] We arrived in Zürich; he took me to a rooming house for the night. . . . [H]e said, "I'll take your satchels to my store; in the morning, we'll see what to do with you." I couldn't sleep all night. [Next morning he goes to the synagogue and asks to sing a prayer.] The gabbai said "Make it quick; you know, lunch." As I started singing, the gabbai said, "Don't make it so quick, we want to listen." I delivered the goods. They were astounded. . . . These twenty-five people went out into the streets and sang my praises to everyone they met. . . . They went straight to the gabbai of the Millershul, that was the shul of the *frume yidn* ["pious Jews"] and they said, "you must hire this young man for the Sabbath. . . ."[11] [His success leads to an offer to split High Holidays with the local hazzan.]

Sunday they called a meeting . . . they told me to go in the other room while they will discuss the matter of hiring him. . . . I was no fool; I decided to listen in through the keyhole. "A young man who is not married cannot daven for us." [12] What am I gonna do now? So I decided there and then to say I'm married; what else can I do? I must confess, I lied. . . . I wrote to my sister, that she should write letters to me; I'll say that's the letters from my wife.

[While davening the first day of Rosh Hashanah, he sings an extraordinary "Shir hamalos" prayer.] At the Shir hamalos before Borchu I let myself go; I poured out my heart. Somehow it came out so that people couldn't get over it. They never heard such a Shir hamalos . . . it was improvised, it wasn't a set composition. . . . After Rosh Hashanah, [people who missed it] said, "You must sing that Shir hamalos." I didn't know what I said; I didn't remember how I did it. . . . So what to do? I sat down and composed a Shir hamalos . . . and when I was through, they said "*That* was the Shir hamalos?" They were very disappointed—it cost them 500 francs and they didn't get nothing. . . . Sometimes the improvised is much better than the one which is set.[13]

I made a lot of money in Zürich and they wanted to marry me off. . . . But I still had to get the American visa [which he couldn't get there]. I went to Germany. . . . [then] I went to Amsterdam. I davened in Amsterdam, and I made a lot of money. In one synagogue they recommended me to another. . . . [He met] a diamond dealer, a great influential man. . . . "If there's a man who can help you, it's Langedijk;

he sends diamonds to America, he's a very good friend of the American consul. . . ."[14] So he went over with me to the consul, and he told him, "This young man is a great singer from Hungary . . . and maybe you can give him an out-of-order visa." There's a quota, but for artists and people of renown they give him a visa if he can be a credit to America. . . . [S]o Langedijk says to me, "Sing something for the consul." So I sang for him the aria from "La Juive." I knew if I sing for him "Hashkivenu. . . ." [He laughs.] . . . So I sang him from "Tosca." He says, "Yes, I see, the man is a great singer . . . I can ask Washington to empower me to give me the right to make an exception."[15]

Langedijk told me, "Don't hang around here" [waiting]. I wanted to cover Paris too while I'm at it. . . . I made a big hit; I gave concerts, I sang all over Paris, especially in the Rue Pavé shul, which is the biggest Orthodox shul. Anyway, the president had his wife's sister, he wanted me to marry [her] and he worked on me I should take the job at the Rue Pavé, become the cantor of Paris and get married. . . . [T]hey were very rich people. . . . I was all set . . . [when] I heard from Langedijk— bingo, I got the visa. I was happy like a lark. I said to the president, I'm sorry; I'm going to America. . . . He was very sad and very angry at me.[16]

On the way to America, the *mashgiakh* ["kosher supervisor"] was himself a little hazzan. He used to sing me all Yosele [Rosenblatt's] things; every record of Yosele's he knew. . . . [On arrival] I called Yosele. "Reb Yosele, you remember the two boys you took from Verbo?" . . . "Come right over. . ." So I said, Yosele, I know all your records. . . . [A]fter I sang [a Rosenblatt piece], he says, "How would you like to daven in my shul this shabbes?[17] This shabbes is a great bar mitzvah, one of the officers of the shul, a prominent man, has his son's bar mitzvah; I can't make it." Will I daven? I'm tickled to death; my first shabbes in America, I'm davening in Yosele's shul—can anyone ask for more?

[Vigoda eventually became the successor to Yosele Rosenblatt at Congregation Oheb Zedek in New York, his first major post in America.]

David Koussevitsky

Before I came to this world [in 1912], my father, when he got married, he bought himself a little violin . . . and my brother Moshe, the oldest . . . he used to play to him, and the next one was born. Then Moshe was old enough to pick up that violin; he started to play it. And so on. Now we were four brothers . . . and at that time, the house was full of instruments, violins, five violins, and mandolins, guitars. The boys, anything they saw, they liked. They used to pick it up and bring it home. . . . I played the mandolin, I played guitar, classical music too. . . .[18] At that time, we're getting close to the [Russian] Revolution . . . and [that region of Poland] began to change hands every two months . . . so I had to interrupt it. And then a few years later, we managed to get out, to go back to where we came from, back to Vilna [part of the independent state of Lithuania, 1919–40].

In Vilna there started a different trend already. . . . Moshe already sang in a choir; he was already a tenor. He joined the choir at the . . . *chorshul* ["modern choir synagogue"] and then I joined that choir as alto. . . . We had a good choir [led by] Abraham Bernstein [learning] just by ear. But one day the choir leader announced: "whoever wants to learn to read [music] I'm willing to come half an hour before rehearsal." We used to rehearse every night, right through the year, except for the summer. . . . We had about twenty-five children in the choir; I think I was one of six that were interested.[19] And this started me out. . . . I was nine, ten. I was reading. . . . I attended the *gymnazia ivrit* ["Jewish secondary school"]; the teacher for *zimra* ["singing"] was Bernstein.

At the age of thirteen or fourteen, I joined [the choir]. The choir leader . . . used to give me to write out the parts of various voices. And then I joined the conservatory. . . . Besides solfeggio [vocal exercises] we started theory, harmony.[20] And as time went on, the choir leader used to give me sometimes to take a rehearsal, rehearse the choir. So he encouraged me. . . . I went to the Great Synagogue. . . . During that period, my brother Moshe, with another tenor, they were the two tenors in the choir. [On the eve of] Rosh Hashanah, they went on strike.[21] They wanted an extra $2 or something, and they left. And at the last moment, the choir leader gave me the two dollars. He says, "Go on, take it to your brother." So I took it. This was before the evening services, so he [Moshe] wouldn't accept it. . . . I [sang in a synagogue] with another few boys, and we got ourselves a bass, and we formed a choir. And we davened *sukkes* with Moshe. . . . At the end of the year, he was transferred into the Great Synagogue. Of course, I joined the choir in the Great Synagogue. . . . At that time, my voice was already changing, but the choir leader wouldn't let me go. . . . He became *khazn sheyni* ["assistant hazzan"], the choir leader, and my brother only davened twice a month . . . so I conducted the choir [at sixteen] until about a year, a year and a half later.[22]

Meanwhile, another brother [Simcha] started to daven. It just went from one to the other. He took a position somewhere in Volin, near Rovno, Kremeniec, and had a choir there, a nice choir, but they didn't like the choir leader . . . so I went out there and I worked with him. At the same time I also attended courses at a conservatory there, a music academy. And there I spent close to two years, and then my brother davened in Lemberg [Lwow] a shabbes and he took another position with me.

When I was thirteen, I was already writing music for other cantors. Once, someone knocked at the door and there was a yid [Jew] with a long beard. "Iz Dovid do?" ["Is David here?"] So he came in, pulled out a piece of music. He says to me, "I want you to teach me that." So we sat down, we worked. I taught him the recitative. I still remember the night, it was *Tikanto shabbes* by Rosenblatt. . . .[23] Many cantors used to come to me. At that time, about 1927, my brother [Moshe] became hazzan in Tlomatzker Synagogue in Warsaw [a major position]. There was already a vacancy in Vilna, so we started getting cantors there, to try out. And I had to prepare them for the shabbes. I had to teach them all the solos. . . . The cantors came to try out; [each] had to sing [the local repertoire] except for his own recitatives . . . the choir had to give him [harmonic] support. Hum here and a word there; that's what we were trained for, that was no problem. But to teach the cantor's solo, with the choir, that was my job.[24]

Then my other brother, Simcha, first he was in the conservatory. . . . They were teaching opera, and they formed a company, an opera company. . . . He did *La Traviata*, he did *Butterfly*, and *Carmen*, and started going around. . . . I started working on him, he should become a hazzan. . . . I started teaching him, prepared him for Friday night service. He got married. And they put him into a shul . . . a great success. . . . I started taking him to various shuls, and he was married, he needed *parnose* ["income"], so it was just right. But he didn't know *yontef* ["holiday liturgy"]. Meanwhile, I went out to Kremeniec with the other brother [Jacob] . . . and a few months later, he [Simcha] took a position in Rovno, in place of Zeidel Rovner. And I at that time was already in Lemberg, if you follow. And they [Simcha and Jacob] between themselves, they sort of decided that I could go; and they didn't ask me . . . so I went to Rovno, became the choir leader there . . . and we did a lot of Zeidel Rovner's compositions. Then my brother Simcha . . . couldn't make a living with opera. Someone heard him from Glasgow, England [Scotland], he went to Glasgow. I was left without a choir, without a hazzan. So the government took care of that: they took me into the army, the Polish army, in a shtetl near Krakow, where the present pope was born, Wdowice.

I was stationed there for a year and a half. . . .[25] We had a lieutenant. He sort of looked into the records, and he saw that I was a musician, a choir leader . . . and he wanted to know whether I would undertake to form a group, a choral group. Why not? It would keep me away from something else. And we started auditioning; we got together 100 men, and we had the most beautiful quality. First of all, he gave me melodies that he sang in the churches, like *sanctus dominus* or something like this. I wrote it all down and arranged it for four voices and I taught them that. . . . Any Jewish boy that could sing was in the choral group. Because whenever there was a march somewhere, for many, many miles, I used to arrange for rehearsal. Everyone stayed behind. . . . [In Warsaw] I bought all the Polish songs, you know, the national songs. . . . [W]e had Russian basses. . . . And the general used to come down sometimes and . . . he walked over to me and shook my hand. . . . To me it didn't mean a thing, but to all the *goyim* ["gentiles"] around—they bowed, you know; I was God to them already: "he shook his hand!"[26] This captain [his protector] was transferred to the officers' school. . . . [T]here we started a new thing. And this is how I became an officer, doing nothing. . . . After the six months, I finished as a sergeant; at the end, when we were discharged, I became a second lieutenant.

Then I came back to Warsaw. . . . My brother got a letter from Constantinople, from Istanbul. The cantor there, Shaposhnik, he needed a choir leader [but Moshe said] "Dovid, I don't think you should go there. *Nisht far keyn yidn* ["no place for Jews"]. We all worked together and helped each other.[27] [I went to a voice teacher.] He says, "Look, I got nothing to do with your voice. It sits there, just like your brother's voice, but you've got to learn repertoire [opera, lieder]."

[I went to Lemberg.] We did Rosh Hashanah, Yom Kippur; must have been 2,000 or 2,500 people there. I was all of twenty-three years old. And the papers of course write all the publicity about it, the davening, before and after. . . . The Jewish papers were circulating all over Poland, and I started getting invitations to various shuls, various cities, to come to daven.[28] [I took Rovno, the best offer.] Comfortable income, and I could save a few zlotys. [Davened just twice a month,] I mean there was no other functions. They sold tickets every shabbes I davened. . . . [T]hen I got a letter from a shul in London . . . through two of my brothers already in London, and my mother was in London. My father passed away in '34 [so I went to London in '37].[29]

[Working for United Synagogue] was like a government. Each shul sends their representative, like to the House of Commons . . . it's like the Church of England. . . . They had all their traditional music. They had a blue book that they give you, and they tell you "use it as much as possible. . . ." [Y]ou had to be there every shabbes . . . and [I] taught

in Jews College. I used to share the weekday services with the rabbi.
I did Sunday morning. No layman was allowed to officiate. . . . I had
a problem with the *leynen* ["Torah reading"]. Although I could leyn,
I had to go to the *bet din* ["rabbinic court"] to pass the test . . . and I
passed, but I refused to leyn, because I said, "If I leyn, who's going
to daven musaf [the lengthy "additional" service]? That will kill me,"
I said. . . . I put my foot down with the chief warden of the synagogue,
and they freed me of the [leynen] and that set a precedent already. My
brother was fighting it too. They were free too. . . .[30]

Simon Ackerman, a clothier . . . used to come back and forth to
America, and he told me about [his] shul. "Would you be interested
in coming over?" . . . He gave me a letter to the consul, and they gave
me a visa. And I came. This was '48. [At his New York debut] all the
musicians of New York came . . . the place was jammed. [Mrs. Koussevitsky adds:] In 1946 we heard that Moshe was alive and well, and
arranged to bring him over. . . . [H]e came from Warsaw, they allowed
him to go back to Warsaw [from Russia]. Moshe came without a sheet
of Jewish music from Russia. David spent the entire time writing out
all his repertoire. . . . This is the love of the brothers. [David Koussevitsky continues:] I sat there day and night. And he started singing right
away, concerts.[31]

[Interviewer: How did America strike you?] I was fascinated, and it
brought back my youth. Here's a choir, and they're singing those compositions that we sang in Vilna, because the choir leader came from
Odessa, he was in our shul nearly fifty years [Hans Zalis]. . . . In the
beginning I felt a little strange davening facing the congregation . . .
but I got used to it. . . . I started getting invitations to sing all over the
country . . . sang weekends and during the week.[32] I used to go to
South America . . . six weeks once I spent . . . all around Buenos Aires,
to Montevideo, to Brazil . . . and in Peru, Lima. . . .[33] The concert had
liturgical music, it had Yiddish, especially in Buenos Aires . . . and I
sang in the biggest halls and opera houses, in municipal halls or theaters. In São Paulo . . . my manager went to the City Hall to approve
the program . . . and they wouldn't approve it; every program is supposed to have a national song in their language, in Portuguese. I said,
"Go out and buy a popular song." He went out and he brought me a
song. I look at the words and I can't make out anything. I called down
for a bellboy, he would help me . . . and I sang it that night . . . and
people were on their feet.[34]

Isaac Goodfriend

I was born [in 1927] in a town not far from Lodz, Piotrkov. I was born
into a very Hasidic family. I grew up as a Hasid, with *peyes* ["earlocks"],

the whole bit and my father was a ba'al tefillah, not as vocation; he did it for fun. Of course, he davened every day, and I as a child used to help him out, what you call a *meshoyrer*. Since I was five, my father used to take me to the [Aleksander] Rebbe [a major Hasidic leader]; we were related with the rebbe, we come from great *yikhes* ["lineage"]. So, as far as the basic knowledge of cantorial *khazones* ["cantorial art"] [it] was there, it was a natural, it wasn't something that I had to go out and learn. I grew up with it. We lived about a half a block away from one of the largest [synagogues], the *shnaydershul* ["tailors' shul"], the *shustershul* ["shoemakers' shul"]. The choir conductor was Professor Sachs who, by the way, I think was killed in the Lodz ghetto; in the ghetto he had the choir and a symphony orchestra and performed operas in Yiddish, you know.

The Hasidim had a yearly [only for High Holidays] ba'al tefillah, you know, nobody else, because of his knowledge, of his piety, and also his vocal ability; Hasidim don't go for khazones, they go for somebody who can inspire them instead of acrobatics.[35] They had a choir, male choir, of course, also Hasidim. I was privileged enough to be at every rehearsal with them before the High Holidays because I used to know the melodies. Every year they composed new melodies [by] the one who conducted the choir; his name was Getsl Zeyde;[36] he perished in the same ghetto where I was. . . . They used me as sort of a fill-in to see how the harmony's going to sound, and everything was melody. There were more melodies without text than with text. They fitted in the text into the melodies; they picked up songs, like marches, secular, but they sort of "yiddishized" it, and to those people in those days, the melody meant very little. It was simply an embellishment. The words and the interpretation meant a lot.[37]

My parents sent me [to yeshiva] when I was eleven years old, in Sosnow. We'd conduct the services. At first, a boy was not allowed to conduct services because he has to have a beard, he has to be thirty years old, he has to be married, you know. And in the ghetto we had services in my house, my grandfather's house; we had enough people within the family to make up more than two minyanim [quorum of ten]; we were forty people in one house. I was never permitted to play like the other kids who were not up to par as far as observance, so we used to get together, put on a towel instead of a tallis, and have our own choir, Saturday afternoon.[38]

My father died when he was forty-one years old, and I became the provider of the family at the age of sixteen and a half, in 1941. And then in '42 I lost everybody, in the ghetto, and I am the only one who survived, and plans were not in my mind. Survival was, so one day I escaped from the camp. I jumped over the fence. And I was hiding with a Polish farmer outside of the city until the Russians came in 1945.

There was no future for the survivors in those days because we didn't trust the world, so we lived from day to day. [In Zailshaim DP camp] is the first time I conducted services officially, and this I'll never forget. People who knew my family, knew me as a child, they remembered me when I was named, or when I was circumcised, or they came to my father's house. So three people walked over to me . . . and they called me the way they used to call me at home. "We want you to daven musaf, Rosh Hashanah, conduct the services." So I said, "I'm not, how should I say, 'fit,' because I'm not observing now, I'm not observing *nothing*, I'm *denying* everything." They started to talk to me, tears are coming down their cheeks. "There's always a time to repent. Let it be *now*. We, the congregation, are going to influence *you*, instead of you influencing us."[39] I said, OK, so I conducted services. I cried more than actually chanted. This was an episode, a single episode that I did, and then I went my way, and back to the normal, or quasi-normal, way of life.

My wife found out she had a sister in Paris, so I smuggled [across the] border, and then landed in Paris. I became a tailor, so the weekends I went to the hazzan [at the synagogue on the] Rue Pavé, so I did a little singing in a choir. I worked very hard in Paris, sixteen, seventeen hours a day in order to survive. I didn't want to stay in Europe, and we wanted to emigrate; make a long story short—the States. I was under the Polish quota; they said it'll take three, four years. If I go back to Germany, it'll be easier. OK! Went back to Germany.[40]

So of course shabbes I went to shul, and it was one of the synagogues that the Germans did not burn on Kristallnacht [in 1938], and suddenly I see that nobody is continuing the service. They're walking back and forth, the committee; there's nobody to read the Torah. I went up and I read the Torah, and they ask me, "Cantor, please, finish the service. You see we are in a bind." I finished the service. Before I took off my tallis, they want me to sit down. "Please consider becoming our cantor." Sure enough, I accepted, and I received the first written contract in 1950 just for davening shabbes, and of course the Holidays. And they [the Jewish community] assign to you which synagogue you participate. Let's say if I daven the Russian sector one shabbes, the following shabbes I had to daven in the American sector.

In '52 we came to Montreal; still couldn't get to the States. In '56, we came to the States [after having] performed operatic roles on television and recitals [in Canada]. I ended up in Cleveland, and in 1965

I left Cleveland and came to Atlanta, and I'm there since . . . and of course my famous highlight officiating at the presidential inauguration in 1977. In the history of the U.S. a cantor *never* officiated at an inauguration. I knew Carter before he was governor of the state, and of course I was involved in the campaign in a small way, so it happened. It was a thrill. People asked me, "How did you feel? What did you think?" I said, "I was numb, I didn't think; I was only worried that I shouldn't forget the words." I was appointed later on to the President's Commission on the Holocaust, and now I'm serving under this President [Reagan] on the Holocaust Memorial Council.

While Koussevitsky and Goodfriend were adjusting to postwar life in America, the cantorate was undergoing far-reaching and historic changes, as detailed in the following two chapters, which round out part 1.

NOTES

1. What Vigoda means by "cantor" here is unclear, in that we do not have a precise line of demarcation between part-time and full-time, between *ba'al tefillah* and *khazn* (the Yiddish term). Could someone who was a *khazn* also be a shochet? Another Polish-born hazzan says no: "Shochet-cantor? I don't know. For a ba'al tefillah more, a ba'al tefillah who was a shochet was a shochet-ba'al tefillah" (C.I.). Perhaps the move Vigoda's father made was to raise his status and to become just khazn.

2. This nicely summarizes the second-class status of the hazzan, as compared to the scholar, which has carried over into America both in mainstream Judaism—rabbis have higher status and more pay—and among the Orthodox, who maintain their low evaluation of the sacred singer.

3. Rosenblatt came because he was hired by the father of the groom, who lived in the city. The anecdote illustrates the urban-rural interchange that so characterized later eastern European Jewish history and which denies the notion of the isolated shtetl so common among American Jews. It is also a nice vignette of the young Rosenblatt, still willing to take local boys on as meshoyrerim in eastern Europe, before his meteoric rise to international stardom.

4. Here we have a hint of the impact of the *haskala*, the secularizing, Europeanizing movement that slowly spread eastward from early nineteenth-century Germany. Early on, Vigoda felt the impulse to get up and go west, which eventually became an obsession.

5. The jump to Cluj is unexplained, but points up the mobility possible within the Austro-Hungarian Empire, as does the standardized nature of the *matura* exam.

6. The multiethnic Austro-Hungarian army was—to some extent—a homogenizing agent, and we have here the first example of song as a key to open closed doors, which becomes a leitmotif of the narrative.

7. The shrinking of post-Versailles Hungary forces Vigoda back to Budapest, where he undergoes the common disillusionment of Jews prepared to secularize who find an unaccepting Christian society. He must stay within the ethnic boundary to become a professional—a hazzan—and stays there permanently.

8. America as a constant presence in eastern European life is illustrated here; Vigoda is lucky to get a vacancy created by emigration.

9. This shows the power of the *kehillah*, the organized Jewish community, whose head had to approve all "civil servants" such as hazzanim, in addition to the endorsement of the congregation in question, which Vigoda nicely opposes to the American free-for-all attitude. He sees it as negative, since the American *balebos* is only interested in musical results, not character references and testimonies to Judaic knowledge. The whole scene is reminiscent of the reasons ordained rabbis did not come to America until the 1840s—it was a "wild land."

10. Vigoda's decision to take off rather than face kehillah censure marks him as an adventurer by temperament. He did not explain the choice of Zürich, which seemed almost random. His immediate rescue by a fellow-Jew shows the strength of ethnic networking, as well as the tremendous edge the possession of a talent—here, sacred singing—can have in the struggle for economic survival.

11. Among other things, this lightning success highlights the uniformity of taste across wide areas of the Jewish landscape: the good burghers of Zürich are just as appreciative as those of Budapest—or anywhere else Vigoda sings, for that matter. Presumably, commercial recordings aided this homogenization of taste, although we have no data to tell us how well this might have worked for Vigoda in, say 1865 or 1900 instead of 1921.

12. Data are scanty about the importance of this requirement in America, although it probably played little part in hiring outside strictly orthodox circles. Nevertheless, one hazzan (C.D.) notes that he was not comfortable in his first position in the 1930s as a single person; he moved to another job and returned to the original post when he got married.

13. This illuminating anecdote touches on a topic detailed in chapter 11: the importance of improvisation as the test of *hazzanut*. Hazzanim were split among those who carefully molded a preset repertoire and those who performed spontaneously, with each having its professional advantages and disadvantages, and many mixing both genres of sacred song.

14. In many ways, Vigoda's narrative parallels Artur Rubinstein's account of his early life in almost the same period. Rubinstein, a middle-class Jew, had mastered the piano as his special skill, and his tales of instant success arriving in town as an unknown or of playing for consuls to wheedle visas, often with a wealthy patron as intermediary, sound just like Vigoda's anecdotes.

15. Here we have a practical illustration of the usefulness of learning classical music as well as cantorial. It is also a conceptual category, however, as in another Polish-born hazzan's remark that "I wanted not only to be a cantor; I wanted to be a musician" (C.I.).

16. The Paris episode shows off the high status of the star hazzan, who could be married off to the "boss's daughter" the way Talmudic whiz kids were given cushy marriages in eastern Europe. Vigoda's dogged interest in America is particularly striking in the face of such inducements.

17. Vigoda's shrewd appeal to Rosenblatt's egotism gives us an inside look at cantorial politics, just as the shipboard cram session tells us how popular recorded versions were at the time. Rosenblatt was at the height of his powers, but shortly thereafter suffered terrible financial reverses as a result of ill-considered investments, and he eventually had to resort to the vaudeville circuit to repair his fortunes, only to die prematurely in 1933.

18. The interchangeability of musics is again illustrated here. It seems from accounts like this that certain families were musically oriented; what is remarkable is their flexibility. Of note here is the fact that the shift from violin to voice is not just a question of instruments, but of crossing the secular-sacred line.

19. This marks a turning point; from here on, he becomes a music resource person due to the technical skills gained from Bernstein, a noted musical figure in Vilna. Childhood stories like these are invaluable for showing how a music culture recruits volunteers for defined niches, and how talented youngsters rise to the bait.

20. The Sulzerian revolution of the mid-nineteenth century meant that knowing classical compositional techniques, if only in rudimentary form, became essential for certain cantorial styles, though purely intuitive, improvisatory hazzanim could get by through the older methods of rote plus well-trained local solo voices who knew how to back up individual styles. The fact that *any* respectable hazzan needed choral support was taken for granted and helped draw the line between the ba'al tefillah and the hazzan.

21. This suggests that by the interwar period, the class consciousness of the Jewish proletariat had diffused even to meshoyrer circles. Zavel Kwartin's autobiography (1952) cites other examples of this trend.

22. By now, David is finding a special niche: choir director/arranger. This could be due to a number of factors, which were perhaps combined: because his older brothers' fame took away the limelight; because they needed help in building repertoire and running choirs; because he was not a great singer; or just because he liked the work.

23. Rosenblatt reappears here as a model, even for hazzanim in deepest Poland, probably again underscoring the impact of recordings.

24. This is an elegant summary of the standard practice of the time which, unfortunately, was never studied *in situ*, so can only be hinted at in oral-history reminiscences by a band of hazzanim whose numbers decrease yearly. Unfortunately, David Koussevitsky was one such veteran—he passed away in 1986, not long after giving this account of his life.

25. Koussevitsky's army tale is remarkably reminiscent of Vigoda's story of a Jewish boy's rise through the ranks via song. Both told the story with relish, enjoying the way each outwitted the usually anti-Semitic, restrictive nature of the army in which he served.

26. Physical recognition by state authorities in the form of handshakes, embraces, or kisses is often cited in Vigoda's collected legends of the hazzanim as true proof of success, not surprising given the usual distance between governmental figures and Jews, and given the former's attitude towards the latter.

27. Culture, not distance was the problem here, as one brother had already moved to far-off Glasgow. Though in point of fact Turkey was not particularly anti-Semitic, it probably seemed much too foreign from the Jewish point of view (i.e., non-Ashkenazic).

28. The power of the popular media and advertising was just as effective in Poland as in the United States at the time. Competition and standards were at their peak in Poland then; a trade journal for hazzanim (*Khazonim-velt*) even flourished briefly in the mid–1930s.

29. David's success, coming after two brothers had departed, might have made him willing to stay on in Poland had the year not been 1937.

30. This account of the restrictiveness of English synagogue life recurs in the oral histories of other American hazzanim and seems to have figured in pushing some of them to leave for America. Similar complaints are voiced about the cantorial life in South Africa, though today the accelerated dissolution of that Jewish community would probably make emigration seem attractive anyway.

31. David's unusual talent of remembering and reconstructing Moshe's repertoire is extraordinary and truly testifies to the remarkable loyalty among the brothers.

32. David's alacrity in adjusting to America was helped by the renown of the family; for garden-variety hazzanim, the postwar transition was far from easy.

33. David also remarked that he was able to use Yiddish everywhere on these travels. Some Latin American cities, notably Buenos Aires, preserved eastern European Jewish culture longer than in the United States.

34. Again, one is reminded of Rubinstein's memoirs, which contain long sections on his conquest of Latin America, where in some ways he was more successful than in the United States.

35. Several Polish-born hazzanim grew up in Hasidic circles, and some confirm Goodfriend's feeling about the difference in prayer styles: "at the Hasidic, there are certain inflections of *dveykus* ["adherence to God," a mystical principle] of tremendous enthusiasm, ecstasy, which did not have any place in the synagogue" (C.I.).

36. We know very little about men like Getsl Zeyde who produced the music for Hasidic "courts"; the impact of their music, however, has lasted in two ways: through hazzanim like Goodfriend who remember what they heard, and through the offshoots of their work preserved and reinterpreted in Hasidic circles in America today, which have heavily influenced synagogue music in the last decade or so.

37. This is part of the well-known Hasidic doctrine of "making sacred" melodies from the outside; see Koskoff (1978) for its persistence in America.

38. This internal separation among Jewish households was not just European, but extended to America at the time—and has become an ever more prominent feature today with the rise of right-wing Judaism. Musically, it implies the favoring of some repertoires over others, very important in the future development of hazzanim.

39. This is a powerful example of conscious deformation of the usual model of the hazzan influencing the worshippers, the often unspoken corollary of the notion that the sacred singer is just the "messenger" of the congregation, carrying its prayer to God.

40. Goodfriend's retracing of Vigoda's route of 1921 in search of an American visa shows how similar immigrant stories can be across the decades in certain respects despite enormous differences.

4

~.

1950s–1970s: Postwar Professionals

> Professionals represent the most rapidly growing occupa-
> tional category in highly developed modern economies,
> and the end is by no means in sight.
>
> —Wilbert Moore, *The
> Professions: Roles and Rules*

When the Jewish-American community woke up to find its homeland
destroyed, the impact was profound in many ways, some of them still
unsuspected and certainly unresearched. For the cantorate, it meant
fundamental regrouping and reorientation. Within a few years, the
three branches of American Judaism established training programs and
associated professional organizations. Hazzanim decided to bootstrap
themselves into legal and social recognition and took giant steps toward
professionalization. All this activity happened under specific historical
circumstances that have made it particularly vital to the future of the
cantorate worldwide. First, the European cradle of the American cantorate had just been annihilated, so America became the largest Jewish
population center. Second, the Jews living around the Mediterranean
and in western Asia moved from their homelands to Israel, a country
practically without full-time hazzanim.[1] Finally, the Orthodox wing of
American Judaism, staunch supporters of the cantorate in the immigrant era, have become progressively less interested in the institution.[2]
So today the bastion of the full-time cantorate, considered worldwide,
is the core of some 400 Conservative and Reform professionals, struggling to maintain themselves in the face of declining synagogue attendance and to perpetuate themselves at a time when being a clergyman is not a shining goal of young Jewish professionals.

Against this background, the accomplishments of the postwar era
stand out in sharp relief. To understand what professionalization means,
here is an "official" definition by a sociologist, George Ritzer, followed
by a point-by-point breakdown of how the definition fits the cantorate:[3]

Where a person lies on the individual professional continuum depends on how many of the following he possesses . . .[4]: a) general systematic knowledge; b) authority over clients; c) community rather than self-interest which is related to an emphasis on symbolic rather than monetary rewards; d) membership in occupational associations, training in occupational schools, and existence of a sponsor; e) recognition by the public that he is a professional; f) involvement in the occupational culture (Ritzer 1973:62).

Individual-professional continuum

Professionalism begins at home: it is the individual hazzan's stake in this type of self-definition that counts, particularly in an occupation of such small numbers whose clients often bypass the professional associations. For although we are discussing the organized cantorate here, perhaps most of the "cantoring" in America is done by part-time, unaffiliated contract labor who often have other professions. Thus the decision to become a "100%" hazzan means placing oneself on one end of a professional continuum. As we shall see when surveying part-timers, congregations tend to call anyone "cantor" who leads services for pay.

General systematic knowledge; training in occupational schools

Over the generations, professionals, lay leaders, and observers called for a school for hazzanim,[5] as in this 1904 plea, timed for the centennial anniversary of the founder of modern cantorial music, Salomon Sulzer: "Brethren, if you have your cause and the cause of Judaism at heart, you cannot more befittingly commemorate this centennial birthday of the great master than by establishing a *school* for cantors where young men of musical ability shall be trained in every branch that is requisite for a modern cantor" (Mose 1904).

As we have seen, it was not until the lesson of the Holocaust sank in that schools were actually founded.[6] The Reform's School of Sacred Music (SSM) of the Hebrew Union College-Jewish Institute of Religion was the first (in 1947), followed by the Conservative's Cantors Institute (CI) of the Jewish Theological Seminary (in 1951) and the Orthodox's Cantorial Training Institute (CTI) of Yeshiva University (in 1954).[7]

But even with the existence of schools, what is "general systematic knowledge" for hazzanim? Basic to all programs, of course, has been an insistence on the student's ability to lead services, still defined as the core of the profession. Even here, though, there are questions: How many of the possible services should a student learn? Does one need to know weekday afternoon services as well as the major holiday liturgy?[8] Then there is the issue of sufficient expertise to take on choral directing and the performance of large, complex twentieth-century compositions, particularly relevant to Reform synagogue work, but recommended to all hazzanim by Joseph Freudenthal, founder of Transcontinental, the main publisher of synagogue music: the hazzan "must become a better musician. He must realize that knowledge in musical theory and composition has become imperative. . . . You expect your mechanic to know something about the construction of a car, though he does not know how to build the car. You expect your country doctor to know about the latest drugs and developments in medicine although he does not need to be a skilled surgeon" (Freudenthal 1972:87). Note Freudenthal's comparison of the hazzan to the local auto mechanic or doctor, a sign of the general American expectation of expert knowledge and professional affiliation.

The hazzanim themselves raise many other issues of "systematic knowledge"; One young professional urges more attention to therapeutic work:

> [There is] a special program which has used Cantors Institute students almost exclusively to visit various special wards at Montefiore Hospital in the Bronx, New York. It is through this program that a tremendous impact has been made on some of the young men graduating from the CI. Several recent graduates have decided to pursue professional degrees in counseling and health-related fields as a result of this program. I am not asking you all to go out and get professional degrees in music therapy. I am recommending that you use available resources to educate yourself. . . . One course could change your life and your ability to meet the needs of people who desperately need you (Chomsky 1982:15–17).

While this young hazzan argues from the point of view of congregant needs, one older leader thinks about curriculum in terms of recruitment and placement: "Our organizations must become more zealous and determined in recruiting candidates for our cantorial schools. It will require a rethinking of the curriculum and the priorities of the cantorial schools [to include] courses in education, psychology, art, dance, musical instruments (beyond the required piano), drama, poetry, as well as in Yiddish and in accelerated courses in Hebrew, to say nothing of computer skills and social work" (Rosenbaum 1984:59).

Meanwhile, the schools now stress an increasing knowledge of what is loosely called "Judaica," meaning a wide understanding of the texts, practices, and folkways of Judaism. This is a new notion of professionalism: after all, in America the rabbi is supposed to be the repository of Jewish wisdom. The Judaica thrust reflects a two-pronged process: congregants know less and less of the tradition themselves, so rely increasingly on their clergy—the "Jewish specialists"—for answers.[9] Simultaneously, the laity has slowly grown more concerned about its ignorance, so looks for guides to reverse the process of cultural loss. To meet the challenge, in 1985 the SSM became a graduate program, partly to spend less time on teaching musical skills, now a prerequisite for entry, and more time on Judaica. Today, future hazzanim have to spend a year in Jerusalem, just like rabbinic students—and this is the *Reform* wing. The hope is that this new orientation will add to the hazzan's marketability and also help in his adjustment on the job: "As cantorial students take more and more classes with rabbinical students—why shouldn't more and more of our congregations choose to have a clergyperson who adds a special cultural dimension instead of an assistant rabbi who has no special musical expertise?" (Sager 1984:44–45). As another young hazzan puts it: "We do services together while we're still in school. There was a time when the rabbis had nothing to do with the cantors; they didn't meet up with their first cantor until they were out of school. Now they already know how to work with them while they're in school" (H.I.).

A 1984 course syllabus from the SSM shows that the "reality factor" of fitting in to congregational life has become part of education as well. Session 1 takes up the basic issues of the "Cantor as Clergy" and then moves into details of the working life: "—His/her Place in the Congregation, in the Community; Proper Attire, behavior, speech; proper pulpit behavior; visiting sick, houses of mourning, etc. . . . .—Working with: Rabbi, Educational Director, President, Executive Director, Office Staff, Choir Leader, Choir, Organist, Other Cantors in the Community and Region, Sisterhood, Men's Club, etc., Youth."

Perhaps the "etc." is the most telling of the listings; congregations today might demand almost anything of their clergy (see chapter 7), so there is no easy way to train someone for every eventuality. As one young hazzan puts it, "Many things you never learn in school you use, and many things you learn in school you never use" (I.D.).[10]

Existence of a sponsor

The sponsor is a delicate issue in the case of the cantorate. The training programs were placed in the seminaries of the three branches of American Judaism, but only after intense lobbying and with somewhat indifferent results in terms of sponsorship. The Reform and Conservative schools have not been headed by hazzanim, always a sore point. Simply put, the professionals feel that the seminary leadership is never really interested in the schools, or at least not interested enough.

Membership in professional associations

We have already cited the less-than-powerful interdenominational Far-band and the small Board of American Hazzan Ministers (1925). These early organizations lacked the essential prerequisite for a strong professional association: graduates of training programs, who carry their credentials and sense of fraternity into professional activism. The Conservative's Cantors Assembly (CA, 1947), the Reform's American Conference of Cantors (ACC, 1953) and the Orthodox's Cantorial Council of America (CCA, 1960) provide a home for those with the strongest urge for affiliation and a basis for a variety of efforts aimed at improving the cantorate's status in American life. As the oldest and most politically active organization, the CA was in the forefront of the battle for professional recognition. Samuel Rosenbaum, the CA's guiding spirit for over two decades, cites three interlinked aspects of professionalism (headings mine):

> *School.* We established a school not only because we wanted to be sure that there would some day be hazzanim to follow us, but because we wanted the world to know that hazzanut is not something you acquire by osmosis, or by listening to records. We established a school because it meant status and respect and dignity to be a member of a profession that required recognized scholarly and academic credentials. . . .

> *Placement and standards.* We established, and enforced with some degree of success, a set of ethical and professional standards by which we expect our membership to live. We have taken placement out of the grimy hands of managers and have worked diligently to convert it to an orderly, fair and productive service. . . . We have been most successful . . . in securing some important personal benefits for the hazzan, unheard of a short thirty years ago: retirement, health, disability. . . .[11]

> *Repertoire.* We instigated, nourished and supported a flowering of synagogue music in the 50's and 60's unlike that of any other single period in the history of the cantorate (Rosenbaum 1978:46–48).

Rosenbaum contrasts today's situation with that in the so-called golden age of the cantorate, the days of the superstar hazzanim:

> It was a golden age only for a small number of gifted hazzanim who flourished in that period. But for the journeyman hazzan, for the everyday synagogue hazzan, it was a time of scrounging for a living, of singing from scraps of music tossed to them by the stars or by their imitators; a time of copying records, of worrying about tenure, of enduring abysmally degrading placement practices and of living in constant fear of dismissal, with no one to raise a voice in objection (Rosenbaum 1978:46–48).[12]

What does it take to become a member of the CA and the ACC? Graduation from the denominational schools will do it for you, or you can take an exam to join if you have already served in a congregation for a set number of years. The comprehensiveness of the Reform exam is evidence of the high goals the profession sets for itself:

> 1. Oral comprehensive in traditional and Reform synagogue Music. 2. Written examination in liturgy. 3. A written examination in the history and theory of Jewish Music. 4. A written examination in Jewish history, literature and thought. 5. A written examination in Hebrew competence. . . .

> The examinations do not cover practical matters in detail: counseling, education, conducting, and the like. It is assumed that you have achieved competence in these areas in your "life experience" at the congregation where you serve. In fact, the Certification Examination is available, as you know, only to people who have thus served a Reform congregation full-time for at least five years ("Certification Examination Procedure," SSM 1985).[13]

The major job of the trade associations remains placement, including monitoring of contracts and disputes. Since 1985, the Reforms and Conservatives have agreed to honor each other's cantorial credentials, so there is a kind of cross-listing of jobs.[14]

Community rather than self-interest

Ritzer links the community-interest factor to orientation towards "symbolic rather than monetary rewards." This description is particularly apt for professional clergy—of whatever religion and denomination. Those purely out for self-interest and money will hardly find satisfaction in the cantorate. Although salaries have improved (now at the $25,000 base level, up to perhaps $60,000 at the largest and most generous synagogues), the job is far too demanding to attract a young professional simply for the money. In terms of status, the standard situation implies the possibility of conflict with the rabbi, hardly an ideal situation for someone looking to be an American "number one." Community orientation is an absolute necessity, or the congregation will rapidly lose interest in its hazzan. Finally, one must have a deep and abiding commitment to the strongest of "symbolic" rewards, spiritual satisfaction, or the worshipper-clients will be disappointed. At the least, this means leading a model life and having one's family live in a goldfish bowl. At the most, it means being a charismatic figure in the pulpit. But more than that, it implies a responsibility to the profession itself, bringing us to the question of internal policing, which is called "ethics" by professionals.

From the start, the associations have been very concerned to monitor and control the activities of members. Let us return to Maxwell House Coffee, whose tie to the cantorate became off-limits by the early 1950s, as reported in the minutes of the Executive Council of the CA: "It was reported that [a member] appeared on a radio program sponsored by Maxwell House Coffee and allowed his name to be used for the purpose of endorsing this product. A letter is being sent to him warning him that this is a serious violation of our by-laws and that he must never again commercialize his sacred office by advertising in any manner unbecoming the dignity of our profession" (12 Oct. 1953). After negotiations with the company and the hazzan, an official policy was created: "Commercials shall be made only at the opening and the closing of the Radio program. This means that as soon as the actual program of Synagogue Music begins there will be no interference of any commercial nature. . . . The closing commercial . . . includes words to the effect that Maxwell House Coffee is the choice of Cantors. Our executive Council objects to this statement. . . . Hazzanim who appear . . . will not endorse Maxwell House Coffee" (CA Executive Council minutes, 1957).

In the 1960s, the CA was more concerned about members with questionable second incomes. The temptation to add to one's synagogue salary has been steady throughout American history, as we saw earlier. Formerly it was only congregational boards who worried about this; nowadays the professional associations are also concerned: "In reply to charges that he was engaged in the insurance business, Hazzan X submitted a letter of explanation. He indicated that he had for a short time, during a period of vocal incapacity, sold insurance to supplement his income. He has regained his voice and for more than a year has been out of that business. . . . The Executive Council voted to quash the allegation" (CA Executive Council minutes, 12 Sept. 1967). The CA has a real stake in the issue of outside income, as it strikes at the heart of the hard-won notion of full-time professionalism. Yet reality can force professional associations to be flexible: "Also discussed was the growing number of situations in the larger cities where positions are gradually being downgraded because of the fact that congregations are aware that their hazzanim have outside sources of income. While the CA demands that men be exclusively engaged in hazzanut, men who teach allied subjects, even if they do so outside their congregations, have been permitted to continue these outside activities" (CA Executive Council minutes, 19 June 1968). Here teaching, another professional activity, is approved, as opposed to activities like selling insurance, even though outside work may cause a deterioration of the cantorate's status. As in all ethical matters, drawing lines about permissible professional behavior is ambiguous, as specific cases show:

> Two years ago a fine young guy from California had to leave his position because they found he was also in the real estate business. That bothered the congregation, and it also bothered us, because at that time we still hadn't come to the realization that maybe this guy had to earn a little more money in order to get by living in California. Maybe today he would not have been asked to leave. I think what we did was, we put him on as a non-active member. . . . He's being reinstated by the way (C.E.).

As for other reasons for throwing hazzanim out of the CA: "There have been people who have been lost go for nonpayment of dues. I remember a very funny case of a guy who was an assistant cantor. . . . He would leave his shades up for example and he would be seen flying around the house in the nude. . . . He did all kinds of crazy things and I remember dismissing the guy. There are crazies in every organization" (C.E.).

Authority over clients

In the case of all clergy, authority over worshippers is a particularly ambiguous component of professionalism: needing a minister or hazzan is hardly like needing a lawyer or an architect. This is both a strength and a weakness in terms of professional power. The fact that clients—congregations—feel their spiritual life demands an officiating presence is a source of real strength. Particularly in the case of the hazzan, worshippers can do without clergy, so presumably are willing to show respect for their chosen voices. On the other hand, it is easier for congregants to change their minds and decide they no longer recognize the legitimacy of the clergy's demands on their pocketbooks or their consciences. After all, the authority that the clergy represents is moral rather than medical, legal, or technical, the more recognized sources of power in modern American society.

Recognition by the public

Recognition of the hazzan by the public is a twofold point, depending on whether we mean the public at large or its representatives, the legal authorities of the state. Let us take the first, much easier question. American society, no matter what its members think individually, tends to defer to clergy, whether in the form of Hollywood's lovable priests and compassionate battlefield chaplains or in everyday terms of address such as "Father," "Reverend," "Rabbi." Also, since the establishment of liberal Protestant activism, the public expects the clergy to articulate social concerns and to be in the spotlight. This means that rabbis—and sometimes hazzanim—are not only expected to be available to the media on national and international issues, but also to engage in interfaith events that strengthen the public image of America as the land of Protestant, Catholic, and Jew (Herberg 1960). These occasions are marked by commentary, both public and private; two excerpts from one hazzan's scrapbook can illustrate: "At any other time or place it might have seemed out of place for a Catholic priest to consecrate matzo bread wafers and kosher wine at Mass. But as part of the Jewish-Catholic experience . . . it seemed necessary and exciting. . . . Cantor R.S. of Temple Emanu-El gave the commentary on the significance of the Jewish Seder" (*Southern Cross* 1975). "As a professing Christian and a practicing Methodist, it gave me distinct pleasure to sing with the choir at Temple Emanu-El . . . during the high holy days of this year. . . . The old traditions are very much alive in Judaism and I felt quite at home with much of the liturgy of Rosh Hashanah" (submitted by F.E.).

The Jewish community delights in every instance of interfaith acceptance, including recognition of a local hazzan's technical expertise, a true sign of appreciation of professionalism: "One of Boston's leading eye, ear, nose and throat specialists regularly sends patients to [Hazzan G.S.] for therapy. And recently the Harvard Health Plan accepted him as an approved vocal therapist. . . . Cantor S.'s most recent challenge has been in helping the chairman of one of Boston's largest corporations regain his voice" (Freedman n.d.a).

But public recognition is usually more noticed within the Jewish communal world, a veritable beehive of activity from political to philanthropic to recreational. In a small community, the hazzan can became a major public figure with a remarkably gregarious lifestyle, as reminiscences about one very active hazzan, Hirsh Chazin, show: "Pa was the father of Mizrachi [a Zionist organization] in Perth Amboy and its president for 54 years. He was chairman of the Hebrew School. He was the founder of the Yeshiva, the day school. . . . My father was active in every cultural activity in Perth Amboy for all of those years. . . . Besides being a full time hazzan he was a full time shochet [slaughterer]. . . . In addition to all that, Pop was an insurance agent for New York Life Insurance Co." (Chazin 1981:10).

Hazzanim may use the regional chapters of their associations as leverage to gain more community recognition: "Our main goal this year [in the New England Region of the CA] was a concerted effort to have the community at large recognize the value of the hazzan. To accomplish this, all meetings involving Jewish community affairs were attended by officers of the Region. Some positive results have developed. A meeting with Funeral directors was held discussing the importance of the participation of the hazzan at funerals and unveilings" (Gluck 1980:67). Such efforts have been going on for decades; here is a 1956 initiative: "Assurances were received by our office from the Bloch Publishing Co., the Hebrew Publishing Co. and the United Synagogue, that a line for the Hazzan's signature will be added to the wedding certificate in their next printing" (CA Executive Council minutes, 3 Dec. 1956). We will examine the hazzan's role within the intense world of synagogue life in more detail below for good reason:

> Jews far more than Christians use their synagogues and religious institutions as social rather than as religious centers in the usual sense of the word. The available evidence uniformly reveals that by and large Jews are far less observant than Christians when it comes to participation in worship. At the same time it is clear that synagogues and other institutions with a religious aura are doing relatively well within the Jewish community. As Marshall Sklare has pointed out, they are doing well precisely because they serve social far more than religious purposes (Elazar 1980:26).

Thus both "authority over clients" and "recognition by the public" are as tightly interconnected with the nature of Jewish communal organization as they are to internalized notions of individual "clients" about the nature of the clergy.

The second aspect of recognition, creation of a niche in the American legal system, deserves some treatment here as well, as the professionals consider this one of their major triumphs. Acknowledgment of the rights of the Jewish clergy under law goes back to colonial times. In 1710 Abraham De Lucena, hazzan of Shearith Israel, wrote to the governor of New York and New Jersey to claim very specific privileges:

> The humble petition of Abraham De Lucena, minister of the Jewish nation . . . sheweth that yho're petitioner's predecessors, ministers of the Jewish nation, residing at the city of New York, by reason of their ministerial function, have from time to time been exempted by the government, not only from boarding any office[r] civil or military . . . but likewise been excus'd from severall duties and services upon the inhabitants of this city. . . . [So he asks for] like priviledges and advantages (quoted in Marcus 1961).

Given American tolerance, rights could be extended to Jewish clergyman on the principle of "hazzan equals minister." When synagogues began hiring rabbis as their nominal leader, the role of hazzan/cantor became ambiguous. Generations went by before the new breed of hazzanim felt they had enough muscle to demand equal legal rights with the rabbi. The strength they mustered for a twelve-year legal battle in the 1950s and 1960s came from two sources: first, the Cantors Assembly now presented a united front of a major group of professionals. Second, the role of the hazzan had shifted to that of full-time clergyman from the earlier sole role of prayer leader; the star hazzanim had appeared only occasionally, as fund raisers and uplifters. True, Vigoda was able to wangle a visa as an exceptional artist, but Harry Truman failed when he tried to use the legal standing of the clergy as grounds for preferential status in the case of a refugee hazzan in 1938:

> I understand that, under the immigration laws, ministers of all religions are allowed to enter the United States as non-quota immigrants. . . . Rabbi Solomon [of the Kansas City congregation] informs us that the Cantor is privileged to perform marriages, bury the dead and conduct the religious rituals in the Synagogue. The Rabbi is superior to him only in that he preaches the sermons and decides questions in Jewish religious law. . . . I will appreciate anything that may be done to expedite the issuance of his visa ("A Letter from President Truman" 1978).

Truman might have found his job easier after World War II, when the new breed of suburbanized Jews founded hundreds of new congregations and demanded more and more duties from their hazzanim. Thus on paper it would seem that the hazzan was as much of a clergyman as the rabbi; the problem was convincing the courts.

The first case, on behalf of Gershon Ephros, fell through in 1964, but the language that the defense used ultimately proved convincing in two later landmark cases, that of Abraham Salkov for tax exemption (1966) and of Stuart Kanas for draft deferment (1967). The lawyer in the Ephros case, M. S. Fisher, used the following line of argument:

> In fact, the rabbi was previously and often exclusively "the interpreter of Jewish religious law and head of the Jewish court," and the Cantor in Judaism is closer than even the rabbi to the priest or minister. . . . Our law allows for varieties in church organization, religious leadership, ministry and experience. The office of the Jewish Cantor, the Hazzan, may seem strange; it may or may not fit the image of a minister of the Protestant sect or of the Christian faith. Improper construction of the Social Security Act, and violation of religious liberty would result if the Cantor, the Hazzan of the Jewish faith, were denied status as minister under the act (Fisher 1964:7).

Whereas Mitchell tried to stress the differences between rabbi and hazzan, in the Kanas case, the issue seems to have boiled down to their coequal status, apparently a more convincing argument: "The record shows that the registrant co-officiates with the rabbi at services of worship, conducts funerals and, perhaps, marriages, teaches Jewish principles to children, and supervised all music at the synagogue" ("A Second Landmark Case" 1968:12–13). Notice that music comes last in this list of duties, cementing the notion that the hazzan is by now much more than a sacred singer. It was not until the final 1973 Silverman case that the full range of the hazzan's professionalism was brought to bear in achieving legal status. Several interesting issues are raised in the judge's decision, including the questions of ordination and home vs. school training: "It did not matter that he was not ordained, as a rabbi is, because Judaism recognizes a dual ministry of rabbi and cantor. . . . Petitioner received his early training . . . under the direction . . . of his father and brother, both of whom were cantors. This manner of training . . . has been followed throughout the history of Judaism and is still in use today, although formal schools have increasingly been utilized to provide such training" ("A Landmark Case" 1973:20–21). Next, the judge takes up professional affiliation, allowing this as an important factor even though the hazzan remains a "lay" leader:

> Petitioner also possesses a certificate or commission issued by the Cantors Assembly of America showing him qualified to serve as cantor in the conduct of Jewish religious services. The Jewish religion is a lay religion . . . [and] has no theologically required hierarchy having control, dominion, or jurisdiction over its sacerdotal functions and religious worship. Yet, many formally organized congregations . . . employ professional rabbis and cantors to conduct religious services ("A Landmark Case" 1973:20–21).

This is a liberal judge: he allows for possible absence of formal training and even concedes that this is a religion without a recognized ecclesiastical hierarchy. He is, however, convinced by the equality of hazzan and rabbi, even going into details of costume:

> In the synagogue, there are equal pulpits for the cantor and the rabbi. Both . . . wear similar ecclesiastical robes which distinguish them from the rest of the congregation. The interpretation of Jewish law . . . is the only function reserved solely to the rabbi, [while] the cantor expresses the prayers and longings of the congregation to God. He must have extensive knowledge of Jewish law and tradition and his excellence is judged by the sincerity of his expression of his congregants' prayers. . . . It would appear that Cantor Silverman provides ministerial services functionally equivalent to those performed in Christian ministry. . . . The fact that Judaism assign this work [including teaching, weddings, funerals] to two classes of professionally trained and qualified men will not be used by this Court to deny the benefits of section 107 to one (the cantor) merely

because other religions have merged such duties into a single group ("A Landmark Case" 1973:24).

Involvement in the occupational culture

Whether hazzanim are involved in a culture of their own is a limited concept for the cantorate, since their numbers are small and denominational distinctions still dominate or, as one hazzan succinctly put it, "the only thing American cantors have in common is that they lead services" (C.B.). However, inter-sect impulses have always been present; recently, the trend has accelerated rapidly: "A major development in 1985 was the first combined Seminar of the CA and the ACC. I look forward to the day when we will establish a 'United Congress of Cantors' (or some such designation) to augment our independent structures, similar to those combined structures which enable our brethren in other spheres of Jewish activities to address common concerns and mutual interests" (Smolover 1986:2). Nevertheless, individuals may find it hard to straddle the gap: "I'm not a member of the cantorial group of Reform which I quit. . . . When I heard . . . at a convention: 'check if you want kosher food,' the next day they had my resignation" (C.G.).

The reference to the "structures of our brethren" underlines the extent to which hazzanim use other Jewish professionals as their primary reference point, rather than general American professionalism. Each denomination is a set of nested organizations representing special areas of professional interest:

> There are professional groupings within the Conservative movement: the Rabbinical Assembly, the Cantors Assembly, the Jewish Educators' Assembly, National Association of Synagogue Administrators, Jewish Youth Directors' Association. On placement committees . . . sit representatives from the Jewish Theological Seminary, Cantors Assembly . . . and United Synagogue [the umbrella organization]. Probably the most important link [between CA and United Synagogue] is placement; it's a bread and butter proposition, so it's crucial to all factions concerned, congregations and cantors. They have other liaisons with the Seminary; a prayerbook commission will call in members of the CA like Max [Wohlberg] and Sam [Rosenbaum] to sit and deliberate with them on the development of prayerbooks (A.I.).

The question of whether hazzanim are consulted in every aspect of denominational decision making is of enormous symbolic importance to the leaders of the cantorate, who do not hesitate to raise their voices whenever they feel slighted.

Summarizing professionalization, here is another sociologist's definition, one which suits the cantorate's own view of what it has tried to accomplish: "Professionalization might be defined as a process by which an organized occupation, usually but not always by virtue of making a claim to special esoteric competence and to concern for the quality of its work and its benefit to society, obtains the exclusive right to perform a particular kind of work, control training and access to it, and control the right of determining and evaluating the way the work is performed" (Freidson 1973:22).

The cantorate *is* now an "organized occupation" for the first time. It can certainly claim "special esoteric competence." The particular preoccupation of the postwar cantorate has been precisely a "concern for the quality of its work," including efforts to control "exclusive rights, training, and access." However, as always, it has little or no authority over the definition of "its benefit to society," which continually waxes and wanes from the laity's point of view, and even less over "the right of determining and evaluating the way the work is performed" beyond attempts to force congregations and denominational bodies to accept the contract terms and bargaining rights of the organized cantorate.

Finally, a quick survey of the parallel Protestant process is worthwhile to add perspective to this portrait. As Donald Scott has mapped it, the track goes from strong authority over a small local community in the eighteenth century through professionalization (in our sense) by the mid-nineteenth century, with pressure for change from congregants being one of the main driving forces:

> During the early decades of the nineteenth century . . . deference disappeared as the relationship became less formal and more immediate and personal. . . . This change . . . reflected the altered and intensified demands that parishioners had come to place upon their pastors. Not only did they want to be edified, they also demanded considerable personal and individual attention. . . .

> [By the 1840s] the clergyman . . . was perceived as someone who offered a service to a set of clients who demanded continuing performance and who would not hesitate to dismiss him if his performance fell below standards which they had given themselves the power to set. . . .

> By the 1850s . . . the clergyman's essential orientation . . . was now towards the profession. It created him, sustained his sense of himself as a clergyman, defined his role and provided the most important community of which he felt himself a part and by which he distinguished himself from other groups in the society (Scott 1978:121, 123, 155).

Society's official view of this process, the legal definition, is part of our background as well: "The Supreme Court of the United States has recognized a clergyman as a professional man, not a 'laboring man,' and as such 'entitled to respect, veneration, and confidence' " (Michaelsen 1956:280).

That it took the Jews an extra century to catch up with this Protestant model might show how encapsulated an ethnic group can be, but exclusiveness is too easy an answer. It is worth repeating that contingent historical forces (waves of immigration, the Holocaust) can wreak havoc on a minority's internal life. It was far easier for the Protestant ministry to unfold in a coherent manner than it was for the cantorate. At the same time, Protestantism itself hardly provides a static yardstick against which to measure the cantorate's evolution: "One of the striking things about this [post-1850s] period is the extent to which the Protestant ministry has reflected new cultural patterns and ideals. The culture-accommodating ministry is a common type" (Michaelsen 1956:253). "In complex societies . . . the minister has taken on an ever longer list of duties. . . . [P]astoral directors had oversight of extremely complicated congregational organizations and found themselves dispersing and distributing their energies through a variety of administrative tasks that were seldom anticipated in Christian history" (Marty 1972:153–54). In other words, establishing oneself as a profession does not guarantee a peaceful social niche. America is too volatile to allow any group to content itself with standard solutions. Like all social processes, professionalization is improvisatory, reshaping available ideologies and practices the way turning a kaleidoscope reshuffles its colorful components. Whether this is good or bad depends on your point of view: "Many Protestants have made virtues of these necessities and argue that lack of clear job descriptions for laymen and clergymen will continue to bring them together and make them ready to take on the unanticipated tasks which the world presents" (Marty 1972:153–54).

This upbeat assessment of the problem professionals face is rare in the Jewish world; most hazzanim would prefer to deal with less complexity—and perhaps the reader might share this view—but nothing is more interesting than trying to grasp a cultural process in all its perverse variety.

To understand professionalization in detail, we must examine the workplace—the synagogues of America—which is the subject of part 2. Before that, we need to bring our survey up to date by reviewing the profound changes the 1960s–1980s brought to the cantorate.

NOTES

1. A number of hazzanim have either come to America as a second land of immigration after going to Israel from Europe or are native-born Israelis; in both cases, many "did not see any possibility of professional or any other development in Israel; . . . I could not make a living as a cantor in Israel. Not even half a living. Not even a quarter of a living to pay for furthering my education" (C.I.).

2. I do not mean to say that the Orthodox have had no interest in or impact on the recent cantorate, but all sources agree that the decline there is sharp and the prognosis bleak. Nevertheless, the Cantorial Training Institute (CTI) has recently been supplied with fresh funds and a new director (Bernard Beer) and hopes to reassert itself after a period when its very existence was threatened (see Nulman 1986–87 for a history of the CTI).

3. Of course, it would be nice to have a more fully developed model of religious professionals as a subgroup within this general definition, but I do not find we have yet answered the questions posed by Yinger over twenty-five years ago: "Who become religious professionals? . . . What role conflicts do they face? How are variations in training, income, and identification with others manifest in their activity? To what degree do they prevent or initiate changes in religious belief and practice as a result of the interactions within the colleague group?" (1961:163). The following chapters address some of these issues in a limited way for one group of religious professionals.

4. Ritzer's stress on an "individual" fitting onto a "continuum" is particularly helpful for a very small, even esoteric profession like the cantorate, where the biographical and the professional are more tightly knit than, say, in large-scale cases like teachers or the military.

5. Early appeals, like Leeser's mid-nineteenth century editorials in the *Occident*, were aimed at what turned out to be rabbinic training; it took the separation of duties to make the case clear for a need to train *music* specialists.

6. Though establishing programs met resistance within denominations, in retrospect, the need is expressed in almost evangelical terms, as in this 1987 Orthodox statement: "The surviving remnants of Jewry throughout the world looked to the United States not merely for salvation and liberation, but also for renewed spiritual and cultural values" (Nulman 1986–87:2).

7. The effort to convince the Jewish Theological Seminary to establish its training program began at least as early as 1924, using an interdenominational committee: "For the first time in the history of American Jewry, Cantors representing orthodox, conservative and reform congregations met in an all-day conference for the purposes of devising ways and means of how to improve the music of the synagogue, and how to secure for our divine service a more dignified and impressive rendition [leading to a recommendation for] the establishment of a Cantors Seminary under the direction of the Jewish Theological Seminary and a delegation going to Cyrus Adler [Chancellor of the JTS]" (Goldfarb 1925:3–4). Even this effort did not succeed until the Holocaust

drove the point home, and a group of activists made another push, as Max Wohlberg describes in an interview: "We approached [Cyrus Adler] with a group, I think . . . Beimel and Glantz, myself, and David Putterman [among others]. . . . And he favored it, but . . . he died, and a little later on we approached Finkelstein [who] seemed favorable, but it took a few years and ultimately was established thanks to the activities of Rabbi Albert Gordon . . . [who] assumed the executive directorship of the United Synagogue . . . plus David Putterman, [who are] probably the arch creators."

8. From the ethnomusicologist's point of view, one of the key issues is whether institutional teaching reshapes the old oral tradition approach, since in several world music cultures—for example, in India—observers have noted a sharp distinction between apprenticeship and classroom modes of instruction. The evidence is mixed in the cantorial case; to a great extent, oral teaching continues within the training programs, as one hazzan-teacher says: "By example. This I found to be the most successful method of teaching. . . . I also taught a class where all the students heard one student perform a service, and they criticized the student, and I threw in my two cents about that criticism" (C.I.). On the other hand the CTI, in a review of its history, makes a point of stressing that the program's founder, Karl Adler, "believed that Jewish music should no longer be taught in a haphazard manner" (Nulman 1986–87:3), and was opposed to teaching by rote. For the effect on repertoire itself, see chapter 11.

9. This reliance on the authority of experts is surely one of the strongest signs of professionalization.

10. What cantorial students think about their training would be a suitable subject for a separate study; in the Project interviews, opinions ranged widely from satisfaction through the following sort of cynicism: "At HUC [Hebrew Union College] you have to have some basic requirements in playing an instrument (piano, guitar, flute, whatever), voice training, musicianship, Hebrew training, sight-reading. . . . For all that knowledge and prerequisites which is necessary, the salary isn't that good" (C.G.).

11. Statistics bear out this notion of success in placement, but do not indicate total victory: fifty-eight percent of congregations reported they turn to the professional organizations for job candidates, but twenty-two percent still do not, and the large percentage that left the question blank—twenty percent— perhaps indicates an even greater degree of nonconformity to official placement procedures.

12. In addition to goals such as Rosenbaum enumerates, professional associations can be quite assertive in staking a claim within the denomination, as a reading of the basic goals outlined in the 1984 Constitution of the ACC makes clear:

"1) Through its ministry to serve the congregations with which they are affiliated in the conduct of their liturgy, their religious education, and ministerial efforts." Here a professional association seems to conceive itself as the collective Reform clergy in all matters liturgical, educational, and ministerial.

"2) To provide the cantorate and the individual cantor with the organizational means where, by elevating its own status and the effectiveness of the cantorate, its primary purpose can best be achieved." Here the appeal to self-interest is couched in terms which make it clear that what is good for the cantorate is good for Reform Judaism.

"3) By encouraging the creation and publication of new liturgy, texts, and educational materials, to directly influence the development of the Reform Jewish Movement in America." Here the cantorate stakes a claim as a major player in the politics of the denomination.

13. Among the Reform Jews, there is "associate membership," extended to those who choose not to take the certification examination but who aspire to ACC membership while they work in congregations. The ACC board debates this issue repeatedly, and the School of Sacred Music gets involved as well, showing how close to the bone the issue of credentials is to professionals and their sense of self. Being an associate member is not exactly a comfortable position, as one hazzan reports: "It's not a matter of knowing more or knowing less than they [full members] do but coming from outside, coming into the circle. . . . I feel at times left out. I don't know the jokes from the School of Sacred Music. . . . I don't have the camaraderie that builds up over four, five years at the SSM shlepping books and studying and worrying about tests" (H.B.).

14. Details of placement can be quickly summarized for the ACC. A congregation pays dues for the cantor (.086 of the salary) and a $50 placement fee for every request to fund an office staff. The organization provides a chapel and an accompanist for a visiting congregational committee, which may arrive in New York from as far away as San Francisco. The ACC places cantorial students only in congregations with less than 400 families to avoid competition between junior and senior hazzanim. The average contract now is two years, though the ACC is pushing for five. About ten to twelve percent of hazzanim "shift around a lot," giving constant work to the ACC staff. Some congregations still want a large voice, while others look for other skills. In general, they tend to prefer younger candidates, who are perceived as being cheaper and more malleable; hazzanim over fifty are hard to place. The interview season is February to May, a bit earlier in these organized times than in the chaotic interwar period when auditions droned on through the hot summer days. Today, contracts are firmed up by June 1 (J.F.).

5

~~~~~~

1970s–1980s: New Trends, New Gender

Some saw me as a pioneer, some as a renegade.
> —Elaine Shapiro, first female
> music student at the Jewish
> Theological Seminary

My parents always told me, whatever I wanted to do, I
would be able to do.
> —Barbara Horowitz, first
> ordained female cantor

The 1970s and 1980s have been a period of great turbulence and in-novation in the American cantorate. Two trends have, literally, grabbed the headlines. First, a spiritual reawakening has led to a period of intense redefinition of American Judaism and renewed commitment by many individual Jews, including hazzanim. Second, as part of re-structuring identity, women have found a niche at the heart of ritual, culminating in the ordination of female rabbis in both the Reform (1975) and Conservative movements (1985) and of female hazzanim among the Reform (1976) and Conservative (1987). Both of these trends show the usual Jewish penchant for close tracking of Christian cultural activity, one of the few constants in the cantorate. Of course, these new directions have caused considerable confusion, conflict, and even pain.

These changes are nested within the concept of American ethnicity, itself a concept always on the move. As immigrants, groups have been singled out for special treatment by the mainstream, always suspicious of the latest entry. If a European-origin group is lucky, it stops being pointed out after a while; then its identity becomes voluntary and symbolic. For the Jews, not typical Europeans, this neutral condition naturally arrived later, perhaps not fully until the 1960s. Today, the Jews are, officially, part of the majority, since the census does not list them as a minority, certainly a rare if not unique occurrence in Jewish history.[1] This means that Jews, like other Euro-Americans, have a chance to reinvent themselves culturally on the basis of internal choice rather than outside pressure. In the case of a voluble and splintered group like the Jews, this refashioning of self goes on almost daily. Each week's newspapers bring fresh accounts of breakthroughs and backswings, making it hard for the scholar to see the forest for the trees. So our analysis here is provisional and largely historic: predictions can be left to journalists and culture critics.

It helps to start with figures. In 1971, among American Jews, "11 percent identified with Orthodox, 42 percent with Conservative, 33 percent with Reform, and 14 percent had no denominational identification"; and "50 percent were synagogue members," a drop from sixty-six percent in the 1950s (Waxman 1983:184–85). Fourteen years later, in 1985: "According to the sociologist Egon Mayer, surveys show that about 10 percent of America's 5.5 million Jews are Orthodox, 32 percent are Conservative, 23 percent are Reform and about 35 percent identify themselves as 'just Jewish'" (Berger 1986). The main story these numbers tell is that American Jews keep dropping out of the organized movements; the increase in unaffiliated Jews is striking. Otherwise, the denominational landscape looks much the same: Reform and Conservative are still separated by a nine-point gap, and the Orthodox hold at around one-tenth of affiliation, showing a very tenacious right wing that is, by default, much more prominent. The problems with statistics is they cannot measure level of commitment, extraordinarily high among the Orthodox, as everyone recognizes: "The 1960's were a turning point for Orthodox Jewry in the United States, the years when this distinctly minority portion of American Jewry developed its own style and program, became much more assertive and self-confident, as well as more public" (Schick 1983:190).

This new Orthodox drive has deeply marked mainstream Judaism, both in America and in Israel, and impacts the identity of hazzanim, who are now pastors as much as singers, even more than the laity: "Orthodoxy is the fastest growing movement in American and the most active. . . . [T]he enthusiasm of this group is infectious. . . . I envy them their regeneration and I would want very much to see a similar return in Conservative ranks. The return to fundamentalism in religion need not be limited to Orthodoxy" (Rosenbaum 1985).

Indeed, the mainstream has shifted right, probably part of a generally perceived American trend of the 1970s, underscored by the election of a "born-again" president in 1976 and the resurgence of fundamentalist political activism.[2] While this general Christian mood has affected both

Conservative and Reform, it has been more evident among the latter, since it represents the acceleration of energy which had been gathering for some time: "About 1928, we note the beginnings of a new direction in the Reform rabbinate in which there is a conscious effort to uncover traditional elements for the enrichment of Jewish life. It is an over-statement, but, nevertheless, suggestive to say that the entire move-ment retains little of its origins except the name" (Polish 1983:319–22). This works itself out in the service itself, which used to stress decorum, a carefully regulated congregation who chimed in on hymns and reverently listened to its star preacher-rabbi and well-trained choir. Today, however: "A majority of Reform rabbis now favor incorporating more traditions; some even advocate merger with Conservative Ju-daism. Services today are likely to include a generous quantity of He-brew and have the musical portion conducted by a cantor with or without the assistance of a choir. . . . A definite trend toward freer self-expression by the congregation and a more favorable attitude to ritual seems apparent" (Meyer 1978:164).

Notice the inclusion of the hazzan as a core aspect of change: the sacred singer is literally the voice of tradition. In the postwar period, 150-year-old Reform synagogues have found themselves shopping for a hazzan for the first time. But the new Reform Jews do not just add a musical leader; they look for wider change. True, they want more "tradition," that is, a more Conservative-looking service, but they also want more energetic input from the laity, participation of women as leaders, and a greater acceptance of interfaith couples. The formula has worked: "The Reform Jewish movement has experienced a period of sharp growth in the last ten years. . . . The number of Reform syn-agogues rose in ten years to 791, from 659, while membership in that period rose 23 percent" (Berger 1985).

As Reform grows more traditional and lively, to a certain extent it becomes less distinguishable from Conservative, which also seeks in-ternal revitalization: "I don't see much difference between the average Conservative second or third generation and the average Reform sec-ond or third generation American. Whether institutional chauvinism will keep us apart—that's *an andere mayse* ["another story"]"(I.D.). "There has been an increase in mergers between congregations of sim-ilar orientation. But mergers have also taken place between congre-gations of different denominational affiliation. The trend began in the smaller communities and is now apparent in larger centers of Jewish population as well" (Wolfe Kelman, quoted in Friedland 1978:218). Needless to say, the Jewish clergy is not happy about this trend: "I heard in two instances where the Conservative and Reform congregations mixed very successfully. . . . It would mean a combination and reduction of congregations, also less jobs for rabbis and cantors, and I'm not for that" (C.G.).

The economic crunch and growing fundamentalism are only part of the story. The liberating spirit of the 1960s, coming from the Left, put institutional Judaism on the defensive before the attraction of Orthodoxy attacked it from the Right. The most notable development along these lines was the creation of the *havurah* movement in 1968, by a group of "young rabbis and graduate students in Boston who 'felt estranged from American society, as exemplified by the Vietnam war and mass culture, and from the Jewish community, as exemplified by what they considered to be its inauthentic bureaucratic institutions' "(Riesman, quoted in Waxman 1983:213).

What is a havurah?[3]

> A havurah is a small community of like-minded families who group together as a Jewish fellowship for the purposes of providing each other with social support and pursuing their own participatory programs of Jewish study, celebration, and community service. *Havurot* (pl.) are generally small, ranging in membership from ten to twenty-four families who meet regularly, at least once a month, often in members' homes on a rotating basis. Some develop and function independently of any formal Jewish organization, while others are affiliated with synagogues (Waxman 1983:213).

From the Jewish clergy's point of view—whether Reform or Conservative—left-wing havurot represent an enormous challenge: "I think the best of our young people, the most religious, the most spiritual of the young people . . . are saying they don't like the 2,000 family congregation. They hate its bloody guts. They won't darken its door except under protest [except] for those things which are very carefully made smaller, more personal, more connecting, and within which they work with some individual who makes a difference to their spiritual life" (Hertzberg 1972:88). Since the hazzan is one of those "individuals," it is clear the new breed of congregants will carefully judge their chosen voices. Part of the challenge also emanates from the youth movements and summer camps of the Conservative and Reform movements, centering on Camp Ramah and National Federation of Temple Youth (NFTY) respectively. These spiritual enclaves began in the 1950s as a way of harnessing the vitality of young Jews and getting them actively involved in creating their own spiritual environment, presumably as a step towards synagogue affiliation. The problem was that the youth movements created what anthropologists would call an age-grade cohort, a group with its own interests and traditions that was not excited by returning to the standard service of the "2,000 family congregation." Within the Conservative movement, the split among hazzanim over the legacy of Camp Ramah is sometimes extreme, as the following quotes from a younger and an older CA member show:[4]

> *Pro-Ramah*: Is there a Ramah tradition of tunes? Yes. But then there is also a German tradition, an eastern European tradition, a Chicago tradition, a Philadelphia tradition. . . . Who is to say that one tradition is really superior over another? Is being a song leader such a reprehensible activity which we must face with only the most stubborn resistance? . . . I don't think so (Tilman 1976:169).

> *Anti-Ramah*: Much of the poison that we get back to our congregations comes from innocent children who have been infected with vulgar melodies at camp. These come back to haunt us and to taunt us. . . . The Ramah concept was a sound one [but] not everything about Ramah was perfect. Particularly bad . . . was the liturgical musical tradition which developed over the years. . . . [S]ome 20 years later, we are meeting rabbis, congregants, and even hazzanim who have been raised on summer camp Judaism, who grew up on it, and have tried to make the camp spirit work in the real life situation . . . in which the Jewish professional is seen as a year-round camp counselor (Rosenbaum 1976:68, 88–89).

Many, particularly among the Reform, steer a middle course: "I use that stuff in the service. . . . I don't do it on a regular basis, but I will often sing something that the kids know. When I say the kids, I mean kids of youth group age, high school age kids. . . . And the adults find it appealing as well. Of course, I don't jazz it up on the pulpit, the way I might in the classroom or when I'm working with my children's choir. But the melody is still theirs" (D.H.).

For the professional, the flourishing of spiritual subcultures within the community represents an escape from the authority over clients supposedly granted by education, ordination, and the power of fraternal associations. All this threatens the gains the cantorate won so painstakingly in the postwar era. Naturally, hazzanim are much happier when the urge for roots and "belonging" makes itself felt in greater synagogue affiliation:

> I do see young Jewish couples yearning for some kind of attachment to the institution of the synagogue, looking to the synagogue to help them feel a sense of community. . . . They are living high-pressured career lives, the adults. The kids are involved in 85 million extra-curricular activities. The parents, the grandparents are far-flung, or in Florida or someplace. And these families want something static, something that means a spiritual home. A place where they can learn, where they can congregate, if not

worship. Where they can study together as family and experience the richness of Jewish tradition together with all other comparable groups" (D.H.).

Why did this movement grow when it did? The hazzan just quoted agrees with many observers that it's partly "because of the black pride movement of the sixties that Jews have become desirous of more self-knowledge. They want also to be proud of their origins." In other words, whereas the fresh breeze of the sixties blew some young Jews straight out of the synagogue into alternate affiliation, it caused others to seek shelter within that traditional haven, the ethnic church, a situation that has continued into the 1980s.

Yet one can never rush to an easy analysis of Jewish trends without considering the overall American scene. Studies of the "baby boom" generation (born 1943–54) shows an interest in religious affiliation is widespread among all groups: " 'We are witnessing a resurgence of religious involvement as many of the prodigal sons and daughters of the 1960's return to more active participation,' said David A. Roozen . . . who directed the study. 'As people move into later stages of their life . . . they're looking to more stable, more lasting kinds of values, and they find the church supportive of that' " (Berger 1986).

Yet this shift towards the church and synagogue is double-edged; the number of dropouts is also growing in the key 31-to-42 age group: "What we have is an increasing polarization among baby boomers in regard to religious participation with an increasing proportion at the high and low extremes and fewer in the middle" (Berger 1986). The findings of this interfaith study tally well with the apparently contradictory accounts hazzanim give, citing both declining attendance and increased participation. What does all this mean for houses of prayer? "Many churches and synagogues have tailored their programs to attract this age group. But Dr. Roozen cautioned that the group, once engaged, was also changing the way the houses of worship do business" (Berger 1986).

Yet as helpful as national studies can be in locating Jewish trends on the mainstream map, they cannot account for particular in-group motivations. One hazzan points to the intellectual as well as emotional appeal the synagogue broadcasts to the professionals who now make up much of its constituency, hardly a factor noticed by Dr. Roozen:

> So many young men, middle-aged men, older men even, became Bar Mitzvah x number of years ago, and that was it. Now they're saying . . . "Here I am a nuclear physicist with a twelve year-old's Jewish education. I can't reconcile that. I'm going to take adult education courses in my

synagogue." It has nothing to do with God. . . . I think what it has to do
with is an intellectual curiosity, a desire for alignment with one's heritage,
identification with one's people, in light of the Holocaust and . . . the State
of Israel (D.H.).

This hazzan is part of a broad outreach effort to the seekers: "In my
congregation we have a very elaborate adult education program, with
the finest rabbinic professors coming to teach in our synagogue. . . .
We have a whole adult school with a fancy brochure, and . . . huge
enrollments" (D.H.). What is the payoff to the hazzan of this type of
educational activity? "So our service is a *service*, because the people
who want to study, do come to class" and can follow services (D.H.).

Beyond the intellectual curiosity factor, two highly emotional, dis-
tinctively Jewish issues are cited above: the Holocaust and the state of
Israel. This is not the place to psychoanalyze American Jewry, but it
has become a well-accepted notion in the 1980s that history has brought
the Jewish-Americans to a new stage of self-definition. On the one
hand, they can no longer think of themselves as immigrants or post-
immigrants, since the Old World is gone. On the other, while they
once worried over being non-Israelis, recently they seem no longer
worried about staying in the Diaspora.[5] While this might make Jews
comfortable, it looks as if it also makes them a bit uneasy as to the
real content of being an *American* Jew. Since the hazzan works in a
major—perhaps the primary—center of self-identity, the synagogue, he
or she cannot escape dealing with the new liveliness and the current
groping for a sense of "who we are."

In later chapters we shall see how this conflict works itself out in
the workplace, in the sanctuary, and in the mind of the hazzan. For
now, we must note the ambiguity of gender in the last sentence of the
previous paragraph, which causes us to turn to yet another area of
turbulence and innovation: the entry of females into the profession.
The move to certify women as hazzanim is part of a general trend
towards increased female participation in Reform and Conservative
ritual, which, as Elazar and Monson have noted, is closely related to
the havurah movement as part of the "repersonalization of the synagogue" (1981:28). They point out a forerunner of today's feminist
issues—the question of whether women's place is in the kitchen or the
choir: "Looking at an earlier example of the expanded role of women,
there are cases where the introduction of mixed synagogue choirs in
Conservative and Reform congregations brought the traditional family
Friday night dinner to an end in homes where women had to choose
between conflicting obligations" (Elazar and Monson 1981:29). The
mixed choir issue is older than Elazar and Monson imply. In 1855

Solomon Jacobs's article on "Ladies' Singing in Synagogue" raised some eyebrows on the subject. Using customary rhetoric, the author starts with a commentary on Jewish law: "We now wish to make a few general remarks on this prohibition for females to sing in choirs. Our Talmudists had the example of heathen communities before them—they saw that the mixture of male and female at public worship was productive of immoral consequences. . . . [T]hey were afraid that public worship might degenerate into the mere concert where men go merely to hear fine singing; hence the prohibition." Now Jacobs gets to the moral of the lesson: "It was to save the Synagogue from that very state to which, alas! it is now fast ending, viz., converting our places of 'public worship' into the concert room, where women are to be the 'prima donnas' and men are to be entertained with their delicious warblings" (Jacobs 1855:541).

What Jacobs points to in Jewish tradition is the great suspicion of the female voice, bound to lead men astray. In eastern European daily life, for example, young women were not supposed to sing in the presence of men whom they might be allowed to marry—in other words, they could perform only for close male relatives.[6] Sholom Aleichem has a lovely description of a girl's broad range of songs, and how it was limited as she grew older; notice that cantorial items come first on his list: "Until she reached the age of fifteen or sixteen, Rochele used to sing free as a bird; no matter whether a *Nakdishcho*, a *Kevakoras*, a Hasidic melody or an orchestral tune. Whatever she sang with her pleasant voice and modest ways was a delight to hear" (from *Stempenyu*, my translation). If Rochele's singing around the house had to be curtailed, imagine how much more upsetting this seductive presence would be in the synagogue, if only as part of a mixed choir. To actually allow a woman to *lead* services would have seemed inconceivable to Jacobs's generation, and still is for Orthodox Jews anywhere. However, there actually were women performing sacred song in public—if not in sanctuaries—before the 1970s. They appeared on discs and the popular stage—Sophie Kurtzer, Sheyndele "the Hazzante" (from the Yiddish word for the hazzan's wife)—but were considered an oddity, a vaudeville item, and were much derided by the profession: "A variety show is on its way to Broadway wherein an actress dons a cap and talis and intones prayers from our sacred service. . . . It is also high time to put a stop to the shameful phenomenon, the so-called professional 'hazzante.' I cannot picture it happening among Methodists or Episcopalians" (Wohlberg 1977). The appeal to Protestant decorum is far from accidental, betraying the "what will they think of us" issue as part of the problem. As late as 1957, the Executive Council of the

Cantors Assembly routinely protested a television appearance by a woman performing sacred songs: "on the Ed Sullivan television program which was to have represented Jewish music in celebration of Jewish Music Month. Her performance was found objectionable. . . . The Jewish Welfare Board took full responsibility for her endorsement . . . and assured the [Executive] Council that such mistakes will not be repeated" (CA Executive Council minutes, 1957).

So far, the history as written by men makes it appear that women never had positions of authority in the synagogue. But one recent study challenges that assumption, pointing out that several ancient inscriptions seem to indicate that there *were* women leaders, and that careful examination of available sources will make it "impossible to mistake male Jewish attitudes towards women for Jewish women's history" (Brooten 1982:150). Brooten's study is part of a larger, intense reevaluation of women's role in Judaism, an offshoot of the general women's movement in 1970s America. At all levels of organized Jewish life, the pressure of accommodating the new female militancy has caused strain and fracture, undoing even very old alliances: "The Jewish commission that has approved rabbis as chaplains for the U.S. armed forces since World War I broke up yesterday over whether a rabbi who is a woman can serve as a military chaplain. The breakup came when the nation's major Orthodox rabbinical group . . . announced that it was withdrawing . . . because Reform Judaism independently approved a woman as a Navy chaplain" (Goldman 1986b).

The move of women into leadership roles has been painstaking. Of course, the Reform movement was the groundbreaker: "Reform Judaism has since early in the nineteenth century called for the equality of women in modern Jewish life" (Borowitz 1978:31). By 1975, ninety-nine percent of Reform congregations had women count as official members of a *minyan*, the necessary quorum of worshippers, as opposed to forty-seven percent among the Conservative. The area of reading from the Torah at services was breached more easily, being ninety-nine percent for Reform and eighty-nine percent for Conservatives the same year (Elazar and Monson 1981:25). The really crucial issue has been admitting women to the rabbinate, which the Reform did in 1975, and the cantorate, in 1976. By contrast, the Conservatives ordained a woman rabbi in 1985 and allowed a female hazzan only in 1987.

The problem posed by the woman as siren, distracting the serious worshipper, seems relatively minor. Yet as an issue in current interpretation of Jewish law, it is a microcosm of Orthodox practice. Discussing the issue of whether "a woman's voice is forbidden to be heard in any case," an Orthodox hazzan explains the problem: "Rabbi So-loveichik doesn't agree with this, but Rabbi Moshe Feinstein does; he's the decider for the majority of the very religious Jews. . . . Both of them have legitimate sources. But the thing is, you see, the more stringent opinion is the one that is becoming prevalent in the religious world, especially as the Orthodox world is becoming more right wing" (E.A.).[7] Yet there is a point of Jewish law that comes closer to the heart of the Orthodox objection to women hazzanim. The core problem is the fact that while men *must* perform many religious obligations, women do not have to. This situation links up with part of the role of the hazzan: to "cover" for the congregants so they are not responsible for their errors or omissions. As one hazzan explains:

> The cantor is . . . the intermediary, if there is such a thing in the Jewish dictionary. There isn't, but he's representing them, let's say. . . . [C]an they, will they acknowledge a woman being their intermediary? A person who is not *khiuf*, obligated to observe commandments . . . can she make some-body else *yotse*, relieved of the responsibility, if you are not *obligated* to do that? This is a halakhic [legal] problem. And of course everybody agrees you cannot be a witness at a conversion certificate, at a marriage certificate . . . there is no doubt about it (C.G.).

The question that seems natural to raise is: what if a woman took the obligation on herself, so made herself equal to men? "She has to take it on lock, stock, and barrel. That means three times a day, and at the right time with tefillin [phylacteries] and tallis. That's it. And once she does it, she can never absolve herself of it. . . . No one has ever done it, that I know of . . . except for Rashi's daughter [in the eleventh century] and some other strange people" (E.A.).

Among some Conservative factions the halachic argument continues to carry considerable weight: "According to Rabbi Ronald Price of the Union for Traditional Conservative Judaism (UTCJ), 'For the Seminary to ordain women as cantors would be a serious mistake as well as a more serious violation of Jewish law than ordaining women as rabbis. From a halachic perspective, leading the prayer service is more crucial than teaching' "(Ruby 1987:9).[8]

The 1987 turning point arrived none too soon for students like Marla Barugel, one of a handful of women who chose to go through the entire Jewish Theological Seminary training program at the Cantors Institute knowing they could receive only a bachelor's degree in sacred music without the diploma of hazzan awarded to their male classmates.[9] Why would a woman put herself in this situation? "Barugel grew up in the Conservative movement and the Camp Ramah program. She taught high-school French and worked as a credit analyst in the international division of a major bank before deciding to study for the cantorate. . . . 'I chose not to go into the Reform cantorate because I do not want to compromise my religious philosophy. I see myself as a traditional Jew, and want to see this issue resolved halachically' " (Ruby 1987:9). In other words, she wanted to stand her ground within her denomination: "She noted that 'a lot of women have been forced to make that compromise, and accept positions in Reform congregations because of a lack of jobs for women as cantors in the Conservative movement' " (Ruby 1987:9).

With thirty-nine women in the rabbinical class in 1986, it became increasingly hard to deny accreditation to women in the Cantors Institute.[10] Yet no one should imagine that revolutionary change comes easily. Being a recent issue, the entry of women has aroused strong emotions in male hazzanim from the earliest advances into synagogue participation: "I know one gentleman . . . a very gifted hazzan, who is leaving his congregation . . . one of the reasons being that they want to make a move in the left direction and that is, allowing women to the Torah, being counted in a minyan, and it's very difficult for him, so he has to look for an orthodox congregation where that doesn't exist" (C.G.). Another old-time hazzan makes no bones about his feelings: "I think by nature men are more concerned with things spiritual" (H.C.). For some, the emotion is partly based on musical nostalgia, a regret for voices past: "Women will *never, never* be able to emulate the hazzan of the golden era. They'll sing nicely, they'll sing sweetly, but that's all. I think [Conservative] congregations will be ready for them, but the *kahal* [community] as I knew it in my younger days is gone" (E.J.).[11]

Such complaints, even the argument about halacha, does not get to the bottom of the problem, according to some male hazzanim: "People hide behind the halacha to hide what really is the bottom line, which is sexism, and not even so much sexism but self-protection. The people who might not be as qualified as they should be are afraid that a woman might take their job away from them" (D.B.).[12] But even those who are qualified worry about the simple question of supply and demand:

> Most of my colleagues, I think, feel comfortable with women being cantors, people my age [early-mid-thirties] . . . but it is nice when congregations know that there's a shortage of cantors; it really makes it easier. Especially in [a small midwestern city], to negotiate a contract. I mean, I did a little bit of interviewing. I looked at a couple of congregations this year, and they were just devastated . . . supply and demand works in the cantorate just as it does in the rest of society, and that's what's going to

dictate the salaries. But if it's flooded by a lot of women, who knows what would happen? (E.G.).

After all, he points out, the numbers involved are small: "How many cantors would it take to turn the picture upside down for there to be a surplus of cantors? You know, if they tell you there are fifty positions and fifteen people looking for cantors, so they haven't filled thirty-five positions—I mean thirty-five is really a very small number: fifty more cantors would turn the whole thing around. That's why it's such a delicate situation and that's why people are concerned about women becoming cantors" (D.B.).[13]

How and why did women get themselves into this confrontational situation? No doubt partly as a result of the Christian model, as abetted by the women's movement. For Protestants, the growth of women as a force in the clergy has been explosive:

> The 1985–6 Fact Book on Theological Education shows that 26 percent of Protestant theological students are women, as against 10 percent 13 years ago. "America is looking toward a clergy that is half women," said Adair Lummis, co-author of the 1983 book "Women of the Cloth." . . . Harvard Divinity first accepted women in 1955, but there was no significant increase in their numbers until the late 1970's. In 1971, 11 percent of the students were female; by 1981, the number was approaching 50 percent (Goldman 1986a).[14]

To understand the Jewish case from the inside, we must turn to women's own accounts of their motivations and career development, and there is no better source to begin with than Barbara Ostfeld-Horowitz, the very first women to receive a degree from the School of Sacred Music and then successfully to hold down a full-time job (where she has been for over a decade): As a child "the more I observed the duties of our cantor, Martin Rosen, the more I decided that that's what I wanted to do when I grew up . . . I saw that he directed choirs. . . . I saw that he sang services. I thought it was a very dramatic sort of career. And I was always complimented when I had a solo as a child. . . . My parents had always told me that whatever I wanted to do, I would be able to do. They never said 'A little girl can't expect to do x, y, or z.' " But Horowitz made no further strides toward training until she was seventeen, in 1970. Having heard that a female student, Sally Preisand, was at the Reform's rabbinic school, she went in for an interview: "I was seventeen. I had never gone to Hebrew school. . . . I had been confirmed. I attended synagogue regularly. As far as my Judaic background, it was a child's Judaic background. . . . They put a Hebrew prayer book in front of me and I said, 'I'm sorry, gentlemen,

I can't read.' And they were astounded. Why they accepted me, I can't tell you." Having been accepted, she confirmed the school's faith in her by completing her degree and getting jobs:

> A year after I graduated in '75, I started at Beth El of Great Neck, and I've been there ever since. And that is the largest Reform congregation on Long Island, with some 1400 families. . . . I almost think that the reason they selected me for the position was because I was a woman, and they wanted to make a statement about women in leadership positions within Reform Judaism. There were upwards of thirty people interviewed for the position. And I think that one of the things going for me was, not only was I a woman, but I was the first woman cantor. And I think that my synagogue likes having first feathers in its cap.

In other words, both at the school and the synagogue, there was a perfect matchup between the Reform movement's interest in innovation and an immensely eager, talented young woman's drive for professional fulfillment. At least Horowitz implies this meshing of interests: "Even the good old classical Reform congregations, where cantors were regarded as anathema because they represented the shtetl and *shokling* [swaying while praying] and davening and all that other stuff that everybody wanted to get away from have been hiring cantors these days. And the influx of women cantors provides many congregations with the opportunity to equalize their pulpits, and to please half the members of their congregations." We have heard this notion of "pleasing the women" before, first as part of the drive for mixed choirs, then as part of the reason young native hazzanim had the edge on Old World men in interwar America. The history of women's contribution to the synagogue atmosphere has never been written, but even these slight insights indicate it would show significant female impact. But that influence is modified by the fact that it is only "half the congregation" that is pleased: "Also remember that a woman cantor is not the threat to a congregation that a woman rabbi is, I regret to say. A woman cantor is not lethal because she's doing what is OK for a woman to do, namely she's singing, she's praying. She is not burying your dead. She is not marrying your sons. She is not preaching to you, which is very hard for many people, I regret to say, to take. A woman cantor is innocuous. Much as I would love to be more controversial than I am, I'm not."

For the Reform, then, the situation is exactly the reverse of the Orthodox position. For the latter, a woman could be a rabbi more easily than a hazzan, since being an expert in legal matters is more neutral than having your voice resound through the synagogue or "covering" for men's prayers. For cautious members of the Reform, on the other hand, the rabbi is the authority figure in the synagogue, hence should be a male, whereas there's no problem with a women raising her voice or leading the prayers. Nothing could be more typical of American Judaism than the perfectly logical, historically grounded way in which both these factions have arrived at their positions, or the fact that they represent polar opposites. Even for the Reform, however, the granting of power to women may have its limits:

> We have an assistant rabbi who was ordained several years ago from the Cincinnati school [Hebrew Union College]. We get a lot of comments about too many women on the pulpit, because the president of our congregation is also a woman. So therefore it's three women and one man on the bima ["pulpit"], and most people, don't really care. A number of people, and certainly some vocal people, do complain about it. And because of that imbalance, I do believe that when we hire our next assistant [rabbi], he will be a man; I'm certain of that.

How a female hazzan gets along with a male rabbi is a matter addressed by another young woman professional:

> Women work well with men. After all, think about the way we're brought up. In most roles in families the woman learned to take a little bit of a submissive role. Two men together, it's difficult, so I think that a rabbi likes working, many times, more with a woman. . . . She's better able, psychologically, to know how to handle a man's ego. . . . I've learned, because a woman learns how to manipulate in her own way. . . . I wouldn't want to work with a woman rabbi . . . difficult to work with the same sex, you know; it's the same as when you put two animals together, two of the same sex, and they start biting each other. . . . Men are better at handling a woman; will take more time and patience than they will with another man (H.I.).

If women do fit in well, is it possible that they will take over the profession, at least among the Reform, as happens to certain fields when women are suddenly allowed full access? Whether the cantorate will become a women's profession is a question many hazzanim discuss, particularly now that the student body at the School of Sacred Music is almost exclusively female. Barbara Horowitz is not worried: "The standards [at the school] are very high; the reason that it is so difficult for even a very qualified person to get into the SSM is because the influx of women students has upgraded the level of the average candidate. . . . If for a decade, the balance is uneven, there are more women than men, I think that in time that will even itself out. I mean, after all, for centuries we were excluded, not only from the cantorate, but from everything." An ancillary question is whether women are or will be underpaid or be underachievers if the field is considered a female one. The American experience of women entering professions shows that "systematically, they were paid less, advanced more slowly, and regarded with less esteem" (Glazer and Slater 1987:11). Horowitz says no: "As far as I know, women cantors receive the same salaries as male cantors. I earn more than my husband—did you get that? But that's because I've been at my congregation longer than he has. I know almost all of the women out in the field, and I know what they're making, and I know what my male colleagues are making. I don't think there's any difference whatsoever." Others report different experiences, one women saying she had to leave a congregation due to low pay, "in the student range," since they used the "well, you have a husband line," saying they were doing her a favor to "let me express myself" (J.C.). Men have another perspective on the hiring issue. One thinks that women will gravitate to part-time jobs in smaller synagogues because they have husbands (H.B.). Another has decided that few men go into the cantorate these days because it does not pay enough for men, who feel they should be the primary breadwinner, whereas women are satisfied with less (G.F.).

The truth probably lies in the middle, since the job situation is organized on a synagogue-by-synagogue basis, with wide variation. Let us just examine one corner of one northeastern state, and the differing situation as perceived by two women. One female hazzan feels trapped into her role, sure that if she has a child her congregation will downgrade her status and salary, treating her as "a woman."[15] Just a few miles away, another full-time *hazzanit* (the new Reform term) who is already a mother says her synagogue is remarkably supportive. The difference probably lies in the fact that the first woman's congregation is elderly, hence more conservative on women's issues, while the second hazzan's workplace is a suburban temple with many professional woman congregants, one even being instrumental in introducing statewide maternity leave. A third young woman simply assumes that there will be no problem: "I wanted a profession that dealt with people, where there would be some sense of respect for someone else. . . . I also thought that it was a good profession for a woman, that I could still be a mother someday and have a home, and yet still have a wonderful career that would give me enough time to do both" (H.I.). She already has a somewhat maternal approach to her work: "I love taking a kid that comes to me, who's angry, who's anti-this and anti-that, who's already involved in hard rock, and already deciding upon his future with the influence of other teenagers. . . . I guess I must attract them, because by the time that their bar or bat mitzvahs have come along, they really have changed a lot. They look at me as someone they worship and love. . . . They start dressing like me, and looking like me, and talking like me." The quick accomplishment of these energetic young women has changed the American cantorate irrevocably among the Reform, and has begun to influence Conservative Jews as well.[16]

To conclude this chapter on recent change and current conditions in the American cantorate, a quick survey is in order, a kind of group portrait of the profession within the three main branches of American Judaism: Reform, Conservative, and Orthodox. One way to summarize the situation is by the placement situation. For the Reform and Conservative movements, a shortage of hazzanim is evident, but for different reasons. The Reform have experienced a strong move towards traditional Judaism, resulting in a greater interest in hiring hazzanim. A full third of the Reform hazzanim responding to the Project survey reported that their temple had no full-time hazzan five years ago. Placement figures show the same trend:

> Every year we have approximately twenty-five to thirty-five congregations that apply for cantors, and we have no more than half that many to provide congregations. But of that, half already, let us say, fifteen, twenty cantors, half of those are musical chairs. Which still leaves those congregations looking for cantors. [Even though] the salary level of cantors have increased to where they're comparable to the academic field, 40s and 50,000s are pretty good norms (I.H.).

Since the number of students is smaller at the Conservative training program, the problem is even more acute, though the entry of women will presumably swell the ranks soon. Among the Orthodox, both supply *and* demand are down; on the right wing of American Judaism, the decline of the cantorate noted in the last chapter has only accelerated in recent decades. In response to whether there will be any Orthodox hazzanim by the end of the century, one Orthodox hazzan was glum: "I don't know. First of all, the wealthy synagogues, like Fifth Avenue Synagogue . . . Beth-El Temple in Borough Park, maybe it will still keep going. The problem is, they're losing their members. . . . [But] I would say that 90% of the orthodox synagogues in the United States do not have full-time cantors, and 5% part-time and 5% just for the High Holidays. . . . There's going to be a low . . . in which we're going to say, 'hey, the [Orthodox] cantor's gone completely' " (E.A).

Reasons for this decline vary with the subdenomination involved, since scholars distinguish three types of Orthodox Jewish-Americans:

Modern Orthodox, Ultra Orthodox, and Strictly Orthodox (Helmreich 1982). The Modern Orthodox are largely made up of professionals who "participate fully in the larger society. . . . [T]hey are observant in that they eat kosher food, abstain from work on the Sabbath, pray every day and celebrate Jewish holidays as prescribed by Jewish law" (Helmreich 1982:53). For these people, who have either rediscovered or recently turned to a very traditional Jewish way of life, the hazzan is largely irrelevant; they tend to organize their synagogues on an egalitarian basis. The situation is well described in Samuel Heilman's classic 1976 study of one such congregation, which he calls Kehillat Kodesh: "At Kehillat Kodesh which, unlike larger, more affluent congregations, has no professional cantor to lead prayer, all male members take turns in the role. Unlike the gabbai [a key organizing functionary] and the president, the cantor is a relatively temporary role. . . . Essentially the role of hazzan requires that a male above the age of thirteen stand at one of the two pulpits and lead the congregation in prayer. . . ." However, the communal feeling that lies at the core of membership does not allow a designated hazzan to dominate: "As he leads, he is also led; the interactional interdependence between congregation and hazzan is thus perfectly synergetic. . . . In a sense, the members become quasi-hazzanim, in that they anticipate not only the words but often the tune which the hazzan traditionally uses at the ends of prayers. . . . [E]very quasi-hazzan, no matter how inspired, blends his voice into the general hum of the congregational prayer" (Heilman 1976:87–89).

So lack of a professional hazzan is not a matter of money, but of an ideology based on nonhierarchical group feeling: "The shul is a dynamic rather than a static reality, a fluid and shifting structure made up of a series of interlocking involvements and activities" (Heilman 1976:214).

The second branch of right-wing American Jewry, the Ultra Orthodox, has other reasons for not needing the hazzan. This group consists of Hasidic sects based on the teachings of charismatic rabbis who formed "dynasties" around "courts" named for their European place of origin (Satmar, Bobov, Kotsk, etc.). The Hasidim have never been interested in the hazzan, since they rely on their spiritual leader, the *rebbe*, and tend to view the hazzan as an unwanted leftover of normative eastern European Orthodox Judaism. The Hasidic ba'al tefillah may be a very soulful singer, for the Hasidim highly value music as a direct channel to holiness, but he is not a professional or an ordained musician.[17]

The third category of right-wing American Jew, the Strictly Orthodox, are more scrupulously observant than the Modern Orthodox, but are not Hasidic adherents. They tend to be heavily influenced by the atmosphere of the yeshiva, the intellectual religious day schools based on the Lithuanian model, which grew dramatically in strength and influence in post–World War II America. In yeshiva life, learning comes first and the aesthetic, perhaps sensuous, leadership offered by the hazzan is not likely to be valued.[18] Indeed, for some of these fundamentalists, "hazzan" is a pejorative term, and the sacred singer is the butt of jokes.[19] Thus none of the branches of contemporary Orthodoxy favor the cantorate, a sharp shift from the immigrant synagogue's total absorption with the mystique of the sacred singer.[20]

It is time to move from the unfolding of the cantorate to an analysis of its inner workings, to the interplay of hazzan and worshippers and the internal feelings of the sacred singer, facing a congregation and perhaps God. Remember that the institution of the cantorate really has no inherent history, being subject to rapid and decisive shifts initiated by a volatile constituency. It is the story of improvisation and self-definition carried on synagogue by synagogue, hazzan by hazzan, with immense latitude for local tastes and interests. So we end our time-based survey here and begin our examination of the variety and complexity of being hazzan, anytime and anyplace in America.

NOTES

1. This situation was recently formalized by the May 1987 Supreme Court decision allowing Jews and other nondistinguished minorities (such as Arab-Americans) the right of recourse to antidiscriminatory law.

2. I will tend to move back and forth from national to Jewish trends and countertrends in this chapter, but one should not put too much stock in comparisons. While one respects the Yiddish saying *vi es kristelt zikh, azoy yidelt zikh,* ["as it goes among Christians, so among Jews"], one can always see the Jews going their own way, based on millennia of distancing themselves from coterritorial ways.

3. The following is a stripped-down account of a complex Jewish-American trend; for a close look at some of the "prefabricated" approaches to Jewish commitment among young professionals, see Weissler (1982) and Prell (1987).

4. Ramah is a sensitive issue at many levels, such as the question of whether the hazzanim were frozen out of the planning or chose to stay out of a development they could have influenced.

5. The cantorate's relationship to Israel has a particular poignancy. Both the CA and ACC sometimes hold their conventions in Israel, where they end up seeing themselves as guardians of tradition, since there is no parallel local cantorate with which they can interact. Israel has almost no full-time hazzanim, for economic and ideological reasons. For Americans to represent an "Old

World" to Israelis is certainly odd. At another level, hazzanim will have congregations commission pieces from Israeli composers or integrate Israeli material into their services as a matter of emotional obligation, backed by various degrees of commitment in the 1980s.

6. This tentative conclusion is an extrapolation from the data of Barbara Kirshenblatt-Gimblett's Yiddish Folksong Project, as buttressed by observations in fiction and elsewhere.

7. The increased rigidity of right-wingers surprises even older Jews; in forthcoming research, Jenna Joselit (personal communication) has found that the interwar American Orthodox identified themselves as much socially as in terms of observance, and felt alienated from today's hard-liners. My own work with hazzanim indicates that the Orthodox-Conservative line was vaguer in the second generation than the Conservative-Reform division, a situation totally changed today.

8. Even after the announcement that JTS would admit women, Rabbi Price continued to voice his objections to the legal ruling used to buttress the decision: "halachic jargon is being used to mislead the Jewish public. . . . [I]t is sad to realize that the once great and halachically-oriented Conservative movement now follows the lead of the Reconstructionist and Reform movements" (Price 1987).

9. Until 1987 the Conservatives went only as far as the 1974 ruling that it was theologically possible for rabbis to be able to choose a woman as sheliach tzibbur. The vote was very narrow and few Conservative congregations picked up the option of selecting a woman.

10. Indeed, the Cantors Assembly has yet to take its step: allowing women full membership, and sources tell me that rearguard opposition will go on for some time.

11. From the hard-core professional point of view, traditional men have many gripes about the entry of women, even in a tangential area like the role of the clergyman's wife: "The whole idea of women's lib, you know, or the women's movement has caused many more problems for our men because whereas the cantor and the rabbi's wife used to be an integral part of our job, it no longer is. Very rarely today is a cantor's wife or a rabbi's wife involved in the synagogue" (C.G.).

12. The path of women into the cantorate parallels other roads to recognition to a certain extent. Glazer and Slater's 1987 study of the entry of women into four professions shows both similarities and differences to the cantorial model. Their summary remark that "the process by which a group of occupations was transformed into powerful and rewarding professional endeavors occurred independently of women's interests" (4) certainly tallies, as does their observation that "beyond the outright exclusion that kept them out of certain graduate and professional schools, they also confronted more subtle barriers" (11), which may be happening at the moment. Of the four "favored mechanisms for career management" (14) not all are relevant for the cantorate. "Superperformance" does seem to mark the new generation of women, but is not necessarily a help in congregational life; "subordination" does occur, as noted

below; "innovation" is not really open, beyond the novelty of being a woman hazzan; and "separatism" is not possible in this profession as it was, say, in the development of women's colleges.

13. Male sensitivity about the devaluation, as well as the lack of economic competitiveness, of the cantorate if it becomes perceived as a female profession is well-grounded in sociology of the professions: "When a majority of those in a profession are of one sex, the 'normative expectation' develops that this is how it *should* be. The model of the practitioner then takes on the personality and behavioral characteristics associated with that sex" (Kaufman 1984).

14. How favorable the situation "out there" is for Protestant clergywomen is open to question, as is the issue of how permanent the boom will be: "Female graduates are finding initial jobs, as pastors in rural areas or assistant pastors in big cities, but second and third jobs, in positions of greater responsibility, are more difficult to come by. Ms. Lummis predicted that the enrollment of women in divinity schools would soon level off. 'The major increase has already happened,' she said. 'There was such a large backlog of women waiting to get in.' [But another authority] said she expected the number to keep rising. 'There is an awful lot of momentum left to this movement,' she said" (Goldman 1986a). Similar ambiguity about projected feminine progress marks the Jewish case as well. Nevertheless, Project data show that sixty-three percent of respondents among the Reform feel that the profession will be mostly women within ten years.

15. This would follow the old American approach: "exclusion and differential treatment of women were reinforced by the strong societal assumptions about women's place in the home" (Glazer and Slater 1987:13). Whether this remains true or whether certain women have internalized this assumption and act upon it is hard to say.

16. It is hard to say more, in mid-1987. A handful of Conservative congregations did accept female hazzanim before the Jewish Theological Seminary's decision to ordain, but women did not always last well in those jobs.

17. See the interlude for the Hasidic beginnings of some European-born hazzanim active in America today. The infiltration of Hasidic tunes into the standard American synagogue's repertoire in recent years is yet another example of the impact of the revived right wing. Second-generation Conservative and Reform Jews viewed the Hasidim as somewhat embarrassing relics of the past, whereas today mainstream Jews seem to think of the Hasidim as the "authentic" Jews and their lifestyles are lovingly described in publications like the *New York Times* and the *New Yorker*, a sure sign of access to acceptability.

18. The attitude of Conservative and Reform hazzanim towards the Orthodox world runs the whole gamut from respect to revulsion, very largely based on upbringing. Some who grow up Orthodox have made careers in mainstream synagogues partly as a matter of practicality and may still consider themselves "Conservodox," choosing positions where they can stay closest to the Right. By and large, the dividing line is literally that: the separation between male and female seating that marks off the Orthodox world which, conversely, keeps right-wing hazzanim from taking jobs in mainstream congregations, often at

considerable financial sacrifice or at the risk of becoming strictly part-time or amateur.

Not every hazzan brought up Orthodox finds the right-wing context sympathetic; a young Conservative hazzan has provided a down-to-earth explanation of why he would never "go orthodox," despite the apparent allure of singing to an informed group of listeners: "I've had a few occasions to officiate in orthodox congregations, and I've . . . thought to myself, you know, that's really where a cantor can feel a sense of fulfillment, because you're dealing with people who are committed to Judaism and people who know how to daven, and many of them *will* understand the text, and they *will* understand what you're trying to do with the hazzanut. They *will* understand why certain texts are happy and certain texts are sad. But then you go into the synagogue and there's so much noise, and so much talking, that they don't even hear you! And then to make matters even more difficult, they won't allow you to use a microphone. And I don't find that fulfilling. . . . And I grew up in an orthodox congregation. I know what's going on. They talk about the ball game, they tell jokes and . . . they are just as bad as Conservative and Reform Jews about being out of the synagogue by a certain time" (E.G).

19. This attitude probably helps explain the struggle at aptly named Yeshiva University (YU) over the issue of a cantorial training program described in chapter 4. Interestingly, among Orthodox respondents, three times as many hazzanim checked off "private" or "family" for source of schooling, and only two cited the YU program as their sole training. None of these hazzanim had been trained at the Conservative or Reform schools, showing how extensive the sectarian demarcation line has become.

20. One musical result of this stance has been the near-elimination of cantorial music from the Jewish airwaves in New York. Old-time sacred singing has been replaced by new-fangled Orthodox popular styles, ranging from day-school children's choirs through religious rock and roll.

An unidentified early American hazzan in period dress. Photo courtesy of the YIVO Institute for Jewish Research.

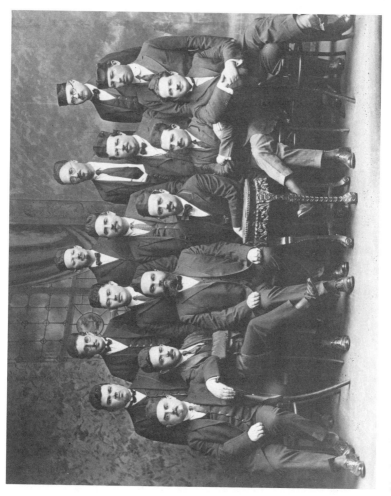

Unidentified and undated group of hazzanim. Photo courtesy of the YIVO Institute for Jewish Research.

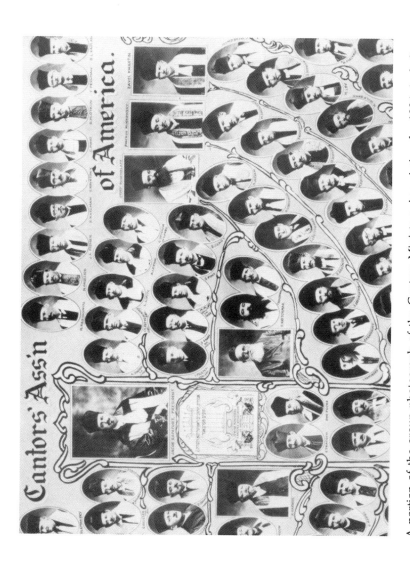

A portion of the group photograph of the Cantors Ministers Association for 1924, including Zavel Kwartin *right* and Pres. Jacob Rapaport *left*. Photo courtesy of the Cantors Ministers Association.

Yosele Rosenblatt, the most celebrated hazzan of the twentieth century, ges-
turing toward Jerusalem, undated (probably late 1920s). Photo courtesy of the
YIVO Institute for Jewish Research.

The Wonder Twins, star cantors, undated. The twins are typical of the family/ novelty marketing of hazzanim in the interwar period. Photo courtesy of the YIVO Institute for Jewish Research.

Moishe Oysher, a star of the Yiddish theater and a celebrity hazzan, undated. Photo courtesy of the YIVO Institute for Jewish Research.

Poster for "The Voice of Israel," a commercial anthology film of cantorial stars, 1934. Photo courtesy of the YIVO Institute for Jewish Research.

Publicity photo from "The Voice of Israel:" Adolph Katchko with the stock choir used to back up all of the film's stars. Photo courtesy of the YIVO Institute for Jewish Research.

Publicity photo from "The Voice of Israel:" Zeidel Rovner with a boy hazzan.
Photo courtesy of the YIVO Institute for Jewish Research.

Announcement for a boy hazzan's appearance, undated. Photo courtesy of the YIVO Institute for Jewish Research.

left Yiddish newspaper advertisement for a concert in Brooklyn by Moshe Koussevitsky, undated. Concerts are listed for both *ma'rev* (evening service) and *sefirah* (period between Passover and Shavout) because tradition proscribed musical events during sefirah. Photo courtesy of Barbara Kirshenblatt-Gimblett.

right Yiddish newspaper advertisement announcing the hiring of the celebrated hazzan Pierre Pintchik: "Bronx Jews! Don't wait until the night of Rosh Hashanah! Already today you can supply yourself with tickets to hear the incomparable Hazzan Pintchik who will pray the High Holidays and say *Selichot* accompanied by the famous conductor Mr. Berish and his double chorus" (undated). Photo courtesy of Barbara Kirshenblatt-Gimblett.

PART II

The Cantorate and the Workplace

6

~~~~~~

Finding a Role

The hazzan shall comply with such directions as shall be
from time to time authorized and enacted. . . .
—1790 job description

The cantor serves as a representative of our congregation
and as a role model of Jewish living.
—1986 job description

Up to now, I have described the cantorate as an institution in motion,
unfolding over the generations of Jewish life in America. From now
on, I will try to present it as a timeless profession, anchored in the
world and the work of the synagogue, though of course the historical
perspective will always serve as backdrop to the ethnographic present.
The following chapters cover a vast range of activities, roles, and choices,
represented by evidence ranging from introspective reflection to statistical survey results. The present chapter portrays the many shades
of meaning packed into the phrase "servant of the congregation" as it
applies to any place, any time in American history. Seemingly simple—
the traditional "messenger to God"—the job of hazzan turns out to be
extraordinarily rich in cultural, social, and personal symbolism, ne-
gotiated between the congregation and its chosen voices.[1]

The basic terms of agreement are already quite clear in colonial times:
"Warranted by no hierarchy and graced by no sacrament, [the hazzan]
was simply a layman hired to do a job. . . . The hazzan was in essence
a hired hand who could be penalized—actually fined—for dereliction
of duties" (Marcus 1970a:929, 934). The congregational constitutions
of the times spell out this general understanding, for example, at Shearith Israel of New York in 1790:

> The duty of the Hazzan Shall be to attend at all stated times of worship,
> as hath heretofore been customary . . . and to obey the instruction of the
> parnass presidente . . . and in all things to be considered under the re-
> strictions that the hazzanim heretofore have been under. . . . If the hazzan

should attend on any occasion aforesaid [weddings and funerals] without
such approbation being previously obtained, he shall forfeit to the zadaca
[treasury] for every such offence five pounds (Marcus 1959:190, 158).

It was true for "A Moralizing Layman" writing to the *Occident* in 1847:
"Regarded as a salaried official, whose duties are plainly indicated by
the terms of his contract, the Reader is held to a rigid observance of
mere technical trifles, whilst the greater objects of his service are totally
disregarded. There is a necessity for a thorough reform commencing
at the very foundation of the structure" (1847: 25–27).

But the "thorough reform" apparently never materialized, because
in 1978 we find the power relationship unchanged, and the hazzan
still unhappy with it: "We are led by synagogue leaders who, for the
most part, have only a passing interest in the synagogue, who are
concerned more with upward mobility on the economic and social
ladder; care more about power, authority and financial accountability
than for providing the membership with a spiritual oasis in which they
can renew their lives" (Rosenbaum 1978:49).[2] So there has been no
social shift since the parnas of Newport was called "the ruler of the
synagogue" 250 years ago (Marcus 1959:943). This means that the
hazzan is often at a loss in facing up to employers who represent
powerful, entrenched interests in the congregation and the community:
"I find myself a fish out of water in sitting down and negotiating. . . .
I'm an artistic temperament, not a business temperament. . . . You're
sitting down . . . with a financial wizard, a business person, a person
who's experienced a negotiation—a corporate president, a banker, a
lawyer" (J.E.).[3]

However, as noted in chapter 4, the sacred singer, by virtue of the
office, must possess *some* degree of moral or spiritual authority over
clients or there would be no cantorate at all. However mighty the
balebatim ("bosses"), they may still fear the hazzan's judgement, or at
least look up to the hazzan for moral guidance. The tension over defining the congregant-clergy relationship has produced some of the
more poignant passages in the documentary literature. Here is an eloquent plea for humane interaction by a major mid-nineteenth century
figure, James K. Gutheim, in his inaugural sermon at New Orleans in
1850:

> Mutual knowledge of each other will lead to mutual esteem. . . . Do
> not look upon him [the hazzan] as if he were a spy upon your conduct;
> as if his business were solely that of finding fault with your lives; as if
> he were a monk looking out of his sepulchral den with a green eye upon
> all the things that you hold most dear. He is a man like yourselves, of

the same social affections, the same intellectual perceptions of all that is beautiful in the world around us; of the same general infirmities, incident to human nature. Do not treat him, therefore, with a distant respect, with the cold politeness of ceremony . . . but as one who is to be with you, a sympathizing friend in scenes of trial and of joy, the most thrilling and affecting this side of the grave (Gutheim 1850:77).

This issue of mixed mission, of serving as both role model and friend, is another recurring refrain:

> I'm very conscious of the image that I give to the congregation. . . . I think that they, even though they're my friends and I feel a real closeness to the congregation, there is still a dividing line . . . you're still the cantor and it should be that way. It should be somebody they look up to. When they need you in times of a *simkha* ["celebration"] or in times of sorrow, if that relationship doesn't exist, I think you haven't set a good model for them and you will lose a certain amount of stature and your title as hazzan will not be creditable (C.E.).

> The cantor is . . . a cultural model, he is a religious model, he is an ethical model, he is a model in his community. He has to live a certain way. Not too many of our people do it that way . . . it's a very complicated job (A.A.).

For the hazzan, proof of swaying a congregant, of evoking the proper spiritual resonance, is often the true reward of the profession: "This gal says to me, 'You don't know what you did for me tonight.' I wasn't aware that I was doing anything, so I said, 'what did I do for you?' So she says, 'Well, I've been through Zen, yoga,' and she names a couple of other experiences like that, 'but tonight in listening to you, I really had a feeling that I was glad to be Jewish.' I said, 'O, my God, if I could do that for a few more people, then I haven't lived in vain' " (A.D.).

Hazzanim particularly enjoy the continuity a long and successful cantorial career provides, though it involves an enormous effort on the professional's part:

> Having been there twenty-eight years, I'm so involved in family life. In many cases, three generations I've been involved at birth, bar and bat mitzvah, at weddings even . . . it's really like a large family. Sometimes I find it too much for me. It's a seven day a week business. I would say 80% of the families insist that I be there at a funeral. They call me personally . . . they say "you knew my parents. . . ." Nobody has served this congregation as long as I have. There have been a number of rabbis. The last rabbi, the longest he was there was eighteen years (A.C.).

The many-sided world of work the last few pages presents also gives a sense of stability to the role of hazzan: we are dealing with a powerful servant, with a highly persuasive professional. The balance of this book will focus on the internal world of synagogue life, and on the interior of the hazzan's mind and music. It would be hard to understand those spheres of activity without locating the hazzan within the communal workforce of American Jewry. The hazzan presents a special problem of analysis, being both expressive leader and institutional functionary, and hazzanim have had mixed jobs ever since there have been Jewish communities—there are more tasks to be done than the chanting of prayers. There is the slaughtering of kosher meat, the circumcising of male infants, the marrying and burying of congregants, the visiting of the sick, the giving of sermons, and the teaching of children. Who does all this work? Can a hazzan do it alone as sole clergyman within the synagogue? Is he also a multiple-use functionary in the community at large? If he works with partners, how are co-clergy roles divided? The rest of this chapter surveys these and other questions to fix professional boundaries—in short, when is the hazzan more than a sacred singer? In the nonhierarchical ecclesiastical and communal life of the Jews, there are no "official" answers to these questions—just cultural improvisation dependent on immediate needs, resources, and values. Only by viewing the whole stage—backdrop, wings, and all—can we understand how the social actor plays his part.[4]

Multiple functionary[5]

In 1862 we find Emanuel Marcuson coming to St. Paul after serving in Pittsburgh, Augusta (Georgia), and Portsmouth (Ohio), to be the hazzan, teacher, shochet, and mohel of the community (Plaut 1959:37). The wide-ranging Mr. Marcuson is typical of the garden-variety community functionary of early America. In Utica, New York, in 1851 they hired "a learned Polish Rabbi who wears the national costume. His name is Rabbi Pesach Rosenthal, and he officiates as Hazzan, Preacher, and Shocket [*sic*] and attends to other duties besides" (Kohn 1959:13). This multiple-use dignitary is a figure who never entirely vanished from small-town Jewish America. One hazzan of today vividly recalls his father's work in rural Maine and how it influenced his own beginnings; it is a story that could have been told in eastern Europe or frontier-age America: "[My father's] father was a cantor and shochet and mohel in Poland, and it was transmitted to my father. . . . We had moved to Maine in '46. . . . I would accompany [my father] to the slaughter house, and it was not the nicest sight for a little boy so he would send me outside . . . to sing; he says go out and sing for the cows and the sheep, it's a good way to get started" (I.I.).

Sometimes communal records reveal the brass tacks of this multiple-functionary role as in the case of nineteenth-century Easton, Pennsylvania: "Regarded as a salaried official, [the hazzan's] duties are shochet; conduct school daily for six hours; supervise the *mikveh* [ritual bath] and provide the necessary kettles of hot water; provide a substitute at his own expense during illness or absence; be at the slaughterhouse winters not earlier than seven o'clock and summers not before five o'clock to inspect the meat" (Trachtenberg 1944:145).

Payment for all these duties varied considerably, and contracts scrupulously itemized each, as in this listing of 1846:

> Salary, $100; secretary's fee, $10; teaching fee, 37 1/2 cents a month per child; caring for the mikveh, 18 3/4 cents from each bather; slaughtering, large cattle, 18 3/4 cents each, small animals 6 1/4 cents each; reading the *Megillah* [scroll of Esther] on Purim, $1; naming a female child in the synagogue, 25 cents. In addition, there were small sums to be received for weddings, circumcisions and funerals, for entering the birth and death records in the congregation's books, and for blowing the shofar, an occasional "pre$ent" for a sermon, two tons of coal in winter, and other such bits that were more than welcome to the hard-pressed "spiritual leader" (Trachtenberg 1944:147).[6]

By the 1950s, criticism of the multiple functionary came from the ranks of hazzanim themselves, as professionalization called into question some of the standard practices of earlier times. The leadership of the early Cantors Assembly did not always approve of job overlaps: "It was reported that some of our members are also Mohalim and that they advertise themselves in newspapers and other publications. This is considered a definite violation of our By-laws and not in keeping with our Ethical standards and practices" (CA Executive Council minutes, 3 Dec. 1956).

Despite these strictures, the tradition of being a multiple functionary persists. Some hazzanim still practice as mohalim, one hazzan describing how he learned the skill "in a hospital from doctors," but notes that now it's harder: "you have to go to Israel to train" (E.H.). The same man has also functioned as a rabbi.[7]

Mainstream Americans may have an even harder time than Jews in distinguishing among Jewish clergy, so hazzanim may be asked to perform some surprising roles:

> Cantor [George] Wald [of Sacramento] was awakened at 5 a.m. with a frantic emergency call from the Highway Patrol. The Patrol captain told the Cantor excitedly that a tractor-trailer loaded with 25,000 pounds of Kosher beef ... had been delayed due to blizzard conditions. ... It was

therefore imperative that the "services of a rabbi" be obtained immediately to "bless the meat," the captain said. . . . Cantor Wald was escorted
at breakneck speed to the State Highway Patrol Barracks, where hoses
had been readied for the necessary washing [within the 72-hour limit,
and was] hoisted ceremoniously onto the trailer and the meat was spared
from becoming "trefe" ["nonkosher"] with only minutes to spare ("Calif.
Cantor. . ." 1978).

The notion of multiple functionary offered here extends only to a
combination of ritual duties that include some usually found outside
the synagogue today, such as those of the mohel and shochet. Some
examples above, such as the Highway Patrol saga, show that hazzanim
may also overlap with or take over roles of their colleagues within the
synagogue's walls, such as the rabbi. Another common area of ver-
satility is teaching; even the earliest communities saw education as
basic to ethnic continuity, stipulating it as part of the sole clergyman's
duties. In the last half-century, the teaching role became more complex
with the establishment of supplementary schools as part of the ethnic
pluralism that now characterizes American life. Jews respected the public school for its ability to make their children feel "at home in America,"[8]
but like other ethnic groups, created a network of supplementary schools
to enrich cultural education. Jewish afternoon/Sunday schools, often
located within congregations, mushroomed during the post–World War
II baby boom period, peaked in the early 1960s, and have declined
dramatically ever since.[9] This is far cry from the late 1940s, when the
Reform movement confidently declared it was producing "cantor-ed-
ucators" at its new School of Sacred Music. This hybrid functionary
was thought to fill two congregational needs:

> Two problems faced by an increasing number of Reform congregations
> are, first, how to enhance the beauty and emotional appeal of worship
> services, and second, how to secure much-needed assistance for the rabbi
> of the medium-size congregation in his increasingly burdensome duties.
> These are being solved at once through the addition to their staff of a
> new kind of functionary, called a Cantor-Educator, a product of the School
> of Sacred Music of the Hebrew Union College-Jewish Institute of Religion
> (Franzblau 1955:20).

To get a sense of how important being an educator was a generation
ago, here is an account by a veteran hazzan of the rise and fall of his
hazzan/teacher role:

> I taught. In the beginning it was like a little Sunday school set-up, or
> red schoolhouse set-up when I first came in '48. Then we expanded; the
> kids started to move in. In 1950 we build a brand new school building.

I don't have to tell you what happened to [Long] Island. Already a suburban area, [it] began to expand. The first thing we did do was build a
religious school. After a religious school we built a second story on to the
religious school . . . the lower floor was in 1950. '57 we put up the second
story. Ten years later we first built another sanctuary—we took care of
the kids first. I taught thousands of bar and bat mitzvahs. . . . And right
now it's back again to where it's becoming a small community again. . . .
There is a return, but not to Conservative Judaism. . . . I think it's going
to kill Conservative Judaism until they wake up (F.A.).[10]

Of course, there are still mainstream congregations with thriving
Hebrew school programs; teaching music for Sunday schools is still a
job requirement in many places. A very special variety of teaching,
bar/bat mitzvah preparation, continues to occupy a significant percentage of a hazzan's hours in the workplace (see chapter 7).

Seeing the hazzan as a ritual functionary with multiple roles, both
within the community and in the congregation, provides one perspective on the job. We turn now to the situation within the synagogue
itself: Is the hazzan the only clergyperson, or part of what is today
called a "clergy team" (rabbi plus assistant rabbi[s], hazzan) or "professional staff" (rabbi[s], hazzan, bar mitzvah teacher, Hebrew school staff,
etc.)?

Sole clergy

In early Jewish-American history, the hazzan wore all the hats, not
only leading services as the "messenger of the congregation," but also
acting as the synagogue's representative to the Jewish and non-Jewish
community, the job the rabbi now holds. Despite radical change, the
concept of the hazzan as sole clergy has not disappeared. Occasionally,
a small congregation will still hire such an individual, as noted by the
Canadian court decision validating the hazzan's clerical status: "The
evidence indicated that in certain smaller congregations where there
might be a choice between having either a Rabbi or a Cantor, in many
cases the congregation would choose to have a Cantor without the
Rabbi" ("Canadian Court on the Legal Status of the Hazzan" 1974:38).

Small communities in the United States also used to make do with
whatever type of functionary they could manage, often on a part-time
basis, as in these memoirs of a contemporary hazzan about his uncles
(as earlier, Maine is our example of a remote, clergy-poor area):

They were paperhangers and painters. To them, that was their vocation,
but they loved being a hazzan, so whenever they could, they would go
out of town, on a weekend. They were from New Haven. They would
go as far away as Maine, Pennsylvania . . . the long distance was really

on the High Holidays. My uncle's very proud of being the cantor of Old Town, Maine. That's a little town up near Portland. *And he did everything.* He was their rabbi, their cantor, their Torah reader. A cantor did everything in the old days anyway (E.A.).

Another hazzan still active today remembers functioning as a hazzan/rabbi at age twenty-two. He was such a good preacher that he attracted crowds (E.H.).[11] Barring such exceptional hirings, today hazzanim tend not to have a stake in being sole clergy, since they could have trained as rabbis.[12] We are fortunate to have an essay on the subject by a contemporary hazzan:

> How does a cantor find himself in the position of being alone for a year? It can happen in a variety of ways. A rabbi can retire and not be replaced immediately. A rabbi can go on sabbatical without an interim rabbi being appointed. A search committee can take longer than anticipated in finding a suitable replacement for a departing rabbi. There might even be a situation where a newly formed congregation without the means to support two clergymen opts to hire a cantor first. It has happened! (Freedman n.d.b).

In Stephen Freedman's case, it was his search committee that moved too "deliberately" in finding a replacement. Freedman found himself fully in charge, a valuable learning experience:

> [Another effect] of being without a rabbi was the opportunity to interact more intensively with my congregation . . . but there was a drawback to this increased contact. Because there was no other full-time religious leader, I *had* to be there when needed. . . . I had to accommodate to the best of my ability the many and varied needs of our 750 families. . . . I learned an awful lot about the physical plant. I now know the location of virtually every light switch, thermostat and fusebox. . . . I also learned about the political machinations of the synagogue. I dealt with committees with which I had not had to deal previously. . . . I will certainly remember the fourteen and sixteen hour work days, the seventy and eighty hour work weeks.

What Freedman found out is that the rabbi may get even closer to the basics of congregational life than does the hazzan, and that with greater contact comes increased responsibility, not necessarily more power. After all, both rabbi and hazzan are servants of the congregation. When it comes to a final evaluation of the experience, he remains equivocal: "Was this 'year without a rabbi' a dream come true or a nightmare? It was both, to be sure, an experience never to be forgotten and, hopefully, never to be repeated!"

Freedman's situation was certainly a difficult one for a young hazzan. The more common way the sacred singer becomes the sole clergyman is through the cumulative effect of his personality over time, eventually causing the congregation to view him as *the* pillar of the synagogue. This can happen to any hazzan who stays at his post for thirty years, as several veterans testify, and has happened in the past as well. Reuben Rinder (1887–1966) of Temple Emanu-El, San Francisco, was one such giant:

> He served as the congregation's spiritual leader while [Rabbi] Meyer was in France at the end of World War I. After the rabbi's death, in 1923, he undertook the pastoral duties of the Temple for more than a year until the arrival of Louis Newman. But even when both the rabbi and the assistant rabbi were in residence, it was frequently the cantor upon whom the congregants called to perform marriages and funerals, to counsel the troubled and visit the housebound. His exceptionally long tenure—more than half a century of service at Emanu-El—accounted in large measure for his being asked to perform rabbinical functions. . . . The rabbis, towering figures though they were, came and went. Rinder remained, seemingly forever, as the presence signifying continuity (Rosenbaum 1980:107).

It seems the formula for cantorial predominance is length of service plus charismatic leadership. However, such situations are rare; what most hazzanim today return to again and again is the more common situation of sharing power with the rabbi.

Co-clergy

In Jewish tradition (both historically and today), congregational jobs can be clustered or left single, one to a person. The notion of co-clergy is a flexible one, responding to the spirit of the times or just to immediate needs, like the sole clergy situations just cited. Even the American court system has recognized the problem inherent in clarifying roles in the heat of actual practice: "An ordained rabbi may very well perform cantorial functions for his congregation. He would not thereby change his status to that of a cantor. A cantor also may carry on for a congregation certain religious duties usually assigned to a rabbi. The cantor does not thereby become a rabbi. Each retains his separate status. Each qualifies for recognition of his special status within the Jewish religion by education and training" ("A Landmark Case" 1973:24).[13] There are two kinds of co-clergy situations. One involves the sacred service, which may be parceled out to more than one prayer leader, briefly detailed here, while the other is the rabbi-hazzan interface, which takes more time to discuss.

The eastern European immigration brought with it the idea that the hazzan—the star of sacred song—did only the "juiciest" parts of the service, from the point of view of aesthetic and emotional impact. The more mundane sections of the ritual could be given over to lesser lights.[14] The most general term for a garden-variety reader is *ba'al tefillah*[15] ("master of prayer"), yet the very simplicity of this role is deceptive. Many hazzanim of yesterday and today take pains to point out that the basic chant provided by the ba'al tefillah is the cornerstone of the cantorate, the foundation on which the hazzan builds his lofty sonic structures. As one hazzan puts it, "I don't know if I'd rather hear a good hazzan or a good ba'al tefillah" (E.H.). As indicated in chapter 1, superstar Zavel Kwartin credited a handful of small-town Ukrainian ba'alei tefillah with being the wellspring of his music. Leib Glantz, another giant, said that he had to listen to the layman in charge of services to hear "the real thing" (B.J.).

The ba'al tefillah is often a true layman, simply a "first among equals" who knows the seasonal settings and favorite tunes (what hazzanim call the *nusach*) of the service and is always ready to lead congregants informally, in the manner of today's Orthodox prayer leader as described in chapter 5. In earlier times, the very useful position of ba'al tefillah was variously handled. A local amateur or semiprofessional might do the introductory section of the Sabbath service (*psukei dezimrah*). The following section, the *shacharit*, might still have been too ordinary for the specialized sacred singer, particularly at High Holiday time, so a *ba'al shacharit* was engaged. For the following, elaborate *musaf* section, if the star hazzan was away that week, one would put on a *ba'al musaf* to do the job, who may have been a volunteer or lightly paid servant of the congregation. In addition, someone had to read the weekly Torah portion, so a *ba'al koreh* was called for.[16]

Recently, in the mainstream Conservative synagogue, these functions have often been combined and a single person hired as a "second-string" hazzan, to cover a variety of such responsibilities, including the daily prayers, at which perhaps as few as a minyan are present. This may well be due to the decline of the laity's ability to produce prayer leaders from the mass of congregants. The term for a professionalized ba'al tefillah in recent decades may be *shammash*, using the old term for the synagogue custodian, or might be dignified by the English term *ritual director:* "We have a ritual director. Now our ritual director takes care, basically, of the daily minyan, reading the Torah and . . . he will do the psukei dezimrah, which is the beginning service on Shabbat morning, and he will chant shacharit on Rosh Hashanah and Yom Kippur, mincha (afternoon service), etc., and if I'm absent on occasion, he would fill in. But when I'm absent, there will be no organized choir. . . . He's not equipped to do it musically" (C.E.). A special time for hiring extra staff is the High Holiday period, when Jews who never set foot in a synagogue suddenly descend on the sanctuary in large numbers. This may force the congregation to hire an "overflow" hazzan, or *hazzan sheyni* ["second hazzan"], a term sometimes synonymous with "ritual director":

> We don't have a hazzan sheyni. It's quite unusual for a congregation of our size—we have close to 2000 members. Mainly because I happen to be a very healthy person. I haven't missed more than two and a half or three services in twenty-one years. But we always had somebody on the premises . . . who was in charge of the little synagogue service, which is the daily minyonim, and in an emergency could always be called upon to pinch hit. . . . [For High Holidays] there's a whole other service downstairs. We have two main ballrooms, or shall we call them "overflow services," besides the main synagogue. We have a ballroom that seats close to 1200 people that's sold out every High Holiday, a second ballroom that seats between five and six hundred people [with an added hazzan]. The final selection, at my recommendation, let's say, is made by the committee. It's more like just a . . . ba'al tefillah. . . . The people upstairs aren't as traditional; these are the . . . "three days a year Jews" or "revolving-door Jews" . . . but downstairs in the main ballroom, it's a more traditional synagogue than upstairs (A.G.).

This convenient congregational structure is in serious danger of disruption these days, since the older men who could be "called upon to pinch hit" or serve as "ritual directors" have faded away to Florida or passed away: "The critically valuable ba'alei k'riah ["Torah readers"] and ba'alei tefillah and other secondary synagogue functionaries are dying out and we are doing nothing to replace them. I urge again that summer institutes be convened where lay people could learn the skills of synagogue services" (Rosenbaum 1972:30). This plea of fifteen years back is at yet unheeded, with the lack of Torah readers being particularly critical:

> What we do find that we're lacking a great deal is that the skill of being a Torah reader . . . is fast disappearing. The people who did it are dying out. They were known as shamoshim or the fancy name given to them in local congregations was "ritual directors," because . . . there is a hierarchy. They felt that the shamash was a degrading term, that it really meant being a caretaker for a synagogue. . . . Congregations, when they lose the person they have to read Torah, find themselves in dire straits (C.E.).[17]

This drastic decline in lay-generated specialists represents a radical disjuncture with the past; of course, Orthodox congregations do not face such a problem, as noted earlier.

Of course, the real drama within the synagogue walls unfolds in the uneasy relationship between hazzan and rabbi, a situation that developed after the arrival of European-ordained rabbis in the 1840s. An 1860s description vividly portrays the shift in power from hazzan to rabbi:

> It has been the fashion among many to hold up to admiration, those whom we may call our bishops, supervisors, or doctors of laws [in other words, rabbis] and to disparage equally the more humble laborers who officiate in the Synagogue and the family-circle [hazzanim]. . . . But, while the more learned members of the profession are deservedly honored and, in proportion, better rewarded for their services, it seems only reasonable that the others, who are more constantly in demand, should not have cause to regret that they have devoted themselves to become public servants and teachers. Till lately, they were the only public men among us in all America (*Occident* 24, no. 8, June 1866:105).

From the hazzan's point of view, the rabbi is treated with inordinate respect, following a Christian model: "our bishop." Second, the rabbi is paid more. Thus the hazzan suffers, despite working very hard and being much appreciated by congregants. This American attitude was so entrenched by the 1920s that Zavel Kwartin, at the height of his powers, was hard pressed to squelch the schemes of a young American-born rabbi who sought to trim the hazzan's role. The unfortunate upstart thought he could convince the congregation to cut several prayers from the overlong Orthodox service. Kwartin protested that this would mean "cutting up the *machzor* ["High Holiday prayerbook"] to make modern and dehumanized Jews" (Kwartin 1952:436). Because his High Holiday performances brought the congregation $35,000 in ticket sales, he won the day and the rabbi lost his job.

Kwartin's personal victory was only a temporary one for the cantorate. The role of the rabbi continually expanded in the interwar period, and conflict with the hazzan increased accordingly, particularly as the burgeoning Conservative movement elevated the rabbi to the position he held among the Reform. In 1937 one thoughtful rabbi felt moved to ask for reconciliation between the co-clergymen. Writing a column in a jubilee volume of the Farband, he expressed himself in the elaborate locutions of the much-admired rabbinic sermons of the day: "Jealousy should give way to cooperation. Pride must be crowded out by piety, and vanity make room for consecration, in a mutuality of regard and reciprocity of appreciation" (Schorr 1937:15).

Nearly fifty years later, the Cantors Assembly invited the head of its counterpart organization, the Rabbinic Assembly, to address its convention as part of a new campaign of rapprochement. Rabbinic language again frames the sentiment of reconciliation in Alexander Shapiro's remarks: "All too often, instead of a relationship of common concern and mutual help, relationships between rabbi and cantor have been fraught, in too many communities across the length and breadth of this land, with petty jealousy and ludicrous competitiveness on the pulpit in a world that desperately needs their joint inspiration for the greater good of the Jewish community as a whole." Toward the end of his address, Shapiro shifts to a more personal style, underscoring the human reasons rabbis and hazzanim need each other: "I need the voice that sings, another human being standing next to me, to share with me that terrible, overwhelming loneliness that is part of a life of any human being who seeks to serve the Jewish community."

After all, the rabbi is a congregational servant, just like the hazzan, as another rabbi has pointed out: "The pre-modern Jewish world defined the rabbi as a civil servant, who was a teacher and a sage. The contemporary synagogue defines him as an employee, who is a preacher and a pastor. . . . [T]he rabbi's authority in the synagogue today is only as strong as his hold on the people's affection" (Stanley Rabinowitz, quoted in Karp 1983:246). In other words, both hazzan and rabbi are part of a triangular relationship with the lay leadership, while the mass of congregants kibitzes from the sidelines, as two rabbis note: "The ritual practices of this Congregation have been handed down from Sinai, and neither he [the hazzan] nor I would venture to make any changes. As a matter of fact, if *Moshe Rabbenu* [Moses] would try to tamper with the service, he would immediately be dismissed" (R.B.). "The hazzan is a member of the Ritual Committee of the synagogue and wins and loses votes there no differently than I do" (R.U.).

Job descriptions aside, it is personalities that ultimately set the tone of the relationship, one which may determine the entire mood of the congregation:

> I find a lot of pain when I hear of rabbis and cantors that can't get it together. . . . The congregation feels it too—that's the worst part—the way a child feels when his parents are getting divorced. And you can see their insecurity, and the way they clutch to their parents. I think congregations need very much to look up at their clergy and feel they are secure with one another [but] if they sit up there and they're doing two different things, they're hypocrites . . . because their congregation needs them badly to show them the right way. There's not enough places in this world left to be shown the right way (H.I.).

For the hazzan, the rabbi can be an obsession, as one of its leaders explains:

> I daresay that there is no subject which so dominates conversations, discussions, meetings and seminars of hazzanim as this. No matter where our talk begins, the moment we touch on the things that make us unhappy with our careers, we inevitably fall to finding fault with our rabbis and before long, with all rabbis. . . . Somehow, most of us—even those who have no real complaints—react like Pavlov's dog, and at the first mention of a problem with a rabbi, no matter what the merits of the complaint, we begin to salivate, and chime in with horror stories which we have heard from others (Rosenbaum 1985).

There are two basic sources of conflict in the rabbi-hazzan relationship: personal and institutional. Hazzanim are the first to admit that personality problems can be self-made. One says: "tensions arise out of different reasons—and they're all crazy" (H.F.), whereas another notes that "for every situation where a rabbi has wronged a cantor . . . you can find a situation where a cantor dug his own grave . . . by not being wise, by not using *seykhl* [his head] and some common sense" (E.J.). Similarly, rabbis try to balance their comments, even while complaining about their present colleague:[18] "As bad as he sounds, he's not as bad as the two other hazzanim I've had to associate with in my rabbinate. Lord knows there are plenty of problems in the rabbinate so hazzanim are just one of many. Now that you've heard this, why don't you get him to give a report, too. This hazzan-rabbi business has two sides, you know" (R.P.).[19]

Personalities aside, there is a basic institutional imbalance that aggravates the rabbi-hazzan configuration: salary. The Project data show that of 187 synagogues with full-time hazzanim, only two reported that the two clergy have the same salary. Eighteen percent put the rabbi's salary as ten to twenty percent higher, fifty-eight percent as twenty to fifty percent higher, and twenty-three percent said their rabbi's salary was more than fifty percent greater than that of the hazzan. In a society that equates salary with prestige, such figures reflect a hierarchy within the clergy staff. So it is hardly surprising that this imbalance carries over to fights over turf that spread tension through the corridors of the synagogue. One hazzan even reports throwing sacramental wine in the rabbi's face at a public Passover seder "out in the Midwest" (G.J.), perhaps indicating the level of confrontation that can develop in smaller communities. The demands of the rabbi can sometimes appear ludicrous to the trained hazzan; for example, one rabbi insisting that the hazzan sing, rather than blow, the *shofar* calls for the High Holidays, an extraordinary departure from standard practice. At times the struggle among the clergy becomes intractable and must be referred to the professional organizations for negotiation: "I've been involved in an arbitration suit. It started out in the pulpit with a problem between the rabbi and the cantor, where the cantor was being disturbed by the rabbi who was singing twice as loud as he was, and I do believe he was doing this to harass the cantor. The cantor had been in the congregation eleven years; the rabbi was fairly new. I said, 'look, you've got to win this guy over. You love the congregation and want to stay there' " Yet there seemed no way to bridge the gap: "It became clear to the congregation what was going on . . . and they arranged for arbitration . . . and a rabbinic group was called in and a cantorial group was called in and it was agreed by the rabbis that this rabbi was acting poorly." Despite this victory, things turned out badly for the hazzan: "He won the case but he lost his job. He left his job now, he asked for some sort of . . . severance. . . . My contention was that . . . the man also had to be compensated for the pain he suffered. . . . They've made a financial settlement to this cantor . . . which the arbitrator suggested and now it's up to this cantor to either accept or reject it. . . . I think he should accept it" (C.E.).

The rabbi might see things exactly the opposite way. One rabbi characterizes his former hazzan as a man "of exceptionally strong ego and temperament who defined his role in such an arrogant manner that the congregation would not renew his contract" as opposed to his present colleague, "a warm and humble servant of the congregation" (R.W.). How easily the rabbi invokes that familiar phrase with which we began our survey of the roles of the hazzan in the American synagogue.

The middle ground is probably the norm for most congregations, the ideal being mutual respect. Success may depend either on the hazzan being the senior clergyman, so resting on a secure base of congregational support, or on his or her willingness to acknowledge the rabbi's preeminence: "I worked with three rabbis in my career and I got along with them splendidly, each and every one of them. I understood my role from the beginning. . . . I was raised in that milieu that you respect your elders, that you give *kavod* ["respect"] to your teachers, although I always reserved the right to question and to even occasionally disagree" (A.G.). Or, from a rabbi:

> The hazzan is pre-eminent in the music programming and the structuring of our music in the synagogue. This is in keeping with the general approach of my work in the rabbinate. I favor a "team ministry" where each professional has a defined role in which he is the leader; and he

may co-opt the other professionals to assist him. . . . In keeping with this approach, the synagogue has a five-figure budget for choir and choir director, as well as a separate budget for the purchase of music (R.U.).

Few hazzanim will quibble with the rabbi being the captain of a "team ministry" if the budgetary rewards are so substantial. Nevertheless, music itself can often be a bone of contention. Several rabbinic respondents were far from happy with a purely musical colleague: "A congregation must usually choose whether they desire a fine cantor or a good teacher. They rarely will find both talents in the same person and much destruction can occur both to cantor and students when unwanted arrangements are imposed on both" (R.E.). "Generally speaking, I search for collegiality with the Cantor. My disappointment is with the narrowly focused concerns of a cantorate which concentrates on soloistic interest and is devoid of a larger focus on the community. The image of a Cantor as a teacher of Judaism through the instrument of Jewish music has been suppressed by the image of Cantor as a would-be 'Pavarotti' " (R.K.). "From my own point of view, I find that the whole dimension of music in my synagogue is 'a little much,' too demanding on our budget and on the duration of our Sabbath and Festival services" (R.X.).

Things work much better if the rabbi appreciates the contribution the hazzan makes; some enlightened rabbis are even willing to bask in the reflected glory their hazzanim provide for the clergy staff: "I have congregants that follow me around in groups. My groupies. And he [the rabbi] is proud to know that I've got groupies. I know rabbis that have fired cantors because the cantor became more popular than the rabbi. I don't ever see that being a problem with my rabbi. To him, if I'm good, he's good" (H.I.). Part of the reason for the success of this partnership might be that the hazzan is female, the rabbi male; as noted earlier, this combination sometimes avoids the problems created by the clash of two male egoes.[20] In addition, both are creative clergy and allow time for original work: "I don't see too many rabbis out there that not only let their cantor shine, but know how to create with them. He's a creator, he's a writer. He writes liturgy the way I write music. And together we write beautiful compositions" (H.I.). There can be other reasons for success as well. One rabbi cherishes his hazzan because he can reach a special segment of the congregation: "My cantor now is a young man who is involved on many levels with the lives of the younger members of the congregation with whom he is more of a peer than I am. . . . He has been helpful in dealing with family problems, particularly those young couples who relate to him personally. . . . If [he] has assumed a larger role in congregational life, it is because I have encouraged him to do so" (R.W.). Above all, a common sense of professionalism can lead to harmony: "The rabbi is very understanding . . . we had discussions . . . but not an argument. He said, 'when I hired you, I wanted a professional. I don't want people to tell me what I should do. I'm not going to tell you what you should do' " (C.G.).

In the long run, both hazzanim and rabbis are threatened by congregational budgets, as one rabbi thoughtfully explains: "True, the cantorate and the rabbinate in this country have been professionalized, but in the light of increasing expenditures and declining income, is the American Jewish community better served by these full-time practitioners or can just as much be accompanied by part-time, more efficient clergy?" (R.L.).

This chapter has examined all sides of the multiple functioning of the hazzan in American communities and congregations. The relationship with the rabbi leads into the knotty area of synagogue life, a topic which the next chapter details as we move ever farther into the workplace.

NOTES

1. The following description of the twists and turns of finding a role can be, in part, generalized to the role of the rabbi and, indeed, the American clergy as a whole, as one analyst points out: "Recent assessments of the 'roles' of priests, rabbis and ministers list activities and skills which are virtually interchangeable among the major traditions." He sees this in large part due to the laity-centered and voluntary nature of American religion, which "makes adaptation and proliferation in the activities of the clergy a virtue and a necessity. Traditional functions must be adapted to be accepted by the laity, and new functions must be created to win their continuing support" (Gustafson 1963:75).

2. Rosenbaum assumes that synagogues have a hierarchical structure that gives the top—clergy and lay leadership—the ability to set the tone for congregants. While this is generally true, the very casual commitment of many synagogue members may mean they do not notice much of what goes on and draw their own sustenance from individually created standards of spirituality. We would need major research on the contemporary American synagogue to clarify such issues.

3. To a certain extent, such complaints are part of a larger syndrome of American professionals: "There has been a tendency to construct a 'lo, the poor professional' myth, and to see an irreconcilable conflict between the professional and his employing organization. In this conflict, the professional is seen as inevitably exploited, frustrated and stifled" (Barber 1963:26).

4. Here, as in some other places combining the largely male past with the mixed-gender present, I may slip into "he" as generalized pronoun of reference.

5. Being a multiple functionary is a very old possibility for hazzanim, as Landman notes for medieval Europe: "Neither the low salary scale of cantors nor their low status prevented the communities from demanding the services of the cantors in numerous communal activities. . . . The cantor seemed to be the catch-all for all communal activities for which no one else had been designated" (1972:28).

6. The situation held nationwide, as a brief survey will show: Beth Israel, Houston, Texas, 1887 "desires to engage a first-class Reader, Sabbath-school Teacher, and Leader of Choir" (Cohen 1954:31); "Milwaukee's first hazzanim functioned as rabbis, and *shohtim* and teachers, as well as Readers" (Swichkow and Gartner 1963:46). In Chicago in the nineteenth century the "minister was the reader; he had to perform the marriage ceremony; he had to be present at funerals and offer the prayers there as well as in the house of mourning, and he had to act as shochet. . . . Later on, hazzanim were also called 'Rabbi' at times, not officially in the records, but by the people at large, and they were looked upon as such" (Gutstein n.d.:95).

7. The need to be flexible—to take on extra jobs to make ends meet—highlights the pragmatic side of the being hazzan, historically a major part of the cantorate, as opposed to the idealized, professional-pastoral component so strongly stressed today. In nonaffluent societies, ranging through depression America, the possibility of escaping penury via certain valued skills is always a strong reason for moving into a given field.

8. Moore (1981) has an extended discussion of the way New York's second-generation Jews interacted with and helped mold the public school system. Musically, however, public schools have clung to the "all-American" song repertoire, which means that singing Christmas carols is an area of cognitive, if not musical, dissonance for Jewish-American children. The absence of any ethnic religious music perhaps tends to make the hazzan (and other minority sacred singers) appear more outlandish than if musical diversity were more common in the classroom. Efforts at multicultural music-making usually stay within the politically safe confines of secular song. Meanwhile, the role of music within ethnic supplementary schools remained unstudied until a pilot project, still unpublished, by the American Folklife Center of the Library of Congress in the 1970s.

9. "Enrollment in afternoon Hebrew schools in the New York metropolitan region is steadily declining. . . . Today the enrollment is barely half what it was at its peak, in 1965—about 51,000 students attending 323 supplementary schools . . . compared with more than 96,000 students then. Nationally, the registration has fallen from a high of 540,000 in 1962 to 220,000" (Hardie 1986).

10. The hazzan just quoted is not the only one to point out the denominational nature of the issue: "Enrollment in the largely Orthodox Jewish day schools has been increasing in the last five years, according to the [Board of Jewish Education]. Most of the afternoon schools are affiliated with the Con-

servative and Reform branches of Judaism and help prepare young people for their bar mitzvahs and bas mitzvahs. . . . Educators give many reasons for the decline, but all say it indicates that young Reform and Conservative Jews are turning away from religion. . . . 'One thing is clear [says the head of the board]: a lack of motivation . . . the kids don't want to be there' " (Hardie 1986).

One family interviewed by the *New York Times* summarizes its position succinctly: " 'I like to watch baseball on Saturdays and don't like feeling guilty about it,' Mr. Lane said. Still, the Lanes wanted Eric to be bar mitzvahed. After Eric had dropped out of Hebrew school, his parents also hired a private tutor. 'He is doing this for me,' Mrs. Lane said. 'Frankly, what he decides to do afterward is his own decision.' Eric has already decided. 'I think I would rather play soccer,' he said, 'or maybe take karate or judo' " (Hardie 1986).

11. This seems to have been an "entry-level" congregation, because he remembers using the Reform prayerbook ("English was better") until he could teach them enough Hebrew to use the Conservative prayerbook, which perhaps explains their interest in hiring a hazzan as sole clergy who could lead services, preach, and also teach them to sing the prayers.

12. One as yet unavailable statistic is the number of congregations that hire only a rabbi, not even putting on a part-time hazzan for the High Holidays, hoping that the rabbi can also sing effectively or not caring whether he does.

13. While the present discussion leads into the rabbi-hazzan situation, I would be remiss in not pointing out that the division of appointees within the synagogue staff was quite complex historically, since it is not altogether clear who should be considered "clergy" by modern standards, or who was just "staff." Two case histories from Savannah illustrate the range of possibilities. In the first, from the eighteenth century, the congregation clearly carved up their service needs among a set of appointees: "[They had] a rabbi or hazzan to lead the service, a *shammash* ["sexton"] to administrate and handle the accoutrements necessary for prayer and religious observance and to be responsible for the building and properties; and a mohel/shochet to circumcise male children, as well as to arrange for kosher meat. Other religious 'offices' could be delegated to the laity: the *ba'al tekiah* ["shofar blower"] . . . the *hatanim* (those who read the blessings over the Torah at the Simchat Torah Festival) . . . and the *gabai* (the individual who assigns honors to congregational members who pledge free-will offerings [to the synagogue] in return)" (Rubin 1983:47).

However, during the Civil War/Reconstruction period (1862–71), Savannah was hard pressed to live up to this ideal of a synagogue bureaucracy, and improvised accordingly. There was a failure to lure or agree upon a much-needed hazzan: "Mr. Amram, the shochet, was requested to read the services on Sabbath eve, morn, and Holy Days [for] $87.50 per quarter [while they advertised a salary of $4,000 for a hazzan]. A year later, Mr. Millhauser was requested to act as reader for two hundred dollars per quarter, in addition to his pay as shammash, on condition that he find someone to do the sexton's chores and reimburse the gentleman out of his own pocket 'until we can obtain a regular minister.' [A Mr. Lewin accepted, but resigned after two years due to leading the congregation to Reform too quickly.] Hebrew teacher E. Fisher read the services as the acting hazzan for six months at a reduced salary of $150 per month" (Rubin 1983:47).

The case of Mikveh Israel, Philadelphia, shows an apparently strong interest in a clear definition of jobs: "In the 1798 constitution of Mikveh Israel the positions of hazzan, rabbi, shochet and shamash were specifically mentioned. The hazzan was the chief religious leader, who acted as reader at services, conducted weddings and funerals and was recognized by the non-Jewish community as the 'minister' of the synagogue. The rabbi, not necessarily the same person, was the teacher of the young; the shochet, the ritual slaughterer who supplied the community with kosher meat and fowl; and the shamash, the caretaker of the synagogue and its ritual objects, and a general factotum" (Wolf and Whiteman 1957:244–45).

Despite the bureaucratese of such contracts, American pragmatism found ways to simplify synagogue life: "The board found it a comparatively simple solution for the hazzan to fill the first three posts (hazzan, rabbi, shochet) when possible [and] it was not an uncommon practice to keep such duties within a family, both for convenience as well as for financial reasons" (Wolf and Whiteman 1957:244).

14. This is an old European idea, going back even to Talmudic times, when "the service could be divided into two parts and could be conducted by two separate individuals . . . the first reader . . . recited the morning service (*Shacharit*) on the Sabbath and holidays while the second reader chanted the Additional Service (*Musaf*). The office of this second reader was considered higher than that of the first" (Landman 1972:28).

15. As indicated in chapter 5, it is entirely possible today for a congregation to decide that all they need is a ba'al tefillah, particularly among the Orthodox; the present discussion takes up mainstream congregations of past and present that opted for multiple sacred singers.

16. In early times in Europe, "part of the cantor's duties included his reading of the Scriptural portions. This was true in many, many communities" (Landman 1972:31). However, the decline in Jewish "literacy" has meant that not all hazzanim today can undertake this job. Nevertheless, the ba'al koreh, the Torah reader, is indeed crucial, because all Conservative and many Reform services demand someone with the highly specialized skills of interpreting the diacritical marks over the words on the Torah scroll in a correct, melodically informed way each and every Sabbath.

17. Responses to a 1982 Cantors Assembly questionnaire detail the way this gap is being filled: "Nearly two-thirds of the respondents claimed that their congregation does not hire Torah readers. Rather, they depend upon the service of the trained layman (teens, adults), rabbinic interns, sextons, as well as the skills of the rabbi, cantor, and ritual director. The typical ba'al keriah is a male, either 24 or 65 years of age (an equal number of each). His remuneration for reading on Shabbat ranges from $35-$50, whereas full-time Torah readers . . . may receive anywhere from $6000–25,000 annually. . . . Half of those surveyed have between 1–5 individuals able to function as ba'alei keriah; over 20%,

between 15–20 people; and only a handful (5%) of congregations have 50–75 Torah readers" (Cohen 1984:51–52).

Where do the newly trained Torah readers come from? As usual, there is a very mixed answer. "One-third of the respondents [hazzanim] trained all of their Torah readers. On the other hand, there are an equal number of hazzanim (33%) who have not trained a single Torah reader" (Cohen 1984:51–52).

18. It is thanks to a commissioned survey of 1986 by Abraham J. Karp that I have been able to quote rabbinic opinion about hazzanim. Thirty-four of seventy-nine rabbis contacted responded, representing a wide range of opinion; they were asked general, rather than questionnaire-like questions and were promised anonymity.

19. Rabbinic accounts of hazzanim, as reported in the Project survey, are understandably contradictory in the light of the ambiguity of power-sharing and of division of labor; thus one rabbi reports that "I have the final say, and he defers to me," but also observes that the hazzan "is a colleague who can officiate in the Rabbi's absence" (R.D.).

20. The possibility of a male-female split of power over ritual expression exists in other American religious contexts, such as the "ministry of music" within the Church of God in Christ, as analyzed by Barbara Hampton (1985). In these churches, "labor segmentation along gender lines occurs throughout the church hierarchy with men and women having different, complementary roles," one of which includes women functioning as "Ministers of Music" alongside male pastors. There is a cap on upward social mobility of these women, based on "the congregations' social charter myth on male-female relations." Thus since the ideal women is modest, "few women will become proficient gospel instrumentalists." Institutionally, these ideals are also embodied in church rules: "A musician can occupy no more than the second highest position unless s/he becomes an ordained minister—a status proscribed for women."

The Jewish case has been more radical, in that women were totally excluded from almost all traditionally male ritual domains until the present generation, and have leaped directly into leadership roles—both musical and pastoral—the transitional period lasting only a decade or two, depending on denomination. Whether this is because American Jewry is more quick to shift its ground as a result of outside influence (here the women's movement) or because its largely upper middle-class membership tends naturally towards liberal views about women, is a matter for sociologists to work on; data from white Protestant churches would help here.

7

Defining a Job

To get a job as hazzan, someone has to be offering one. In earlier decades, this was done by newspaper advertisements, or even by word of mouth in a huge community like New York. Aspirants would turn up at the synagogue for a *probe* ["try-out"], which could be a traumatic experience. One hazzan remembers the probe as a form of entertainment for teenagers tending towards the cantorate. In the 1930s, he and a gang of friends would check the ads in the Yiddish press, get dressed up, and walk "all over New York" to hear hazzanim try out for jobs: "You'd walk into a synagogue and see about a hundred cantors sitting waiting in line with numbers like in a chain store. . . . [T]he *gabbai* ["warden"] would stand at the side he would take the *machzor* ["High Holiday prayerbook"] and he would just flip it to a page and say: 'sing!' And then right in the middle of your word, if you didn't make it, he would say *'zol shoyn zayn genug!'* ["enough already!"] Enough. Leave us your name and address" (B.H.). This situation lasted right up to the founding of the professional organizations. In 1949 another hazzan described arriving for an audition in Brooklyn and finding the whole synagogue full: "He was impressed that so many congregants had come to hear him try out for the job. He asked one dignified looking gentleman in the back row where he should go. . . . He was abruptly told to find a seat wherever he could for all those in the Sanctuary had come to apply for the job" (Orbach 1975:3).

This description was provided by a president of the American Conference of Cantors to show the progress the profession had made in placement matters. The rise of the Cantors Assembly and the ACC has meant that placement has shifted away from mass auditions or deals with managers[1] to a matchmaking process between a placement committee and a search committee. The associations try to exert maximum leverage on congregations to live up to basic salary and benefit levels. Synagogues tend to stress their shopping list of anticipated duties, because they expect anyone receiving such support to put in long hours of versatile service. In the sense of specifying duties in exhaustive detail, congregational expectations have not changed since the nineteenth century; for example, here is the 1849 list of duties at Anshe Chesed, New York, where Leon Sternberger was told "To perform the celebration of marriages provided that he has received the written permission thereto from the Board of Trustees and at such celebration to wear his silk cloak. . . . To read on Friday night from *Lekhu neranena* [an opening prayer] until the service is over" (Grinstein 1947:484). A current congregational list of expectations can be just as specific: "A de-emphasis on the organ and the professional choir in order to promote overall involvement. . . . It would be expected that the Cantor would use the Sephardic Hebrew pronunciation. . . . The Cantor will lead services each Friday night and Shabbat morning, as well as all holidays."

Many details of the working life used to be spelled out more concretely than today, when on-the-job improvisation has taken the place of itemized strictures; indeed, only one-half of congregations polled reported using a standard list of job requirements for hazzanim. Nevertheless, areas of competence are often the same as two hundred years back, and criticism for infractions can be as cutting as ever. Take the case of errors in reading Torah. In 1790 it was handled this way: "It shall be the duty of the chazan to peruse the parza ["portion"] of the week in the same sepher torah ["scroll"] which is to be read the succeeding Sabbath or holiday; and that he be allowed 2s.6d for each error he may find out and correct in the same, by the owner thereof, and pay a fine himself of 5s. for any error that may be discovered in the same when read in public by any person" (Marcus 1959:191).[2] In the 1970s, the same issue may arise on the job, rather than in the contract; the results may be just as devastating to a rookie hazzan: "It was a difficult year. I had to read Torah every week. Although I was good at it, in the beginning of the year it took me fifteen hours a week to prepare. . . . Afterwards the rabbi would come over and not in a mean way, in an instructive way, say, 'You know, you made six mistakes this morning, and these were the mistakes.' His intention was positive: it was to increase my knowledge, but it wasn't—they watched my corpse" (D.B.).

The lesson here is that contracts are only guidelines; practice is what counts, when the congregation and its servant take each other's measure and work out a compromise—or fail to. Several sources mention increased mobility among today's younger hazzanim, who may lack the *zitsflaysh*, the stick-to-it-iveness that a clergy position requires. The shortage of professionals makes it possible to move around more freely than in earlier decades, and a young hazzan may even choose to drop in and out of the calling.[3] Dissatisfaction may simply be the result of a number of small issues:

> We did not agree on how to do things. . . . I think Hebrew should be properly accentuated. . . . Well, they weren't so convinced about that; they want the bar mitzvahs to chant as much of the service as they possibly could whether they knew what they were doing or they didn't know. If they didn't know, the rabbi would stand at his pulpit and reproach the kid through the services and it really was disgusting . . . and I kept fighting against it. And my predecessor . . . who was not a formally trained cantor had them doing Saturday morning service with sheet music, and I said no, only from a prayer book. . . . We had a lot of disagreements, and so it ended in the middle of the year. . . . I came back and spent the remainder of that spring with my parents, worked as a sound technician for my friends' rock band . . . and then I got a position where I am now (D.B.).

The lack of agreements on the noneconomic aspects of the job partly explains why the associations' model contracts and guidelines spend more time on the question of length of vacation and amount of severance pay than on details. For example, the ACC's statement begins with generalities: "Duties. All cantors exhibit a unique combination of special talents and abilities. The Duties herein described will therefore reflect the *general* areas of concern, the *unique* talents and abilities of each cantor, as well as the special needs of each congregation." On the Conservative side, the United Synagogue, the denomination's umbrella group, leaves it up to the rabbi and hazzan to work things out: "The Cantor shall also serve, in consultation with the Rabbi, the religious pastoral, cultural and educational needs of the congregation" (United Synagogue of America 1973).[4]

The Cantors Assembly's advice to job candidates crisply enumerates what the modern professional expects in a contract:

> It would be well that you take along with you as a guide for discussion during negotiations, the simple headings of the various topics as a reminder. These are: duties, length of term, renewal, compensation, pension, health, Blue Shield and Blue Cross, major medical, illness and disability, housing, vacation, mergers, liquidations, convention costs, moving expenses, arbitration, renewal notices, severance payment, termination, retirement, Freedom of the pulpit, a suitable private office, allowance of time for study and communal and civic activities. Remember, the Cantors Assembly officers and Joint Placement Committee are always ready to help you (Belskin-Ginsburg 1974:95).

Conversely, the professionals seem a bit weary when discussing the congregations' demands:[5] "First when I became active in placement, it was not unusual for a congregation to ask for a cantor-teacher. Always there was a tendency to have what we call a hyphenated job; cantor-youth director, cantor-teacher, cantor-sweep-the-floor, just to say something" (C.E.).[6]

With all this give-and-take between professional and client, it is not surprising that hazzanim themselves do not necessarily agree on what you need to get or keep a job, even in the case of what would seem relatively straightforward: having a "good" or "big" voice, as the following complementary remarks make clear: "If you don't have a big voice, you don't get a big job" (G.F.); "If you have a good voice, you can kind of skirt the other problems" (H.H.); and "When a congregation hires a cantor, it's an audition. That's what they listen to first. Then after they decide 'that's a great voice,' after that moment, that's taken for granted. Now, 'what else can you do?' . . . So that for which they hired you, they put into their back pocket" (I.H.).[7]

This type of discussion underscores the basic gap between the immigrant era, when voice/aesthetic leadership was the prime criterion for success, and today, when what it takes, above all, is dedication to synagogue life: "You have more validity on the pulpit if you know them on a personal basis" (H.J.); and "You know, you can sing all you want, but the fact of the matter is that you can have a cold one week, and you might not sing your best, or it's lovely and it's fun, and it's hopefully helpful to make other people pray and all this, but it doesn't necessarily form the bond which is necessary to be effective in congregational work. I would say: relationships" (G.F.).

The idea that pulpit work, the basic job requirement, is not the most effective means of accomplishing the hazzan's calling today is concisely summarized by one thoughtful professional: "Nobody relates to me through the prayerbook; at best, they relate to the prayerbook through me. . . . I spend so much time getting ready for something that touches people in kind of a hit or miss way. . . . Not only does the service take a short amount of time, but I'm convinced that by the time the people get in their cars, most of the effect is gone. . . . The things that last are the other kinds of human contact I have" (F.E.).

Viewed this way, even the onerous task of comforting a bereaved family can provide particular rewards: "[At a funeral, I had a] very satisfying feeling . . . really directly connecting with people who have a religious need and of being able to satisfy that need [which] I almost never get at a shabbat service" (G.B.). Even those who find this approach alien admit they are not typical: "I don't have an intense relationship with many, just a few. I don't consider the synagogue my life, like a lot of people do. My family is my life. Composing is my life. And the synagogue is my job and I do my job well and that's it. I'm not the kind of guy that goes in for organizational stuff. . . . I'm an atypical hazzan, let's put it that way" (C.C.).

The expectation of "organizational stuff" goes beyond the boundaries of the synagogue: "A hazzan today cannot be just associated with his congregation. He really should be community-minded. How one does it ? Well, he works for [Israel] bonds, he works for Hadassah, he works for B'nai Brith, he works for ZOA, he works for so many other organizations" (J.B.).

It is often the case that the spirit of American religious pluralism puts particular pressure on isolated Jewish communities to be the local standard-bearers of Judaism: "We do between eight and a dozen [Passover] seders a year for churches. . . . [T]here are 164 Christian religious institutions listed in the Yellow Pages [and] just one synagogue, so we're really in the middle of a lot of fairly conservative fundamentalist Christianity, and we do a tremendous amount of interfaith work" (D.B.).

While ecumenical activity is "kosher," other sorts of community commitment can lead to trouble, as the same young hazzan found out:

> The first year I came here, at the end of the year Carter had reinstituted draft registration. We had a large meeting in one of the churches downtown, and we did a mass draft counselors' training. I was interviewed by the local newspaper, and it identified me. . . . The day that the article appeared, I wasn't there; I was scheduled to leave for my month's vacation. I got two phone calls that morning, one from the rabbi, and the other one from the Klu Klux Klan. The rabbi said . . . "leave town, or go away on your vacation" (D.B.).

In this case the rabbi backed up the hazzan, who was not fired, and the two of them continue to be politically active; not every hazzan who goes out on a limb is so lucky. Yet, by and large, congregations are satisfied with their hazzanim, particularly in terms of productivity. The Project survey showed that half of the synagogues reported their sacred singers did "pretty much" what they were hired to do and thirty-four percent felt the hazzanim was doing more than expected, while only seventeen percent felt he/she was doing less than anticipated. Only one congregation out of six said it would be looking for a new hazzan in a year or two, and since much of that turnover is probably due to imminent retirements, the level of satisfaction with present personnel seems high.

Having surveyed basic attitudes and activities, we can turn to the nitty-gritty of the job: the division of the work week into categories of activity, and the hazzan's feelings about each type of work. This is the only part of the Project that produced quantifiable data, the result of a questionnaire answered by 141 full-time professionals, all members of the Cantors Assembly, American Conference of Cantors, or Cantorial Council. One set of questions dealt with the hours spent on each aspect of the job, which are summarized here under four headings: (1) music, meaning time spent preparing for services, rehearsing choirs, etc; (2) education, which primarily includes bar mitzvah training but also includes adult education and Hebrew school responsibilities; (3) pastoral, including attendance at weddings, funerals, hospital visits, *shiva* ["house of mourning"] visits, and other events in the life of congregants; and (4) clergy, which describes hours of administrative work within the synagogue. Because a large number of synagogue presidents (210) also answered a Project questionnaire asking them how hazzanim spend their time, we have a control on the sacred singer's report from the lay leadership point of view. Of course, both sets of responses are hardly definitive, because the hazzanim were asked to estimate time, not punch a clock to register hours spent, whereas the lay leaders were asked what they thought their hazzan *ought* to be doing with his/her time. So what the descriptions below represent is the professionals' guess about their workload and the clients' ideal of what the clergy's work week should be.[8]

Music

Full-time hazzanim apparently spend few working hours on what might have been thought to be the core of their work: music-making. Not counting the time spent on the pulpit, the average respondent spends about five hours a week preparing for performance, with nearly forty professionals saying they spend no time at all on this work sector. There is congregational agreement on this, since the average lay leader's figure was also five hours, though none suggested the zero-hour figure some hazzanim reported. Because later chapters take up the nature of pulpit work and musical organization, this category needs no further comment here, except to point out a further subdivision within music-making: "choir and other chorus groups." This is vague, since a certain amount of choral work may prepare a specialized ensemble for performance at services, whereas other groups may be more recreational in nature. Both congregations and hazzanim report and average of three or four hours a week expected or spent on this branch of aesthetic leadership.

Education

There is a fair amount of agreement between professional and client as to how much time it takes or should take to teach, though the lay leadership on average expects about sixteen hours a week versus the twelve generally reported by hazzanim. Again, an important difference is in the zero category, where a significant number of hazzanim, but very few lay leaders, report no hours spent on education. Apparently, teaching takes up a large part, the lion's share in some cases, of the work week. Hazzanim talk about this aspect of the job in interviews, because most of the hours involve taxing one-on-one interaction in the form of bar/bat mitzvah instruction. The reaction to this situation is extremely varied, partly due to temperament but also to demographics: the number of children per year who will reach the age of thirteen in a given congregation. This may have to do with the makeup of the membership. Is this an old-timers' synagogue slowly drifting towards Florida, or a congregation on the edge of suburban spread during a baby-boom period? If the latter, the numbers of children processed can be monumental: "When I came . . . in 1963 we had 119 bar mitzvahs the first year, not including about 25 bat mitzvahs, and that kept on for eight to ten years, always over 100 bar mitzvahs every single year. I hate to use the word, but it was like a factory. . . . We had close to a thousand children in our Hebrew school in those days that I had to work with . . . on an individual basis" (A.G.).

The essential quality of doing bar mitzvah work is the intensity of the personal relationship, as one senior hazzan who has done over 1,800 bar mitzvahs in thirty years at one synagogue points out: "The cantor, if he takes his job seriously, is the only one in the synagogue who meets with the child on a one-to-one basis" (B.G.).

The hazzan's response to this very demanding job requirement, then, may vary with a number of factors, including how much he/she has to handle personally. In many congregations, there are assistants, "preparers," so that the hazzan only has to put the finishing touches on the child's performance. While the workload probably dictates the professional's attitude, personality also plays a large role, as the following contrasting accounts of bar mitzvah work by two veterans show:

> I would never give up the teaching of kids, because that's my contribution and my way of embracing and being an integral part of this congregation. These kids grow up and remember me and I've endeared myself to them. . . . What I'm doing is trying to instill some kind of image of myself as a religious being who can be a friend, who has a commitment to Judaism, that I'm not an old fogey, that I'm not square, that I'm aware of the world around me. . . . What I want to do for that kid is make him

feel that when he walks into any synagogue in the world, that he's gonna walk in and feel right at home (C.E.).

I find that in 98% of the cases . . . after the bar mitzvah you don't see the family, you don't see the kids, and all those hours and hours of study really . . . were in vain. And I feel there should then instead of that there should be more perhaps study of the text, biblical text, Jewish history, of current issues, and that would be more worthwhile than to try to drum into a kid hours and hours and hours of a *musaf* service of which he does not understand the meaning of the words, even though he may have a beautiful voice. And I think it's really a waste of time. I've come to that conclusion unfortunately after so many, many years (D.S.).

One way of measuring satisfaction through bar mitzvah work is through congregant response. In an earlier chapter, we cited parental letters of praise as a coveted reward; the children themselves may also voice their pleasure, as in this quotation from a school "report on a person who studies and teaches Torah as presented to the eighth grade speech class": "In conclusion, I would like to say that I am really fond of this man. . . . He really makes me feel that he is interested in me and wants me to do well. . . . I'm not sure that my singing voice is good enough, but I might try to be a cantor some day too" (F.E.). The fact that the report is by a girl about a male hazzan, whom she can view as role model, says something about the contemporary situation.

Pastoral

For questionnaire purposes, "pastoral" includes the two areas labeled "hospital and condolence visits" and "weddings, funerals, and other ceremonies." For convenience, "counseling" was also included, because it is a personal-service area as well. Like other job components, pastoral work is extremely variable, ranging from a sizable number who seem to shun it altogether through extremely dedicated individuals who spend upwards of twenty hours a week in close touch with the congregants. The oral history accounts of professional life do show this to be perhaps more a matter of personality than contractual obligation. As we have seen, territorial disputes with the rabbi may also be involved in this category, because the rabbi, as the counterpart to the Protestant minister, may consider pastoral work to be his/her turf.

By and large, the demand on the part of the lay leadership is, in this category, stronger than the reported time spent. Synagogues, it seems, would like to see their hazzanim "out there" with the membership, though none imagine such a commitment could take up more than twenty to twenty-five hours, and some think it is not necessary at all.

The average of hours expected—about nine—however, is the same as reported by Conservative hazzanim, and just a couple of hours a week higher than the figure for Reform and Orthodox.

Clergy

There is maximal agreement among the parties that hazzanim neither spend many hours on administrative work nor are they expected to; all groups report under three hours weekly. This probably stems from the rabbi-hazzan difference: the hazzan may make an appearance at committees, but it is the rabbi who runs the show. It is unlikely that many sacred singers thirst for a greater share of the administrative burden, although they doubtless would not mind the accompanying amplification of their voice in synagogue affairs off the pulpit and in the corridors of power.

Although the statistical base for this study is significant, it is not authoritative, because it is the first survey of its kind; it appears here as a guideline for considering the hazzan's workload in all its variety. For what emerges is just that: a diverse work week, placing a variety of demands at irregular hours on the professional. From the ideal of the charismatic aesthetic/religious service-leader through the patient transmitter of ancient chant to children, from the skillful committee member to the consummate consoler and celebrant in the rites of passage, the hazzan is on the job and on the spot throughout the day and the week, as summaries of the workload show:

> The specific musical duties involve me during my so-called working hours, Friday evening, Saturday morning, Saturday afternoon. I do not know too many cantors function Saturday afternoon in the synagogue, but we do have a Torah reading program which I instituted which involves about 400 youngsters that I'm in charge of and responsible for. I don't teach bar mitzvah myself, but I'm responsible for the program.

> There is a professional choir which I am responsible for which sings every Friday and Saturday for the whole year excepting for two months during the summer, and for the holidays there's an amateur choir which I conduct of sixty voices; it's celebrating its eighteenth year now. There's a youth choir each year of about 60 or 65 children which I'm also involved in. . . .

> I get up early. . . . I usually get up at about a quarter to six in the morning. That's when I write. . . . I go to the synagogue and take care of paperwork; it's a large congregation and I have things to do and a secretary to give instructions to.

I'm very involved with families in terms of bereavement, sickness, health; I often call congregants to find out how they are, when I notice they've been ill. I visit the hospital four, five times a week. I am constantly at *shiva minyanim* [services at a house of mourning]—people die—where in other congregations the cantor may not be as involved and the rabbi may not be as involved, but Rabbi R. felt it's very important that we should all be involved very, very closely, and so the concept of a family, extended families, is most of my life now in the cantorate (D.T.).

What changes from job to job is the specifics, not the kaleidoscopic nature of the work experience:

[Starting a new job] I'll be responsible for training some fifty kids during the year for bar mitzvah with two auxiliary staff that I will supervise. Perhaps a prayer class that I will get the kids started with so it won't be entirely individual work. There's an adult volunteer choir which I'll be responsible for, both directing, choosing music, and organizing and the like, hopefully promoting. And apparently some teaching. I'll probably be working with the second grade in combination with the two rabbis of the congregation. And also teaching adult education, and also supervising the music program in the religious school.

Those are just the specific things that are written down. There are certain things that don't get written down that are always included in the job. You always are involved, if not initially . . . in funerals and weddings and, hopefully, *brit millot* ["circumcision rituals"] . . . because you become more involved in the life of the community. . . . One of the things that I have done in other positions that I very much enjoyed is to become involved with basically the geriatric community—old age homes, Jewish old age homes [plus] outreach to the community at large (G.F.).

All in all, it is not easy to summarize the role the hazzan plays. We have seen that throughout history the American synagogue has expected a variety of skills from its professionals, and in recent decades the level of demand has sharply risen, almost to the burden placed on the multiple functionary or sole clergyman in the eighteenth and early nineteenth centuries. To the extent that hazzanim will continue to be popular in the United States, it is hard to imagine that congregations will expect any less of them.

From this general picture, we now move inward, to the part of the job that most ties the hazzan to Jewish history: leading services. Though hazzanim may claim that their heart is not in pulpit work, it is the true testing place; no professional who is inept at running a ritual can hope to keep a job. In the final analysis, despite the routine nature of the weekly service, if only at High Holiday time, all sacred singers feel a special calling, the true vocation of being a hazzan, to which we now turn.

NOTES

1. Being outside the control of the associations, part-time hazzanim may still engage middlemen.

2. In earlier times the absolute obedience of the sacred singer to the lay leadership was also spelled out in terms of fines for infractions, as in the 1790 Constitution of Shearith Israel: "None but *yahidim* ["first-class members"] shall be intitled to the aforesaid prevelidges [*sic*]. . . . [I]f the hazan should attend on any occasion aforesaid [weddings and funerals] without such approbation being previously obtained, he shall forfeit to the *zadaca* ["treasury"] for every such offence five pounds" (Marcus 1959:160).

3. In 1987 the United Synagogue and the Cantors Assembly fell out, leaving placement solely in the hands of the CA, quite a burden for the hazzanim who do professional chores such as placement in their spare time.

4. However, the Project survey showed that mobility is still not the norm; of synagogues that had full-time hazzanim in the last ten years, there is an even chance that they have had only one hazzan. Only nineteen percent reported hiring more than two hazzanim in the decade 1976–86.

5. It would help if we knew more about congregants; if we could answer basic questions posed by Yinger: "What does it mean 'to belong' to a church—is it the sort of segmental contact that one makes with many associations or is it a close personal attachment? How does this vary among the adherents of various religions, among classes, among those with different personal needs?" (1961:163); we know very little even about the Jewish situation in these terms, let along the general American scene.

6. Part of the diversity on the lay leadership side may result from the variety of ways congregations structure the hiring process. The Project survey produced the following breakdown of how candidates are chosen (based on 141 responses to this question): president only—22%; president and ritual committee—6%; president, ritual committee, and special committee—8%; president, ritual committee, rabbi, and special committee—16%; rabbi, ritual committee, and special committee—9%; and rabbi only—6%. All the other possible combinations of the above players, including "all except president," received no mention. Of course, the fact that the questionnaire was addressed to presidents may skew the results somewhat, but the variety of responses is what is important here. Also worth noting is the fact that the average congregant is infrequently allowed input into the hiring process (40% "yes"; 54% "no"), or even systematically asked about attitude towards the hazzan (30% "yes"; 65% "no").

7. This lack of clarity as to what really counts extends to the lay leadership. In the Project survey, synagogues reported the following set of preferences, when asked for the single most important quality in which their hazzan ex-

celled: good voice—38%; all purpose musical organizer/teacher—39%; clergy work—21%. Nearly one-fifth filled in "all of the above." Notably, only two percent checked "Work/standing in the Jewish/general community," indicating the hazzan is not the communal figurehead that the rabbi often is.

8. Denominational differences show up in the data, since the questionnaires were separately addressed to the three professional organizations, but the responses indicate minor, rather than major differences, along the following lines: (1) bar/bat mitzvah training less prominent among Orthodox; (2) "other educational" higher among Reform; and (3) hospital condolence visits higher among Conservative.

8

~-

Life in the Sanctuary

If it comes out from the heart properly, then it will enter
the heart of the listeners.

—C.D.

To make prayer meaningful for whom it is not a *mitzvah*
["obligation"], that's a damn hard job.

—H.I.

The heart of the cantorate is the sanctuary, the sacred space in which
the hazzan and the congregation construct ritual events on a rigorously
regular basis governed by an ancient liturgical and weekly calendar.
By looking at the sacred singer's part in creating and maintaining the
worship service, we will try to probe the heart of the hazzan. We have
discussed contracts and conditions, roles and rabbis, but we cannot
move into the real core of the work until we understand what goes on
in a hazzan's mind preparing for and performing a sacred service. The
present chapter approaches this sensitive issue from the point of view
of the hazzan-congregation interface; part 3 looks at the service from
the point of view of its music.[1]

Being a hazzan is a vocation, and at times this word must be taken
literally: a calling. Some hazzanim feel a sense of mission constantly,
some rarely, but for all it is an issue that infuses at least part of their
work, particularly what happens on the pulpit. The bulk of this chapter
relies on the Project's bank of oral histories, but we need to start with
the tradition's own commentary on the hazzan-congregation relationship: the prayer called *Hineni*. This is performed only at one point in
the year, during the High Holidays, at the beginning of the *musaf*
("additional") service for Rosh Hashanah and Yom Kippur, so it is
placed for maximum effect, since "the liturgy of the High Holy Days
is . . . the most fervent and solemn of all Jewish worship convocations"
(Millgram 1972:226). It is in this season that the impact of the sacred
singer on the congregation is the strongest, both in former times and

in our own.[2] One hazzan notes that while he receives compliments about his musicality for the weekly Sabbath service, on the High Holidays the praise is for the "experience." Virtually every hazzan will concede that preparing for the "Days of Awe" is indeed the most serious ritual work of the year. For many hazzanim over the generations, intoning the words of the Hineni has been the touchstone of feeling for the task of representing High Holiday worshippers before God. The Hineni is extraordinary in being an individual, not a collective, prayer, as the liturgy itself clearly indicates: "Because Hineni is a personal prayer and not part of the prescribed liturgy, it ends with a benediction in which the *shem* (mention of the name of God) and malkhuot (mention of the kingship of God, *melech ha'olam*) are omitted" (Klein 1979:197). Since "the first person plural is the nearly universal voice of Jewish liturgy" (Mintz 1984:414), this singularity of the Hineni is particularly striking. After all, "one is never allowed to forget . . . that a person's prayer is efficacious only because of one's speaking from within one's membership in a community" (Mintz 1984:407). What it means to be a hazzan, then, is to be situated in the innermost layer of the community, singing out from the very core of the congregation as, paradoxically, an individual who animates the collective yet remains a part of it. As we shall see, this insider-outsider duality can create real tensions for the sacred singer.

The Hineni is so central to cantorial consciousness and to the cultural definition of the role that it deserves full quotation.[3] It opens with a simple statement of the hazzan's position at this very moment and of his role as sheliach tzibbur, messenger of the congregation: "Here I stand, impoverished in merit, trembling in Your Presence, pleading on behalf of Your people Israel even though I am unfit and unworthy for the task." Next, the sacred singer prays for guidance, stressing the immense responsibility shouldered and the interdependence of hazzan and congregation: "Therefore, gracious and compassionate Lord, awesome God of Abraham, of Isaac and of Jacob, I plead for help as I seek mercy for myself and for those whom I represent. Charge them not with my sins. May they not be shamed for my deeds; and may their deeds cause me no shame." The following passage summarizes the traditional personality requirements of the hazzan, and God is entreated to remain open to what is now called "my" prayer, underscoring the "magnifying glass" role in which the hazzan concentrates and intensifies the entire force of collective worship, whose heat should now ignite, consuming all blocks to the efficacy of prayer: "Accept my prayer as the prayer of one uniquely worthy and qualified for this task, whose voice is sweet and whose nature is pleasing to his fellow men.

Remove all obstacles and adversaries. Draw Your veil of love over all our faults. Transform our afflictions to joy and gladness, life and peace. May we always love truth and peace. And may no obstacles confront my prayer." In a final peroration, the hazzan appeals to the Lord to accept prayer "for the sake of" the righteous, thus summoning the whole weight of the community to tip the scales in favor of the sacred singer's petition: "Revered, exalted, awesome God, may my prayer reach Your throne, for the sake of all honest, pious, righteous men, and for the sake of Your glory. Praised are You, merciful God who hears prayer."

The Hineni is the only prayer of the entire liturgy in which the hazzan stands alone to address God directly. Though not all congregations and hazzanim include it in the High Holiday services, those who do feel it is a special moment: "The Hineni is a prayer that really gets to me. . . . It really brings you back to your roots as a hazzan, to your roots as a Jew, to your roots as the messenger of the congregation" (G.A.). This feeling cuts across all lines: Ashkenazic or Sephardic, male or female, old or young, full-time or part-time. At times the experience can be literally electrifying: "While I was saying this portion [Hineni] something struck me which started up here. And it was like two insulated wires that went down my back, right to my heels. It was amazing. I was like in a grip and I was tightened and I was chanting here. If there is such a thing as communion with the Almighty, I think I experienced it that morning" (M.A.). But if the hazzan is not galvanized, it can cause real anxiety, as the same singer testifies: "The next year came. A month before the holidays, I know I'm going to be the cantor and I can't wait for that day to come when I'm going to experience the same thing. Flat! The feeling never got to me again" (M.A.).

This experience of an amateur hazzan with the Hineni provides a wedge for entering the internal world of the sacred singer. Over the years, the hazzan must confront his/her own deepest emotions every week, not just once a year. Of course, the question of the hazzan's role seemingly could be answered by the phrase "sheliach tzibbur," but that would only beg the real question: what does it mean to be a "messenger"? The answer varies from hazzan to hazzan and shifts according to where the congregation is on the spectrum of observance. In the Orthodox realm, where each congregant is intensely intoning on his own behalf, the hazzan may be an amateur or a part-timer. Even if he (always male) is a full-timer, he is felt to be no more than a first among equals. Gone are the days of eastern Europe, when a pain-wracked, anxious congregation turned to its virtuoso "messenger" to convert their collective longing into an eloquent and effective plea to the Almighty. As an American rabbi said to an immigrant hazzan in 1948, "Cantor, you're a wonderful cantor, you have a beautiful voice, but—don't cry so much" (I.F.).

When we move to the Conservative and Reform worlds, the decrease in general congregational knowledge means that the hazzan is not just the one who covers for you if you make a mistake, not only the person who can do the prayers more beautifully and effectively, but may be the *only* one who really knows what's going on. This large question of hazzan-congregation interaction can be symbolized physically, since the placement of people in a sacred space is of crucial importance to ritual. Though extensive study of the physical aspects of the cantorate, from the role of synagogue architecture to the choreographed movements of the clergy, would be in place here, lack of data and space will allow just one reference to this important component of the profession. In the synagogue throughout European history, the *bima*, the "platform or table from which the scrolls of the Torah are read," is "the principal influence on the synagogue's plan" and is "the primary focus of attention" (Krinsky 1985:21). The bima stands in relationship to the Ark, or *aron kodesh* (the Ashkenazic term), where the scrolls are kept. While traditionally the bima, from which knowledge flows, tended to "compete with the Ark" (Krinsky 1985:21), part of the nineteenth-century Reform heritage was an "apsed" placement of bima and ark close together at the eastern end of the synagogue. Thus the rabbi and/or hazzan, standing on the bima, instruct and dominate the congregation and control access to the Torah, as opposed to alternate arrangements such as having the bima in the center with the congregants surrounding the officiant, both having to travel back to the Ark to retrieve the Torah. The new arrangement is almost theatrical, as the bima becomes a stage and the worshippers, now in fixed rows, tend to turn into an audience.

An interesting corollary of the bima-Ark dominance, which has become standard among non-Orthodox Jews in America, is the question of which way the hazzan stands. Should the congregation's chosen voice face the nearby Ark, thereby symbolically allowing the congregants' prayers to travel through him/her to the east as the "emissary," or face the worshippers as a leader imparting knowledge and exaltation that flows from the source through the officiant to the masses? One of the key moments in the evolution of the hazzanic role in America was the gradual shift towards facing the congregation, most likely a Protestantization of the choreography of ritual. The available sources do not give us a clear picture of the evolution of this approach, nor is the question completely resolved today, but the way hazzanim talk about the issue can be powerfully suggestive of their inner feelings: "I have never faced my congregation. I have always faced the aron kodesh. I feel that way I'm the sheliach tzibbur and they are a congregation, not an audience. . . . When they built the new building in 1967, there was a whole thing, should I face the congregation, should I not face the congregation. Because we had gone from a small congregation of 185 seats to building a sanctuary which holds 350 with an expansion for another, perhaps, 900 seats" (F.A.). In this case, the hazzan was able to use his seniority to insist on his own way of leading services: "In the committee . . . one guy got up and said 'we're going to tell him that he has to face us.' So then the president said to them, 'No, in this particular case [he] will tell us.' And he was strong enough, and he won out" (F.A.). Nevertheless, this particular hazzan is wily enough to know how to achieve a compromise that will please both himself and the congregation: "So the compromise on Rosh Hashanah, Yom Kippur was, which I like very much, which still dates back to my times in the traditional Orthodox congregation, I daven in the center of my congregation. Where the electric walls open up, they put a platform in the center behind the permanent seats, and my choir is around me" (F.A.). In this way, the hazzan has found a way to echo his childhood synagogue, and quite literally to resonate with his own past in the congregation:

> The music that I use is some of the music which I used when I was a child; it's all by rote. My choir consists of some thirty young men now, and young women, college graduates some married, that started singing with me when they were in my Hebrew school, at age seven and eight. . . . They come back each year for like a sing-in, like, you should excuse the expression, Christmas, the *Messiah*. . . . They say, "if we're not there Rosh Hashanah, we're gonna be there Yom Kippur." They stay at friends' homes—they have to sing in our choir (F.A.).

The care with which this thirty-eight year veteran of the cantorate has composed his High Holiday services is typical of the painstaking efforts professionals make to create a proper atmosphere for any worship service. For Jewish prayer is more than just a set of printed phrases to be intoned ritualistically:

> Jewish prayer is both a text and an experience. As a text, Jewish prayer is a prayerbook, a classical written liturgy, a structure of words and ideas, which, like any text, is open to literary and theological analysis within the terms of the historical periods that produced [it]. As experience, Jewish prayer also incorporates the several means by which the text is brought to life: what takes place in the inner, subjective world of the worshiper

during prayer; the communal arrangements and nonverbal techniques of the practice of prayer; and the contemporary interpretations of the meaning of the text of the liturgy (Mintz 1984:403).

Mintz's elegant summary of the worship situation only implicitly includes the two main components we will be focusing on: the figure of the sacred singer and the fact that prayer is *sung*, is by nature *musical*, in Judaism. This means that the hazzan, if chosen by the congregation, is one of "the several means by which the text is brought to life," and that he/she uses the principal tool of the trade: music. In vivifying the text, the professional has at hand numerous service-building strategies that we will examine in detail below. The key word insiders tend to use for their craft is "balance" in satisfying themselves and their congregants. Satisfaction, traditionally, was defined in terms of *kavanah*: "Whether a person concentrates on the religious message of the words and invests them with emotion and meaning, or whether one prays hurriedly and out of habit while one's mind wanders to other affairs— this is the difference between praying with kavanah or without it" (Mintz 1984:426). Continuing his analysis of kavanah, Mintz points directly to the role of the hazzan without even mentioning the sacred singer: "In a general sense, kavanah indicates the interpretive axis of prayer, that which is heard and meant when the words are uttered, and how that meaning changes over time and among individuals and communities . . . it is the subjective margin that allows the prayerbook to be meaningful and useful at times of both national emergency and personal crisis, in confronting both collective responsibilities and the individual moral life" (Mintz 1984:426).

There are two ways in which this quotation feeds directly into our concerns. First, the sense that the meaning of prayer changes "over time and among individuals and communities" explains the tremendous variation we will be seeing in looking at Jewish-American worship services. Second, the fact that we are looking for an "interpretive" approach to the prayerbook points directly toward the activity of the chief interpreter, the hazzan.

This brings us back to the duality of the hazzan's situation in the prayer experience, the simultaneity of being both a professional, "chosen voice," and an individual Jewish worshipper. One of the standard questions asked in interviews for the present study was: "When you lead services, are you also praying for yourself?" This question startled many hazzanim, who paused reflectively before replying. Their answers reveal a broad range of interior states and strategies, and are best summarized by indicating the range of responses, which sketch out a continuum from those who feel they cannot be themselves while also being a "messenger" to those who very determinedly stake out their own territory on the pulpit. We start with those who find it hard to find themselves:

> Unfortunately, like somebody said, when you become a cantor, services aren't services any more for you—they're your job. I work all Shabbat. I mean, you know, everybody else prays on Shabbat, but I work. If I have a Shabbat off for whatever reason, the last thing I want to do is go to temple. I mean, I'm in temple all the time. If I weren't a cantor, I'd love to go to temple. . . . I'm too busy doing the service to pray myself. *I* might not feel God when I sing, but some other people do (C.I.).

Though hazzanim recognize what they would like to experience while leading prayers, they acknowledge that it is difficult to achieve: "It's those moments, it's those peak experiences. . . . Sometimes you have to take a step back from it, describe it, like 'was God in this place and surely did I know it or did I not?' More times than not, I don't think about it, which isn't good of course. We get bogged down in the mechanical . . . in the staging, in the show business, in the theater" (G.G.).

One hazzan recounts an incident that gives us a good idea of problems and solutions of professionals facing an indifferent congregation: "I remember one Shabbat in the traditional service I was particularly angry, because there was just a lot of kibitzing. I have colleagues who bang on the *amud* ["pulpit"], you know, and that's not me. The emeritus [his predecessor] would stare, he would just stop and stare, and I've done that too, but I'm just not that type. So I simply turned around and finished davening facing the *aron* and shut everybody out and said 'let's go for it' myself" (G.G.). His exasperation brought an unexpected response from the congregation: "And afterwards: 'Oh cantor, it was *wonderful,* you sang so great,' and 'it was, like, you know, it was such a prayerful feeling.' I guess what had happened was, even though I was terribly angry . . . it wasn't a matter of 'listen to me,' it was a matter of 'I need to pray, and you guys are screwing around out there.' So I just turned around and did it" (G.G.). Some professionals just hope for the best: "I just assume, and maybe wrongly so, that if I can forget about the rest of the world and create a sense of kavanah for myself, then perhaps they'll come along" (M.F.).

The notion of being dulled by routine, or *keva*, is a well-known problem in Jewish discussion of prayer, being discussed by rabbis as well as hazzanim. Some clergy note that congregational indifference extends to apathy towards all of creation, so feel it is their job "to raise their consciousness, to not take things for granted. This is, if everyday things that we take for granted, we shouldn't, and God has created them, and as far as I'm concerned, they're miracles" (D.C.). Others are cynical about the possibility of creating kavanah from the pulpit: "When I go up to the pulpit to do my thing religiously, I'm praying for me. In doing so, I hope I can relate to you. If you don't want to be moved no matter what I do—forget it. There's a lot of people [who] don't like Pavarotti—what can you do?" (G.E.).

Some who once tried to appeal to the mass of congregants have turned sharply in the other direction, like this hazzan who began as a professional at a tender age: "Lately I see where I really daven for myself, the last years, where I, *I* count. I daven for myself. Not 'if I take you along please come along, please. . . .' I'm no more a *pleaser*, not the managerial thing, but rather *I* count, *my* prayer" (B.A.).

Through a highly intense delivery of prayer, a histrionic hazzan may feel that he is able to transmit his kavanah without appearing to pay attention to the listeners: "I am unaware of the congregation. I do what I do for me. When I daven, I don't look at the congregation. If I want to close my eyes, I'll close my eyes. If I want to dance when I'm doing a Hasidic tune, I'll dance. If I want to jump a little bit, I will jump a little bit. Whatever I do communicates to them . . . through me, as a person . . . and they are caught up with me" (H.F.).

This description dramatically underscores the fact that in many mainstream American congregations, the hazzan is hardly the messenger of the congregation to God, but rather the message of the prayer comes "through me" to them. In interviews, hazzanim avoid the word *audience*, but there is no question that worshippers are more likely to be onlookers rather than participants these days: "synagogue life itself has become a spectator sport" (B.B.). One hazzan goes so far as to brand the whole process non-Jewish: "People view the clergy the same way the Catholics view the clergy: as the intercessor between God and man. . . . It's a totally alien view of Judaism" (B.B.).

Shouldering this responsibility makes it very hard to concentrate on one's own prayer experience:

> I get my satisfaction during the service each time I sing. I really do pray. I close my eyes almost all the time and I enter the music and the worship. And I take advantage of every momentary period of meditation or silent devotion. And I've learned, practice hard, how to meditate and take advantage of those moments. So that even though announcements, and a sermon, and all of these things move me afield from my worship experience, I can at least get enough out of it to feel that I have [prayed]. But I have to work hard to create it. I would find congregants have to have a murderous time doing it. . . . I use up an enormous energy warding off that which interferes (I.H.).

The distractions are numerous: "People walking in at the wrong time. An announcement from the pulpit at the wrong time. A sermon which has to do with politics and stuff, which—yes it's important—but they're doing it a hell of a lot better on television. But what is worse is that the message we deliver is: *that's* important, worship is marginal, ancillary, *es makht nisht oys* ("it doesn't matter")" (I.H.).

Perhaps this is why some hazzanim prefer a quiet crowd, finding it easier to "get into yourself" with an audience that's "stone-faced." They "can be obnoxious," but if they're "complacent, I can do anything I want—be in whatever world I want" (H.H.). On the other hand, recognizing the potential for distraction, the sacred singer's job might simply be to force the congregants to focus on the task at hand—prayer: "What the cantor can do is jar the worshipper . . . it wakes the congregation up. . . . It's so easy for the mind to wander" (E.G.).

The real question raised, however, is whether the congregants' feelings are really all that important, a possibility suggested by another viewpoint: "As a cantor, you cannot be responsible for what the congregation feels. That's not your job. Your job is to be responsible for what you are feeling, and for what you are saying. And let them feel what they feel. You can't be out there and inside yourself at the same time. Does that make sense? So, when I step up on the bima, I don't think, 'now I'm taking all of you in my arms and praying for you.' That's a lot of bull" (H.I.). This can lead to a certain internal intensity for the same hazzan: "The easiest Yom Kippurs for me have been the ones in which I was praying, when I was leading the service, because I'm very involved in what I'm doing, and I'm not hungry" (H.I.). The possibility also arises that the sacred singer can literally internalize the dualism of the experience: "I do daven for my own purposes as well. As I 'feel' a prayer, I render it. Sometimes I feel as if the worship experience is a sharing between the left and right sides of the brain, and I let myself go back and forth between dominances" (F.E.). Though this state seems complex, it might convey itself to the congregation: "As a leader, I feel that I have been elected by the people to 'orchestrate' the experience for them, so it is perfectly appropriate for them to experience what I happen to feel at the moment" (F.E.).

Of course, the defining case for interaction is the presence of a congregation. Declining attendance at the weekly service can drastically affect both the hazzan's and the worshippers' sense of self: "When there are the fewest people there I really have to work hard because I want to overcome the gloominess and pessimism that those that are there feel by looking around them and seeing few, so you try harder. . . . No amount of money can help you overcome . . . coming in week after week looking at an empty congregation" (E.J.). This can become a serious issue in the minds of professionals: "I think that guys are concerned about, if they're thirty, thirty-two years old, whether or not there is a future in this profession for them for the next thirty-five years. You know, in my congregation of over 600 families, if we have thirty-five people on Friday night and thirty-five on Saturday morning, are we going to be getting a minyan in ten years?" (E.G.).

Yet no matter how small the hazzan-congregant group, there is a third, ever-present party who also shapes the inner experience: God, mentioned only sporadically so far. A question put to interviewees was: "Where is God in the process?" which at times evoked even more surprise than the question about praying for oneself. Again, response varied enormously across denominational, gender, and age lines.[4] One hazzan simply feels God is omnipresent, so needs little comment, beyond a generalized evocation of a superordinate force: "I think God is everything that I discuss. I think that when we are together at a service, I think God intertwines in and out of everything we do. . . . The idea that we can believe in something one day a week bigger than ourselves, to me, is God" (H.I.). If God is there, does he need us? "God *does* need our prayers, and that's why we're an *am kadosh*, a holy people, and chosen in that sense. I don't know—I really *don't* know. I'd hate to say that God doesn't need our prayers. But whatever our prayers are, ought to be acceptable to him if they're done with the proper intention" (D.B.).

Caught in an ambivalent mood, this young hazzan tries to find a positive answer: "God has been listening to the same prayers for six hundred to a thousand years, so maybe they're being a little bit abridged [now, but] there are more people praying to God now than ever before, so He may be a little bit busier" (D.B.).

Yet the fact that much of the congregation does not believe in God, even if the hazzan does, can be very present in the sacred singer's mind. One remarked that he is satisfied with a service if for two minutes, one congregant doubts the "fact" that there is no God (M.B.). This modest expectation is cited by another hazzan as being part of his cantorial education: "One of my teachers once said: if you could influence one congregant a little bit with one selection, then you've done quite a bit" (G.A.). Yet another wonders if even this is possible: "I hope I can lead them to some sort of feeling with God. I'd *love* to have them have a religious experience. Sometimes that's asking a little too much, especially from Reform Jews" (H.H.). The problem is compounded if even the sacred singer has doubts:

I am not their emissary to the Almighty. As a matter of fact, I'm an agnostic at best. But I do believe in Judaism. And I do believe in prayer, believe it or not. Because I believe that prayer realigns a person with what's important in life. And I believe in the texts which I sing. . . . I, singing "adonai hu ha-elohim" ["the Lord is God"], despite the fact that I'm an unbeliever—I acknowledge an awe of the intricacy of nature and of humanity . . . the miraculous nature of the human soul (D.H.).

Whatever one calls "God," there certainly is a triangular play between the hazzan, the congregation, and a third power in the sanctuary, and the interaction can change as a career progresses:

Now as I am maturing [at thirty-eight], I surely am different. . . . Once upon a time, I felt myself engaged in direct conversation with God, even as people converse one with another. In a way, that made it "natural" sometimes to plead—e.g. in Hineni, Kol Nidre, *Matai timloch b'tsion* ["when will you rule in Zion?"] I felt quite literal about the approach of the siddur ["prayerbook"] . . . but today my theological feelings are so much more complex . . . that my conversation has as much—sometimes more—to do with the people with whom I am praying than [with] the One to whom I am praying. And now I feel that the voice is the medium of the message—and sometimes the message itself (F.E.).

Which way the message is flowing through the messenger and how the direction flows between the sides of the brain is not easy for a practitioner to summarize in a short interview; so far, we have only fragmentary evidence about this extremely complex and fascinating process, and almost no literature from other religions and cultures to guide us toward an understanding of how a prayer leader feels, thinks, and works. The hints we do have indicate how all-encompassing the role might be; one hazzan follows the age-old Jewish technique of evolving a point of view from an etymology: "I feel . . . that a hazzan has to understand, a *hazzon*, a vision. He has to be a seer. He just can't look at his present situation; he has to think of all the ramifications of what he says or does" (C.A.). The ideal situation, as understood by the traditional hazzan, can best be summarized in the words of one veteran: "I want to evoke response, I want to inspire them to pray, I want to establish a mood. I want to interpret the words of liturgy for them, through me. I am the sheliach tzibbur. . . . The old corny line: the rabbi carries God's word to the people and the cantor carries the people's word to God. . . . At the same time, if you are inspiring them, the message goes the other way. . . . A message comes from me to them, inspires their prayers; it's a kind of magnificent interplay" (A.A.).

Another old-timer sees an immense attenuation of the spirit just cited, certainly in terms of the religious nature of the service:

We, today, the rabbi and the cantor, go towards the congregation and say, "Come to us, let us pray," whereas it used to be in Jewish life that all of us together, the rabbi and the cantor and the congregation, would all come and stand before God. Today, more often than not, our congregations are not even thinking of God. . . . The life blood of prayer has disappeared because we are engaged in the ridiculous task of trying to attract the congregation; and as we attempt to make the service more and more attractive, the services become less and less Jewish. Judaism in America as been diluted to something of a club in which all of us are members. . . . We must serve the religious needs of our people and stop attempting to serve their social needs (Shames 1984:40–41).

Some young hazzanim have a much more informal notion of their mission: "That's my job—to make people feel happy in the synagogue . . . giving them a nice feeling, a good experience" (I.D.). Or: "They've come out of a whole week of problems, and you just want to take them away from those problems, [try] not to lose them [since some even fall asleep]" (G.H.). Or simply: "My congregation needs to be soothed. I don't want to call it hot tub, but. . ." (C.B.). How does one counter this mood? "The purpose of the synagogue and of the hazzan especially is to access people subconsciously" (D.B.).

We have surveyed a wide range of personal needs and of solutions to the role of sheliach tzibbur. To see how the professional puts these varied feelings into practice, we need to detail carefully the true craft of the cantorate: service-building.[5] One hazzan has said there are only three requirements for success: (1) understand yourself; (2) know your congregation; and (3) acquire a decent library (J.B.). We have just made a stab at the issue of "understanding yourself," and part 3 will look into the library, so what we need to grasp in detail is what a hazzan means by "knowing the congregation," the focus of the next section of this chapter.

One thing most hazzanim know about their congregations is that worshippers do not want to work overtime: "People don't have the patience to wait until Saturday 12:30 or 1:00. When I sang with Zeidel Rovner as a child [in the thirties], we finished the Musaf at a quarter to three" (A.H.). In practical terms this means that if you're the hazzan in a town dominated by a Big Ten university, you try to finish early on football Saturdays. It also means you may organize your whole service, or even workshops at your annual convention, around the question of time. Strategies abound:

I find that you don't need a lot for a good hazzan to really keep his congregation interested. He can use plain nusach [a davening style of chant], then all of a sudden, two lines to take off, give a little bit, calm down. In other words, you have to be a little bit of a psychiatrist, a psychologist also. When they start looking at their watches you know they want to get out. So the first thing you do is you speed up. And all of a sudden you take off. And they say, "Gee, that sounds nice." You go right down, you speed it up and you get them out. "Gee, he got us out on time." And if you run over five, ten minutes, you tell them, "I'm a human being. I have to cough too" (F.A.).

But it's not so easy as all that, since professionals feel a sense of loss when they condense their contribution: "By cutting the service, it's like saying, I don't like the third act of *Aida*. You really don't need it. Take two of the arias, put them in Act Two. Take 2 of the arias and put them in Act Four; the rest of it is blah, it's nothing, it's drab" (F.A.). The comparison to opera is not accidental; as part of their commitment to classical music, many hazzanim use it as a yardstick: "If you're doing Mozart, no matter what, you're not going to change the tempo . . . but in a religious service, if you come upon a paragraph and it's ten minutes of one and you're going to finish by one, if you had a concerted piece you were going to do with choir, you might easily say, 'I'm going to knock that out,' and just chant right through it . . . and when you do that, all kinds of terrible things happen. You make mistakes [in proper delivery of text]" (C.E.).

Beyond the bare issue of time, there is much more to know about the congregation. One is that they may be either indifferent or even indignant. One hazzan has noticed that congregants can be angry at the hazzan for reminding them of spirituality, but maintains that "that is a prime function of the cantor." This viewpoint is in the spirit of an oft-quoted talk, "The Task of the Hazzan," delivered in 1957 by the immensely influential modern Jewish thinker Abraham Joshua Heschel. Delivered at the Cantors Assembly's convention, the talk was particularly addressed to the professionals. Heschel bluntly describes the enormity of the hazzan's challenge: "One must realize the difficulties of the Cantor. The call to prayer falls against an iron wall. The congregation is not always open and ready to worship. The Cantor has to pierce the armor of indifference. . . . He has to conquer them in order to speak for them" (Heschel 1972:65). Piercing people's armor can arouse negative emotions, as a veteran hazzan knows well: "The American Jewish community today comes to a congregation purely with not much education in the liturgy. So very often they're sung to, or performed at . . . and yet in a way perhaps they're angry at themselves for not knowing. So their anger or hostility is shot out at saying that 'well the organ doesn't allow us to participate, or the choir takes over. . .' but that's not really the truth" (C.E.).

Indeed, there are several active players here, including the choir. This is usually just another group of congregants, since outside soloists are commonly hired only for special occasions, and they can be as sticky as the rest of the professional's clients: "I've got to please all three c's: congregation, choir, cantor" (I.D.). Complaints about choirs can be heartfelt: "Everything that I've done in the synagogue has always been met at first with opposition from the choir. The people you'd think would be willing are always the ones to say, 'Oh cantor, this is too hard, we'll never learn this,' and how the hell do you approach it. You really have to coddle those people to make them come through for you. . . . They behave unbelievably poorly; they talk during rehearsals, and you know, it's unprofessional" (C.E.). Of course, the choir has its reasons, as does the organist, who is usually an outsider and often non-Jewish: "You have to remember that you're working in a synagogue situation, and even though they're paid, they're not paid earning them a living, and you need them. . . . Anywhere from $10 to $17.50 a service, which includes a rehearsal. The organist gets $35 a service, which is also very modest. At the end, they do love it and there's the reward of performance" (C.E.). One way around the choir is to use children, but you have to know how to handle them too:

> I've developed a certain rapport with the kids and I have a waiting list to get into the choir . . . they come from all the shuls. . . . I get 98% attendance at every rehearsal. . . The secret is to reward them properly, and not with money. . . . It's very difficult to get a kid to come on Sunday morning to a choir rehearsal when the sun is shining and he wants to play baseball . . . so I make a contest and I give out baseball equipment for attendance, for singing, for behavior, for everything; you get a certain amount of points for each thing (D.R.).

How then does the hazzan get enough satisfaction from the service while confronting the congregation and perhaps even the choir? "I have to satisfy my ego, so I do some recitatives where I know they'll enjoy them, e.g. *matai timloch be tsion* ["When will you reign in Zion?"] because my heart *is* breaking; there isn't a day that I can't pick up a . . . newspaper and not read about something that's breaking my heart" (E.H.). Of course, one can also be pleased when congregants are: "That's my job—to make people feel happy in the synagogue . . . giving them a nice feeling, a good experience" (I.D.).

Like other professionals, hazzanim measure satisfaction partly by the testimony of clients: a kind word after the service or a letter of thanks. Probably every hazzan saves a file of tributes such as the following:

> I just wanted to thank you personally for your davening and your work with the choir during the recent High Holy Day services. . . . It's not an easy job to lead such a variegated congregation in prayer, given the mix of pseudo-orthodox daveners and megaReform spectators, but I thought you did it superbly. I personally found myself responding to the davening more than in recent years.

> When we leave for Florida we shall miss Temple—and its wonderful environments. Especially will we miss the beautiful, spiritual cantorial services you render.

> We want to thank you especially for taking Liz under your wing, and helping her to prepare her [bat mitzvah] portions. . . . [N]ervous though she was, she gained confidence from your presence on the bimah and performed beautifully. You were not surprised! You do it so well, so often! [letters to F.E.].

Despite such gratifying tokens of appreciation, hazzanim often express a nagging feeling of dissatisfaction on purely personal grounds: did I meet my own standards? There is also a degree of cynicism in assessments of congregants' praise. "Let's say you've conducted services at a bar mitzvah, and you see people sitting there with closed prayerbooks, and you see people in a shul that you know you're not going to see again until Rosh Hashanah-Yom Kippur. They come up and pay you a compliment. The only thing that that will probably mean is that they've enjoyed your voice. It probably doesn't mean that you've inspired them to prayer" (E.G.).

Though this hazzan is sensitive to the question of kavanah—inspiration—much of the tug-of-war between hazzan and congregation centers on issues of aesthetics and control. One of the constants in the history of the cantorate is the extent to which the congregation views the hazzan as the musical-aesthetic leader. At one end of the spectrum the congregation may yield to a dominating sacred singer, which can happen in any denomination at any time, while at the other end, the worshippers override the professional:

> Imagine that you are singing with a congregation and you hear some sounds that it throws you out completely off key. I have to continue because I want to sing. I realize from the commercial point of view it might be good, the participation, but I think from the artistic point of view it dies.

> I would grow to hate myself if I gave in to their desire to do more and more of that stuff [summer camp music] because one should teach and raise the congregation's taste (M.F.).

Faith in your own taste can be vindicated if only a handful of congregants sit up and take notice: "There are times when you do things that are interesting to you and very often nobody picks up on them. But you always have a couple of people who have radar ears" (B.B.). Yet the professional can have just the opposite reaction if the "real" listeners object to the hazzan's taste: "They eat ham on Yom Kippur, but if they come to shul and hear an organ, they think it's a church. . . . [At a wedding] they'd rather have a violin kvitching ["squeaking"] off-tune playing 'Sunrise, Sunset' or some such *shmate* ["junk"]" (B.B.).

Strategies for achieving aesthetic goals vary, but that there are strategies is very apparent.[6] One hazzan uses smiles and eye contact to settle down the congregation but may then surprise them by singing an important prayer himself, instead of letting them read it, with startling results: "it changed the whole mood from bright pink to deep blue" (H.B.). When hazzanim articulate their interactive strategies, they convey something of the complexity of their craft: "I carry the piece in my pocket and wait for the right collection of people to do it for. . . . It's up to me to direct the moods, to tell them how to fell at a given moment. So part of my own mood is not necessarily how I would respond to the particular prayer, but rather to the pacing of the service and how I feel the congregation should feel at the given moment" (F.E.).

This means the hazzan has internalized congregational response to such an extent that his anticipation of their reaction is self-fulfilling. The same veteran's ideology/theology is very precise on the subject of the worship service and his role, which goes beyond the aesthetic: "I do believe that the miracle of prayer is not based upon the answers to our prayers, which may or may not be forthcoming, but rather that twenty or two hundred or a thousand people with *very* disparate intentions and feelings can collect themselves together and share an experience with their heritage . . . and I am the conductor/director of that experience" (F.E.).

To achieve this admirable goal takes a great deal of hard work, which expresses itself in the ways the hazzan educates the congregation. The professional needs to teach the clients how to participate, or the interaction both want will be missing. From Heschel's point of view, education is a two-way street: hazzanim must educate themselves to teach their congregations. "In order for Cantorial music to regain its dignity, it will not be enough to study the authentic pattern of our musical tradition. What is necessary is a *liturgical revival*. . . . The Cantor must constantly learn how to be involved in what he says, realizing that he must also teach others how to attach themselves to the words of the liturgy" (Heschel 1972:62, 67). Or, as a hazzan puts it: "Almost everything [the hazzan] does is educative" (D.C.). Remarks like this show just how far we have come from the immigrant-era view of the hazzan, who was not supposed to teach—every congregant knew the texts and the rules—but to beautify the obligation of worship, to elevate the event, to transcend the trivial—which might result in a revelatory *interpretation* of the text, but not an elementary primer on prayer. Today, from the pulpit's-eye view, there are really two kinds of education: (1) teaching congregants the basics; and (2) introducing something new. Although both activities have an idealistic component, each provides the sacred singer with a certain type of personal satisfaction. For example, for a hazzan who grew up in Europe, having the worshippers know basic tunes substitutes for the old gratifying feeling of being backed up by a group of daveners: "I want them to know the melody . . . next week again, and the week after, until they're acquainted, and they start humming along, and they sing. And this is what I like. It sort of warms, [provides] a contact between me and the congregation. Some hazzanim, they make fun of the congregation. No, that's wrong . . . you don't have to do the alarming things all the time" (F.C.).

Hazzanim teach either in specially arranged sessions or at the service itself:[7] "I realize that I don't have people like my grandfather out there, you know, who are going to know what I'm doing. I really have to spoonfeed it to them. So sometimes what I'll do is take a paragraph and instead of doing a straight cantorial thing, I'll intersperse the Hebrew with English. I'll interpret it for them as I go along" (M.F.). The professional hopes this education will have a payoff: "You have to teach them and tell them beforehand what you're going to do. This makes it easier for them to listen to it, understand what you are striving to do; that you're not just up there improvising, that you are in fact singing a classical masterpiece" (D.F.).[8] However, there are many obstacles to educating the congregants. The methods just outlined assume a group of "regulars," but this core of worshippers may simply not exist:

> Out of 1000 families you have 100 families that rotate coming often. The rest come on rare occasions, they come for special occasions. . . . 10% of the people (I think it's been recognized 7%, but go 10%) are people that come on "a regular basis," meaning once a month . . . and from that there's a nucleus that comes twice a month. But that's it. And then you might find ten families who really come three times out of the month, which is pretty good, but that's a small group (I.H.).

So trying to introduce a new tune may take some time:

Even if I have an opportunity to announce "we're going to do the 'adon olam' that's an old Sephardic melody instead of the Gerovich . . ." by the fifth verse they will have sung it. OK, great accomplishment, right? But next week only 10% of those who were there last week are there. So we've got to do the whole thing over again. . . . [Y]ou either sing the same "adon olam" for six months, so that they'll all learn it, or else they're not going to learn it (I.H.).

New teaching techniques may require innovative technologies, a solution recently pushed by the president of the Cantors Assembly in an article addressed to the laity: "The invention of the videocassette now makes it possible to introduce Jewish families to High Holy Day services and orient them to the music and the form of worship. I think we'll find that making use of the TV tape as a tool of Jewish literacy will evoke a heightened degree of participation in the services and make the synagogue and its rituals more attractive to our congregants" (Hammerman 1986).[9] One of the main obstacles to educating congregants remains synagogue politics. This involves the issue of whether the congregation sees the hazzan as the guardian or the architect of the local minhag.[10] In all cases, an incoming professional has to walk on eggs, as quotes from both a Reform and a Conservative hazzan show:

I said to myself . . . you want to be here for a *long* time, so you've just got to be extremely patient and take the educational process as slowly as you can. . . . When we do services at school [School of Sacred Music] it's always making the best selection from among the best composers, and so on, and when you come here and you sing anything but the Sulzer *shema* [the standard tune] somehow you have not provided a worship experience for your congregants . . . it's not worth the fight (J.E.).

When a young cantor goes to a new synagogue he might not be able to practice his art as he's been taught it. As a matter of fact, they may give him a cassette and be told, "this is what we sing here." I think the cantor today has got to strive for that balance between seeing what the congregation wants and singing what he feels is important to preserve (D.F.).

The question of innovation encompasses two notions, both expressed above. One is the idea that, as musical/aesthetic leader, the hazzan should be introducing the "best," which may include newly composed or nonstandard repertoire. The other is the sense that "tradition" might itself be novel for a congregation that does not know the great works and melodies of the past: "It seems logical to me it's the cantor's responsibility to preserve the art of the cantor, and to keep alive the vast

library of liturgy that we have. And it's fallen into disuse largely because of the advent of congregational singing" (D.F.).

It seems the important thing is to get members of the lay leadership
on your side as you slowly infiltrate your concept of the ideal service,
as we hear in one tale of trying to add an unfamiliar traditional prayer:

> First it's brought up within the ritual [committee] meeting. Now in this
> case, everyone wanted it but one of the old diehards, one of the folks
> who was early on in the formation of the synagogue; he was very much
> against it. We explained that it enhanced the service, just like all music
> enhances the prayers, and that perhaps we could find a way to do it once
> a month, or twice a month. I think that's the way these things really will
> have a chance to develop. We haven't done it yet. But after the ritual
> committee, then it's brought up to a full membership meeting. And I am
> inclined to think that somewhere along this year I will be chanting the
> *Avot* (M.F.).[11]

This push to add a single prayer is part of a three-pronged attack, the
first being the sort of campaign just cited, while the second is a pre-
service prep session: "I have said I'd like to have maybe once a month,
fifteen minutes before the service, anyone who's interested in congregational participation to come at 8:15. And we'll learn a new song or
two . . . and that night the choir and I will do it, and then we'll do it
the next week, and pretty soon it'll be part of their repertoire as well
as mine" (M.F.). The third component of the master plan for innovation
is the "cantor night": "The other thing is that I'd like to have cantor
nights, which means maybe every two months or something like that,
let it be a night where I can do all new music, if I so choose. Next
week will be the familiar things; this week she's doing new things"
(M.F.).

All this long-range planning implies the continuity a full-time job
can provide. To provide perspective, it helps to look at the world of
the part-time hazzan.[12] Some part-timers frankly acknowledge a lack
of repertoire and variety: "Since I don't do it full-time, it's not a full-
time profession, I really don't have the time to make a full effort to
get more material. so my material is, I think, pretty standard. It's not
constantly changing and I'm not constantly updating it" (J.H.). Beginning as a part-timer can be somewhat accidental, in which case you
have to scramble: "My first cantorial position was a *kolbo* ["jack of all
trades"] on the High Holidays for an old age home . . . where my
grandmother happened to live. . . . This was my second year in college,
and they were looking for someone, and because my grandmother was
there . . . someone put two and two together and asked me about it,
though I had never done the whole service. I had to go out and get

those tapes and learn it starting in a professional capacity" (K.C.). However, some things come easier to the part-timer: "I think there are far less rivalries between temporary hazzanim and rabbis; on the contrary, they are seen much more as a team . . . the temporary hazzan is more pliable and able to do what the congregation wants, like a temporary in any case; I mean, you don't expect a Kelly girl to come and tell you, 'well, I think this is a better way of doing things' " (J.J.). Or as one who is a dentist by profession puts it: "I've personally never had a problem with anyone. Especially if I let them do whatever they want, and say 'yes sir, no sir.' And listen, I'm in and out once a year, and I'm not about to cause any problems or give them a hard time" (J.I.).

While the man just quoted finds it easy to be a dentist-hazzan, another medical professional has had identity problems: "I think at the outset it was confusing, more: 'what is this guy doing? I never heard of a doctor who sings, where is this guy from, what kind of an alien being is this combination'—but I'm accustomed to it" (K.A.). It is particularly hard to build up a consistent sense of self if you constantly shift service types and denominations: "I davened now in Reform, Orthodox, Conservative, Orthodox in Israel, you name it, Contemporary, you know, the ones . . . where we had music playing in the background. This last one was Reform so I had to learn a whole lot of new Reform melodies . . . which was kind of fun. . . . In this last place I had to read torah, haftorah, and blow shofar as well. So I was exhausted" (K.B.).

Why would anyone take on this responsibility? "There's the show biz side of it. I really enjoy being on a stage, and I'm basically a ham. . . . The other part has to do with my feelings towards my father. . . . And thirdly, I feel closer to what's happening, I feel more of the holiness of the day. And then there's the remuneration . . . which can be good" (J.I.).

For some, deciding whether to work as a hazzan at all is an open question. One part-timer, an environmental consultant, takes job only if he anticipates personal satisfaction: "The first decision is, do I want to daven this year . . . especially now that I have a family and two kids. . . . [A]nd [my wife] is not enjoying the High Holidays because I'm up on a bima and she has the kids. . . . So once I decide I want to daven, generally the things I'm looking for is a person I enjoy working with and a congregation that I enjoy davening in, because I do enjoy davening" (K.B.). Some part-timers are drawn to the work simply because they grew up davening and leading services: "My father's father was a rabbi . . . both my mother's family and my father's family were from what would certainly be considered Orthodox backgrounds. Grew up in a home where we . . . sang *zmirot* [home Sabbath songs] every Shabbat, and I first got heavily into singing and harmonizing around the dining room table and while washing the dishes in the kitchen, and then was in the Junior Congregation . . . and started being a Junior Hazzan and *ba'al kriah*" (K.D.).

For others, mastery of material is only the starting point toward approaching the task of being a hazzan, even if it is only seasonal work: "I find that when I do connect, things start to melt away and also using relaxation techniques that I know, breathing, knowing how to release tension in areas of my body, also taking the whole month before. . . . I do a lot of emotional preparation, writing, personal though, it's kind of clearing myself out. If I don't take care of my own personal agenda first, how can I take care of what I feel the collective agenda to be when I get in front of people" (J.H.). As a part-timer, this hazzan feels he can reach real heights, but also worries about his adequacy: "When I'm feeling very spiritual and when everything is working and all the gears are lubricated, I can get into this kind of shamanistic mood, and so far I haven't burnt myself. But my initial perceptions when I do the work are that I am not worthy, that probably somebody else could be found who could do it better . . . that they're going to find something wrong with what I do" (J.H.).[13]

Of course, full-time hazzanim might talk the same way, but would not last long in any job if they continued to feel these emotions. Total commitment to career includes collaboration with the congregation and the rabbi, mastery of repertoire, and a somewhat more intangible comfort with one's role that only a long-time professional can achieve, based on a sense of comfort in the sanctuary and the synagogue every day, all year, over time. Of course, this involves social and political activity, teaching and counseling, choir management and budget balancing, and some part-timers are simply not interested in those aspects of being a hazzan: "I would not want to *have* to teach all the bar mitzvah lessons. I would not want to *have* to play the politics of a shul, kowtowing to certain people and performing the tunes that they want to do" (K.D.). Or, simply: "I certainly don't have any of the moral obligation to be a pillar in the community that the hazzan does" (K.C.).

It is true that part-timers and full-timers differ on the question of whether work off the pulpit can be satisfying. Some hazzanim openly say that their work outside the sanctuary is more important to them. Yet anyone who agrees to stand up and lead services is in some way inextricably linked to a long chain of service-builders and soul-stirrers, must have a self-conception as "chosen voice." The core of that notion lies in the relationship to the congregation, but also—and perhaps most deeply—to a tradition of the music itself, to which we now devote the final section of the book.

NOTES

1. Of course, the "music" includes its immediate context—the charged atmosphere of worship—as will be clear from the discussion in part 3.

2. "The importance and religious significance of the Days of Awe led the communities to demand higher qualifications than were ordinarily demanded throughout the rest of the year. Furthermore, during this period, they were highly insistent that none of the usual qualifications sought in a cantor were waived and that none of the disqualifying factors be present" (Landman 1972:29).

3. I am using the current Conservative translation (Harlow 1972:27).

4. This is one area of responses that illustrates my policy towards noncontextualized quotations. Were I to cite a non-God remark as being a young Reform woman, I believe it would do more to create a stereotype than to indicate a statistical or interpretive reality at this stage of our knowledge of the population under study.

5. The variety of services presented weekly and at festival times in American synagogues over the past three hundred years is too diverse to cover comprehensively. There is also too much going on at any given ritual event to be adequately discussed here, as our focus is not on the service per se but on the hazzan. It is quite possible, and would be extremely timely, to envision an entire volume on the nature of the Jewish-American—or, for that matter, any mainstream American—worship experience. Ideally, one would also like extensive input from the chorus of congregants, whom I am viewing only through the eyes of the clergy.

6. One method to ensure satisfaction is to use almost exclusively the music you compose: "85% of *all* melodies used in my congregation, the congregational singing or cantorial renditions, are my own compositions" (C.I.).

7. Hazzanim may arrange special teaching events, and advertise them, using the cantor's column in the congregational bulletin, a prime place for the professional to reach his clients: "In my last article, I raised the point that relatively few of the laity in Conservative congregations are able to participate in a traditional davening type of service. . . . [H]ere then are some alternatives . . . 1) extract the highlights of the weekday morning service and read them aloud, either in unison or responsively with the one who is leading the service. . . . The results were positive. We found that most of those who attended services, even . . . only occasionally, were now able to participate. . . . Some learned to serve as the leader by simply coming every morning" (Stein 1981:6).

This approach—offering text drills—apparently works well with the "regulars": "We carried the idea over into our Friday evening services. Most of the prayers not chanted by the Cantor and choir or sung by the congregation were again read aloud in the Hebrew, either in unison or responsively with the Rabbi. We found after a relatively short period of time that many of our 'regulars' whose ability to read Hebrew was limited had learned a number of prayers by heart" (Stein 1981:6). This method of teaching prayer skills is a common practice: "I must tell you that in the last two, three years, those that have been attending my minyanim ["prayer groups"] mornings have increased their fluency. As a matter of fact, they know half of the *shacharit* by heart, by rote" (D.S.).

8. Of course, there is a certain amount of condescension implicit in many hazzanim's remarks in this vein, part of professional life rarely commented on in the literature and hardly surprising given the knowledge gap involved, particularly in the case of ritual.

9. Yet another way of increasing involvement is to create a multitude of services. Lincoln Square Synagogue, in the heart of upscale Manhattan, offers a wide range of tailormade worship sessions each Sabbath, geared to youth, women, "heavy" daveners, light participants, etc. Sometimes these services can focus on learning, as experience at another synagogue shows: "the Saturday morning service is the vehicle for kids to become b'nai mitzvah. But for those people who don't need to see three children, you know, reading from the Torah for the first time, we've begun a minyan service. . . . [T]his is held in our congregation's museum. It lasts maybe an hour and a half. And we have between 20 and 30 people who come every week, people of all ages. We have some very elderly people for whom it is the focal point of their week. We have some young couples and we have a good many middle-aged people. It's been on of the most interesting innovations. . . . It's much more learning than devotional. The big service begins at 10:45 and is over between 12:30 and 12:45. This begins at 10:00 and is over by 11:30" (E.D.).

10. This is one of the constant issues of the American cantorate, going back to its beginnings; it is briefly discussed in chapter 9 as part of the larger question of congregational participation.

11. The data available from the Project tend to be more anecdotal, in some ways, than one would like. One can collect many stories like the preceding, which seem to indicate the hazzan is politically active in getting his/her point across with the lay leadership, but the questionnaire addressed to synagogue presidents strongly supports the view (70%) that the rabbi is really in charge of structuring the service.

12. Full-scale survey of all the "cantors" of America was an unattainable goal. The hundreds (thousands?) of men and women who do some "cantoring" constitute too large and too scattered a group to include systematically. Fortunately, Jeffrey Summit's survey of the Boston metropolitan area gives us at least a point of departure for this valuable topic, and the following quotes are from his fieldwork data. One further point: full-time hazzanim have an extraordinary dislike for part-timers, for a variety of reasons ranging from the obvious distrust professionals have for those they consider amateurs at the same trade through uneasiness over lost employment possibilities. Among the Reform, for example, there is the oft-told anecdote of the cantorial students'

boycotting a prestigious New York congregation that never hires full-timers. For the Conservatives, there is the intense distaste for the Women Cantors Network, a support group of largely nonmatriculated part-timers, where amateur status and gender coincide to set off the alarm among conservative male full-timers. Notice here how gender alone is not sufficient to specify the dynamics of a professional situation, a topic to be developed in a separate article in preparation.

13. It would be worth taking the preceding quotation literally and comparing the hazzan to the shaman, but I do not find the comparative literature viewing shamanism from the insider's perspective abundant enough to do so. One might argue that the ancillary obligations of the contemporary hazzan just listed (synagogue politics, etc.), make the hazzan's case different, but I am not sure that practicing shamans do not have to cope with similar sociopolitical contexts.

Convocation for the inauguration of the Cantors Institute at the Jewish Theological Seminary, 1952. Left to right: Max Routtenberg and Louis Finkelstein, both of JTS, Hazzan David J. Putterman, and Hugo Weisgal, composer and faculty member. Photo courtesy of the Cantors Institute.

Concert crowd at the 1954 convention of the Cantors Assembly. Photo courtesy of the Cantors Assembly.

Banquet at an early Cantors Assembly convention. Photo courtesy of the Cantors Assembly.

Awarding of Cantors Assembly citations for the twenty-fifth anniversary (1979) to five distinguished hazzanim, including Isaac Goodfriend (second from left). Photo courtesy of the Cantors Assembly.

A special award given to Hazzan Samuel Vigoda, 1969. Photo courtesy of the Cantors Assembly.

Hazzan Max Wohlberg and Hazzan David Koussevitsky. Photo courtesy of Max Wohlberg.

Max Wohlberg at work, teaching cantorial students at the Cantors Institute of the Jewish Theological Seminary. Photo courtesy of Max Wohlberg.

Graduating class of 1970, School of Sacred Music of the Hebrew Union College-Jewish Institute of Religion (Reform), with three men on left, two school officials on right. Photo courtesy of Hebrew Union College-Jewish Institute of Religion.

Graduating class of 1987, School of Sacred Music of the Hebrew Union College-Jewish Institute of Religion (Reform), flanked by four school officials (two on either side). Photo courtesy of Hebrew Union College-Jewish Institute of Religion.

The first joint ordination of a married couple at the School of Sacred Music, Jodi Sufrin and Roy Einhorn, 1983. Photo courtesy of Jodi Sufrin and Roy Einhorn.

Hazzan Bernard Beer teaching a cantorial student at the Yeshiva University training program (Orthodox). Photo courtesy of the Belz School of Jewish Music, Yeshiva University.

Practicing a cantorial chorus at Yeshiva University. Photo courtesy of the Belz School of Jewish Music, Yeshiva University.

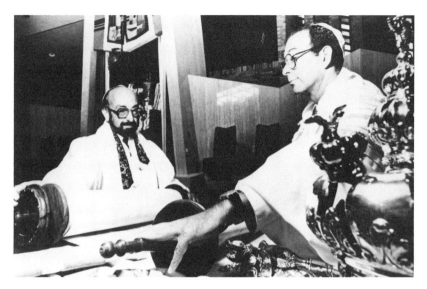

Hazzan and rabbi: Hazzan Morton Shames and Rabbi Herbert Schwartz meet over the Torah. Photo courtesy of Temple Beth El, Springfield, Mass.

Hazzan Morton Shames prepares children for performance. Photo courtesy of Temple Beth El, Springfield, Mass.

Composer Max Helfman exhorting a Cantors Assembly banquet to further the cause of composed sacred music, 1963. Photo courtesy of the Cantors Assembly.

A hazzan and choir take a bow with Jan Peerce, the Metropolitan Opera star and a role model for hazzanim, undated. Photo courtesy of Temple Beth El, Springfield, Mass.

PART III

The Cantorate and the Music

9

~~~~~~

The Music of Participation

I have worlds of music to choose from.
—H.S.

All the Jews from all over the world came together in
America so obviously it's a blending.
—E.A.

This final section of the book shows the ways that the figure of the
hazzan is intertwined with the survival of Jewish sacred music. I will
not present highly detailed musicological analysis, nor give a comprehensive history of either liturgical music or hazzanut, the art of the
cantorate. These three chapters take the insider's view as much as
possible, borrowing titles and content from the way sacred singers think
about the music of the worship service, which they tend to categorize
under three headings: participation, concert services (which I am calling
presentation), and improvisation. *Participation* refers here to music/
services in which the hazzan shares the responsibilities with the congregants; *presentation* to preset services, ranging from classic composition through trendy pop-based events; and *improvisation* to those
moments of the service when the hazzan feels most ties to the ancient
tradition of hazzanut and fewest constraints on creativity.

"Participation" is directly related to the issue of control within the
ritual event, a knotty question throughout American history, which
varies across time within one denomination as well as among groups—
including the Ashkenazic-Sephardic subethnic boundary—at any given
time. Among the former, many hazzanim point to the growth of the
Young Israel movement in the interwar period as the birth of the participation movement.[1]

The seeds planted by this group sprouted in the interwar period
when the Young Israel movement began to blossom, as a veteran hazzan recalls: "I davened a couple of years in the Young Israel of Brooklyn

when I was a kid. . . . Young Israel was originally started for young Jews; that's why it was called Young Israel. And they started what is considered today Modern Orthodox Judaism. They started the congregational singing . . . very seldom did a cantor ever daven in a Young Israel; always ba'alei tefillah, members of the congregation" (D.R.).[2]

Reform congregations have also slowly taken on the participatory mode as their basic service type: "The Reform movement . . . replaced the highly dramatic orchestration of the organ-choir-reader-cantor complex and adopted informal, congregationally active modes of worship, emphasizing simple songs of American and Israeli youth" (Hoffman 1982:161).[3]

Thus right across mainstream American Judaism, the laity has insisted on raising their voices and cutting back the sacred singer's contribution. By the 1970s, the leading professionals began to protest at the curtailment of the cantorate: "In the last decade, we complained that our people were not 'davening.' In this decade the hazzan is being added to the company of non-daveners. To put it bluntly, hazzanim are heard less and less, doing what it once was considered their sacred duty to do: to lead their congregation to achieve sincere prayer" (Rosenbaum 1976:87). What then became of the hazzanic role in this analysis? "They are becoming song-leaders, *ruach* ["spirituality"]-instigators, guitar-players, hand-clappers, Amen-sayers; in short, entertainers. Less and less is heard of the sound of hazzanic chant; more and more is heard of the rhymed and rhythmic word" (Rosenbaum 1976:87). What Rosenbaum refers to and Hoffman calls "simple songs of American and Israeli youth" is repertoire coming from two main sources: the youth movements of the Conservative and Reform wings (United Synagogue Youth and National Federation of Temple Youth, respectively), in particular, their summer camp programs, and the catchy melodies of the Hasidic movement, either in their original form or, since the 1970s, in the popularized Israeli versions of the Hasidic Song Festivals. Mainstream hazzanim consider each style a threat. Veterans do not enjoy this particular notion of congregational participation, seeking to maintain a veto power over what happens within the sanctuary, literally the "holy of holies" for hazzanim: "Within that framework [congregational singing] you still have to present something tasteful . . . not that type of music [Hasidic] where the words are not present and becomes almost like a singsong, like a hoedown, whatever you call that. . . . At other meetings—men's club, sisterhood functions—you can experiment . . . but within the synagogue walls when you do chant the liturgy I do feel that some semblance of order and certainly taste should be always present" (M.F.).[4]

Most hazzanim return repeatedly to the word or notion of "balance" to indicate their attempt at finding the middle road between cantorial and congregational domination; what differs, then, is the percentage suggested: "I think that a successful cantor can make his congregation listen as my congregation listens. It's really two-thirds listening; two-thirds of the singing has to be done by the cantor who inspires them while they listen. . . . My congregation may sing a good third of the time, but half of the time with me. But when I get to my solo passages it's mine, and nobody says, 'Oh God, why is he singing so much'" (A.A.).

Another hazzan says that "balance is really the key to any successful service," which for her means fifty percent familiar congregational tunes, twenty-five percent solo "for my own enjoyment," and twenty-five percent music "I want them to learn" (H.H.). Yet another likes "at least fifty percent congregational participation" and "ten to fifteen percent strictly cantorial solo," with the rest varying (G.F.). The formula for success, of course, implies negotiation and compromise between the sacred singer and the congregation, often with the rabbi as an important player in determining overall balance. That the metaphor of play is an appropriate one emerges from quotes such as the following: "I never had a problem as far as music because for every congregational melody, I have six or eight versions. And the congregation plays a game: which one is he going to use today? So I never find it boring" (A.C.). And presumably neither does the congregation, so the hazzan may get more leeway in the items he/she chooses for cantorial display.[5]

Thus the controversy over participation is a microcosm of the philosophy of service-building and, like so many other parameters, describes a very extensive continuum from full cantorial control to extremely strong congregational dominance. Because it would be impossible to survey the whole range of participatory music, this chapter takes up two prime examples of texts where today's worshippers expect to be able to raise their voices, both from the Sabbath service: *Lecha dodi* from Friday night and *Tzur yisroel* from Saturday morning.

Lecha dodi

The text of *Lecha dodi* was composed by Solomon Alkabez in 1529. Alkabez was part of the circle of the mystical philosopher Isaac Luria (1534–72) in Safed, a town in the Holy Land. Luria's interpretation of the central mystical text, the Kabbalah, "dominated Jewish life . . . by the seventeenth century" and, according to Gershom Scholem, was the last religious movement in Judaism, the influence of which became preponderant among all sections of the Jewish people in every country of the diaspora (Millgram 1975:491). For Alkabez, "the best-known liturgical poet of the Safed circle," writing a hymn could have immense liturgical consequences because "each prayer became a mystical weapon with infinite power." Lecha dodi "is the climax of the *Kabbalat Shabbat*, the prayer unit in which the congregation welcomes the Sabbath before the official Friday evening service."[6] Lecha dodi begins with a short passage that then becomes a refrain repeated after each verse: "Come, my friend, to meet the bride/ Let us welcome the presence of the Sabbath."

Lecha dodi, then, represents a colorful segment of Jewish history and displays all the wealth of the prayerbook, with its strands from various eras and styles of worship. The musical possibilities for the hymn are similarly rich. Since every denomination and congregation sings Lecha dodi, the notion of "local minhag" (customary usage) prevails, though denominational songbooks may make a specific suggestion.[7] For the Project, members of the Cantors Assembly were asked to sing their "favorite tunes." The results from the ninety-three hazzanim who responded show all the variety one might hope for: they sent in 184 variants, some singing as many as five different tunes for the hymn.[8]

The distribution of tunes followed a pattern typical for several of the items we asked for. There were a couple of heavy favorites, some common tunes, some rare, and others only sung by a single hazzan. Specifically, one variant garnered fifty-two citations and another fifty-one; two other tunes were sung sixteen and eleven times respectively, one tune turned up four times and two others twice, and 38 melodies made solo appearances. We will look at a few variants to show the repertoire pools they represent and to give an idea of the diversity in setting a short text; only the refrain of Lecha dodi will be considered.

The most commonly sung tune (fifty-two entries) was the Sulzer, and its companion, the Lewandowski, was one of the second-rank tunes (sixteen). These date back to the origins of the modern cantorate, generally dated at Sulzer's appointment as chief cantor in Vienna in 1826. They are both in waltz time, perhaps reflecting the central European milieu, and in a major key, the modality much more common in central and western European Ashkenazic music than in the East, where other, more Balkan and Levantine sounds are also heard (examples 1 and 2).

The second most frequently cited melody (fifty-one) is of unknown origin (example 3) and contrasts with Sulzer-Lewandowski dramatically. First, it is in a minor key, suggesting an eastern European origin. Second, it is in a meter of four, and third, it has an extended second section that resembles the style of many Hasidic tunes. The fact that

Example 1. Salomon Sulzar, *Lecha dodi*

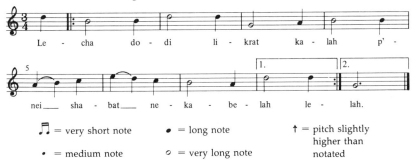

Le - cha do - di li - krat ka - lah p' - nei___ sha - bat___ ne - ka - be - lah le - lah.

♪ = very short note   ● = long note   ↑ = pitch slightly higher than notated

● = medium note   ○ = very long note

Example 2. Lewandowski, *Lecha dodi*

Le - cha do - di li - krat ka - lah p' - nei___ sha - bat ne - ka - be - lah le - lah.

Example 3. Second most-commonly submitted melody

Le - cha do - di li - krat ka - lah p' - nei sha - bat ne - ka - be - lah, le - cha do - di li - krat ka - lah p' - nei sha - bat ne - ka - be - lah. Le - cha do - di le - cha do-di li-krat ka - lah le - cha do-di li-krat ka - lah, le - cha do-di li-krat ka - lah p' - nei sha-bat ne-ka - be - lah.

the two most popular tunes are of different geographic and musical orientation, and that one is by a known composer and the other is anonymous, typifies the variety and the layered sense of repertoire in the music for the liturgy.

In the second rank of popularity, along with the Lewandowski there is a clearly Hasidic tune (eleven entries) with a lively, syncopated rhythm far from the rather stately sound of examples 1 and 2 (example 4). It is perhaps not surprising to find a number of Hasidic-oriented melodies for Lecha dodi, since the Hasidim have been the main preservers of the mystical tradition from which Lecha dodi sprang, with all its emphasis on the immense potential of the sung prayer to bring the worshipper closer to God.[9]

"Sulzer-Lewandowski" and "Hasidic" are two of the basic repertoire pools hazzanim informally define when discussing the range of available musics. Among the other Lecha dodi variants submitted, we find most of the remaining pools: "Israeli," "contemporary composer" (e.g., Ben Steinberg, Paul Ben-Haim), "my own," and even a melody from Salomone Rossi, the pioneering seventeenth-century Italian Jewish composer.[10] Adding to the diversity of settings, two hazzanim thoughtfully included the version of Lecha dodi commonly reserved for specific times in the liturgical calendar. One sang the variant for the three Friday nights preceding *Tisha b'av* ("ninth of the month Av"), the official day marking the destruction of the First and Second Temples and other catastrophes, when the joyous Lecha dodi tune is changed to mark that solemn season. Another gave a version for "the month of Elul," the period of the High Holidays, singing a Lecha dodi straight out of the appropriate melodic sources for that period (example 5).These two hazzanim deftly illustrate the persistence of seasonal variation in melodic types which we will examine in chapter 11 as part of the key concept of *nusach*.

Summarizing Lecha dodi, we come up with a few helpful points of orientation in the area of musical choice for a participatory prayer: (1) as a congregational tune, the notion of "favorites" is shared by congregation and hazzan. The latter may insist on "my tune," but will also give congregants popular melodies. Most—probably all—hazzanim have more than one Lecha dodi up their sleeves; (2) the sources for

Example 4. Hasidic-style *Lecha dodi*

Example 5a. Seasonal variant: *Lecha dodi* for three Friday nights before
Tisha b'Av

Le - cha   do - di   li - krat_ ka - lah   p' - nei   sha - bat   ne - ka - be -
lah,   le - cha   do - di   li - krat ka - lah   p' - nei   sha - bat   ne - ka - be - lah.

Example 5b. Seasonal variant: *Lecha dodi* for the month of Elul

Le - cha   do - di   li - krat___ ka - lah   p' -
nei___   sha - bat   ne - ka - be - lah.

this widespread hymn are just as varied as one might expect; (3) even
this stock item shows some sensitivity to seasonal change within the
liturgical year; and (4) the pattern of choice among a sample of ninety-
three contemporary hazzanim is not random—there are two ranks of
popularity, scattered favorites and isolated tunes. This weighting is
partly due to congregational choice, but also shows cantorial individualism, so nicely illustrates the worshipper-sacred singer dialectic at
the heart of the music of participation.

Tzur yisroel

Unlike Lecha dodi, with its colorful and datable history, Tzur yisroel
is a more conventional passage from the middle of the Saturday morning service, closing the *Shema* section of the liturgy and making the
transition to the *Amidah*, which begins with silent prayer.[11] It restates
Israel's faith in the Lord and asks for release from the sufferings and
diaspora of the Jews: "Rock of Israel, arise to Israel's defense. Fulfill
Your promise to deliver Judah and Israel. Our Redeemer is the Holy
One of Israel, the Lord of hosts is his name. Praised are You, Lord,
Redeemer of the people Israel" (Harlow 1972:123).

The prayerbook does not dictate whether this passage is to be rendered solo by the hazzan or sung by the whole assembly. In America

today, it has become a congregational tune in most Conservative synagogues. What is more, a single melody for this text has captured the
fancy of a vast majority of congregations. Of ninety-three versions
collected in the Project sample, seventy-two were the same tune. This
means that Tzur yisroel is useful for looking at two things: (1) how
differently a hazzan might sing the same consensus tune, and (2) what
other choices might be available for a minority.

Example 6 is the most common way to sing the standard melody.[12]
If you sing it to yourself, you will notice its rhythmic regularity: it is
a "metrical" tune. This is not surprising; Werner notes that "of all
Jewish traditions, *minhag ashkenaz* contains the largest share of metrical
melodies, and the more recent the tune, the stronger its propensity
towards metrical structure" (1976:5). How recent is the popular Tzur
yisroel tune? No one today seems positive about the origin of the tune
despite its popularity. Extensive questioning of hazzanim produced a
tentative view that it might have been composed by Zeidel Rovner
(1886–1943), a cantor-composer discussed in earlier chapters who was
influential in America in the interwar period. The fact that the melody
has become "traditional" shows that hazzanim can be just like their
congregations: within a short period of time, they forget the origins of
a tune if it is not printed in a standard text. The fact that this melody
is *not* published is surprising for such a popular tune and shows how
strong oral tradition still is in the cantorial world. Hazzanim still learn
from each other, even if the teaching may take place in an official
training program.[13]

The tune seems to have four lines, following the text division. Melodically, the first and third lines—A and C of example 6—are very
similar, and B and D also resemble each other. No wonder this tune

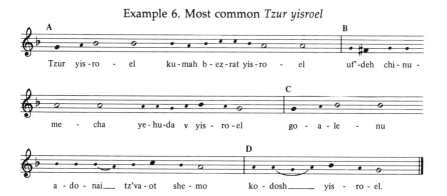

Example 6. Most common *Tzur yisroel*

is so popular—it is very easy for any congregant to learn after only brief exposure. The parallelism between the two halves of example 6 (A+B, C+D) leads some hazzanim to carry out the similarity completely, making a totally symmetrical tune, as in example 7.

Given this basic structure, hazzanim turn up quite a number of small variations, giving individualism its due within a predictable melody. Examples 8, 9, and 10 show three personal ways of singing the same tune; departures from the norm are starred for easy identification. Example 8 has a rather popular pickup for line openings and a tendency to leap up to a note higher than usual at the end of lines C and D. That this is done symmetrically shows a tendency to generalize particular ways of melodic thinking. Example 9 introduces another symmetrical approach at midline. Example 10 is more unusual in creating new turns of phrase stressing the note *b*. All these individual ap-

Example 7. Symmetrical version of *Tzur yisroel*

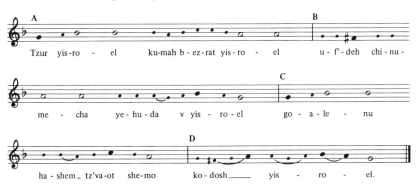

Example 8. Personal variation of *Tzur yisroel*

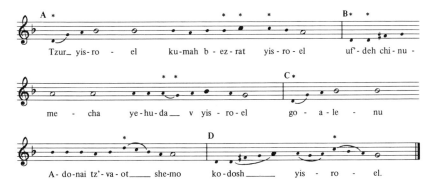

Example 9. Personal variation of *Tzur yisroel*

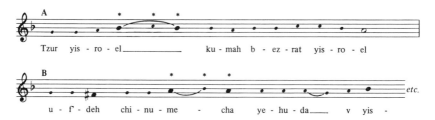

Example 10. Personal variation of *Tzur yisroel*

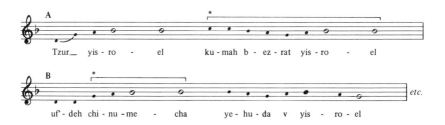

Example 11. Text accent shift in *Tzur yisroel*

Example 12. Text accent shift in *Tzur yisroel*

proaches are acceptable and show where a hazzan can locate creativity even within the bounds of a stock tune.

One sort of melodic variation may force the hazzan into shifting the accentuation pattern of the Hebrew text, putting the emphasis on the wrong syllable. This is considered bad form in our times, as a corollary of professionalization, but was hardly an issue in previous generations, particularly in the work of the virtuoso hazzanim. Examples 11 and 12 illustrate this issue. In example 11, the melody pushes the accent on *tz'vaot* from the third to the second syllable, paralleled by the just-earlier shift from third to second syllable on *adoshem* (a more pious substitute for *adonai* for the name of God). In example 12, the stress shifts from the third to the fourth syllable of *chinumecha*.

Another issue of text delivery once standard, now problematic, is whether any words or syllables can be repeated. The great hazzanim of the past repeated syllables, words, and whole passages at will to produce long, dramatic musical lines that often moved their listeners to tears. Today even Orthodox hazzanim and worshippers protest at the slightest bit of word repetition, partly on aesthetic grounds but mainly because it "drags out" the service. In our Tzur yisroel sample, a very small amount of word repetition turned up as a personal approach, as in example 13, where *kodosh* ["holy"] is sung twice for emphasis, perhaps reminiscent of one of the most striking passages in the Sabbath liturgy, the core of the *Kedushah*, where "*kodosh, kodosh, kodosh*" is a central phrase ["Holy, holy, holy is the Lord of Hosts"].

Finally, there are the twenty-three collected settings of Tsur yisroel that avoid the standard tune entirely. Remarkably, no two of these versions are the same. This strengthens a general pattern we saw in Lecha dodi of considerable consensus, but substantial individualism. As usual, more than one repertoire pool is represented. We have the "contemporary composer" pool in the form of the Tzur yisroel setting from Bloch's *Sacred Service*, a highly influential piece. Another hazzan uses what he calls the "Zionist" version, presumably from an Israeli tune source. But most of the nonstandard melodies are from what hazzanim call the "traditional nusach" pool (see chapter 11), being very cantorial in quality. In essence, this means there is too much detail and display for the setting to be congregational. In this way, the professional sets him/herself off as the musical/aesthetic leader—if the congregation allows—by foregoing the standard tune. Example 14 is an elaborate example of the cantorial approach to Tzur yisroel. So complete is this hazzan's sense of a large, overall form that he cannot wind down to ending on the required *g* without including the text of the *bracha* ["blessing"] that follows the Tzur yisroel text.[14]

Summarizing Tzur yisroel, it stands as a fine example of widespread acceptance of a standard tune. The tune being by now very nearly anonymous, it represents the persistence of oral tradition in the modern

Example 13. Word repetition in *Tzur yisroel*

ko - dosh yis - ro - el   ko - dosh____ yis - ro el

Example 14. Personal variation of *Tzur yisroel*

A
Tzur yis-ro-el   ku   -   mah   b - ez - ras yis-ro-el_____

B
u - f'-deh   chi - nu - me - cha   ye - hu - da___   v yis - ro -el_____

C
go-a-le   -   -   nu   A - do- nai   tz'- va os   she-mo

D   *bracha* extension
ko-dosh_ yis-ro - el.   Bo-ruch a - tah A-do-nai go al____ yis-ro   -   el.

cantorate. The fact that one-quarter of Project respondents sang their own, largely cantorial settings despite nationwide agreement on a single congregational melody tells us that the hazzan-congregation dialectic is still lively.

Having surveyed the music of participation for the Ashkenazic mainstream, where it has been a minority approach traditionally,[15] it is important to complement the discussion with a brief survey of the Sephardic-American situation, quite different in many essential aspects. While a thorough study of this pioneering and still lively branch of American Judaism lies beyond the scope of this book, it would be remiss not to point out that Ashkenazic practice is not universal, particularly in the context of the present chapter. As noted earlier, Sephardic practice of the London-Amsterdam variety was the earliest and long the most influential model of the worship service until the Reform and East European models came to prominence. In terms of participation, the terms are set quite differently in the western Sephardic tradition, as described by David DeSola Pool, a rabbi and scion of one of the great Shearith Israel families:

> The hazzan remains the leader in prayer . . . while pleasing musical rendition is expected of him, he is not called on to sing the involved note groupings of the Oriental Sephardi tradition, or the coloratura cadences often heard in Ashkenazi synagogues. Hazzan and choir guide the congregational singing . . . but essentially the service of worship remains with

the congregation. Indeed, in some of the most familiar and best-loved hymns, the choir is expected to follow and not lead the congregation (DeSola Pool and DeSola Pool 1955:157).

Back in 1866, Isaac Leeser supported this view when he described the ease and power of Sephardic hymns, which he ended up preferring to his native German service: "The tunes are such that nearly every one with the least voice and the smallest musical taste can participate in them and, what is more, they are of that popular nature that they seem to be the very utterance of a whole people's thankfulness and entreaty. . . . Those who composed the tunes . . . knew what would inspire and excite the mind. . . . [The hymns] will haunt the memory and imagination for ever when once heard" (*Occident* 24, no. 8, Nov. 1866:340–41). Continuing his analysis, Leeser very helpfully contrasts the Sephardic and German styles: "The German Minhag is, indeed, not without tunes of the same fascinating tendency . . . but they are mostly for the Hazzan, and the congregation is neither capable nor expected to join in the singing, and thus they lack the element of popularity."[16] Abraham Lopes Cardozo, just retired after forty years as the sacred singer of Shearith Israel, fills out the picture: "A Sephardic hazzan is not a cantor in the Ashkenazic sense, but rather a reader and a leader of the services. In many Sephardic congregations the *hakham* or the rabbi also not infrequently acts as reader" (Cardozo 1960:40). Because of its simplicity and its limited range, the Sephardic chant facilitates and invites congregational participation with the hazzan serving as leader.

The organizational counterpart to this situation is the job description: at Shearith Israel, the figure likely to be called "cantor" elsewhere is "assistant hazzan," the title Cardozo held, with the rabbi still being considered the hazzan. Apparently this means the rabbi can feel free to take the juicier liturgical items for himself, including the main plum of the year, Kol Nidre.[17] In a sense, the rabbi, understood in modern American terms, has taken on something like the traditional hakham's authority, while the "cantor" has the lower status the hazzan was accorded in earlier centuries. In any case, the hazzan would not get to do elaborate vocalizing, since the essence of the Sephardic hazzanut is meticulous correctness with no improvisation.[18]

Finally, before leaving the Sephardic context, it is vital to remember that the western Sephardic tradition, though the first in America, is only one of many Sephardic and Asian traditions that stand out from the dominant Ashkenazic approach. Along with the great wave from eastern Europe, a parallel stream of Jews from the Mediterranean arrived, who were not part of the patrician Shearith Israel crowd and who created their own service types: "In September 1915 . . . there were more than twenty Sephardic services going on in New York City for the High Holidays. . . . [By 1920 they] held thirty different services" (Angel 1982:32–33). We lack full description of these small-scale services, except for the clear picture that, like the parallel East European situation, intensely localized organizations thrived. In terms of our current topic—participation—we can at least note that another comparison with the East European scene is relevant: in the Mediterranean tradition, high demands are made on the hazzan, who is expected to display a skillful, perhaps even virtuoso, knowledge of the musical system, based on complex melodic structures that parallel the Middle Eastern modal *maqam* system. Though this aspect of the organization of the service contrasts with the western Sephardic tradition, the tendency to keep the leadership role non- or semiprofessional is shared by both the Mediterranean and the western Sephardim. This means that amateur or semiprofessional status is the norm, with a high level of expectation of those who take on the leadership role. This puts participation into a slightly different light; though the sacred singer should be a true aesthetic-inspirational leader, he is still a first among equals.[19]

Participation in its broadest sense comes down to the issue of whether the hazzan or the congregation is thought of as the architect of the service and the guardian of the synagogue's tradition, a topic which needs a bit more discussion. The notion of local variation, as we saw in chapter 1, was built into Jewish tradition under the term *minhag*, a flexible word applying to local custom in all its richness, from the celebration of holidays to styles of dress, ornament, and music. There are very large *minhagim*, such as the difference between Ashkenazic and Sephardic, and very small ones. To a certain extent, each synagogue has its own minhag in the sense that its members, year after year, insist on certain ways of doing things that are "our way."

In the Western Sephardic tradition of early America, the hazzan was largely viewed as guardian, even when individual contributions were conceded to have value. At Shearith Israel, when the towering figure Jacques Judah Lyons (1813–1877) passed away, his repertoire was left intact: "When he died it was thought that changes would be introduced in the ritual of the synagogue to which he had so long ministered, but . . . although thirty-five years have passed away no change of any kind has taken place" (*Lyons Collection* 1:xxxvi). The extent to which music is felt to stay the same is in the minds of the listeners, and a perceptive ear like David DeSola Pool's has noticed that things change despite the appearance of stability: "Each successive hazzan with a more or less accurate musical ear, or with a penchant for the higher or the lower

ranges, whether he came from Amsterdam, from London, from Suri-
nam, from Gibraltar, or elsewhere, inevitably brought with him to New
York local variations of chanting which often left their mark, however
much he might try to adapt himself to the niceties of Shearith Israel's
own local tradition" (DeSola Pool and DeSola Pool 1955:96).[20]

What is true for Shearith Israel holds for the entire American situation. There are three basic reasons for variety, which have not changed
over the course of two centuries: (1) mobility of membership; (2) mobility of hazzanim; and (3) a penchant for creating a temporary local
consensus, synagogue by synagogue, of "our tradition," all this within
the setting of a country known for immense volatility in its musical
life in a society marked by successive waves of immigration. The music
of participation is one emotionally charged arena for working out these
issues—perhaps even weekly.

Strategies for safeguarding local tradition—what I am calling minhag
here—are occasionally documented, whether for Sephardic or Ashkenazic congregations: "Gustavus M. Cohen, who came from Germany in
1844, was the first hazzan of Temple Emanuel in New York. In 1852,
Cohen was forced to give his successor all of his music, although he
objected that they were either his own works or his own liturgical
arrangements. Evidently he was prevailed upon to give Rubin his work"
(Cohen 1976). Thus was born a Temple Emanuel local minhag. The
idea that a hazzan might be capable of creating his own repertoire,
though it is well illustrated by the preceding quote, was novel to Isaac
Leeser a generation later, indicating how strong the notion of the an-
tiquity of congregational repertoires can be: "The new Polish synagogue was dedicated [in Savannah]. . . . Rev. Mr. Lewin of the Mikva
Israel congregation . . . conducted the service. . . . The melodies, the
paper before us says, were entirely new and were introduced in Savannah by Mr. Lewin. We do not understand this altogether. Perhaps
the reporter meant that they were new to him; or else our friend has
the additional merit of being a composer of original melodies, which
would not be a slight merit in him" (*Occident* 25, no. 8, Nov. 1867:415–
16).

First among equals or innovator at the cutting edge; an artist kept
on a congregational leash or a musical mover and shaker—no one
musical role has been entirely dominant at any given time or place in
America for the hazzan. How people organize their music, even in
terms of performance itself, is often an example of the social order
itself, as ethnomusicology teaches. In a sense, the issue of participation
is itself musical, a fine instance of group improvisation on a grand
scale.

NOTES

1. The seeds had been sown for this approach earlier by a group of young Turks within what was to become the Conservative movement. Members of the Jewish Endeavor Society, including the young Mordecai Kaplan, began as early as 1901 to organize "young people synagogues" in which "congregational singing in English and Hebrew was encouraged" (Gurock 1983:115). Of course, for the Reform, "participation" via congregational hymn-singing had been standard for a long time, and for the Sephardim, as we shall see, the notion of group dominance had its own meaning as well.

2. Though Young Israel was nominally Orthodox, denominational lines were much more fluid then than now. Their willingness to find a theological sponsor to back mixed singing shows their flexibility, and in fact Young Israel seems to have had a considerable impact on the emerging Conservative notion of service-building as well, though documentation is scanty.

3. Lawrence Hoffman, former director of the Reform's School of Sacred Music, sees this trend expanding: "If we assume such people are typical of Americans born in the baby boom of the 40's and 50's, and now just reaching child-bearing age; if we further assume people generally exercise influence over liturgical modes only after their children reach educable age and force their parents to take a stand on Jewish identity; then we can expect this model of worship choreography to expand rapidly in the next decade" (Hoffman 1982:161).

4. To do otherwise seems suicidal to some: "A lot of congregations and even hazzanim are . . . taking the easy way out, by making the whole service congregational in nature which means, in a sense, the hazzan is cutting his own throat. Because . . . they're not really expanding the repertoire even with congregational melodies; a lay person can stand up there and do the service. What do they need a hazzan for? So then, the hazzan in the pulpit will be minimized, his duties in the pulpit will be lessened because they got the service reduced, not to the highest artistic level" (A.C.).

5. This sort of variety can be expanded to include whole services; one hazzan does a five- to six-week cycle of Friday night services, including notes and lectures, including Sephardic, Hasidic, western European, eastern European, and "classical" and contemporary composed services. On the other hand, another professional feels that such diversity is excessive, because the service should be clear and straightforward with no interruptions and jumps, because people expect confirmation of the service as a habit (G.F.).

6. This is part of an elaborate ritual of the Safed circle: "[They] used to form a procession every Friday afternoon and go to the outskirts of Safed to receive the Sabbath Bride with song and praise. . . . [T]his mystic ceremony spread to other communities, where the Sabbath Bride was welcomed not in the fields, but in the synagogue immediately before the Friday evening service. In time the Kabbalat Shabbat was standardized to consist of six psalms, corresponding to the six days of the week, and the hymn Lecha Dodi" (Millgram 1975:502).

7. For example, the Reform *Union Hymnal* has only the Lewandowski setting. The question of prayerbooks and their impact on the cantorate can only be

briefly touched upon in the present study, but offers another avenue for future research, since any siddur is the voice of the denomination that produces it and summarizes the philosophy of a generation—or more—of Jewish-Americans. No wonder hazzanim are always eager to be on the committees that revise the prayerbook.

8. This prominence shows the continued importance of the "Sulzer-Lewandowski" repertoire pool, which includes the contemporary Samuel Naumbourg.

9. Nothing could be farther from the atmosphere of the mainstream Jewish-American service than the Kabbalat Shabbat among the Bratslaver Hasidim in Jerusalem, an indelible musical memory for which I am grateful to Samuel Heilman and Jeffrey Summit.

10. The other pools are "cantor-composer," encompassing a wide variety of composers from the late nineteenth century through the interwar period, who were both active hazzanim and gifted producers of functional sacred song, "traditional nusach," the meaning of which is explored in chapter 11, and something like "modern," including a variety of pop-based or perhaps Israeli tunes of recent origin, many of which can be sublabeled by their composers, such as "a Zim tune."

11. According to Max Wohlberg (personal communication), Tzur yisroel became a popular congregational tune only in recent decades, showing the continued volatility of congregational taste, a feature that marks the entire history of the prayerbook, yet another form of improvisation on sacred text as described in chapter 1. Tzur yisroel's concluding *bracha*, a formulaic blessing, is not included in the musical examples here, but it raises an interesting point. Because this prayer immediately precedes the silence of the Amidah, the hazzan (and congregation) should taper off at the end of Tzur yisroel, ending in a whisper, an eloquent illustration of the precise structuring and execution of the service. The amount of technical ritual knowledge any competent hazzan must master is extraordinary, making particularly clear what an achievement it is to acquire such skills through schooling rather than upbringing, an increasingly common phenomenon.

12. The examples taken from the sample tapes submitted by ninety-three members of the Cantors Assembly represent extrasanctuary performances that do not reflect the dynamic nature of tune singing in actual participatory performances. This is due to two factors: (1) the data bank of live, in-service performances is small, and (2) the stress of this book is on the hazzan, not on the congregation, though the latter deserves full study as well.

13. Responses to the query "Where did you learn your version?" from the group that sent in tapes showed for many selections that interhazzan tune trading is still very much alive as an important source of acquisition, along with printed sources, upbringing, and schooling. Some hazzanim pointedly remarked how much better the atmosphere is for such sharing today than in the interwar period when they had to buy or steal repertoire from cantor-teachers or famous performers. One hazzan told of nabbing Zeidel Rovner's

melodies when he was out of the room—perhaps this is how tunes like the favorite Tzur yisroel began on their path to prominence!

14. His use of the Ashkenazic rather than the now more popular Sephardic pronunciation (*ezras* rather than *ezrat*) also marks this hazzan as rooted in the East European cantorial tradition.

15. Of course, participation is still the watchword for the Orthodox, as described in chapter 5. "Participation" is a tricky word; the traditional Conservative service, with its core of what today's hazzanim call "real daveners," was in many ways participatory, with the hazzan displaying his leadership largely through "recitatives," arialike breaks in the communal action, to highlight a certain text.

16. Continuing the same passage, Leeser raises the professional placement issue that flows from his analysis: "Hence the difficulty of supplying the place of sheliach tzibbur on the great festivals . . . while among the Sephardim it would not take a very long probation to fit any person having a decent voice and a comparative good knowledge of the Hebrew to read the service on all the solemn occasions, or else we for one would scarcely have been able to become sufficiently qualified to officiate, as we have done for a long series of years, having no knowledge of musical annotation and no facility to learn playing on musical instruments" (340–41).

17. Judit Frigyesi (personal communication) adds that "this applies to many European Orthodox Ashkenazi synagogues as well, with the difference that the rabbi usually keeps the *Neila* (solemn conclusion of Yom Kippur) for himself rather than the Kol Nidre."

18. According to Cardozo, in a Sephardic congregation like Amsterdam, a job candidate would be judged not by elaborate chant, as among eastern Europeans, but by his pronunciation and intonation in reading the very taxing Mishnah passage *Bame madlikin*. As noted above, professionalization has led to a similar preoccupation with pronunciation among the Ashkenazim.

19. However, this tradition has been eroded by the majority Ashkenazic model, which stresses professionalization, as can be noted in this report from the Syrian community of Brooklyn: "The cantorial tradition among Syrian Jews in Brooklyn is in flux. Traditionally the domain of talented non-professionals, the position is fast being taken over by professionally trained cantors from Israel. . . . 'In the old country, there were no professionals. In the United States, it's a big business. . . . People today feel you now need a big figure in a robe walking down the aisle. It's the influence of the Ashkenazic tradition' " (Shelemay 1986).

20. This is an old problem at America's oldest congregation; a 1789 letter of one Manuel Josephson caustically attacks variation: "As to our North American congregations . . . they have no regular system; chiefly owing . . . to the smallness of their numbers and the frequent mutability of its members from one place to another. . . . And every newcomer introduces something new, either from his own conceit and fancy or (what is more probable) from the custom of the Congregation where he was bred, or the one he last came from" (quoted in DeSola Pool and DeSola Pool 1955).

10

The Music of Presentation

Without unfolded wings no free development of music and
singing is possible.
—Salomon Sulzer, 1865

The composer has to write music which will strengthen
their shaky ethnic-religious identity.
—Bonia Shur, 1984

One way out of the problems raised by the participation issue is to
circumvent it entirely by using two types of services: (1) completely
composed services, commissioned by congregations from local or nationally known composers; and (2) in-house services composed/pro-
duced by the hazzan, often in conjunction with the rabbi and/or local
musical collaborators. Both service types are highly sensitive to the
contemporary musical atmosphere, perhaps even reflecting short-term
fads, and each offers the congregation a prefabricated presentation.

This chapter will briefly describe both types of service, then move
in to a detailed discussion of one small, key prayer—the *Barchu*—to
illustrate the long and complex interaction between the hazzan and
the composer.

Commissioned services

Commissioned services come in two varieties, which overlap somewhat. At one extreme, we find the respected "serious" composer of
Jewish origin who has either decided to dedicate his/her energies to
sacred music or who is willing to take time out from mainstream composition to respond to a commission from a synagogue.[1] The most
influential model of the latter variety is Ernest Bloch's 1933 *Avodat
Hakodesh/Sacred Service*. Bloch (1880–1959) was a world-famous composer who was prevailed upon to look to his Jewish roots and to write
for the synagogue. His impressive, demanding work demonstrated the

possibility of creating an entire service couched completely in the contemporary compositional idiom, and it cast a long shadow. Hazzanim
mention only Darius Milhaud's 1947 *Service sacre* in the same breath
as the Bloch work, due to the composer's comparable renown. Few
Jewish composers are impelled to write complete services; it is not a
"natural" urge, like it might be for a Catholic composer to decide to
make his contribution to the ancient and ongoing project of setting the
text of the Mass.

At the other end of the compositional continuum we find services
by composers who are closer to the cantorial workplace or who are
hazzanim themselves. In these works, the composers attempt to work
out their personal musical poetics and politics of the service. As an
example, we can take Max Wohlberg's *Chemdat Shabbat* of 1970. Published by the Cantors Assembly, this work attempts to articulate the
professionals' current concerns about participation. In his notes to the
service, Samuel Rosenbaum spells out its ideology:

> One of the things which congregations today seem to want most is a
> wider share of participation in the service. Unfortunately, many American
> Jews cannot participate in the most meaningful way, in the way in which
> Jews for centuries participated, by davening. However, the need is there
> and it is legitimate. It is up to hazzanim and rabbis to devise a service
> which is at once true to Tradition, but which, at the same time, will permit
> even partially illiterate Jews wider participation. (Wohlberg 1971).

The solution to this dilemma is an artfully composed service that will
give each party its fair share of the musical action: " 'Chemdat Shabbat'
is a unique answer to this need. It is a service conceived, from beginning
to end, as an antiphonal, cooperative venture between hazzan and
congregation.... Like all good things it will not be acquired easily.
Congregations will need to undertake to study the parts which the
composer has assigned to them and the hazzan will require the discipline of chanting his sections just as the composer has written them
in order that the maximum effect be achieved" (Wohlberg 1971). In
short, for a meaningful truce between hazzan and congregation to take
place in the conflict over participation, both sides must lay down their
arms and agree to collaborate. How frequently works such as *Chemdat
Shabbat* are performed is hard to tell, since no one monitors the weekly
service across America and sales figures do not reflect the standard
practice of saving the congregation's money by xeroxing. Interviews
with hazzanim indicate some enthusiasm for the composed service as
an occasional special event to attract an audience of urban synagogue-
goers who enjoy going to concerts. Hazzanim tend to be ambivalent

about commissioned works because the congregation has to feel its scanty arts funds have been well spent and, at times, because they have to respond to a composer's demands instead of their own. On the other hand, they relish the showcasing of their talent and taste.

Locally composed services

There are two kinds of services that spring out of local circumstances: (1) the local "traditional" service, which has evolved over time, discussed in the previous chapter. In a sense, every weekly service across America is a jointly composed local production; and (2) the special service made by local musicians, often reflecting a current trend, to which we now turn.

In terms of the first type—jointly created by a number of influential clergy and their congregational supporters over time—it is very helpful when a congregation decides to publish its idiomatic service, as did Adath Jeshurun of Philadelphia on the occasion of its 125th anniversary in 1983, in the form of a record album with extensive notes. The history of this particular congregation and service—as everywhere—is a compendium of various developments, and because the album summarizes the situation concisely, it can stand as example of a large-scale process.

Begun along Reform lines, Adath Jeshurun quickly gravitated towards the emerging Conservative movement under its rabbi from 1910–60, Max Klein. This history is mirrored in the unfolding of the local service, as the record notes by Hazzan Charles Davidson explain:

> Throughout much of A.J.'s early history, the Congregation worshiped using the *Abodath Israel* prayer book which was edited by Rabbi Marcus Jastrow of Philadelphia [an important "liberal" of his day] and Rabbi Benjamin Szold of Baltimore. It was originally issued in German in 1864, and then translated into English a year later.
>
> [In 1951] the Congregation first used the *Seder Avodah* which was edited by its rabbi, Max D. Klein. . . . Rabbi Klein included traditional Hebrew prayers which had been omitted from the Jastrow and Szold prayerbook, retranslated the *Siddur* into a felicitous, poetic rendition, and modified the traditional text to reflect his theological and philosophical perspective.

This completely personal approach to the prayerbook explains the distinctiveness of A.J.'s service and offer a fine example of the basis for a locally composed service, here done largely by the rabbi, who also wrote hymns, with later additions, particularly since the hiring of a full-time hazzan, Davidson, who is a prolific composer. Somehow, composition and participation are both stressed this way: "A visitor . . . will note . . . the unique style of congregational participation.

Whereas in most traditional Synagogues the worship Service alternates between individual devotions paced by the cantor's leadership of opening and closing sections, the Service at A.J. is conducted largely through unison worship. Whether in English or in Hebrew, the Congregation prays the Service together." Adath Jeshurun's special service, then, is a fine compendium of the possibilities latent in localism, which can build up an extraordinary sense of loyalty to a unique minhag.

We turn now to the second type of local service, the all-at-once production responding to current conditions. Many recent in-house developments respond directly to the intense search for "relevance" that characterized much of American society in the mid–1960s to mid–1970s. As rock became the major musical idiom for youth, those who wanted to attract the young created new genres. The much-touted musical *Jesus Christ Superstar* showed it was possible to legitimize the trend and to use it for new ends, highlighting a tendency in American churches to introduce a variety of folk and rock services. Synagogues were not far behind, true to the Jewish spirit of domesticating the surrounding musical styles. One of the key figures in bringing new sounds into the Reform synagogue was Raymond Smolover, hazzan, composer, and long-term leader of the American Conference of Cantors. His *Edge of Freedom: A Folk/Rock Service for the Sabbath* was performed in conjunction with a group from NFTY, the Reform summer camp program. In his notes, Smolover frankly explains his interest in working with young people:

> I realized that we had been asking our children to accept our God and the God of our fathers, and what He sounds like. I realized after almost twenty years of teaching them the sound of my God, that I must listen to the sound of theirs. I dared enter their world aware that I may be respectfully tolerated, amusingly indulged, or murmuringly ignored. They welcomed me. It may be that the Folk/Rock Service is not completely their sound nor my own. It may be what happened, when their God met mine (Smolover n.d.a).

Smolover has created a series of such services, explaining the need for "religious rock . . . a new term, chosen to express a tradition as ancient as the chanting of scripture, as joyful as a Hasidic nigun and as contemporary as folk/ and jazz/rock"[2] (Smolover n.d.b). He has also attempted to bridge the interfaith gap through this style with *Where the Rainbow Ends* (1972), which garnered favorable comment from the heads of the ecumenical Protestant, Catholic, and Jewish organizations.

During the 1970s, the Reform were not alone in experimentation. Sol Zim, hazzan at a Conservative synagogue, created *David Superstar* in 1974. On the liner notes, the major Jewish radio producer in the New York area, Art Raymond, was effusive in his praise: "TIMES CHANGE, PEOPLE CHANGE, and if we are to grow we must learn to change with the times. Today SOL ZIM'S 'DAVID SUPERSTAR' is a REVOLUTIONARY IDEA but fifty years from today this, too will be TRADITIONAL" (Raymond 1974).

The conflict between the notion of the commissioned contemporary music service and the "relevant" in-house service is nowhere clearer than in remarks by David Putterman in 1969. At Park Avenue Synagogue, Putterman was the foremost champion of bringing renowned composers into the synagogue through a long-term program of commissioning Friday night services from the best-known contemporary composers (such as Aaron Copland, Leonard Bernstein). Not all the composers accepted, but many famous people did. Writing from this vantage point, Putterman decries the rock service:

> Can one imagine the Hazzan on the pulpit in front of the sacred arc, flooded by psychedelic multi-colored lighting effects . . . accompanied by electronics, as he gesticulates, waves, shakes his face and body in affected pseudo sexual contortions in order to emphasize the frenetic rhythms of rock and roll? We must reject the notion that "anything goes," or that we must "be with it." We must not demean our houses of worship. The pulpit is not a stage, a religious service is not a performance, the Hazzan is not a performer (Putterman 1969:23–24).

Yet many younger hazzanim disagree; as one puts it, "anything that turns Jews on is good for the Jews; [later they can] move to another level" (H.H.). Though the "with-it" service has been pronounced a thing of the past, a fad, it has remained as a musical resource available to any hazzan who finds it useful. One San Francisco Bay area hazzan has continued to create a jazz service, noting that it raises synagogue attendance from 35–40 worshippers to 500 on a Friday evening. Premiered in 1984, Bruce Benson's jazz service was lauded by Michael Isaacson, an important contemporary synagogue composer: "The plaintive saxophone of Kenny G echoes Benson's stylized chant with good natured warmth. Cantor Benson's quest in redefining Synagogue music in America is to be applauded; for it is only by energetic musical activity that a truly representative sound can be found. The Cantor's mission is ours as well: To make a statement that says our worship is of this time, place and condition—This is our Jewish musical legacy for future generations" (Isaacson 1986).

Rock and jazz are not the only media for special services, whose content is limited only by the hazzan's imagination and the congregation's budget. Various other experiments have flourished, especially in the "relevance" era. For example, during the black consciousness period, one hazzan did a multimedia service called "Torah like it is," featuring multiple slide projections with appropriate sermon and music commenting on the black-white conflict in America (F.I.). Others have turned to nonpolitical genres, such as the children's choir service. In the late 1970s, Jerome B. Kopmar found he could focus a great deal of attention on music in the synagogue in a small community (Dayton, Ohio) by creating an immensely active children's choir program. As the choir's recording with Jan Peerce (a role model for many hazzanim) describes it:

> The Beth Abraham Youth Chorale . . . has achieved a record of accomplishments that is unique in the American synagogue. They have toured the United States from Coast to Coast as well as Canada, England and twice in Israel. . . . In March, 1980, the Chorale was featured in a special documentary on the CBS National Television network. . . . The Chorale's role in the development of new music for the synagogue [premieres of twelve commissioned works] has earned its members . . . an unprecedented five consecutive Solomon Schechter Awards, symbolic of the highest achievements in music programming in the American synagogue (liner notes to *Across the Generations* 1983).

The question that arises about any variety of special service is how lasting an effect it can have on a given congregation's attitude toward the service, the real payoff from the point of view of hazzan, rabbi, or lay leadership. How many times will people come to hear one rock service, or how long will they continue to be delighted at seeing their children take over the pulpit? Much the same question comes up when discussing any sort of service innovation with hazzanim, one of whom is rather dubious about the long-term impact of fiddling with tradition:

> The synagogue is the graveyard of prayer instead of the life and fountain of the Siddur. Rabbis, hazzanim and concerned laymen have not been unaware of the problem. A great many cures have been suggested and tried . . . let us make changes in the service because it is the fault of the Siddur. Let us find some gimmicks: have it start later, finish earlier, make it short, make it long, more English, less Hebrew, more announcements, less announcements, short sermon, long sermon, study session, more children, less music, more readings, etc., [but] the service is not a classroom but a sensitivity session which can only be created through a sincere, artistic, unified experience and accomplished by a devoted professional (Kula 1974:40–41).

Having surveyed the basic headings of the music of presentation, we can turn to close examination of the core of this category, the commissioned service. A comfortable way to survey such a vast topic is to look at just one piece as set by a representative group of composers over three centuries. Of course, this will not provide a comprehensive analysis, but will touch on how composers view the hazzan in creating Jewish sacred music.

Our case study for composition is the *Barchu*, a formal call to prayer. It cannot be said without a minyan being present. It has a small, but key role in the liturgy: "The *Barchu (Invitatorium)* and its subsequent response constitute one of the most important doxologies, since it is recited twice daily in the course of the morning and evening prayer. Furthermore, it is the initial formula before grace [in a different form] after each meal and before each public scriptural reading" (Werner 1959:281).

The hazzan intones "Praise ye the Lord, who is to be praised," and the congregation responds "Praised is the Lord; He is to be praised for ever and ever." Since the hazzan is also praying for him/herself, he or she repeats the congregational response. Thus this key opening item is a microcosm of the interaction between "messenger" and congregation.

The Barchu is also a good point of entry for the hazzan-composer dialogue: it is short, pithy, and crucially situated. As an overture to the service, particularly the Friday evening service that begins the observance of the Sabbath, the Barchu literally sets the tone. All major and many minor composers have contributed Barchus, so there is no shortage of examples, from the seventeenth century to the present. Since Friday night is the traditional focal point of the Reform synagogue's week and was until recently also the center of Conservative observance, there has been a good market for this particular service for decades.[3] This demand helps explain the abundant supply of composed settings.

We will survey fourteen composers' versions of the Barchu, including: (1) settings by cantor-composers, who are thus wearing two hats; (2) compositions by professional composers, who must take the hazzan's role into account; and (3) the role of the choir, since the response to the hazzan's call is often set for a chorus.[4]

Salomone Rossi

We start with history, with the understanding that the past is part of the present. This notion is embodied in modern adaptations of the work of Salomone Rossi (c. 1565–1628), the first important Jewish composer of modern times. Isidor Freed, an important modern composer whose Barchu is found below, arranged Rossi's work and describes him in the preface:

> Rossi wrote a collection of thirty-three religious songs to Hebrew li-
> turgical texts. These were printed in 1622 under the title *HaShirim Asher
> LiShlomo* (The Songs of Solomon). This is the earliest known published
> volume of harmonized Jewish music. The style is almost entirely Italian
> Renaissance; but here and there a minor cadence intrudes which distin-
> guishes his sacred music from that of his Christian contemporaries. . . .
> We know that he was highly regarded by his contemporaries, for he
> collaborated with Claudio Monteverdi, then also attached to the Mantuan
> Court (Freed 1954).

Rossi wrote for chorus, in the true seventeenth-century manner, and
his works are often performed as benchmark compositions of Jewish
sacred music in European art style. However, the purely choral structure is alien to today's hazzan-choir model. Furthermore, Rossi did not
set all the texts commonly used today, so Freed reshaped Rossi two
ways, setting new texts to the music and rearranging the setting: "The
task was to find Rossi music that could be molded into our liturgy,
both in spirit and in rhythm. . . . It is the hope of the transcriber [Freed]
that this effort to preserve the basic character of Rossi's music will find
favor in the eyes of our synagogue musicians. . . . The changes have
been limited to re-arranging the music in such fashion that it can be
presented by the musical forces found in the average American synagogue—Cantor, four-part choir and organ" (Freed 1954).

Example 15 gives the original opening of Rossi's Barchu in its three-
part choral setting. Example 16 is the Freed arrangement; the choral
response is the same for both. Freed has taken the soprano line of the
Rossi and set it for solo cantor, with the organ filling in the soprano
and baritone voices. The musical effect, of course, is quite different
from the original.

Freed's emphasis on "cantor/choir/organ" as the basic American
synagogue forces applies to Reform and some Conservative congregations only. Many Conservatives do not favor the organ, and no Orthodox do. Not all synagogues have choirs, as it depends on the energy
of the hazzan to recruit and sustain one and the will of the lay leadership to support it financially and morally. Many hazzanim think of
a permanent, professional choir as the ideal, and many composers
assume that if a congregation is interested enough in Jewish art music
to commission or perform modern music, they will hire a choir.

Salomon Sulzer

Sulzer played a pivotal role as the "father" of modern synagogue music. Picking up where Rossi left off, Sulzer aligned Jewish sacred music
with mainstream European composition. He was particularly crucial in

Example 15. Salomone Rossi, *Borchu*, No. 1

Example 15. continued

Example 16. *Bor'chu* arranged by Isidor Freed

Example 16. continued

establishing the importance of the choir: "The institution of a regular choir in the Synagogue has proved to be a sacred and fruitful one, and has become a well-established general practice," he was able to say by the time his first volume of compositions was published in 1839 (quoted in Werner 1954). Werner sees Sulzer as universally applicable today: "The cantor of an Orthodox congregation will find in Sulzer's work at least as much valuable recitative-material, as the cantor of a Conservative or Reform congregation will find of cantor-cum-chorus compositions" (Werner 1954).

Example 17 gives Sulzer's Barchu. Despite Sulzer's modernism, he was also careful to collect and preserve traditional material and weave it into his settings. Two features worth noting are the resolutely Western major-mode sound and the inclusion of the chorus nearly throughout, underlining Sulzer's philosophy. Of secondary interest is the dramatic structure he provides through the dynamic markings, which show little swells at the opening, then an abrupt shift to forte, as well as the tempo shift from *lento e religioso* to *andante*, signs of Sulzer's being a son of the Romantic age of European composition. Also noteworthy is the highly Protestant nature of the choral cadences, particularly the final "amen."

Benjamin Grobani

From the historical backdrop of Rossi and Sulzer, we now move to settings of recent decades. We will begin with "cantor-composers," those local hazzanim who regularly contribute to the sacred music repertoire. Often, they are commissioned by their own synagogues to produce works which will then become part of the local minhag. Grobani's 1966 service is a typical example of this repertoire pool; suitably, it is introduced by his rabbi: "Cantor Benjamin Grobani has completed a full quarter of a century of service as Cantor of Temple Oheb Shalom of Baltimore. . . . [He was] schooled in outstanding musical institutions, such as the Cincinnati College of Music and the Curtis Institute of Music . . . [and] associated with . . . the Philadelphia Grand Opera Company" (Grobani 1966). Rabbi Shaw introduces Grobani's classical music credentials first, outlining the familiar hazzan-opera connection, then turns to his cantorial background: "A boy soprano, he began singing in his earliest years in the choirs of famous cantors in Europe and this country. . . . [He] has written extensively in the field of synagogue music for the festivals and holidays; and with this Friday evening service he further enriches Reform Jewish music" (Grobani 1966). "Reform Jewish" here means composed music, as opposed to the Con-

Example 17. Salomon Sulzer, *Barchu*

servatives' "traditional nusach" source that the Reform have only recently begun to accept.

Grobani himself chooses to emphasize his cantorial lineage over classical training: "To my father, my first teacher in hazzanut, in whose choir I began singing at the age of five years, I owe much of the inspiration that brought forth the music of this service" (Grobani 1966).

Grobani is, then, an ideal example of "cantor-composer:" one who has grown up with the tradition, then learned to adjust it to the craft of classical composition. His Barchu (example 18) illustrates a reliance

Example 18. Benjamin Grobani, *Borchu No. 1*

on early art music models, like Sulzer, and perhaps also the influence of opera in the cantorial melodic line. Technically, it makes few demands, so would be quickly available to the average synagogue forces. Musically, the opening in minor and final cadence in major shows the ambivalence of key that will turn up repeatedly in our examples. According to Max Wohlberg (personal communication), the Barchu was traditionally in the major everywhere except Lithuania, meaning that broad region of northeast European Jewish culture centered on the city of Vilna. Why the Lithuanian minor version has become the favored setting for the Barchu in the United States is one of those mysteries of Americanization for which we have no answer.

Arthur Yolkoff

"Cantor-composers" do not always write just for their own congregation. Arthur Yolkoff's Barchu was commissioned for the children's choir of Jerome Kopmar, cited above as an example of type of "presentation" service. In his preface, Yolkoff links his compositional work to his job as hazzan:

"Working with adult and junior choruses over a number of years, has made me aware of the need for liturgical music written specifically for young people. . . . The challenge was greater than I had anticipated. . . . The music would have to melodically interesting, unpretentious yet challenging, grammatically correct and true to the spirit of each text" (Yolkoff 1966).

As a direct outgrowth of his professional experience Yolkoff's work shows another side of being a "cantor-composer." This is particularly the case in the Barchu (example 19), where he has eliminated the hazzan from the service in favor of the children. Musically, Yolkoff adopts the same modal solution as Grobani, beginning in minor and ending in major. Since this the way that Bach is often interpreted, it is a gesture toward classical music, but at the same time represents a compromise within the Jewish tradition between eastern and western European approaches to the Barchu. His insistence on "grammatically correct" Hebrew shows the influence of current practice, and the method of providing a constant rhythmic figure to unify the music is common in many "unpretentious" contemporary settings.

Rounding out the "cantor-composer" approach, the contribution of the choir-director/organist should not be overlooked. They provided virtually all the music for the classic Reform movement, and continue to play a role in some congregations.[5] When clergy and lay leadership have agreed to commission a new service, they may naturally turn to

Example 19. Arthur Yolkoff, *Bar'chu*

Example 19. continued

ruch_ A-do-nai ha-m'-vo-rach   l'-o-lam__ va - ed.

ruch_ A-do-nai ha-m'-vo-rach____   l'-o-lam va - ed.

their own musician. He may have already contributed to the local minhag, as in the case of a Philadelphia congregation:

> A major event in our Jubilee Year celebration was a special Friday night service for which *Simchat Shabbat* was composed. In seeking a composer for the service, Cantor Neil Newman and I [Rabbi Aaron Landes] turned to Mr. Joseph Meyerov, the gifted choir-director and organist at Beth Sholom, who had composed music for many individual prayers which became significant and beloved parts of the Beth Sholom music tradition. . . . [T]he decision to publish "Simchat Shabbat" was made by the lay-leadership of Beth Sholom as a contribution to the field of Jewish liturgical music (Landes n.d.).

Heinrich Schalit

With this version, we move from the "cantor-composer" to the "contemporary composer" category. Schalit (1886–1976), Viennese-born and highly trained in twentieth-century styles, emigrated to America in 1940 as part of the great wave of central European Jewish intellectuals and artists. Several of these immigrants have had a lasting impact on Jewish sacred music. Schalit produced a large amount of sacred music in the United States, some of which has found a permanent home in Reform congregations. Schalit was quite aware of the significance of the hazzan, as he says in the introduction to his Friday evening service, a major work which appeared first in Germany in 1933 and was reworked and republished in America: "The important role of the CANTOR is demonstrated by the fact that out of the twenty-six selections in this book, fourteen choral pieces have cantorial solos, and five numbers are solo selections without choir" (Schalit 1951).

Schalit's Barchu (example 20) even has its opening organ passage marked as "optional," allowing the hazzan's unmediated voice to open the service. True to Western tradition, it is in the major throughout. A descending bass line underlies the cantorial solo, a simple, effective device many composers rely on to support harmonic motion against the nonharmonic traditional chant. The ornamental twists of the melodic line pay tribute to the old-time hazzan's means of expression, in line with the composer's philosophy. At the same time, he suggests that "the practicability for 'Congregational Singing' [is] indicated in the response to the BOR'CHU," thus allowing for all three parties—hazzan, choir, and congregation—to play a part in the service.

Lazar Weiner

Weiner (1897–1982) was unique among American Jewish musicians, acting as teacher, choral director, pianist, and composer, even being an instructor at the Reform cantorial training program. He wrote art songs based on modern Yiddish poetry, but was equally adept at setting the liturgy. His 1971 *Shir l'yom hashabos* was an outgrowth of David Putterman's energetic commissioning program at the Park Avenue Synagogue, mentioned earlier as an outstanding example of how sacred music has been created in recent decades. Weiner manages to combine "traditional nusach" style, featuring elaborate cantorial flourishes, with modern harmonies in his very brief Barchu (example 21). The piece moves unambiguously into the Eastern minor as the "piano, con devozione" of the hazzan's solo shifts to the "forte" response of choir or congregation.

Max Helfman

Like Weiner, Helfman (1901–63) was an East European by origin, coming to America in 1909. Classically trained, he devoted himself to Jewish music and was particularly influential as director of the Brandeis Music Camp (1945 on), where he taught a generation of younger Jewish-American composers, including Gershon Kingsley, whose Barchu appears below; he also helped found the School of Sacred Music, so had considerable influence on the musical training and taste of Reform hazzanim. His works have been widely adopted.

Helfman was particularly aware of the basic eclecticism of Jewish music, discussed in the preface to the 1950 service from which we take his Barchu (example 22): "Many and diverse are the elements that

Example 20. Heinrich Schalit, *Bor'chu*

*The "Bor'chu" may also start here.

Example 21. Lazar Weiner, *Bor'chu*

make up the music-fabric of the synagogue service. Most of our prayers have their musical as well as liturgic tradition; their own mode, melodic idiom, form and character. . . . Obviously, such kaleidoscopic changes of moods, modes and motives make a pure stylistic continuity difficult to achieve" (Helfman 1969). One virtue Helfman finds in this situation is its dramatic possibilities: "To some extent, however, the difficulty is, in this impressively pageant-like portion of our liturgy, counter-balanced by its inherent dramatic sweep and vitality. It is this dramatic element that I have here primarily sought to capture" (Helfman 1969).

In Helfman's Barchu, the drama is indicated by the marking "with quiet intensity"; apparently he sees the call to prayer as a deeply felt yet subdued preparatory gesture. The chorus echoes the hazzan's melodic line, giving primacy to the sacred singer. Helfman chooses the Western major mode, despite his Eastern background, again indicating the way European roots intertwine to create an American approach.

Miriam Gideon

American-born of German background, Miriam Gideon is an important American composer of secular music who, by taking a position on the

Example 22. Max Helfman, *Bar'chu*

Example 22. continued

faculty of the Jewish Theological Seminary in 1955, has influenced three decades of Conservative cantorial students. Unlike Helfman, Gideon feels comfortable with a "unified" style—her own personal compositional idiom—in her rare settings of sacred music. Her Barchu (example 23) is a model of the purely contemporary approach to the text, being in an atonal idiom. This, along with the delicate counterpoint, probably put the Gideon setting well beyond most regular synagogue choirs, so would be suitable for synagogues with a strong interest in professional art music, certainly a small minority of congregations, or

Example 23. Miriam Gideon, *Bar'chu*

for concert performance. Every year brings Jewish Music Month, and many congregations feel the need to mark the occasion with special concerts or "Jewish Music" services, which may include newly commissioned works or revivals.

Paul Ben-Haim

German-born Paul Ben-Haim is the Israeli composer most performed in the United States, so stands for a special category within recent

Example 23. continued

trends. Though commissioning music from Israelis has perhaps declined, it has been one of the many ways congregations pay tribute to the Jewish state. In 1966, the NFTY commissioned a Friday night service, the source for other Barchus included here. Inviting Ben-Haim contrasts with NFTY's recent prominence as an important force for pop-based religious music. NFTY was cited above as a collaborator with Hazzan Raymond Smolover in creating a rock service. Such turnabouts are typical in the volatile world of Jewish-American culture.

Ben-Haim, a meticulous modernist renowned for integrating Jewish/

Example 23. continued

Middle Eastern style into Israeli art music, straddles the fence in this service, generally allowing for a great amount of flexibility, as his preface shows:

> I have tried to set the prayers to music in as simple and modest a style as possible to express the spirit of the Jewish liturgy. . . . According to the request of the commissioning body I gave an especially simple character to the concluding hymn. . . . The Cantor may be sung by a high baritone

Example 23. continued

or tenor. The accompaniment has been set either for organ or for nine instruments; if the choir is composed of more than 20 singers and an instrumental accompaniment other than organ is used, the string body should be increased accordingly (Ben-Haim 1968).

The proliferation of instructions, which extend for another para-graph, is typical of many composers' prefaces, since there is no way of telling who might adopt or adapt a given work. There is a need for such flexibility, because budgets and expectations vary enormously from synagogue to synagogue, like everything else in congregational life.

Ben-Haim's Barchu (example 24) allows the hazzan a traditional, free recitative statement, but its tonal structure is nontraditional and it is supported by complex modern chords. The choral part, true to NFTY demands, is extremely simple, set in unison, but also has a definitely twentieth-century tonal basis.

Frederick Piket

Piket's music is part of the current Reform repertoire. It can be extremely simple, stripped down to essentials like the Barchu given here (example 25). Hazzan and unison choir are largely restricted to large

Example 24. Paul Ben-Haim, *Barechu*

Example 24. continued

leaps in a fanfare style, while the accompaniment reiterates the same rhythmic figures in each measure, making the music highly accessible and remembered by almost any congregant.

Samuel Adler

One special category of composers consists of men who are sons of hazzanim. We noted this possibility for "cantor-composers" earlier,

Example 24. continued

but it holds for some "contemporary composers" as well. Ben Steinberg, a favorite Reform composer today, acknowledges a strong debt
to his father: "Much of the music in this volume was inspired by the
improvisations of my father, Cantor Alexander Steinberg, of blessed
memory. Like other Cantors of his generation, he kept Jewish music
alive by devoting his entire life to the beautification of synagogue song

Example 24. continued

and the preservation of its traditions. Melodic fragments of his prayers are the foundations for many pieces in this work" (Steinberg 1964).

Samuel Adler is the son of a major Reform "cantor-composer," Hugo Chaim Adler, and is well known as a secular composer, educator, and author. His Barchu was regionally commissioned by six Reform con-

Example 25. Frederick Piket, *Bar'chu*

gregations in the southwestern United States and is tailored to local circumstances: "I set out to write a Service which would serve the needs of these rather small institutions. The reason for the multi-purpose character of this Service is that many Congregations do not have a mixed chorus but only a solo voice or a unison chorus or a Cantor and unison chorus, or a similar medium to render their Service music" (Adler 1965). Adler is also interested in denominational flexibility: "*Shiru Ladonoy* is designed to be used by both Reform and Conservative Congregations and has been tried in both situations" (Adler 1965).

The resulting Barchu (example 26) combines contemporary tonal structures with melodic simplicity for both "soloist" (possibly hazzan) and unison chorus. The call and response are set off markedly by dynamics (soft to loud) and by a generally rising versus descending melodic line for the two parts, each having a distinctive tune, another way to make the music accessible and easy to remember.

Example 26. Samuel Adler, *Bor'chu*

Isidor Freed

Freed (1900–1960) is another German-origin composer whose works are standards in the Reform repertoire. Long before the recent, controversial eruption of Hasidic tunes into mainstream services, Freed felt the appeal of the Hasidic spirit, though the innovation was controversial enough to require a rabbinic introduction in 1954: "The seeming paradox of Hasidic music in a Liberal American Temple calls for an explanation. Two years ago Dr. Freed and I [Rabbi Judah Cahn] were planning the Annual Music Festival for Temple Israel. The program was comprised of five great musical traditions. One of these . . . was, of course, the music of the Hasidim" (Cahn 1954). This experiment paid off: "The response of the Congregation was so warm and full-hearted that it prompted us to make the Service part of our repertoire" (Cahn 1954). The sources Freed drew on were published collections and the Hazzan's recollections: "Most of the traditional melodies of this Service are recorded in the Zalmanoff and Idelsohn Anthologies of Hassidic music. The *Mi Chomocho* tune was remembered by Harvin Lohre, who until his recent retirement was our Cantor" (Cahn 1954).

Freed's novel service differed sharply from today's Hasidic incursions, which come from the large, vigorous Hasidic community itself or from the Israeli Hasidic Song Festivals. Similarly, the Barchu (example 27) is very tame in comparison to the current notion of Hasidic, which often extends to nontext syllables (*yom-bom-bom*) or even hand clapping. Freed's approach is to underlay the Hasidic tunes with regular harmony, keeping the "classic Reform" sound alive in the organ part. He increases the cantorial role by having a call-response pattern for both lines of text. This is perhaps reminiscent of the important role among Hasidim of the ba'al tefillah prayer leader, and perhaps gives this Barchu a "folksy" quality.

Gershon Kingsley

Our two final examples represent the pop-influenced end of the "recent trends" spectrum. Gershon Kingsley and Michael Isaacson are two of the most successful composers of this new style. Both have worked extensively in commercial music, and the former was an early advocate of the Moog synthesizer: "Gershon Kingsley was already an established composer, arranger, and Broadway conductor when he became intrigued with the musical possibilities of the electronic synthesizer. . . . [H]e then began creating Moog music for popular records, commercials and films. And now, perhaps most lovingly, he expresses his commitment to the heritage of hebrew liturgical music in *Shabbat for Today*" (Kingsley 1968). Kingsley's Barchu (example 28) starts with a cantorial call backed by steady offbeat rhythmic accompaniment, then moves to an even more syncopated, pop-based choral response. Then the Barchu fades into a Rabbinic reading using English text, underlining

Example 27. Isidor Freed, *Bar'chu*

Example 28. Gershon Kingsley, *Bor'chu*

Praise God's works.

And the Heavenly Father approved of the angels' words and soon thereafter, He created man, gifted with the muses. This is the ancient story, and in consonance with its spirit, I say—it is God's peculiar work to benefit man, and man works to give Him thanks.

Example 28. continued

Example 28. continued

Praised be the Lord to whom all praise is due_____ for - ev - er and
ev - er__ and ev - er__ and ev - er._____

Shout joyfully to the Lord all the earth. Serve the Lord with gladness, come into His presence with singing, know that the Lord is God; it is He who made us and we are His. We are the sheep of His pasture. Enter His gates with thanksgiving and His courts with praise. Give thanks to Him, praise His name. For the Lord is good, His love endures forever and His faithfulness.

the modernism of the work. Finally, the hazzan and choir return with the Barchu text in a new pop-sound setting.

Michael Isaacson

Like Kingsley, Isaacson represents the ascendancy of the folk/popular medium and has thoughts about it as well: "The musical mood of the contemporary synagogue has traveled from the postwar experimentation of classically trained composers of primarily European origin, though the gallant, but isolated efforts of a second generation American group, to what is now a popularistic free-for-all of folk settings by young Jewish Americans who have gone through camping experiences" (Isaacson 1977). However, Isaacson is interested in the next phase: "I am optimistic that the next decade will bring a new wave of musical offerings that synthesize the popularism and relevance of today with the classicism and rich heritage that has been handed down to us" (Isaacson 1977).

He feels that his own experiences are a microcosm of recent trends: "My own music . . . has pursued just this synthesis. Since Eastman I've taught college students, been a temple music director and now compose for the media. I've studied a great deal of twentieth century music and have learned with some anxiety that the eclecticism of our time precludes any sure direction for a 'school' of composition" (Isaacson 1977).

The theme of eclecticism, pronounced earlier by Max Helfman as a necessary part of composing Jewish sacred services, resurfaces here. Jewish composers are always facing up to the question of eclecticism and responding either by acknowledging its force in their work or—like Gideon—defying it by sticking to their own personal style, regardless of popularity.

The Isaacson Barchu represented here (example 29) is a guitar setting, in English. Isaacson's patron is once again NFTY, here in its folk phase: "*Avodat Amamit* was commissioned by the NFTY during the summer of 1972. . . . The particular design of this service insures both beginning guitarists and more advanced classical guitarists of finding joy in the accompaniment material. With the increased emphasis in congregational singing, it is my hope that these folk-like tunes will give pleasure and new meaning to worshippers of all ages" (Isaacson 1974). The guitar is the emblem of the summer-camp syndrome and as such is scorned by many older or more traditional hazzanim, just as it is embraced by a younger group of sacred singers. Isaacson specifies "voice," not "cantor" for the text line, allowing for any service milieu, so his work is appropriate for the havurah age of informal/improvised services as well as the sanctuary. Again, ambiguity and adaptability are necessary to modern sacred music.

A good way to summarize this musically very diverse chapter is to concentrate on its title: music as *presentation*. From the hazzan's point of view, whether dealing with a composer's vision or writing for the synagogue, you must constantly think of others' demands before your own. Viewed this way, presentation is not that different from participation. Many composers of Jewish sacred music are in the same boat. Any hazzan or composer who charts an individual course does so at his/her own risk, since congregational acceptance is the key to future employment, commissions, or performance. So in this realm of professionalism, as in the others surveyed earlier, flexibility, a wide range of choices, and the constraints of interaction remain the key themes. For

Example 29. Michael Isaacson, *Bar'chu*

Example 29. continued

Example 29. continued

the individual musician, the task is always to balance compromise and creativity. In the next and final chapter, we will focus on improvisation, the area of the repertoire where the hazzan has more leeway, and which expresses the deepest cultural values of the cantorate.

NOTES

1. Actually, commissioning is very often done by a consortium of synagogues to defray costs, as examples below will indicate. In the Project survey, a surprisingly high number of Reform hazzanim—forty-one percent—reported they have commissioned music. Of course, the Reform depend much more heavily on precomposed music than do the Conservative or the Orthodox, but it is still indicative of the hazzanic power of persuasion that so many professionals have convinced their consitutuents of the need to help produce new music for the sacred service.

2. I am grateful to Judit Frigyesi for pointing out that this appeal to the earlier "revivalist" appeal of Hasidic music here should not lead the reader to assume that the rock movement is substantively similar to Hasidism's eighteenth-century way of stirring souls through music. The reference here is part of the general mainstream interest in finding a genealogy for its current trends.

3. The question of when services are scheduled is an interesting, but untapped, chapter in the story of the cantorate. In America, the weekly service has ranged from Friday night to Sunday morning across time and denominations. Today the Conservatives' initial concentration on Friday night has tended to yield to Saturday morning for a variety of reasons (e.g., shift from a congregation of small-businessmen to professionals). Friday night is still the main Reform moment, though it appears that Saturday is increasing in importance, perhaps partly due to increased stress on bar/bat mitzvah highlighting.

4. Of course, there are also musical ways of categorizing the examples here in terms of a distinction between those versions that tend toward being settings of traditional tunes and those that represent novel compositional material. For present purposes, however, the notion of "presentation," from the performer's (hazzan, choir) point of view is what counts.

5. There is a professional organization—the Guild of Temple Musicians—affiliated with the Reform's American Conference of Cantors, and members attend the ACC convention.

11

~~~~~~

The Music of Improvisation

We have followed the hazzan through history, through the professional pathway from schooling to workplace and finally into the sanctuary itself, where we have listened to sacred singers comment on their feelings and choices. We have surveyed the songs and strategies hazzanim draw on to build services, and the constraints congregations impose on creativity. The present, final chapter zooms in on the expressive area nearest to the traditional hazzan's sense of self: the music of improvisation.[1] This will require a two-part approach: an exploration of *nusach*, a professional term which is also a cultural concept,[2] followed by examples of nusach at work in improvised—and individualized— sacred song. Combining a core concept, based on interpretation of sacred text, with the free play of individual sensibilities is part of the Ashkenazic cultural pattern outlined in chapter 1, so this chapter stresses the continuity of the cantorate and rounds out this volume by cycling back to its beginnings.

Exploring Nusach

Nusach is a tough term to grasp,[3] but anyone who wants to understand the cantorate from the inside has to make an exploratory journey into what sacred singers think of as their home territory. The approach taken here is simply to give the reader a guided tour, using the words of the professionals themselves under topic headings that suggest the extensive field the term covers; all quotes, including those from secondary sources, are by hazzanim.[4]

Nusach as tradition

> To me, the *nusach hatefillah*,[5] Eastern European, this is what I was raised with. . . . I would say this was my father's and my grandfather's and my grand-grandfather's. Because this is what I heard from my home and my father heard from his father. . . . I would call this "traditional chant" (A.E.).

The hazzan has got an unbelievable responsibility to the past and . . . to preserve the future and he is the synthesis, he puts it all together. He's the catalyst to see to it that it continues and is preserved properly and it's insulated against foreign elements that try to destroy it. So where we talk about nuschaot [plural] . . . when I pick up a piece of music, this is exactly what I'm looking for. Where is that thread that ties me down with what was a hundred years ago or fifty years ago? (A.B.).

Nusach is the folk melody of the synagogue (B.A.).

Since one must approach prayer in a joyful mood appropriate melodies were employed to infuse joy in both singer and listener. These melodies (and musical modes) which have become our nusach, the "traditional" music of the synagogue, were scrupulously adhered to. (Wohlberg 1974).

The origin of nusach

In regard to the prayer service, [nusach] signifies a pattern or an established form of a text. When a text was removed or copied, that text or copy became known as nusach. Hence, forms of texts in prayer books belonging to different rites (e.g., nusach Ashkenaz, nusach Sefard . . .) are known as nusach hatefilah ["nusach of the prayer"] (Nulman 1975:189).

There are very ancient nuschaot . . . there are those nuschaot that came into our prayers at a later date . . . there are melodies that appear in our prayers from the era of the Minnesong (11th–14th centuries) which influenced the Hazzanim . . . then there are the various differences in the nuschaot of our people of the same origin such as the nusach of Polish Jews, the Lithuanian Jews, or the differences between the Sephardic Jews of London and of Amsterdam, etc. (Fuchs 1969:3).

The basic nusach is the shtibl [Hasidic] nusach, that's the authentic nusach. What the hazzan does is embellish it, and try to make it sound as professional as possible (D.R.).

The nature of nusach

In theory, nusach means: "mode," "form." Nusach is a form. It has a broader sense: "a way of doing things" (A.A.).

The nusach is the cement that holds the service together (C.H.).

Nusach is our stock in trade (B.G.).

I don't think nusach can be eclectic. I think nusach should be nusach. You're having one nusach, you stick to that nusach (D.R.).

Where nusach is in the service

When I was a child, if you were deaf—no, not deaf; if you were dumb and blind, you couldn't smell, but you could hear—you could go to shul and find out what day of the week, what season of the year [because of the nusach used] (E.C.).

Nusach is at the ends . . . nusach is not at the beginning or in the middle (J.B.).

[Asks his teacher] "What is nusach?" and he said to me, "If you were to take a cat and throw this cat up into the air, this cat would turn this way and spin over and somersault, but it would always land on its four feet. This is nusach. You can do whatever you want within the piece. You can even modulate out of the key, as long as you return to the traditional nusach and end in the nusach" (A.G.).

The ending is something that has to give you the feeling that you're not going to start nusach afterwards in a different room; you have to lead into it (F.B.).

I'm here in the nusach, and they like it, and I get support from the rabbi. In fact, before Tal or *Geshem* or before *Neilah* he announces: "watch the special music for that Kaddish or for that music," that it expresses the mood which is coming for that service. And he points it out. That's a very relaxed situation. So then they begin to notice (M.F.).

Learning nusach

[I use] the nusach which I learned when I was a child from my father in my hometown in Czechoslovakia and to this day for the last twenty-seven years, I am doing the same nusach (M.J.).

The two pieces [I recorded for you] contain pure nusach, whch I guess I have picked up over the years through listening and reading music. I have no idea where or when I *absorbed* them (M.G.).

I'm a strict adherent to nusach. And it's a studied adherence. And I'm grateful to the Seminary program, for Max Wohlberg particularly, for showing me where to find the right nusach and for teaching it to me (D.T.).

Sometimes you listen to a good ba'al tefillah, it's fascinating. I can sit and listen to them forever, and learn a lot [about] nusach, because they don't do any hazzanut [cantorial art], but nusach. They come from some part of the world that they used to do it one way (F.C.).

Nusach in the workplace

This synagogue is more than sensitive to nusach. I will only tell you that every year that I've been here, the *balebatim* ["lay leadership"] who come from various locations in Europe sit down and quiz me every year on nusach. They want to make sure they know that I know what *that* phrase is for *Neilah*, or in the High Holiday davening, or whatever (E.D.).

Once we were interviewing . . . someone to do the overflow service . . . so my lay leaders went to listen to this fellow . . . an excellent voice. I heard him from outside the door; I said "my job is up for grabs—that's it." He was terrific, he was really good. . . . Then they asked him to sing something from the *Neilah* service, and he did what he was taught. He did a cantorial recitative. They came out of that meeting afterwards: "Nobody in America knows nusach; they don't know it at all!" Of course, they didn't take him (E.A.).

In my particular synagogue I have tried to retain as much nusach as is possible. Number one when it comes to selections in the prayer book which deal with biblical passages, for example, like the Torah reading, like the *V'ahavta* or the *Vayomer*. . . . I must tell you, that in the last two, three years, those that have been attending my minyanim, mornings, have increased their fluency . . . and also what I am planning to do is to, for a while, to have them sing with me the endings of the prayer with the real nusach (D.S.).

I can't see myself or any hazzan, a professional hazzan, discarding nusach or using a Friday night nusach for Rosh Hashanah or for Passover. [Interviewer: Would the congregation know if a substitute used the wrong nusach?] Yes. Whether they would care, I don't know (C.D.).

Some of the stuff that they learn at [Camp] Ramah, which I feel is not in nusach, and they come back in some cases, to plague their cantor who perhaps is doing it in nusach and doing it well, and they'll say, "Oh, you're all wrong! At Ramah, they do it this way!" (D.R.).

Nusach in the Reform movement

The nusach will never have the same power in the Reform worship experience as it does in the Conservative, but its presence is increasing and, I believe, is a potent source from which we all draw strength and inspiration (Sager 1984:46).

There has been an undeserved importance placed on nusach [at the Reform training program and] how best to communicate the message of prayer. . . . Absolute nonsense that nusach does that. [Those who think so will end up] in a museum (F.J.).

It would seem to me, I know, simply from a survival point of view, a cantor will survive far longer on the Reform pulpit without nusach, than he will without a voice (I.H.).

Personalizing nusach

> We have to dress a man who's five foot two, but he's so many inches wide, but he's got to look good in it. So anybody can just stitch together a suit, but the suit has to look proper on the person. This is our problem when you get individuals [composers] who are not familiar with nusach (A.B.).

> I like the Hebrew. I like traditional nusach. I like old recitatives. I'll take something from Joshua Lind and clean it up: I'll change the accentuation, I'll reduce the amount of textual repetition, but the *neshome* ["soul"], the *ta'am* ["flavor"], the taste, the feel, the *soul* of that old style recitative . . . (D.B.).

> I make my shabbes ["Saturday"] morning a Jewish happening, and I am not stifled in any way with nusach because nusach—I'm a free bird (D.F.).

The foregoing quotations suggest nusach is involved in everything from hiring through youth relations, viewed as anything from a discipline gratefully accepted to a hindrance proudly rejected. Nusach is so basic as to be a job requirement, but not in every denomination; it is simultaneously musical and political. It is learned, but it might be "absorbed." Nusach should automatically tell you what season it is, yet performing "traditional nusach" can mean "cleaning up" and "reducing" a famous teacher's approach, as long as the "soul" is kept. Meanwhile, the real master of nusach may not even be the hazzan— the artist—but the "ordinary" ba'al tefillah, perhaps just a volunteer prayer leader. Finally, as background it is very much worth noting that nusach originated as a *textual*, not a musical term, and that it might imply much more than either text or tune: "way of life."[6]

The only point of agreement is that nusach is the emblem of tradition and that it somehow specifies, stipulates, or situates a musical moment, perhaps in a particular locale. Tangible and ineffable, musical and somewhat mystical, nusach is worth a long look, which we will do next through concrete musical examples. We will examine two selections from the Project sample: (1) the opening of the *Ashrei* for the *Selichot* service; and (2) the paragraph beginning *Uvchen ten pachdecha*, part of the Rosh Hashanah liturgy.[7] We will not be attempting thorough musicological analysis, but seeking principles that link nusach and its practitioners with the general themes of the present volume.

Opening of the Ashrei for Selichot

The Ashrei is Psalm 145, which begins "Blessed are they who dwell in the house of the Lord, for they shall sing his praises forever." It is an important item in the liturgy: "Because Ashrei sums up the Jewish doctrine of God, the Talmud urges that it be said three times daily (B. *Ber.* 4b). Hence it is said twice at the morning service and once at the afternoon service" (Klein 1979:33).

Like other prayers that recur, the Ashrei has variable significance according to the season, which means its musical setting—part of what nusach implies—will also vary. Selichot is a particularly weighty service: "Selichot, or penitential prayers, are recited before the morning service during the month of Elul and between Rosh Hashanah and Yom Kippur . . . the Ashkenazim [begin] on the Sunday before Rosh Hashanah" (Klein 1979:178).

Because the Selichot service begins with the Ashrei, and because Selichot is the opening of the entire High Holiday period (also known as "Days of Awe"), we might expect hazzanim to carefully prepare this particular setting of the Ashrei. Like the Barchu (see chapter 10) that initiates the Sabbath, the Ashrei literally sets the tone—but here it is for an entire season, the holiest of the year. The ninety-three available renditions of this item show an immense variety at some levels and great uniformity at others, just as we might expect of the cultural pattern in question. We will look at just six examples, each representing a legitimate, yet distinctive approach to setting the compact text, just the opening line of the Ashrei.

Uniformity in the ninety-three variants is clear enough: all end on what is transcribed here as g. This supports one of our original quotes: it is at the endings where one looks for nusach in the strictly musical sense. Yet a further distinction is needed: nusach mandates endings only for pieces in the "gravitational field" of nusach. Our Ashrei, due to its key placement in the liturgical year, is naturally one of those spots controlled by nusach. Many other slots in the vast yearly round of sacred music are "nusach-free"; for example, it seems that metrical songs have zero gravity, to extend the metaphor.

So the Ashrei for Selichot is anchored; this would be one of those items you would ask a candidate to sing, and on which you would base a judgement of competence. But there is more to the nusach here than where you end. Because eighty-nine of our ninety-three variants also begin around g, there is a general sense of departure and return: Max Wohlberg feels this is another basic feature of the concept, though again, not always applicable. With this background, we can now approach our six examples of the Ashrei.

Example 30 is the variety of performance hazzanim call "straight nusach," here of a particularly plain variety. A mere thirteen seconds long, it is nearly the shortest of the variants. The hazzan *chants* rather

Example 30. *Ashrei* variant

Example 31. *Ashrei* variant

Example 32. *Ashrei* variant

Example 33. *Ashrei* variant

than sings, covering only three pitches all told. His only concession to decorating the text is to place two notes on the syllable *lu*. Example 31 is in the same "straight" category, being rather circumscribed and short (eleven seconds). Here the hazzan agrees with the first singer in choosing *lu* as the place to expand a bit. Both on *lu* and in general, he carries the tune a bit farther than in Example 30. Though these two versions are similar in approach, notice that one ends *b-g*, whereas the other concludes *a-g*. Thus although each features departure and return and is "in the nusach," one sees the possibility of *choice*, here being how to get back to *g*.[8]

Example 32 expands the options in a number of ways. First, we have the opening *d-g* figure, shared by forty-four of our ninety-three variants, hence a popular choice. Stretching the time out to twenty-three seconds, this hazzan finds time to take an entire breath on *od*, holding the tune at the level of *b*. Altogether, four syllables have more than one pitch, giving a much more fluid sense of melodic line.

Example 33 is more dramatically different. Starting up on *d*, it continues down, back up, then way down before coming to rest appro-

priately on *g*. This hazzan manages, in just fourteen seconds, to create
a parallelism of phrases by having both *rei* and *od* follow the same
melodic turn of phrase, letting the listener concentrate on a strictly
musical structure that has nothing in particular to do with the text.[9]

Example 34 takes us far from "straight nusach" to what hazzanim
call a "cantorial" or "hazzanic" style. The former could be done by
any ba'al tefillah (professional or volunteer), whereas the latter is the
specialty of the hazzan alone. After a modest opening phrase, this
sacred singer shows off his vocal dexterity, extending the phrase to
thirty-two seconds to include swoops, glides, trills, and climbs before
settling back down on *g*.

Because seventy-six of our ninety-three singers make a point out of
od, perhaps we might look into a text linkage. After all, a basic premise
of our analysis is that the hazzan is one who interprets text carefully
and beautifully. In fact, *od* is the "forever" of "they shall praise your
name forever," so it seems suitable for it to be the most protracted,
embellished syllable of the text line. Here we have a fine example of
the cantorial feeling for *hiddur mitzvah*, beautification of a necessary/
meritorious act: the hazzan acts out exactly what the text suggests,
which is to praise God at length, and does it in the appropriate manner:
beautifully. That the *lu* of *yehalelucha* is also ornamented is again mi-
metic—the English "hallelujah" comes from this verb of praise.

Finally, example 35 shows yet another possibility of interpretation.
Heretofore, all our examples have stayed in the same tonal frame (*g-
a-b-flat-c-d* as the basis of the tune), another hallmark of nusach: the
appropriate "sound" for the Selichot service.[10] Yet twenty-three of our

Example 34. *Ashrei* variant

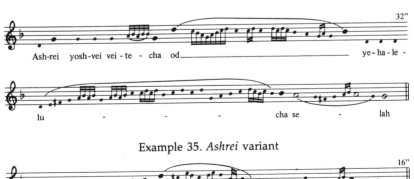

Example 35. *Ashrei* variant

ninety-three examples take the path shown by example 35, which is to shift the sense of tonal orientation by temporarily introducing a radically different sound (*g-a-b-flat-c-sharp-d*), then returning to the familiar for the necessary conclusion. Such departures do not take the piece out of nusach, according to Wohlberg, who views them as "instinctive" improvisations by talented hazzanim. Should these intuitive constructions impress other professionals, they may become favored versions; we will see this process at work in our next selection.[11]

This brief look at a single line of text-setting begins the process of unpacking the concept of nusach. The need to end the piece in the right place is universal, as is a strong tendency to start it in the same place, allowing for a sense of departure and return. The examples illustrate the range from "straight" through "cantorial" nusach and from a single to a multiple tonal orientation within "the nusach," showing the variety of individual approaches to prayer leading. There are many ways to beautify this particular text while staying within the basic, consensus guidelines.[12]

Even taking a few steps into the territory of improvisation—looking at just one line of text—makes clear how wide the area of choice is for slots in the service left open to individuality, as compared to the prefabricated items discussed in chapters 9 and 10.

Uvchen Ten Pachdecha

We will now move to a medium-length passage from the High Holiday liturgy. Greater length means greater scope for constructing melodic designs. We will be looking both for clues to nusach and to the process individual hazzanim go through in putting together personal versions of a standard text.

In the voluminous Rosh Hashanah repertoire, particularly in the *musaf* ("additional") section, there are numerous inserted passages heard only at this important time of year. A set of three paragraphs hazzanim simply call the *Uvchens* (each begins with the word *uvchen*, "thus") is not a major item; it is possible to chant right through them or, in a non-Orthodox synagogue, to sing them on one day of the holiday and omit them the next.[13] Nevertheless, if they are to be planned into the service, they will have to be done with the seriousness that any part of the High Holiday service demands. The text (in the current Conservative translation) reads: "O Lord our God, let all Your creatures sense Your awesome power, let all that You have fashioned stand in fear and trembling. Let all mankind pledge You their allegiance, united wholeheartedly to carry out Your will. For we know, Lord our God, that Your sovereignty, Your power and Your awesome majesty are supreme over all creation" (Harlow 1972:251).

This paragraph stresses God's power and the necessity for mankind, united, to bring his will to fruition. The succeeding Uvchen paragraphs speak of the coming of the Messiah and the end of days, so taken as a whole, the Uvchen insertions carry an important message. Our question is, How do sacred singers approach such a text through the medium of nusach? Again, we turn to the ninety-three hazzanim of the Project sample, from which six variants will serve as illustrations (examples 36–41).

The first difference between the Uvchen and the Ashrei just examined is that known hazzan-composers' work now turns up in the sample, which includes thirteen appearances of Adolph Katchko's version and five of Max Wohlberg's setting of the Uvchen text, a significant percentage of the total. Katchko was one of the premier hazzan-teacher-composers of the interwar period. His legacy of pieces, often handed out in the training programs as models of nusach, is very much alive.[14] So if thirteen of our ninety-three hazzanim brought the Katchko Uvchen to our sample, it is not surprising. By contrast, the Wohlberg has been taught in the Conservative training program only within the last decade, so its widespread adoption shows the impact of the newer, institutional mode of teaching.

This piece (example 36) has an overall shape that suggests a rhetoric of interpreting the text. It is marked into phrases, following the consensus of all ninety-three versions as to where major breaks should come; e.g., eighty-nine variants make a pause on *masecha*, the end of phrase A. Katchko uses Phrase E to make a grand gesture to illustrate the text's message about all mankind uniting to do God's will. He also dramatizes the closing phrase, H, by dipping down to *d* to build an impressive final cadence for the piece. Katchko has other expressive devices as well, such as the change of tonal orientation at F, familiar to us from the Ashrei example above. Other gestures, such as a "reciting tone" on one pitch at the opening of the piece, are common to over one-third of our recorded variants. These tendencies to express text in certain ways are part of the general concept of nusach as well as being personal trademarks of a particular hazzan-composer like Katchko. It seems the more one looks into nusach, the more levels one finds at which it operates.[15]

To see what individual hazzanim do with standard models such as the Katchko version, we can take one singer's variation. He admits

Example 36. *Uvchen* variant

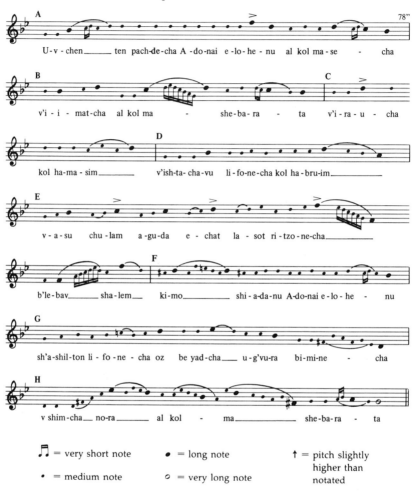

♫ = very short note   • = long note   ↑ = pitch slightly
                                          higher than
• = medium note   ○ = very long note   notated

that his version is based on Katchko, but says it includes his own ideas
as well as those he learned from a hazzan in whose choir he sang as
a child. Example 37 gives this Uvchen setting. Phrases E and F bear
some resemblance to the Katchko Uvchen, stressing the same passage
as the expressive high point, but the rest of this version differs markedly. The opening reciting tone is on *b*, not *d*, the closing does not
have the long swell up from *d*, etc. This approach bears out Wohlberg's

Example 37. *Uvchen* variant

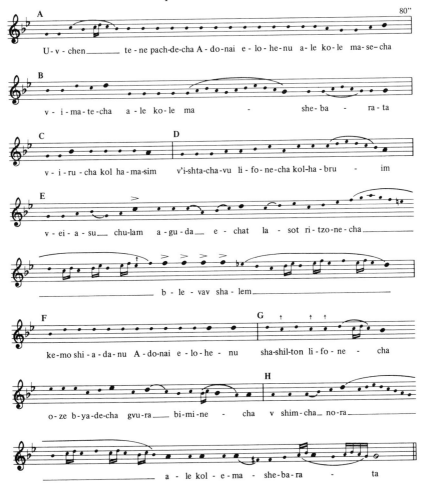

comment that inspired versions of particular hazzanim become part of "tradition" for later sacred singers. These striking settings represent the nusach in a memorable way but, like other elements of the culture, allow for further improvisation on the basis of the text. One learns from the masters, but is not bound by their approach, as in the study of the Talmud.

We turn next to the other "model" variant, that of Max Wohlberg (example 38). Interestingly, Wohlberg conceived of this version not so much as a finished "piece," but as an illustration of the type of nusach students should have for the entire section of the liturgy in which the Uvchen is situated. Consequently, he "packed" a variety of phrases and approaches into it and was somewhat surprised to find it had become the version for a number of younger hazzanim. For the congregations involved, the Wohlberg version is now the "traditional" Uvchen. In this way, classroom nusach has become a standard source in our times, though the process of transmission is not particularly different from the older musicways.[16]

The Wohlberg version is less "dramatic" than the Katchko in that it does not rise and sink so obviously, nor have extensive written-out melismas (long ornamented passages). Nevertheless, there are common features: (1) the highest pitch is in Phrase E; (2) there is a tonal shift in Phrase F; (3) a reciting tone style characterizes the opening phrase; and (4) sections have distinctive melodic lines that stick in the mind, here in Phrase G. And, of course, like all ninety-three variants, the

Example 38. *Uvchen* variant

piece ends where it should, on *g*.[17] Tendencies, approaches, finalities: this is where nusach resides.

Our last three Uvchen examples represent family and regional traditions as well as musical variation. The first hazzan (example 39) learned his version—as well as the rest of his repertoire—from his father, a hazzan from Warsaw. Musically, it is notable for its extensive use of sequences—melodic lines made of similar phrases pitched a step higher or a step lower, creating a chain-like effect throughout Phrases E, F, G, and H.[18] Here overall melodic form seems to take precedence over highlighting of a specific passage of text. Hazzanim and their works can be placed along a "interpreter-beautifier" continuum which, somewhere along the line, includes the ba'al tefillah-hazzan boundary. Also noteworthy is the final cadence on the word *uvchen*, suggesting a flow into the following, second Uvchen paragraph, rather than the usual

Example 39. *Uvchen* variant

decisive stop on *mashebarata,* the last word of Uvchen ten pachdecha. This occurs in a number of versions, supporting the notion that here we see nusach in fluid, rather than contained, form.

Example 40 is a German version, learned "from 1928 to '38." This hazzan is clear about his notion of how to "represent the innate Jewish spirit and the classical tradition of Jewish liturgy": "The *origin* of the music is difficult to pinpoint; these are not 'original' compositions, but extended motives that mirror the image of the prayertext or the spirit of the festival it represents" (M.H.). These remarks jibe with Wohlberg's sense of "intuitive," creative musical thoughts that add up to memorable text settings. The exquisite sense of appropriateness always characteristic of the concept of nusach is well expressed here as well. In the setting, we can spot an interest in a "hummable" tune at the ending—Phrase H—a metrical melody typical of German nusach. Being a regional variant, it includes tonal material heretofore unheard, in Phrase G (the *a-flat-g* gesture). The tendency to keep returning to the upper register, rather than saving it for midpiece climax is different

Example 40. *Uvchen* variant

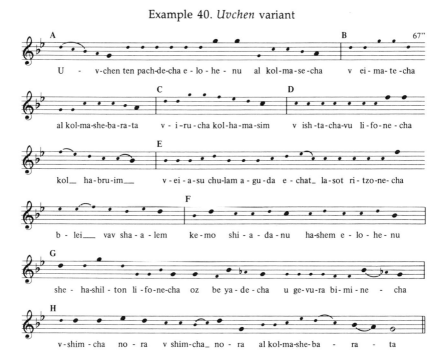

than, say, the Katchko and Wohlberg approach as well, implying a different rhetorical approach to the text.

Finally, one more eastern European example learned by absorption: "Since I was very young I sang in Choirs with the greatest Cantors of Europe. In addition, my father, [he] should rest in peace, brothers, grandfather and uncles were all Cantors. So this piece of music is a natural outgrowth of the Synagogue music from my youth—not from a specific teacher, book or record" (M.I.). Example 41, though eastern European like all but one of our examples, is sharply different in a number of ways. It favors heavy concentration on the upper *d-f* area, not important for our other examples, and uses *c-e*, then, as an alternate area, also novel. The tonal shift (including a *c-sharp-b-flat-a* turn) comes way at the end, instead of just after midpiece. The reciting-tone feeling is particularly pronounced and, as in example 39, the singer moves on to the next Uvchen—here with the *d-f* figure, instead of concluding solidly on *g*. So some gestures have become familiar, even through looking at a few variants, whereas others immediately stick out as

Example 40. *Uvchen* variant

individual or regional. Nusach, finally, can be seen as a fixed system, based on sacred text, which allows for time- and space-based variability and personal exploration.

We can draw no real conclusions from even ninety-three variants of a passage like Uvchen. Because no one sampled cantorial music systematically before 1939, we have no solid grounds for comparison with an American counterpart. All we have are fragments, crumbs from the great banquet of Ashkenazic sacred music that lasted for a millennium. For contemporary America, though, our sample is helpful, because it happens to contain an elegant balance of participants in terms of age, country of origin, and type of training in which no single variety of hazzan predominates: it is truly a cross section of today's professionals. Although it cannot tell us anything definitive about the cantorial art, it certainly has helped us trace the outlines of nusach, our core concept. Having established this basis, we can build on it to make a foray into the last frontier of individuality in sacred song: improvisation.

Building on Nusach: Improvisation

Just as getting at nusach was best begun by a series of quotations, the mystery of improvisation might well be approached in a similar fashion to show the scope of the term:

The requirements for improvisation

[From a 1938 analysis of America by a Polish hazzan:] The older hazzanim . . . say that hazzanic improvisation must be preserved, since it is the soul of *hazzanut*, but only by a handful of hazzanim, those who know their way around improvisation, that is, hazzanim who are drenched in the true spirit of nusach, who know correct pronunciation, have flexible voices which can serve their ends, and who really have a rich imagination (Shelvin 1938).

Even people who improvise, the serious pulpit artist, will have a scheme . . . the jazz musicians also they have a background, they have experience . . . you can't improvise from nothing; you can't take a novice and say "improvise!" (A.C.).

Improvisation doesn't come suddenly. Improvisation is something that you have to develop. . . . You have to work. You have to have the picture of the music in front of you; the notes, how you are working it . . . not just a sudden change from one key to the other; you have to slide into it; it shouldn't be noticed (F.C.).

It's something you've got in your gut, in your heart (E.J.).

The individual craft of improvisation

Since the musical elements of the recitative consist of a limited number of motifs and their variations . . . it is in their selection, combination and emphasis that the individuality of the [hazzan]-composer appears. Thus, the recitatives of Kwartin are pleading, those of Rosenblatt are melodic, Roitman's are intricately plaintive (Wohlberg 1979:85).

Nisi [Belzer's] forte was tefillah (prayerful supplication), whereas Zeidel [Rovner] was in his element and excelled mainly in *neginah* (melodic, rhythmic song). At Nisi's the method and style was declamation, recitation, and what is commonly called "saying" (*zogen*). At Zeidel's the conception and aim was singing and tuneful chanting. Nisi's school was placing more emphasis on recitative, Zeidel's on the other hand was more in favor of melody. To Nisi it was the soul that counted the most; for Zeidel the heart and feeling were predominant (Vigoda 1981:215).

Standing at the pulpit, [Arye Leyb Rutman] would pull out from one pocket and another slips of music paper, on which he had scribbled down some fragments of musical phrases. Only he himself could decipher them. He was able to modulate from one form of scale or mode into another with the utmost ease . . . and it seemed as if he had gone too far astray. . . . At such times, even seasoned professionals were puzzled and used to wonder how in the world he would manage to unravel the maze. . . . But they underrated Rutman's wizardry. He never lost his bearings. . . . As soon as it suited his purpose he was able to execute the necessary retreat and with one adroit maneuver he was back in the original musical mode . . . with the remarkable agility and the graceful mobility of a cat that always lands on its feet (Vigoda 1981:157).

The rhetoric of improvisation

Nisi divides the roles. While the tenors and sopranos are praying and pleading, the bassos and altos are presenting briefs with irrefutable arguments, complaining bitterly about the continuance of the endless exile and demanding a speedy redemption (Vigoda 1981:270).

David Roitman told how he has recently given up the minor scale, that is, arguing through supplication. He says he no longer says *matai timloch betzion* ["when will you rule in Zion?"] with crying, but in major, demandingly: "when, Lord, are you already going to take your hands off your heart and show that you are really the boss in the Holy Land, and no one else?" (Shelvin 1938).

The inspiration for improvisation

If you're talking about improvisation—it's not a *decision* (E.H.).

Many times you're starting a composition, you're going one way, even though it's a set composition, and all of a sudden while you're doing it you say, I'm feeling this at this particular moment. I can't do it that way. I have to do it this way. I have to repeat that word. I just can't say *aveinu . malkeinu*. I have to go back to *ha-malkeinu avinu* also sometimes and reverse the verbiage at that particular time (F.A.).

He [his teacher] would teach me to interpret every word, the meaning of every word. Simply singing it beautifully was not enough. But to feel, you know the meaning: God will take us under his wing, and feel the all-embracing comfort of God [in the "Hashkivenu" prayer] (A.G.).

Sometimes you feel like davening and there are many times I wake up and I say, forget it. I can't daven today. I'm beat, I'm exhausted, I had an argument with my wife . . . then when you open up and you see—oh, *es geyt* ["it's working"], it's going . . . so you take off, you start a composition, you may take off in all different ways. I had my heart attack when I was 38, and so everything wells up. Or my kids are sick. I'm not talking a cold or anything; I have a daughter that has lost a kidney . . . so I felt when I want to say "tear that evil decree up, rip it up," I was giving Him hell. I felt it, you know, and it wasn't just an act (F.A.).

Improvisation today

Excepting in some Orthodox and in a few right-wing Conservative synagogues the singing of lengthy recitatives has become a rarity. In addition to the indifference and/or impatience of the worshippers, too few of the younger hazzanim are vocally, temperamentally and emotionally equipped to do justice to the type of recitative cultivated by hazzanim of a previous generation (Wohlberg 1979:86).

I take snatches of things and build on them. . . . I've developed a style [like] David Koussevitsky with the high stuff on a few phrases and with Moshe Ganchoff teaching me modulation is very good for you if you know what you're doing. And even if you don't know what you're doing, as long as you can get back . . . as long as you keep the tonic in your ear (B.H.).

I haven't done it [improvisation]; I have a problem in that I grew up without hearing hazzanut. So all these notions are really my own. And what I'd like to do is go out now and bias myself entirely by hearing Malovany every week and Davis every week and these guys every week. Yeah, because I've got to know what "real" hazzanim do because I don't *know* what "real" hazzanim do (E.D.).

It seems that improvisation requires two things: extensive background and a personal approach. Without deep preparation, individualism is meaningless; without temperament, training is useless. In short, improvisation is the most demanding sector of hazzanut, the pinnacle of professional skill. Also clear from the above quotations is a sense that improvisation is something that used to be widespread and expected. Whether it is still something congregations value is an open question among hazzanim, and has been at least as far back as 1938, when the following words were penned: "In America, [there are] many Orthodox and Conservative congregations [who] have members who can't grasp the full meaning of an improvised [prayer]. . . . If they could, their children and grandchldren couldn't, and the younger members are the heart of the matter, since they influence the older ones as well. . . . This means that the prestige of a hazzan of the old school is declining" (Shelvin 1938).

However, the Project sample shows that individual diversity within the nusach system is not just alive, but healthy in late 1980s America. The variety of the music examples just analyzed bear witness to this survival of personal style. Of course, few Reform hazzanim are comfortable with improvisation, and many younger Conservatives are simply not prepared for it. Yet even the Reform training program is moving towards greater consideration of the old-time skills, and a significant number of young professionals are interested in expanding their capabilities, as one quote above testifies.

Yet despite the somewhat surprising health of improvisation today, one wonders about its cultural underpinnings. As the quotes above show, in earlier generations, the "messenger" took a very active role, pleading with, or even threatening, God on behalf of his congregation and the entire oppressed Jewish people. Today, the inspiration is more likely to be personal, a situation consonant with an age of comfort and the American stress on individualism. Looked at this way, both improvisation and nusach appear to be representatives of a European tradition that is constantly being reshaped on American terms, a process drastically accelerated by the passing of the Old World. These key components of the old sacred song complex will survive only insofar as they speak to a purely American Jewish sensibility. The longevity of the cultural pattern outlined in chapter 1 and detailed musically here is, however, extraordinary, and as long as Jews feel sacred singers should correctly and aesthetically interpret the words of prayer, it will endure.

So we close where we begin: describing an institution dependent on grassroots support, mandated not by religious legislation, but by popular demand. But we have also seen a body of professionals who, in America, have tenaciously fostered their interests in the name of tradition, carrying their cultural contribution—musical expression and leadership—into the late twentieth century with extraordinary vigor, often some steps ahead of their congregants. Both the demand and the drive will be needed to keep the cantorate alive into the next millennium.

NOTES

1. By "traditional" here I mean not only senior hazzanim brought up in the oral tradition (in Europe or America) that stressed improvisation as a mark of the professional's individuation, but also some younger sacred singers who have grown up in the older musicways. For those who come to hazzanut late in life and go through formal schooling, it is extremely difficult, as in any world musical tradition, to gain the skills of improvisation. As part of the recent rightward shift, improvisation seems to be making something of a comeback in the 1980s despite the dominance of the musics of participation and presentation. Certainly the striking evidence of the Project data impressed all of us with the durability of the tradition despite enormous changes in the cantorate and in Jewish music.

2. Unpacking *nusach* is a task worthy of an entire book; as befits the survey nature of the present study, only the outlines of the problem, as illustrated by insiders' views and brief analysis, will be sketched out.

3. Indeed, some find its ambiguity and its insider status so troubling as to render the term useless. In his major study of Ashkenazic sacred music, Eric Werner, dean of Jewish music research, omits the term from his glossary and index, and dismisses it in a footnote: "The term nusach (Hebrew) beloved by the old-time cantors, does not exactly denote musical tradition. . . . It is regrettable to find the term in the *Encyclopaedia Judaica*" (1976:293). Of course, it is exactly because the term was—and is—a favorite of hazzanim that I have spent so much time on it.

4. Still, any dividing up of a core insider term is bound to be artificial, as is any one gloss for a cultural concept. Experiences such as mine in trying to map nusach are commonplace these days in ethnomusicology, with its recent stress on emic data; but despite all the lip service paid to the interior view, no one has turned up a good methodology for doing so honestly or comprehensively. What the most successful attempts (e.g., Feld 1982; Zemp 1979) do ultimately is demonstrate the excruciating difficulty of working from the inside out.

5. *Nusach ha-tefillah* ("the nusach of prayer") is the full name of nusach and is usually used by hazzanim in formal situations like an interview or classroom.

6. To add to this mixture, here are statements about nusach by the scholarly authors of two standard sources on Jewish worship: "[A]ncient melodies, associated with particular prayers or whole prayer units, are designated as the official nusach, or musical tradition, of the synagogue. . . . When a congregation is about to elect a cantor . . . if he lacks a knowledge of the synagogue nusach

he is considered inadequate for the post" (Millgram 1971:366). "The solemnity of Rosh Hashanah is expressed in the liturgy. Not only the prayers, but also the traditional nusach, or musical rendition of the prayers, helps to create this mood" (Klein 1979:184).

Like the hazzanim, Klein and Millgram suggest a broad cultural resonance for nusach, including the job qualification aspect as well as the sense of "appropriateness" for occasion. Musically, they are vague about whether nusach consists of specific "ancient melodies" or is simply "the musical rendition of the prayers" that somehow helps to "create a mood."

Somewhat more helpfully, Harold S. Powers has pointed out (personal communication) that nusach is analogous to the Latin *modus*, a general cultural term having to do with way of life, which became adapted to musical concerns, like its descendant, English *mode*.

7. For analysis of nusach and improvisation, I am greatly indebted to studies done on other items from the Project sample by Judit Frigyesi, Marcie Frishman, and Lionel Wolberger, for many insights from Louis Weingarden, and for the kind commentary on us all by Harold S. Powers at a staff get-together of 27 December 1986.

8. Of course, by indulging in this sort of analysis, I am leaving the insider's viewpoint elsewhere stressed in this book. Playing many variants of the same item for even so authoritative an insider as Max Wohlberg, he is likely to become impatient, because he hears all the versions as "being in nusach." This is exactly the point raised by Bruno Nettl, commenting on his work in Iran: "Now, when in my experience Persian musicians were confronted with analysis of this sort, they pronounced it correct but found the information only mildly interesting, and not really particularly relevant. I had tried to take their way of looking at their own music further, and had managed to avoid violating their way of approaching the analysis, but I had gone further than they were willing to go, had divided their concepts into units smaller than those they were willing to use. I had given myself some insights into how the music is put together but, on the other hand, I could no longer claim simply to be presenting the system as it presents itself" (1983:97–98).

9. In further musicological study from the Project data, a central issue would be the extent to which strictly musical factors dominate, an issue of considerable ambiguity among hazzanim. Although the notion of text projection and interpretation is important, the purely aesthetic or even sensual side of music-making, so distrusted by rabbinic authorities over time, often comes to the fore, underscoring the ambivalent position of the hazzan as "messenger."

10. I am deliberately avoiding the term mode and the debate over the existence and identity of "synagogue modes" which remains a murky area in Jewish musicology. Harold S. Powers, whose work on the concept of mode is widely considered definitive, has counseled me in this direction, to which I lean for various reasons. First, the "modal" theory for Jewish liturgical music is recent (twentieth century) and still molten. As Werner notes, "all the attempts at classifying the prayer modes are very recent and of little theoretical or historical value" (1976:48). Second, younger hazzanim use the "modal" ter-

minology they learned in school, but somewhat as a formula that hardly touches the essence of their craft. Some use "modes" as a synonym for nusach in the sense of endings: "I don't think modes until I get to where I'm going to end" (E.H.). Older hazzanim much prefer to talk about "nusach," "mood," and other features, like ornament (*kneytsh, dreydlakh*). For example, David Koussevitsky: "the *shabbes* ["Sabbath"] creates the mood, more so than the *freygish* [a modal term]"; or "the major can be a majestic sound without the kneytsh." After all, modal terms are only a fraction of the extensive vocabulary of the hazzan (see Avenary 1960 for a lexicon). An appropriate extension of my approach (suggested by Kay K. Shelemay too late for inclusion here) would be a survey of how "modes" are taught in the training programs, thus grounding the term in an ethnographic/ethnomusicological context.

11. In time, such preferred pieces became a part of the generalized repertoire pool called "traditional nusach," the most generalized use of the term. The gradual accretion of "anonymous" repertoire from individual contributions is a worldwide process in the evolution of orally transmitted musics. In the cantorial case, the shift to written, acknowledged authorship only began in the mid-nineteenth century and has never been completed.

12. I like to think of the variety of approaches as a choice of the rhetoric of prayer, a concept that should be worked on jointly by a liturgist and a musicologist.

13. See the appendix for an example of how a veteran hazzan decides what to include and what to omit in the Rosh Hashanah service.

14. Katchko's son was also a hazzan, as is his granddaughter, Deborah Katchko-Zimmerman, the first woman to be appointed as full-time hazzan in a Conservative synagogue. In true East European fashion, her *yikhes*—lineage— has earned her respect despite the cantorial establishment's active dislike of her politics as the founder of the Women Cantors Network, a support group largely for nonordained female sacred singers.

15. An extreme, absurd example was brought to me by Jeff Summit from Israel, where he found a cream cheese label proclaiming the product to be *b'nusach Philadelphia.*

16. The substitution of classroom for apprenticeship has been discussed for several world music cultures, particularly India and Indonesia. No general theory has emerged beyond a general sense that the new order must somehow promote standardization and homogenization. The Jewish-American case is too recent to warrant drawing any conclusions.

17. On the issue of endings, one hazzan provided a useful self-analysis of his version, which makes a more general point: "Note the absence of the 3-note trademark High Holiday ending (5–3–1) since this selection leads into the following, and contains no *b'racha* (the formula-words *Baruch atah adoshem* ["Blessed are Thou, O Lord Our God"]), which according to strict tradition must introduce the trademark ending" (A.D.). As noted above, nusach in one of its technical senses is limited only to certain passages that have key framing and concluding roles in the flow of the liturgy. Thus because *Uvchen ten pach-decha* is just the first of three Uvchen paragraphs, it need not conclude "in the

nusach," but might be musically conceived to flow into the following passage. This itself is another aspect of nusach—here it is an organizing principle that stipulates where narrow "nusach" should be applied. This is a fine example of how nusach operates at various levels of the musical structure simultaneously.

18. Heavy use of sequences marks the golden age of hazzanut in general; it is an easy way to extend, repeat, or emphasize textual passages so is a handy crutch for formal structure, and at the same time it provides handy melodic identification for the listener.

12

~~~~~~

Conclusion

It has taken eleven chapters to give a preliminary survey of the American cantorate in all its variety and volatility.[1] While conclusions would be premature, it might be possible to reflect a bit on the Americanness of that cantorate. This involves distinguishing two aspects of the issue, framed as two questions: What is typically American? and What is uniquely American?[2] For while the experience of the Jews in the United States is distinctive, to some extent it has always paralleled developments elsewhere, from Russia to South Africa, from Mexico to Shanghai. Ashkenazic Jews carry their culture with them, and the creation of a local *minhag* always takes some time. After all, it was not until recently that the Sephardim and Ashkenazim parted ways definitively, and they still share many approaches to the common task of working out the meaning of sacred text in everyday life.

Typically American Features

The American cantorate evolved in the age of modern Judaism, in the shadow of increasing secularism and in the sunlight of increasing civic rights and responsibilities. This experience was largely paralleled in Europe, so it is not surprising that many aspects of the cantorate that seem typically American are not unique to the Western Hemisphere. The American situation was less constrained than the European arena, so perhaps more flexible in its responses, but this is a difference of degree, not kind; Judaism as an experiment in modernism was common to both sides of the Atlantic from the turn of the nineteenth century on.

The typical features of the American process can perhaps be summarized in terms of stability and volatility. Stability has resided in the synagogue system since the very beginnings of Shearith Israel in the 1650s. Each set of congregants has incorporated itself separately, empowering a powerful lay leadership, usually from the wealthiest, most socially prominent families, the two being largely synonymous in America. Internecine feuding within this group might allow for a measure of democracy, culminating in a breakaway movement to form a new synagogue. In all cases, the ruling group hired a clergy staff of varying description, depending on historical and denominational factors, and treated them as servants of the congregation. This simple system of religious governance was only lightly modified by the elaboration of nationwide denominational bodies and has continued to provide the flexibility the Jewish community has wanted in coping with the multiple shocks of modernism and historical change.

Stability is also apparent in the continued ties to Jews of the past and of other lands, a typical but not unique aspect of American Jewry. We have surveyed the survival of European musicways, in the form of a respect for and maintenance of the concepts of nusach and improvisation. The persistence of regional differentiation, as in the multiple subethnic communities of the United States, also underscores the strong survivability of oldtime sacred music-making. The recent, but always strong tie to Israeli culture and music links America to other Diaspora communities and has become a new, but important unifying factor that substitutes for older shared heritages like the Yiddish language.

Volatility arises from the great scope for ethnic and religious expression America allows. American society of course noticed early on that Jews represented something "other," but not as alien as Afro-Americans. Whereas the latter were forced to abandon or drastically modify their indigenous religious practices and were pushed into the Christian fold, the Jews, like dissident Protestant and utopian sects, were extended the right to develop their internal religiosity without outside pressure. The arrival of successive waves of immigration (which has continued into our own times, including Soviets and Israelis, for example) keeps American Jewry lively as currents from abroad keep suggesting, or even forcing, the development of new solutions. At the same time, major historic facts like the Holocaust and the creation of the state of Israel bring about constant internal redefinition. Social change among non-Jews, such as the emergence of the New Ethnicity in the 1960s, stirs the Jewish community to action as it gropes for ways to interpret Christian trends on its own terms.[3] Typically American as this almost frenetic activity may be, it is in many ways matched by the Israeli experience and partially paralleled by western European Jewish communities.

For the cantorate, volatility is obvious in ways described in earlier chapters. Yet stability also emerges from this somewhat anarchic situation through the persistence of the ancient sense of what the cantorate is for. Always a grassroots phenomenon, the drive to support the sacred singer is a cultural potential tapped whenever American Jews feel they need what the hazzan can offer. How that need is interpreted varies considerably from generation to generation, as do most aspects of ethnic life in America.[4] For eastern European immigrants, the hazzan might have been a transitional figure, a star "like Caruso" to hold up as model until Americanization allowed for a Jan Peerce or Richard Tucker to serve as vocal hero, someone whose success in the Christian world could validate and coexist with his authority as sacred singer. Today, the emergence of the female hazzan has coincided with Reform Jewry's embracing of tradition, so that the seemingly radical innovation of women on the pulpit could easily fit into a general reinterpretation of denominational goals. The slot of hazzan was there to be used in this process of rightward shift and was in fact filled by eager candidates. For the Conservative movement, the acceptance of women as sacred singers represents a victory for the left wing, showing what anthropologists call the multivalent—multimeaningful—quality of cultural symbols. In these and other situations the existence of the cantorate has helped anchor American Jewry by providing a highly traditional institution that could act as a shock absorber for social and cultural change.

Uniquely American Features

There are two spheres in which the American cantorate appears as distinctive: musical and social. Musically, the unique quality of the cantorate is the blending of styles and approaches from world Jewry. Although Jewish music is always eclectic, the particular combination of influences that shape Jewish-American music is characteristic only of America, especially in our time.[5] Congregations and hazzanim nowadays may make a special point of rotating services, jumping from Hasidic, Israeli, and Sephardic to commissioned-composed and oldtime cantorial—and enjoy the variety. The intertwining, now inextricable, of strands of indigenous American popular forms is uniquely American as well.[6] There is also the mixing of generational musics, whereby summer camp tunes are brought into the main sanctuary or children's choirs take over the pulpit. This joy in musical innovation is American, as is the radical difference among the simultaneous stylistic pools being tapped.

From the social point of view, the emergence since World War II of a professionalized, highly self-conscious cantorate makes America a special case. Particularly in the light of the disappearance of major European and Mediterranean communities and the Israeli lack of interest in the full-time hazzan, the American experience stands apart as distinctive in all of Jewish history. Never before have the hazzanim themselves taken their fate into their own hands so decisively, and there is no question that this has helped the cantorate to survive, and even flourish, on American soil. Work conditions and self-confidence have never been so positive, and the admission of women to the ranks only confirms the strength of the movement.

Where the cantorate will go from here is of course conjectural, and beyond the scope of this study. On one side are the prophets of doom, who note declining synagogue attendance and the current fad for fundamentalism, which bypasses the hazzan. On the other side, there is the fact that Jewish-Americans do turn to the cantorate when they need to. Whatever happens in the immediate future, there will be chosen voices as long as there are synagogues in America.

NOTES

1. This seems the place, finally, to observe that by using the term "America," I have often included Canada with the United States. Several of the hazzanim quoted above work or have worked in Canada, which, despite some regional variation, has experienced a cantorial history similar to that of its larger neighbor. Differences include later immigration and somewhat greater conservatism in regards to the cantorate. For example, hazzanim tend to cite Toronto as "the old country" in terms of taste and demands made on the hazzan.

2. I am grateful to Judit Frigyesi for suggesting this approach.

3. That the Christian clergy is in a state of constant flux is well summarized by Gustafson: "The ancient must function under the conditions of modernity, and under the conditions of a voluntary system. . . . 'Adaptation was thrust upon the ministers from the beginning,' wrote Sidney Mead of the American clergy. Adaptation will be thrust upon them until the end" (1963:89).

4. Here I am speaking of those ethnic groups for whom group identity is largely voluntary—white, Euro-Americans—as opposed to those American society can easily single out as "different," hence for whom ethnicity is a much more involuntary phenomenon. For voluntary ethnics, particularly since the acceptance of cultural pluralism as the accepted philosophy of social interaction and the rise of the New Ethnicity, the arranging of ethnic boundaries is more a sport than a struggle.

5. This works itself out in quite technical ways, as in the case of items and approaches that are clearly European in origin, but that represent only one strand of the pluralistic music culture of the Old World; hence the choice to privilege one European source over others is uniquely American.

6. This is made explicit by the shapers of contemporary religious styles, like Jeffrey Klepper, but is implicit in, say, the institution of the annual NFTY (Reform youth movement) song contests, which serve as barometers of current taste among younger Jews. Of course, the Israeli influence continues, as evidenced by the hits adopted from the yearly Israel-based Hasidic Song Festivals.

APPENDIX

~~~~~~

Annotated Accounts Of
Service Building

Too technical for earlier chapters, but too interesting to leave out of this book are accounts solicited from two hazzanim of the nitty-gritty of service building—the craft of knowing your sources and shaping a ritual event.

One hazzan is a young Reform woman, the other a veteran Conservative male. The former will discuss her approach to Friday night, still the central service for Reform, and the latter his approach to the High Holidays, mainly focusing on Rosh Hashanah. In each case, I looked for what influences choices as well as the sources of the repertoire.

These two blow-by-blow accounts were not selected for their excellence or typicality, but to show the handcrafted nature of services in all its full detail; to my knowledge, this is the first exercise of this ethnomusicological technique in the literature on Jewish music. Another approach used in the Project was the playing of taped services (kept anonymous) to other hazzanim to get spontaneous critiques.

Planning for Friday Night

The current Reform prayerbook, *Gates of Prayer*, offers ten different Friday night services, an effort by the denomination to demonstrate that diversity of viewpoint is welcome within the Reform movement.[1] Thus, the first choice a hazzan faces is which of the services to use:

> I pick the service every Friday night. The rabbi just likes me to alternate between all of them, so I do whichever one I want. It was that way at the last temple too. I don't think that's usual; I think the rabbi normally picks the service.

> Well, [service numbers] 8, 9, and 10 are children's services, so we don't normally do those. Service #1 is the traditional service, so we usually don't do that one either, so it's between 2 and 7.

Local circumstances, then, dictate the main choice. A focus on children
is probably inappropriate because this is a congregation heavily
weighted towards senior citizens. The "traditional" service leans towards
the Conservative, which would be very much against the grain for
these older, classic Reform congregants.

> Service 6: we call it the "Hiroshima" service; it talks about *v ahavta
> adonai elohecha* ["and you shall love the Lord thy God"]—Hiroshima! the
> bombs fell!" We don't usually do that one.

In this case, hazzan and congregation are united in their apparent
indifference to the political slant of service 6. The Reform movement
and left-wing Conservatives have tended to adopt the social-activist
stance of liberal Protestant churches.

> So that leaves us 2, 3, 4, 5, and 7. Now 7, they don't like because . . .
> usually we do the *Borchu* Hebrew-English-Hebrew-English; that one
> doesn't have the English for some reason under the Borchu, so they don't
> like that one.

Local minhag covers all details, and congregant comfort means it is
easier to pick a different service than adjust to an unfamiliar way of
doing one prayer.

> 2,3,4 and 5 . . . are the ones we generally do, except if it's *shabbat
> teshuva*, then I need the traditional insertion, so then I do service #1.

Shabbat teshuva is the Sabbath that falls between Rosh Hashanah and
Yom Kippur, so is particularly solemn, a fact marked here by a short
excursion into the traditional service.

> OK. So 2, 3, 4, 5. . . . So say I decide well, maybe I have a little bit of
> laryngitis or something, so I'm going to sing "The Sabbath Queen," so
> then I'm going to do service 5 . . . start off on p. 189.

Here the hazzan's own needs can come first, all other things being
equal.

> The first thing in every single one of the services is the candle bless-
> ing. . . . Probably 90% of all Reform congregations in the U.S. use the
> Binder candle blessing. I like [it] but I was tired [of it] so I started using
> Jack Gottlieb's . . . so in the two temples that I've been cantor in, their
> traditional candle blessing is Jack Gottlieb, OK? If I ever didn't sing Jack
> Gottlieb now—who's Jack Gottlieb—he wrote this thing five years ago,
> right? They don't know who wrote it. Of course, I have service notes
> every Friday night telling them who wrote it, but if you said to them—
> all they know is, it's the traditional candle blessing.

This is a classic example of local minhag at work. Although this congregation is very decided in its tastes and will not allow any deviation from certain of its favorites, it apparently has no stake in the candle blessing tune, so lets the hazzan create an instant tradition.

> So then I do "The Sabbath Queen" on p. 190. Now, there's only one arrangement that you can use, and that's the Goldfarb, which you can find in the Coopersmith. Now I have a really beautiful arrangement of "The Sabbath Queen" by . . . [unsure of his name]; he's one of these Conservative cantors; it's real nice, and . . . they like it once and a while, but most of the time you have to do the Goldfarb though. Then you have the *Hatzi kaddish* . . . you have to do the traditional chant. OK, so already, the first things in the service that I've done I do the same every time I do that service, right?

The "Sabbath Queen" case is one of partial control; she can substitute her version occasionally without raising the congregants' hackles. The reference to "the Coopersmith," a well-known tune anthology, is typical of Reform practice, in which turning to published works is the primary orientation. The alternate tune is given as "Conservative" in origin, showing that denominational lines are still very much intact politically, yet permeable aesthetically. The switch to "traditional nusach" for the Hatzi kaddish introduces another layer of repertoire, one for which there is no alternative: "you have to do the traditional chant." This is a short text; the Kaddish or Hatzi kaddish (half kaddish) appears throughout the Sabbath services as a divider between sections of the liturgy. Keeping it in traditional style preserves its demarcating character, because it may be the only section of nusach used in this Reform service.

> Then the Borchu. Now, most temples do the Borchu from the Union Hymnal. This temple did Adler and Schalit; don't ask me how they ended up with those two, so I alternate between Adler and Schalit, and if I'm really feeling brave, I do something like Helfman . . . but Adler and Schalit they'll sing along, anybody else's they won't. The Borchu is one of those prayers that they like to sing along, so I very rarely ever change between the Adler and Schalit.

Participation is the key to choice here; because it's a favorite sing-along tune, it is wisest to let "them" have it their way. This congregation strongly prefers works from the "contemporary composer" category, rejecting the old-time Reform songbook, the *Union Hymnal*, which, though it has been officially replaced, still influences many congregations.

> *Shema*—there's only one Shema; you have to do Salomon Sulzer's Shema.
> If you ever dared do another Shema, you'd lose your job.

This remark underlines the permanence of Sulzer's most famous tune,
cited earlier.

> Now in my old temple, the *V'ahavta*, I always used to sing; that was
> my solo piece. Here they're very traditional oriented, so they want to say
> it. . . . My old temple's in the New York area, so they were much more
> progressive musically, so I could do anything. I could do a Janowski
> V'ahavta, I could do a Freed V'ahavta or Birnbaum . . . here I don't ever
> do it because they like to read it; it's one of the Hebrew passages they
> know.

A new variety of localism emerges here: New York as more progressive
than the "provinces." Among the Reform, one often hears that what
works on the coasts may not succeed in the middle (which might
include anywhere outside New York or California), where the older
Reform tradition holds sway. For example, one hazzan says West Coast
"means mostly guitar-playing cantors" (G.H.). However, this hazzan's
version of progressive merely means other composers from the core
contemporary group, not anything radically new.

> Now, the *Mi chamocha* I change all the time. That's one of my changing
> ones. I usually do Mark Lipson's Mi chamocha or the one from the Freed
> Hasidic service, which probably 80% of all people do. I like to experiment
> with a lot of different ones on the Mi chamocha. I do one by Gershon
> Kingsley, I do a lot of people's Mi chamocha, [but] at the Saturday morning
> service if I don't do the Adler one, the minute I open my mouth and sing
> one note of a different one they get upset and they all start talking.

This is a nice example of a "changing piece," which is largely understood by all parties to be variable in origin—except for Saturday morning, where the congregation is inflexible. For the hazzan, Mi chamocha
is a chance to try out whatever's new and popular, which means that
this view of the piece is national, not just local, because many published
versions keep appearing. In other words, where variability occurs can
also be a fixed part of tradition.

Areas of cantorial self-expression are located at specific points in the
service:

> There's certain pieces that they consider solo pieces and they accept
> you doing a lot of different things . . . those are things they expect you
> to do by yourself so they don't care if you do a melody they don't know,
> 'cause they don't expect to join along anyway.

Moving down towards the end of the service, there are a number of items that do not even enter the picture:

> The other stuff, the "Modim," the "Retsei," most Reform cantors don't chant those things.

Towards the end:

> Then the *Kiddush* you have to do Louis Lewandowski, you just have to. . . . Then the two adorations are on p. 615 and 617. You either do the traditional, or you have "let us adore" in English. . . . *Ba yom hahu* you mostly do "the farmer in the dell," then for closing hymn you always try to pick something that's in the back so they can sing along. Usually you do *Adon olam* on Friday night or *Ein kelohenu* on Saturday morning . . . you see the great selection I'm allowed.

So Lewandowski joins his nineteenth-century contemporary Sulzer as an unavoidable part of the local service. Having to choose between "traditional" (Hebrew) or English is a standard problem in both Reform and Conservative services, a nuance that involves congregational preference and clergy leadership. The reference to "the farmer in the dell" could have been made by virtually any hazzan. The "traditional" (probably nineteenth-century German) tune for this passage bears a certain accidental resemblance to the children's song cited. It has become one of a few tunes nearly universally despised by professionals as part of their claim to aesthetic leadership, an attitude fostered by the training programs.

To summarize, our model Reform service builder is not happy with the constraints on her process of selection, but tries to satisfy her taste wherever possible. The fact that tunes she has introduced have become "traditional" in less than three years' time is certainly one source of comfort and recognition of the hazzan's power. Thus she is simultaneously guardian and architect of the local minhag, which draws on most of the standard Reform repertoire pools.

We turn now to the Conservative approach to the High Holidays, which begins with the *Hineni*, the crucial solo prayer of the hazzan discussed in chapter 8:

> I have a Hineni that I used when I was a student at the Seminary. There were a number given out to me and I learned one and I enjoyed singing it. Now, it is interesting that in the first fifteen years of my stay with this congregation, I did not sing Hineni every morning for the Holidays; I sang it only on the first morning of Rosh Hashanah . . . but then we decided it was important enough to do each day and so recently I

have added another setting of the prayer. . . . I sing one now from Cantor Sam Rosenbaum which is arranged for cantor and choir. The fact that we use an organ at our synagogue also gives me a much greater variety of music to choose from, and that is wonderful; even though I use traditional repertoire the organ is accompaniment and I adapt it from the choral part. Of course, there is no special organ part written in.

Several points emerge here. First, we see the major impact of schooling; the seminary Hineni lasted for many years before he felt the need for a second version. When he expanded, he took a version from a trusted colleague, a very common practice among hazzanim. Second, we have the inner need to sing this confessional prayer more often over the years. This sort of emotional reorientation to the prayerbook occurs constantly among sacred singers. Reinterpretation of sacred texts over a lifetime is the hallmark of old Ashkenazic culture, and this is the musician's way of continuing that process.

Third, there is the question of musical forces. Organ or not, choir or not—these are issues decided jointly with the congregation and often with the rabbi, but ones which are closest to the hazzan's heart as the person responsible for music. In this congregation, it was the laity that endorsed the notion of organ, a fact to which the hazzan had to adapt, which he clearly has done successfully and enjoyably. His way of bridging the gap between the "traditional nusach," which is unaccompanied, and a service with organ is to keep the old-time feeling by disallowing special organ parts.

Aside from the special case of Hineni, there is a general philosophy at work in preparing for the Holidays:

Of course, I go over the service very carefully with my Rabbi to see what we wish to keep in the service and what we wish to eliminate, what we choose to do musically and what we wish to do in responsive reading. There might be some small prayers that we might decide to do in a kind of congregatonal simple tune, responsively with the congregation to keep them involved; not always is the spoken word effective, sometimes a chant can be moving to an audience. You have to sort of plan your music so it is not too heavy with large choir compositions and yet there has to be enough so that you have a feeling you are really presenting a substantial service both musically and that the liturgy is being interpreted well enough so that those people who may not be able to read the Hebrew may feel and understand it more fully. In other words, it can't be a kinderspiel, it can't be play.

These comments underscore the general feeling that the High Holidays require the most preparation and offer the most substance of the entire liturgical year. Outside of the religious reasons for this approach, there is the simple practical matter that most congregants turn up only for the High Holidays, so expect to be impressed. At a mundane level, they are also paying a good deal for these services, so want their money's worth. There is another philosophy at work, with which we are already familiar:

> Obviously since I've taught them, that is the congregation, this service and have sung it for thirty years as their hazzan, it is highly unlikely that I would change the service at a whim because I choose to be creative, or I want to do something else to keep from boredom or even for the sake of the choir. It is a service that the congregation now feels comfortable with and anticipates each year. The evening service really speaks for itself. of course, the liturgy is like every other evening service and of course, the nusach is changed.

Repeatedly, the richness of the High Holiday service is stressed. The materials are so rich that some items are bound to be underplayed or passed over, at least one day. So, for example, we find this comment about the *Uvchen* paragraphs, a special insertion for Rosh Hashanah discussed in chapter 11:

> In going over various parts of the service I might say to the Rabbi concerning the Uvchens; since they come every day in the service; what shall we do with them? They may indeed be a little boring to hear each day and they also come immediately after the Khol ma'minim, for which I use a simple congregational melody so it didn't make sense immediately in terms of the pacing of the service for me to chant the uvchens, so we decided, the Rabbi and I, "why don't we just reverse the prayer—one day I would chant it and one day you might read it?"

In this hazzan-rabbi dialogue, we see how the flexibility of the service is extended by the fact that there are two service leaders and many possible modes of presentation: solo cantorial, choral, congregation-rabbi or congregation-hazzan responsorial, read by rabbi. Each decision triggers another to create an overall service shape, which is often the expression of an ideal: to know very well just what will happen and when. Some hazzanim have an actual timetable they follow for the long, complex High Holiday services and enjoy keeping to it.

Within a sense of overall design, we have the usual selection process, drawing on different repertoire pools, that marked the Sabbath service examined earlier. Again, being a veteran means you tend to expand the variety as you progress through your career. For example, take the case of a key cantorial solo, *Unetane tokef*:

> At the very beginning of tenure here I would do one or two settings of the Unetane tokef. However, I now use one for each day. I add a third

one for the third day which is, of course, Yom Kippur. The three settings
I use I have gotten from different sources. I received one when I was still
a student at the Seminary. It is very interesting to note that things which
you choose to do at the very beginning you very rarely give up. They
become part of you. I then acquired one from a hazzan with whom I sang
as a child in a choir and finally I chose one of the classic settings by Leo
Loew which I found in the Ephros anthology which I find to be extremely
effective.

Childhood and schooling contribute two basic versions, but a third was
consciously selected from available anthologies. The Ephros collection
is typical of the "cantor-composer" category, having a variety of pieces
from different practical sources. Leo Loew (1878–1969) is part of a
special subgroup of this pool. He, along with a few other influential
composers such as Zavel Zilberts (1881–1949), were not hazzanim
themselves, but made a career of producing pieces for the virtuoso
singers like Sirota and Kwartin as well as for the many free-lance
professional choirs of the interwar period.

Thus far we have seen there is a great deal of leeway in choosing
sources for the High Holidays. Yet the hazzan is restricted to what is
in the congregation's prayerbook, which is usually the one dissemi-
nated by the national organization of the denomination. A change in
siddur can make a real difference:

> We are, of course, limited by the prayerbook we use, and we're using
> the Silverman at this point. We are, as of this year, acquiring the new
> prayerbook of the Rabbinic Assembly. Personally, I am happy about it.
> I've used the Silverman prayerbook for thirty years and I am ready for a
> change. The translations are archaic, and people do not really speak that
> way. Perhaps some of the readings in the new prayerbook will indeed
> have a little more meaning for the congregation.

Even within this limitation, there are two areas of choice. One is the
diversity written into the prayerbook by its authors, who anticipate
congregational variety, whereas the other is the selection made by the
local clergy, who have an intimate knowledge of their clientele's needs
and tastes:

> I think we look for the dramatic; which readings would be the most
> effective. Personally I do not enjoy the responsive reading and find them
> ineffective. I often wonder how many people really derive anything from
> them. . . . On the other hand, we are dealing with congregations that don't
> know how to daven, they really don't. Many of them cannot read Hebrew,
> they do not know the significance of the prayers and so you have to do
> something to engage them in the service. I do appeal to them through
> my music, but I am sure that very often they do not have any idea what

I am trying to interpret in the words. Perhaps they may even be bored by some of it. You have to find a careful balance between reading and music.

How do you know if they're satisfied?

I believe that in my congregation they are very happy and pleased with the service. One way that I can be sure is that very few people in our congregation leave before the end of the service.

Moving on in the Rosh Hashanah service, we arrive at serious points in the liturgy for which a choice of how the text is presented is based on an underlying philosophy of interpretation:

One can do many things to have effective dramatic points in the service. After singing the Unetane tokef, if it is a major composition, perhaps a congregational melody for B'rosh hashanah would be effective. The line after B'rosh hashanah—uteshuva, utefilla, utzedeka ["but repentance, prayer and charity will lessen the severity of God's judgement"] can be high-lighted very much if the rabbi were to come in immediately and read the English translation and then a very beautiful melody highlighting those significant words: uteshuva, utefilla, utzedeka. One has to have a feeling of movement, of direction. It cannot really be slow—it has to be big and magnificent. The melody I use I believe to be either Sulzer or Lewan-dowski.

Pacing is of prime importance, as is preparation: the line should be set up in English so the meaning, hence the impact of the interpretation, can be effectively conveyed to the congregation. Using "Sulzer-Le-wandowski" here assures an old-time, very solid and familiar style that can be imposing, like old synagogue architecture.

For each section, then, the hazzan taps an appropriate repertoire pool, with diversity itself as a goal:

There is such a variety that one can use over Rosh Hashanah and Yom Kippur, and by the way, that is a very important part, that the kind of music one uses isn't all from one musical period. If it were, it could be extremely dull. If a symphony orchestra programmed only Beethoven program, that might be ok; the conductor is obviously going to commem-orate something special. But it is rare that you see a program that doesn't perhaps have a seventeenth, eighteenth, twentieth century piece in it. You know, of course, that people will complain about the twentieth century piece but then again, it adds variety. One must make the ear listen, even if they don't approve of it. The same is true in liturgical music. We must try to use a variety of sources, of periods, to highlight all music which was written down through the years in terms of synagogue music.

Here the fact that this hazzan is also an important figure on the local symphony orchestra board is relevant. Where does the repertoire come from?

> When I first came to the congregation, I established that I would have a budget for music, and when all the Jewish music corporations were in business, I had a standing order that all music which was published was to be mailed to me. I wanted to establish a library of music that I could call upon for any occasion that I might need, and of course that would also include music for the High Holidays.

The key piece of the entire liturgical year is *Kol Nidre*, so much so that the clergy talk about "Kol Nidre Jews," who turn up only once a year just to hear that famous piece sung. Choosing your approach to Kol Nidre, then, is particularly sensitive. Many sacred singers stick to the tried and true, that is, the venerable, anonymous Kol Nidre tune that has become a brand name for the Jewish faith, for example, as the emblem of ethnicity in Hollywood (*The Jazz Singer*), or on records of interfaith music (*Perry Como Sings Religious Favorites*) as the representative Jewish item. The classic way to perform the text is to sing the entire passage three times, but this raises problems for our hazzan:

> However, I do not think I would be terribly upset if I were to sing it just once. I'm not sure that the three times, which seems to be the legal formula, is necessarily an effective one. Even though I use three settings—each one adding more excitement and more fervor—I am sure that at times people might feel a bit tired: they are standing. I believe it is effective if one chants simply the first one by himself. Then, maybe, add the organ, and finally the organ and choir so that there is a great deal of interest and also the idea of various key changes as we go along.

Despite the hallowed nature of Kol Nidre performance, then, innovation is always possible, and more is anticipated:

> I'm not sure that in the years to come the Kol Nidre will not be chanted but once. For example, there are other things in the liturgy that I did chant three times, such as *Adonai, adonai* during the Torah Service. I no longer do it three times; I do it but once.

In addition to worrying about continuity, the clergy team freely invents new rituals for local consumption, such as this congregation's handing out of the many ornate Torah scrolls to members of the congregation on the pulpit:

> During the procession prior to the Kol Nidre we feel that there should be a continuity not only in the congregation but a continuity we feel in Judaism. Therefore, Elders of the Synagogue pass down the Torahs to the

children and they often have older people, middle-aged people walking around the synagogue in the procession while I sing B'sheva shel ma'alo. I find it is effective walking around the synagogue with the Torahs while chanting and one hears the sound of the bells, the *rimonim*. As I walk towards the back of the congregation it becomes very dramatic because the voice fades and suddenly I turn back to the Ark and come forward. I believe that drama plays a very important part in ritual in this synagogue. Our synagogue happens to be a magnificent edifice and one must do something that is in keeping with that big, that important, space.

Despite innovation, there seem to be limits on tinkering with tradition:

The Rosh Hashanah service has form. There is a beginning, there is a middle, and there is an end. Since the service could be terribly long, we must again make choices in the section which consists of *malchuot, zichronot,* and *shofrot.* One remembers as children getting out of shul at 2:30. That is not likely to be the case today. We are not going to make every word count and we are not going to chant every single word. Since we want to do the three sections during the holiday, we choose the parts we will do each day and in the long run we will have completed all three sections, so there is an abridgement each day.

In other words, abridgement or even rearrangement does not touch the basic quality of the service. Despite all the detail the hazzan relates in terms of shifting elements and modes of presentation, he concludes:

So you see, the service, the liturgy, really does dictate to us what kinds of music we can use.

This devotion to the tradition still allows one to satisfy oneself:

I am not necessarily upset if one piece of music has to be cut up; there is plenty to sing. One can find so many areas to create a service where the music speaks to the people of their heritage and at the same time invites them to be a witness to the great musical culture of hazzanut and Jewish music. I believe that is truly the goal that a hazzan should have that he translates the great heritage of hazzanut to his people, and certainly the High Holidays are a time when one can do that.

NOTE

1. For full-length commentary on *Gates of Prayer* by the denomination's thinkers, see Hoffman (1977).

Bibliography

The following list represents items quoted in this volume, outside oral history quotations. For the latter, the initials used are pseudonyms. For those wishing further acquaintance with aspects of Jewish music, the articles in the *Encyclopaedia Judaica*, available in many libraries, are a good starting point. For an up-to-date, annotated survey of the literature, see Irene Heskes, *The Resource Book of Jewish Music* (Westport, CT: Greenwood Press, 1985). Standard abbreviations used below include: *JSM* (Journal of Synagogue Music) and *Proceedings* (Proceedings of the Annual Convention of the Cantors Assembly).

Abrahams, Simeon. 1847. "Letter to the editor." *Occident* 5(2):87–90.

Abrahams, Solomon. 1857. "What is a hazan?" *Occident* 15(8):397–400.

Across the generations: Jan Peerce/Beth Abraham Youth Chorale. 1983. Tambur Records TR 601.

Adler, Frank J. 1972. *Roots in a moving stream: The centennial history of Congregation B'nai Jehudah.* Kansas City: Congregation B'nai Jehudah.

Adler, Samuel. 1965. *Shiru ladonoy: Sing unto the Lord.* New York: Transcontinental Music Publications.

Adolf, Martin. 1935. "The paradox of the cantor." *Jewish Music* 2(3):8–9.

al Faruqi, Lois Ibsen. 1986. "The cantillation of the Qur'an." Unpublished ms. prepared for the Project.

Angel, Marc D. 1982. *La America: The Sephardic experience in the United States.* Philadelphia: Jewish Publication Society of America.

Avenary, Hanoch. 1960. "The musical vocabulary of Ashkenazic hazzanim." In *Studies in biblical and Jewish folklore,* ed. R. Patai, D. Noi, and F. Utley. Bloomington: Indiana Univ. Press.

———. 1971 "Music." In *Encyclopaedia Judaica.* Jerusalem: Keter.

"B." 1865. *Occident* 23(1):43.

Barber, Bernard. 1963. "Some problems in the sociology of the professions." In *The Professions in America,* ed. K. Lynn, 15–34. Boston: Beacon Press.

Bayer, Bathja. 1971. "Music." In *Encyclopaedia Judaica.* Jerusalem: Keter.

Belskin-Ginsburg, William. 1974. "A new perspective on hazzan-congregation relationships." *Proceedings,* 85–95.

Ben-Haim, Paul. 1968. *Kabbalat Shabbat: Friday evening service.* Tel-Aviv: Israeli Music Publications.

Berger, Joseph. 1985. "Rise of 23% noted in reform Judaism."*New York Times,* 1 November, B5.

———. 1986. "Conservative Judaism affirms identity tenet." *New York Times,* 22 May, 16.

Borowitz, Eugene B. 1977. *Reform Judaism today, book 2: What we believe.* New York: Behrman House.

———. 1978. *Reform Judaism today, book 3: How we live.* New York: Behrman House.

Brooten, Bernadette, J. 1982. *Women leaders in the ancient synagogue.* Brown Judaic Studies, no. 38. Providence: Brown Univ.

"Calif. cantor—Hfd. native—saves 25,000-pound shipment of kosher meat." 1978. *Connecticut Jewish Ledger,* 12 January.

"Canadian court on the legal status of the hazzan." 1974. JSM 5(2):35–42.

Cahn, Judah. 1954. Introduction to *Hassidic service for Sabbath eve,* by Isidor Freed. New York: Transcontinental Music Publications.

Cahn, Louis F. 1953. *The history of Oheb Shalom, 1853–1953.* Baltimore: Oheb Shalom Congregation.

Cardozo, Abraham Lopes Cardozo. n.d. "Music of the Sephardim." In *Herzl Institute Pamphlet,* no. 15, 37–71.

"Certification examination procedure." 1985. Hebrew Union College-Jewish Institute of Religion School of Sacred Music.

Chazanut. *Geshikhte fun.* 1937. New York: Jewish Cantors Ministers Association.

Chazin, Pinchas. 1981. "Growing up in my father's house." *Proceedings,* 6–14.

Chomsky, Jack. 1982. "The cantor and music therapy." *Proceedings,* 13–17.

Clar, Reva. 1983. "Early Stockton Jewry and its cantor-rabbi Herman Davidson." *Western States Jewish Quarterly* 5(2):63–86.

Cohen, Anne Nathan. 1954. *The centenary history: Congregation Beth Israel of Houston, Texas, 1854–1954.* Houston: Congregation Beth Israel.

Cohen, Herschel. 1938. "Khazonim oyf proben: Bilder funm amerikaner khazonim-leben," *Di shul un di khazonim-velt,* n.p. Warsaw.

Cohen, Irving H. 1976. "Synagogue music in the early American republic." *Annual of Jewish Studies* 5:17–23.

Cohen, Kenneth. 1984. "A statistical analysis of bar/bat mitzvah preparation." JSM 14(1):46–59.

Danielson, Virginia. 1987. "The Qur'an and the qasidah: Aspects of the popularity of the repertory sung by Umm Kulthum." *Asian Music* 19(1):26–46.

DeSola Pool, David, and Tamar DeSola Pool. 1955. *An old faith in the new world: Portrait of Shearith Israel, 1654–1954.* New York: Columbia Univ. Press.

De Vaux, Roland. 1961. *Ancient Israel.* Vol. 2, *religious institutions.* New York: McGraw Hill.

Dolan, Jay P. 1975. *The immigrant church: New York's Irish and German Catholics, 1815–1865.* Baltimore: Johns Hopkins Univ. Press.

Egoz, A. D. 1910. "The magid and the cantor in America." *Morgen Zhurnal*, 27 September, 5.

Elazar, Daniel J. 1980. *Community and polity: The organizational dynamics of American Jewry*. Philadelphia: Jewish Publication Society.

Elazar, Daniel, and Rela Geffen Monson. 1981. "Women in the synagogue today." *Midstream* 4:25–30.

Ephros, Gershon. 1976. "The hazzanic recitative: A unique contribution to our music heritage." *JSM* 6(3):23–28.

Erdely, Stephen. 1978. "Traditional and individual traits in the songs of three Hungarian-Americans." *Selected Reports in Ethnomusicology* 3(1):99–152. Los Angeles: UCLA Department of Music.

Fater, Issachar. 1969. "Gershon Sirota: An appreciation." *JSM* 2(3):16–21.

Faulkner, Robert. 1971. *Hollywood studio musicians*. Chicago: Aldine.

———. 1983. *Music on demand*. New Brunswick, NJ: Transaction Books.

Fein, Isaac. 1971. *The making of an American Jewish community*. Philadelphia: Jewish Publication Society.

Feld, Steven. 1982. *Sound and sentiment: Birds, weeping, poetics, and song in Kaluli expression*. Philadelphia: Univ. of Pennsylvania Press.

Feldman, Anna. 1983. "Yiddish songs of the Jewish farm colonists in Saskatchewan, 1917–1939." M.A. thesis, Carleton University.

Fisher, Mitchell Salem. 1964. "Supplemental brief of claimant appellant." Social Security Administration Case No. NY–5153.

Franzblau, Abraham N. 1955. "The Reform cantor-educator: Something new under the sun." *CCAR Journal* 8 (January): 20–23.

Freed, Isidor. 1954. *Hassidic service for Sabbath eve*. New York: Transcontinental Music Publications.

Freedman, Stephen. n.d.a [circa 1985]. "Cantor's corner." *Jewish Advocate*.

———. n.d.b [circa 1985]. "A year without rabbi." *Jewish Advocate*.

Freelander, Daniel Hillel. 1979. "The development of the role of the hazzan through the end of the Geonic period." Rabbinic thesis, Hebrew Union College-Jewish Institute of Religion.

Freidson, Eliot, ed. 1973. *The professions and their prospects*. Beverly Hills: Sage.

Freudenthal, Joseph. 1972. Remarks in "A forum on synagogue music." *JSM* 4(1–2):81–98.

Friedland, Eric L. 1978. "The synagogue and liturgical developments." In *Movements and issues in American Judaism*, ed. B. Martin, 217–32. Westport, CT: Greenwood Press.

Fuchs, Israel C. 1969. "Some thoughts on the origin of nuschaot." *Proceedings*, 3–9.

Gelbart, Mikhl. 1942. *Fun meshorerim-lebn*. New York: Shklarsky [translation excerpts by Judith and Norval Slobin].

Gideon, Miriam. 1984. *Sacred service*. New York: Transcontinental Music Publications.

Glazer, Penina M., and M. Slater. 1987. *Unequal colleagues: The entrance of women into the professions, 1890–1940*. New Brunswick: Rutgers Univ. Press.

Gluck, Gerhard. 1980. "Report of the New England region." *Proceedings*, 67.

Goldberg, Harvey E., ed. 1987. *Judaism viewed from within and from without: Anthropological studies.* Albany: SUNY Press.

Goldblum, Dr. Shmuel. 1925. "The poet of khazones." *Morgen Zhurnal,* 21 August.

Goldfarb, Israel. 1983. "The cantors conference." *JSM* 12(1):3–6. (Originally published in *United Synagogue Recorder,* January 1925.)

Goldman, Ari L. 1986a. "As call comes, more women answer." *New York Times,* 19 October, 6E.

———. 1986b. "Issue of women as rabbis breaks up Jewish unit." *New York Times,* 18 June, A17.

Goren, Arthur. 1970. *New York Jews and the quest for community: The kehillah experiment, 1908–22.* New York: Columbia Univ. Press.

———. 1980. *The American Jews.* Cambridge, MA: Harvard Univ. Press.

Gray, Judith. 1986. "Choices within available repertory: The interplay of tradition and change, of group and individual ideology in the process of hymn selection." Unpublished paper for Wesleyan Univ. graduate seminar.

Grinstein, Hyman B. 1947. *The rise of the Jewish community of New York, 1654–1860.* Philadelphia: Jewish Publication Society.

Grobani, Benjamin. 1966. *Songs of prayer for Sabbath evening service.* New York: Sacred Music Press of the Hebrew Union College.

Gurock, Jeffrey S. 1983. "Resisters and accomodators: Varieties of Orthodox rabbis in America, 1886–1983." In *The Changing American Rabbinate,* ed. J. R. Marcus. *American Jewish Archives* 35(3):100–187.

Gustafson, James M. 1963. "The clergy in the United States." In *The Professions in America,* ed. K. Lynn. Boston: Beacon Press.

Gutheim, James K. 1850. "The Jewish ministry." Sermon delivered on 19 January 1850, in New Orleans. [Published in *Occident* 8(2):74–82.]

Gutstein, Morris A. n.d. *A priceless heritage: The epic growth of nineteenth century Chicago Jewry.* New York: Bloch.

Hammerman, Saul. 1986. "Fund sought to ease shortage of cantors, improve worship." *Jewish Week,* 23 May, 15.

Hampton, Barbara. 1985. "Yes Lord! Afro-American pentecostal women in the urban ministry of music." Unpublished ms. supplied to the Project.

Hardie, A. E. 1986. "Hebrew schools losing students in New York." *New York Times,* 15 December, 67.

Harlow, Jules, ed. 1972. *Mahzor for Rosh Hashanah and Yom Kippur: A prayer book for the days of awe.* New York: Rabbinical Assembly.

Hayburn, Robert. 1979. *Papal legislation on sacred music: 95 A.D. to 1977 A.D.* Collegeville, MN: The Liturgical Press.

Hays, Samuel. Papers. American Jewish Archives Correspondence Collection, Cincinnati.

Hecht, Simon. 1879a, 1879b. "Chasan und cantor, oder frueher und jetzt." *Die Deborah,* 10 October, 2 and 17 October, 2.

Heilman, Samuel C. 1976. *Synagogue life: A study in symbolic interaction.* Chicago: Univ. of Chicago Press.

──. 1983. *The people of the book: Drama, fellowship, and religion.* Chicago: Univ. of Chicago Press.

Helfman, Max. 1969. *Sabbath repose/shabbat m'nuchah.* New York: Transcontinental Music Publications.

Helmreich, William B. 1982. *The world of the yeshiva: An intimate portrait of Orthodox Jewry.* New York: Free Press.

Herberg, Will. 1960. *Protestant, Catholic, Jew.* rev. ed. Garden City, NY: Doubleday.

Hertzberg, Arthur. 1972. "Is there a future for the synagogue in America?" *Proceedings,* 82–93.

Heschel, Abraham Joshua. 1972. "The task of the hazzan." Talk given at CA convention, 1957. Published, *JSM* 4(1–2):62–68. [Also published as "The vocation of the cantor." In *The insecurity of freedom,* 242–53 (NY: Noonday Press, 1967).]

Hoffman, Lawrence. 1975. "Creative liturgy." *Jewish Spectator* (Winter):42–50.

──. 1977a. "The debate on music." In *Gates of Understanding,* ed. L. Hoffman, 27–35. New York: Union of American Hebrew Congregations.

──. 1977b. "The liturgical message." In *Gates of Understanding,* ed. L. Hoffman, 129–68. New York: Union of American Hebrew Congregations.

──. 1984. *Gates of Understanding 2.* New York: Union of American Hebrew Congregations.

Howe, Irving. 1976. *The world of our fathers.* New York: Harcourt.

Isaacs, Samuel Myer. 1844. "Religious education." *Occident* 1(12):590–94.

Isaacson, Michael. 1974. *Avodat amamit: A folk service.* New York: Transcontinental Music Publications.

──. 1977. "Preface to the second edition." *Hegyon libi.* New York: Transcontinental Music Publications.

──. 1986. Liner notes for *The Jazz Service.* Oakland, CA: Bensongs.

Jacobs, Solomon. 1855. "Ladies' singing in synagogue." *Occident* 12(1):537–42.

Joselit, Jenna Weissman. 1983. "What happened to New York's 'Jewish Jews'?: Moses Rischin's *The promised city* revisited." *American Jewish History* 73(2):163–72.

Kaplan, Mordecai. 1981. *Judaism as a civilization.* Philadelphia: Jewish Publication Society and Reconstructionist Press. (First edition published 1934.)

Karp, Abraham J. 1983. "The Conservative rabbi—'dissatisfied but not unhappy.'" In *The American rabbinate: A centennial view,* ed. J. R. Marcus. *American Jewish Archives* 35(2):188–262.

──. 1984. "From 'hevra' to congregation: the Americanization of the Beth Israel synagogue, Rochester, New York, 1874–1912." Unpublished ms. made available to the Project.

──. 1986. "A century of Conservative Judaism in the United States." *American Jewish Year Book,* 35–94.

Kaufman, Debra Renee. 1984. "Professional women: How real are the recent gains?" In *Women in feminist perspective,* ed. J. Freeman, 353–69. Palo Alto: Mayfield.

Keil, Charles. 1982. "Slovenian style in Milwaukee." In *Folk music and modern sound*, ed. W. Ferris and M. Hart, 32–59. Oxford, MS: Univ. of Mississippi Press.

Keil, Charles, and Angelica Keil. 1977. "In pursuit of polka happiness." *Cultural Correspondence*, no. 5.

Kingsley, Gershon. 1968. *Shabbat for today*. New York: Kingsley Sound.

Kirshenbaum, Jacob. 1938. "Der kamf tsvishn alte un yunge khazonim in Amerika. *Di shul un di khazonim velt*, 14–17. Warsaw.

Kirshenblatt-Gimblett, Barbara. 1982. "The cut that binds: The western Ashkenazic torah binder as nexus between circumcision and torah." In *Celebration: Studies in festivity and ritual*, ed. V. Turner, 136–46. Washington, DC: Smithsonian Institution Press.

———. 1988. "Erasing the subject: Franz Boas and the anthropological study of Jews in the United States, 1903–1942." In *Ashkenaz: An intellectual history of Jewish folklore and ethnology*. Bloomington: Indiana Univ. Press. In press.

Klein, Isaac. 1979. *A guide to Jewish religious practice*. New York: Jewish Theological Seminary of America.

Kohn, S. Joshua. 1959. *The Jewish community of Utica, New York, 1847–1948*. New York: American Jewish Historical Society.

Koskoff, Ellen. 1978. "Contemporary nigun composition in an American hasidic community." *Selected reports in ethnomusicology* 3(1):153–74. Los Angeles: UCLA Department of Music.

Krinsky, Carol Herselle. 1985. *Synagogues of Europe*. Cambridge, MA: MIT Press.

Kula, Morton. 1974. "Confronting the time problem." *Proceedings*, 40–42.

Kwartin, Zavel. 1952. *Mayn leben*. New York and Philadelphia: S. Kwartin Publishing Committee.

Landes, Aaron. Introduction to *Simchat Shabbat*. New York: Transcontinental Music Publications, n.d.

Landman, Leo. 1972. *The cantor: An historic perspective*. New York: Yeshiva University.

"Land mark case, A." 1967. *JSM* 1(2):18–27.

"Landmark case, A." 1973. *JSM* 5(1):20–27.

Leary, James. 1984. "Old-time music in northern Wisconsin." *American Music* 2(1):71–87.

"Letter from President Truman, A." 1978. *Shalshelet* 4(2).

Levy, Alan. 1976. *The bluebird of happiness: The memoirs of Jan Peerce*. New York: Harper and Row.

Liebman, Charles. "The religious life of American Jewry." In *Understanding American Jewry*, ed. M. Sklare, 96–124. New Brunswick, NJ: Transaction Books and Center for Modern Jewish Studies, Brandeis Univ.

Linder, N. B. 1925. "One of the four million." *Der Tog*, 8 September.

Lipitz, Louis. 1937. "The cantorate in Jewish life." *Chazanut: Fortieth Anniversary Journal*. New York: Ministers Cantors' Association of America.

———. 1938. "Farvos hot zikh der amerikaner khazonim-farband ongeshlosen an der arbayter-federatsiye?" *Di shul un di khazonim velt,* 4–5. Warsaw.

Lowenstein, Steven M. 1981. "The 1840s and the creation of the German-Jewish religious reform movement." In *Revolution and evolution: 1848 in German-Jewish history,* ed. W. Mosse, 255–98. Tuebingen: Mohr.

Lyons Collection, vol. 1. 1913. Publications of the American Jewish Historical Society, no. 21.

Malachi, A. R. 1937. "The first hazzanim in America," trans. A. J. Karp. *Hadoar,* 17 September.

Marcus, Jacob Rader. 1959. *American Jewry: Documents, eighteenth century.* Cincinnati: Hebrew Union College Press.

———. 1961. *Early American Jewry: The Jews of New York, New England and Canada, 1649–1794.* Philadelphia: Jewish Publication Society.

———. 1970a. *The colonial American Jew: 1492–1776.* Detroit: Wayne State Univ. Press.

———. 1970b. *The handsome young priest in the black gown: The personal world of Gershom Seixas.* Cincinnati: Hebrew Union College-Jewish Institute of Religion.

Marty, Martin E. 1972. *Protestantism.* New York: Holt, Rinehart and Winston.

McLeod, Bruce. 1978. *Music for all occasions: The club-date musician in New York City.* PhD. diss., Wesleyan University.

Meyer, Michael A. 1978. "Reform Judaism." In *Movements and issues in American Judaism,* ed. B. Martin. Westport, CT: Greenwood Press.

Michaelsen, Robert S. 1956. "The Protestant ministry in America: 1850 to the present." In *The ministry in historical perspectives,* ed. H. N. Niebuhr and D. D. Williams, 250–88. New York: Harper.

Millgram, Abraham E. 1971. *Jewish worship.* Philadelphia: Jewish Publication Society of America.

Mintz, Alan. 1984. "Prayer and the prayerbook." In *Back to the sources: Reading the classic Jewish texts,* ed. B. Holtz, 403–30. New York: Summit Books.

Mirsky, A. 1900. *Selmar Cerini (Steifmann).* London: Londoner Verlagsgesellschaft.

Moore, Deborah Dash. 1981. *At home in America: Second generation New York Jews.* New York: Columbia Univ. Press.

Moore, Wilbert. 1970. *The professions: roles and rules.* New York: Russell Sage Foundation.

"Moralizing layman, A." 1847. *Occident* 5(1):25–27.

Mose, I. 1904. "The cantor as a religious functionary." *Annual Report of the Society of American Cantors.*

Nettl, Bruno. 1983. *The study of ethnomusicology.* Urbana: Univ. of Illinois Press.

Nulman, Macy. 1975. *A concise encyclopaedia of Jewish music.* New York: McGraw Hill.

———. 1986–87. "Jewish music education at Yeshiva University." *Journal of Jewish Music and Liturgy* 9:1–11.

Orbach, Harold. 1975. "President, A.C.C." *Shalshelet* 1(1):3.

Petuchowski, Jakob J. 1968. *Prayerbook reform in Europe: The liturgy of European liberal and reform Judaism.* New York: World Union for Progressive Judaism.

Philipp, June. 1983. "Traditional historical narrative and action-oriented (or ethnographic) history." *Historical Studies* 20(80):339–52.

Piket, Frederick. 1961. *The seventh day.* New York: Transcontinental Music Publications.

Plaut, W. Gunther. 1959. *The Jews in Minnesota: The first seventy-five years.* New York: American Jewish Historical Society.

Polish, David. 1983. "The changing and the constant in the Reform rabbinate." in *The American rabbinate: A centennial view,* ed. J. R. Marcus. *American Jewish Archives* 35(2):263–341.

Prell, Riv-Ellen. 1987. "Sacred categories and social relations: The visibility and invisibility of gender in an American Jewish community" In *Judaism viewed from within and from without: Anthropological studies,* ed. H. Goldberg, 171–92. Albany: SUNY Press.

Price, Ronald D. 1987. "Ordination of women cantors marks break with halachah." *Jewish News,* 6 March, 20.

Putterman, David J. 1969. "Rock'ing the Temple." *JSM* 2(3):22–24.

Raymond, Art. 1974. Liner notes for *David superstar: A Friday evening rock service.* Zimray Records 102.

Rischin, Moses. 1983. "Responsa." *American Jewish History* 53(2):185–204.

Ritterband, L. M. 1847. "Letter to the editor." *Occident* 4(2):548–50.

Ritzer, George. 1973. "Professionalism and the individual." In *The professions and their prospects,* ed. E. Freidson, 59–73. Beverly Hills: Sage.

Rosenbaum, Fred. 1980. *Architect of reform: Congregational and community leadership, Emanu-El of San Francisco, 1849–1980.* Berkeley: Judah L. Magnes Memorial Museum.

Rosenbaum, Samuel. 1972. "Report of the executive vice president." *Proceedings,* 24–33.

———. 1974. "Report of the executive vice president." *Proceedings,* 61–74.

———. 1975. "Report of the executive vice president." *Proceedings,* 58–68.

———. 1976. "Report of the executive vice president." *Proceedings,* 76–93.

———. 1978. "Report of the executive vice president." *Proceedings,* 41–63.

———. 1984. "Looking to the future." *JSM* 14(2):50–61.

———. 1985. "Report of the executive vice president." *Proceedings,* 26–35.

Rosenblatt, Samuel. 1954. *Yosele Rosenblatt: The story of his life as told by his son.* New York: Farrar, Straus and Young.

Rosenfeld, Jacob. 1849. "Letter to the editor." *Occident* 6(11):563–65.

Roskies, David G. 1984. *Against the apocalypse: Responses to catastrophe in modern Jewish culture.* Cambridge, MA: Harvard University Press.

Rossi, Salomone. 1954. *Sacred service,* transcribed for the American synagogue by Isidor Freed. New York: Transcontinental Music Publications.

Rubin, Saul Jacob. 1983. *Third to none: The saga of Savannah Jewry, 1733–1983.* Savannah: Congregation Mickve Israel.

Ruby, Walter. 1987. "Having gone to the wall for women rabbis, JTS still denies ordaining women cantors." *Washington Jewish Week*, 8 January, 9–10.

Sager, Sarah. 1984. "The variety of cantorial experience and practice in the Reform synagogue." *JSM* 14(2):42–72.

Sandrow, Nahma. 1977. *Vagabond stars: A world history of the Yiddish theater.* New York: Harper and Row.

Sarna, Jonathan, ed. 1982. *People walk on their heads: Moses Weinberger's Jews and Judaism in New York.* New York.

Schalit, Henrich. 1951. *Sabbath eve liturgy.* Denver: H. Schalit.

Schick, Marvin. 1983. "Borough Park: A Jewish settlement." In *Dimensions of Orthodox Judaism*, ed. R. Bulka, 186–210. New York: KTAV.

Schorr, Henry A. 1937. "As a rabbi sees it." *Chazanuth: Fortieth Anniversary Journal*, 15. New York: Ministers Cantors' Association of America.

Schorsch, Ismar. 1981. "Emancipation and the crisis of religious authority: The emergence of the modern rabbinate." In *Revolution and evolution: 1848 in German-Jewish history*, ed. W. Mosse, 205–53. Tubingen: Mohr.

Schwarzbaum, Haim. 1969. *Studies in world and Jewish folklore.* Munich: DeGruyter.

Scott, Donald M. 1978. *From office to profession: The New England ministry, 1750–1850.* Philadelphia: Univ. of Pennsylvania Press.

"Second landmark case, A." 1968. *JSM* 1(3):7–15.

Sed-Rajna, Gabrielle. 1975. *Ancient Jewish art: East and west.* Paris: Flammarion.

Seixas, Gershom Mendes. Papers. Hebrew Union College Manuscript Collection, Cincinnati.

Shames, Morton. 1984. "The variety of cantorial experience and practice in the Conservative synagogue." *JSM* 14(2):34–41.

Shelemay, Kay K. 1986. *Sephardic (Syrian) cantor.* Report prepared for the Project.

Shelvin, B. 1938. "Fir stilen in amerikaner khazones." *Di shul un di khazonim velt*, n.p. Warsaw.

Sholom Aleichem. 1942. *Yosele Solovey.* New York: Forverts.

Shur, Bonia. 1984. The composer and the Reform synagogue." A talk delivered to composers and cantors at a special gathering at Congregation Emanu'el B'ne Jeshurum, Milwaukee, 4 November.

Sklare, Marshall. 1955. *Conservative Judaism.* Glencoe, IL: Free Press.

———. 1982. "On the preparation of a sociology of American Jewry." In *Understanding American Jewry*, ed. M. Sklare, 261–71. New Brunswick, NJ: Transaction Books and Center for Modern Jewish Studies, Brandeis Univ.

Slobin, Mark. 1982a. "How the fiddler got on the roof." In *Folk music and modern sound*, ed. W. Ferris and M. Hart, 21–31. Oxford, MS: Univ. of Mississippi Press.

———. 1982b. *Old Jewish folk music: The collections and writings of Moshe Beregovski.* Philadelphia: Univ. of Pennsylvania Press.

———. 1982c. *Tenement songs: The popular music of the Jewish immigrants.* Urbana: Univ. of Illinois Press.

———. 1983. "Some intersections of Jews, music, and theater." In *From Hester Street to Hollywood: The Jewish-American on stage and screen,* ed. S. Cohen, 29–43. Bloomington: Indiana Univ. Press.

———. 1986. "A fresh look at Beregovski's folk music research." *Ethnomusicology* 30(2):253–60.

Smolover, Raymond. 1986. "New times, new hopes, new prayers." *Koleinu,* 2.

———. n.d.a. Liner notes for *Edge of freedom: A folk/rock service for the Sabbath.* Covenant Records 6021 SA.

———, n.d.b. Liner notes for *Gates of freedom.* Covenant Records 6312.

Stein, Stephen. 1981. "The cantor's voice." *Bulletin of Beth El Congregation,* 6. Akron, Ohio.

Steinberg, Ben. 1964. Preface to *Pirchay shir kodesh.* New York: Transcontinental Music Publications.

Steinsaltz, Adin. 1976. *The essential Talmud.* New York: Bantam Books.

Strauss, M. 1851. "Letter to the editor." *Occident* 9(6):323–42.

Sulzer, Salomon. 1954. *Schir zion.* New York: Sacred Music Press.

Sussman, Lance. 1986. "Isaac Leeser and the protestantization of American Judaism." *American Jewish Archives* 38(1):1–22.

Swichkow, Louis J., and Lloyd P. Gartner. 1963. *The history of the Jews of Milwaukee.* Philadelphia: Jewish Publication Society.

Temperley, Nicholas. 1979. *The music of the English parish church.* Cambridge: Cambridge Univ. Press.

"Thoughts on the Jewish ministry, no. V." 1852. *Occident* 10, no. 4 (July):179–87.

Tilman, David. 1976. "Hazzanut as you see it: Today and tomorrow." *Proceedings,* 165–71.

Trachtenberg, Joshua. 1944. *Consider the years: The story of the Jewish community of Easton, 1752–1942.* Easton, PA: Centennial Committee of Temple Brith Sholom.

Turner, Victor. 1969. *The ritual process.* Chicago: Aldine.

United Synagogue of America. 1973. *Proposed revision of the guide to congregational standards.* New York.

Vigoda, Samuel. 1981. *Legendary voices.* New York: M.P. Press.

Vigoda, Shmuel. 1938. "Khazonishe glikn in amerika." *Di shul un di khazonim velt,* 8–10. Warsaw.

Waldman, Morton. 1980. "Growing up in my father's house." *Proceedings,* 11–18.

Waxman, Chaim I. 1983. *America's Jews in transition.* Philadelphia: Temple University Press.

Weiner, Lazar. 1954. *Likras shabos.* New York: Transcontinental Music Publications.

Weinreich, Max. 1980. *History of the Yiddish language.* Chicago: Univ. of Chicago Press.

Weinshel, Hayim. 1891. *Sefer nitei naamanim.* New York.

Weisser, Joshua. 1938. "Der khazn in amerika un der khazn in der alter heym," *Di shul un di khazonim velt,* n.p. Warsaw.

———. 1940. "It's hard to be a cantor." *Der Tog,* 25 September.

Weissler, L. 1982. "Making Judaism meaningful: Ambivalence and tradition in a havurah community." PhD. diss., University of Pennsylvania.

Werner, Eric. 1954. "Preface." In *Schir zion,* by S. Sulzer. New York: Sacred Music Press.

———. 1959. *The sacred bridge.* New York: Columbia Univ. Press.

———. 1976. *A voice still heard . . . : The sacred songs of the Ashkenazic Jews.* University Park: Pennsylvania State Univ. Press.

Wise, Isaac M. 1901. *Reminiscences,* transl. and ed. D. Philipson. Cincinnati: Leo Wise.

Wohlberg, Max. 1971. *Chemdat shabbat: A new Sabbath morning service for hazzan and congregation.* New York: Cantors Assembly.

———. 1974. "Varying concepts of ne'imah and their place in the liturgy." *JSM* 5(3):16–21.

———. 1976. "A unique chapter in the history of the American cantorate." *JSM* 7(1):3–25.

———. 1977. "Hazzanut in transition." *JSM* 7(3): 5–16. (Originally a speech delivered 14 May 1951.)

———. 1979. "Some thoughts on the hazzanic recitative." *JSM* 9(3):82–86.

———. 1984. "Shiru lo: aspects of congregational song." *JSM* 13(2):35–45. (First published in *Conservative Judaism,* Fall 1968.)

Wolf, Edwin II, and Maxwell Whiteman. 1957. *The history of the Jews of Philadelphia from colonial times to the age of Jackson.* Philadelphia: Jewish Publication Society.

Yinger, J. Milton. 1961. *Sociology looks at religion.* New York: Macmillan.

Yolkoff, Arthur. 1966. *Shirat atideinu/song of our future.* New York: Transcontinental Music Publications.

Zemp, Hugo. 1979. "Aspects of 'Are'Are musical theory." *Ethnomusicology* 23(1):6–48.

Zucker, Jeffrey, S. 1983. "Edward Stark: American cantor-composer at the turn of the century." *JSM* 13(1):14–28.

———. 1985. "Cantor Edward J. Stark at Congregation Emanu-El, part I." *Western States Jewish History* 17(3):231–49.

Zwerin, Kenneth C. 1985. "The Cantorate at Sherith Israel, 1893–1957." *Western States Jewish History* 17(2):144–50.

Index

Note on the Recording

The cassette recording of songs discussed in *Chosen Voices* includes the following selections, which follow sequentially on the first side:

Examples 1–6. *Lecha dodi* variants

    Example 1.   Salomon Sulzer, *Lecha dodi*, 0:26
    Example 2.   Lewandowski, *Lecha dodi*, 0:23
    Example 3.   Second most-commonly submitted melody, 0:54
    Example 4.   Hasidic-style *Lecha dodi*, 0:25
    Example 5a. Seasonal variant: *Lecha dodi* for three Friday nights before Tisha b'Av, 0:23
    Example 5b. Seasonal variant: *Lecha dodi* for the month of Elul, 0:19

Examples 6–14. *Tzur yisroel* variants

    Example 6.   Most common *Tzur yisroel*, 0:34
    Example 7.   Symmetrical version of *Tzur yisroel*, 0:30
    Example 8.   Personal variation of *Tzur yisroel*, 0:32
    Example 9.   Personal variation of *Tzur yisroel*, 0:38
    Example 10. Personal variation of *Tzur yisroel*, 0:37
    Example 11. Text accent shift in *Tzur yisroel*, 0:34
    Example 12. Text accent shift in *Tzur yisroel*, 0:38
    Example 13. Word repetition in *Tzur yisroel*, 0:44
    Example 14. Personal variation of *Tzur yisroel*, 1:08

Examples 15–29. *Barchu* variants

    Example 15. Salomone Rossi, *Borchu, No. 1*, 1:16
    Example 16. *Bor'chu* arranged by Isidor Freed, 1:23
    Example 17. Salomon Sulzer, *Barchu*, 0:54
    Example 18. Benjamin Grobani, *Borchu No. 1*, 0:50
    Example 19. Arthur Yolkoff, *Bar'chu*, 1:02
    Example 20. Heinrich Schalit, *Bor'chu*, 1:01
    Example 21. Lazar Weiner, *Bor'chu*, 0:43
    Example 22. Max Helfman, *Bar'chu*, 1:03

Example 23. Miriam Gideon, *Bar'chu,* 1:07
Example 24. Paul Ben-Haim, *Barechu,* 1:10
Example 25. Frederick Piket, *Bar'chu,* 0:29
Example 26. Samuel Adler, *Bor'chu,* 0:45
Example 27. Isidor Freed, *Bar'chu,* 1:05
Example 28. Gershon Kingsley, *Bor'chu,* 1:33
Example 29. Michael Isaacson, *Bar'chu,* 2:16

Examples 30–35. *Ashrei* variants

Example 30. *Ashrei* variation, 0:17
Example 31. *Ashrei* variation, 0:16
Example 32. *Ashrei* variation, 0:33
Example 33. *Ashrei* variation, 0:19
Example 34. *Ashrei* variation, 0:37
Example 35. *Ashrei* variation, 0:22

Examples 36–41. *Uvchen ten pachdecha* variants

Example 36. *Uvchen* variation, 1:22
Example 37. *Uvchen* variation, 1:27
Example 38. *Uvchen* variation, 0:51
Example 39. *Uvchen* variation, 1:01
Example 40. *Uvchen* variation, 1:14
Example 41. *Uvchen* variation, 0:45

Total time, 34:47

The *Barchu* recordings were produced at the Eastman School of Music, 17 May 1987, under the direction of Samuel Adler, with Hazzan Abraham Mizrachi, soloist, and the Eastman Chorus. All of the other recordings were volunteered by members of the Cantors Assembly for the History of the American Cantorate Project. Done locally under differing conditions, the audio quality of these examples varies widely. In line with my general approach toward field recordings and informant choices, the original sound has been maintained as submitted.

The cassette is available separately from the University of Illinois Press (ISBN 0-252-01566-5).

Note on the Author

Mark Slobin received his Ph.D. from the University of Michigan in 1969. He is a professor in the Department of Music at Wesleyan University, president of the Society for Asian Music, and editor of *Asian Music*. He has conducted research in northern Afghanistan, and his most recent work is on American Jewish music, including popular music and folk songs. In addition to many articles in scholarly journals, his publications include the book *Old Jewish Folk Music* and a previous book with the University of Illinois Press, *Tenement Songs*.

Books in the Series Music in American Life